The Doctrine of Election
and the Emergence of
Elizabethan Tragedy

MARTHA TUCK ROZETT

The Doctrine of Election and the Emergence of Elizabethan Tragedy

PRINCETON UNIVERSITY PRESS

PRINCETON, NEW JERSEY

Copyright © 1984 by Princeton University Press

Published by Princeton University Press, 41 William Street,
Princeton, New Jersey 08540
In the United Kingdom: Princeton University Press, Guildford, Surrey

All Rights Reserved

Library of Congress Cataloging in Publication Data will be
found on the last printed page of this book

ISBN 0-691-06615-9

This book has been composed in Linotron Galliard

Clothbound editions of Princeton University Press books
are printed on acid-free paper, and binding materials are
chosen for strength and durability

Printed in the United States of America by Princeton University Press
Princeton, New Jersey

TITLE PAGE: DETAIL OF AN ILLUSTRATION FROM THE STAGING OF
TITUS ANDRONICUS

For my parents

CONTENTS

ACKNOWLEDGMENTS

This book has been in the making for many years, and has changed, as I have changed, with each rereading of the plays. I am grateful to students and colleagues who have listened to and helped shape my ideas during these years, and in particular to my three student assistants, Karen Cherewatuk, Evan Rivers, and Emmanuel Gomes. Their careful attention to detail helped immeasurably, as did the patience and skill of Peggy Cooper, who typed the manuscript, and Linda Sajan and Lauren McCaffery, who helped prepare the index. I am also deeply indebted to Edmund Creeth and William Ingram, for their help at the beginning, and to Norman Rabkin and Susan Snyder, who each read the manuscript and offered suggestions for its improvement. I was also assisted by grants from the College of Humanities and Fine Arts at the State University of New York at Albany and the Research Foundation of the State University of New York. My greatest debt is to my family—to John, for his patience, understanding, and encouragement; to Joshua, for letting me write on Saturday mornings; and to Alexander, who waited to be born until the book was finished.

*The Doctrine of Election
and the Emergence of
Elizabethan Tragedy*

INTRODUCTION

Dramatic tragedy emerged suddenly in Elizabethan England. In the 1560s serious drama was still primarily religious and designed to serve didactic ends; by the end of the 1580s, the transition to an essentially secular, commercial drama had occurred. How and why tragedy came into being at this time and in this place remains a subject of energetic scholarly debate, debate which frequently reveals as much about our attitudes toward literature as it does about Elizabethan tragedy itself. This book joins the debate in at least two ways. From one perspective, it is about the evolution of the tragic protagonist, and his relationship with the Elizabethan audience. This character's increasing ability to summon up complex and ambivalent feelings in the spectator resulted from (although it also helped bring about) the transformation of an essentially religious dramatic tradition into a secular one. From another perspective, this book is about the written and oral material, most of it overtly didactic, that provided the playwrights with so many of their character types, dramatic structures, themes, and rhetorical strategies. In looking at these sources, I am not much interested in their influence on the playwright's personal artistic development.[1] Rather, I am interested in how the

---

[1] Because my approach to the sources places greater emphasis on the audience's expectations than on the process of composition, there will be few references in this book to the traditional source studies which have helped scholars to understand the playwrights' relationships to their literary predecessors. My approach has instead been influenced by such works as C. L. Barber's *Shakespeare's Festive Comedy* and Robert Weimann's *Shakespeare and the Popular Tradition*, and has benefited from the approaches represented in the volume of *Renaissance Drama* devoted to Dramatic Antecedents (N.S. VI, 1973). In his preface to this volume, Alan C. Dessen observes that "For many years the study of Renaissance Drama was largely the study of dramatic sources, influences, and antecedents," but that "inevitably the pendulum swung" and the evolutionary models were challenged as misleading or inadequate. The essays Dessen has collected all reexamine questions of influence, many of them

playwrights reacted to their audience's expectations, and in how these expectations were at least partly determined by the preoccupations of the age. To what extent were the audience's responses to a play shaped by their familiarity with morality plays, sermons, tracts, and histories, or, perhaps more accurately, by the kinds of ideas and attitudes expressed in such works? To what extent did those responses lead to unspoken agreements between playwrights and audiences about ways of presenting characters? And to what extent did conventions of characterization depend upon attitudes about the nature of man's relationship with God or the concepts of good and evil as manifested in human behavior? To answer questions such as these, I plan to reconstruct one set of assumptions which the Elizabethan audience brought to the theatre and hypothesize about its effect on the emerging shape of tragedy. Broadly defined, these assumptions represent a range of culturally determined attitudes toward the self in relation to others; more specifically, they originate in the Calvinist doctrine of election.

The doctrine that God has predestined some persons to salvation and some to reprobation is deeply rooted in the Pauline tradition, as set forth in the epistle to the Romans. Emphasized by St. Augustine and again by Calvin, the doctrine of election taught that all men and women are by nature sinners but that God's free gift of grace has conferred righteousness upon a chosen few, who would come to recognize the signs of election in themselves through a process involving intense self-scrutiny, repentance, and gradual regeneration. The widespread influence of Calvin on sixteenth-century English Protestantism led to an adherence to the doctrine of election that transcended the political differences between the reformers and moderate Protestants. This is not to say that the Elizabethans were strict believers in absolute and unchangeable predestination; inherent in Elizabethan Calvinism, as I will

---

with the expectations and demands of the audience in mind. Taken together, they form an important contribution to our sense of scholarly method in the field of Renaissance drama.

demonstrate in Chapter II, was a politic ambiguity on this score.[2]

At this point it may have become apparent that certain implicit premises lie behind my hypotheses about the emergence of tragedy. The first premise is that when literature is a commercial enterprise, as the Elizabethan drama was becoming during the period this book examines, it is carefully attuned to what its audience wants. However varied or heterogeneous in terms of class or social position, that audience was more "communal" than "random"; that is, it possessed what George Steiner calls a "mythology," the context of belief and conventions which the artist shares with his audience.[3] Some of our best clues to the way this audience helped shape the development of drama will thus be found in the groups or sub-genres of plays (the conqueror and revenge plays, for example) whose shared characteristics result from the audience's expressed preference for certain character types, situations, and theatrical techniques.

My second premise is that popular art forms always address issues of current public interest and debate in one way or another. They constitute one public forum among many, reflecting and commenting upon the dialogue of the time. This, of course, may be an aspect of popular art of which the artist is not wholly conscious, for the presence of topical issues in the text need not be intentional. Rather, it may result from an influence so subtle and oblique that neither playwright nor audience recognizes it at the time. For these topical issues to be religious in origin, in a time of energetic religious controversy, seems natural and indeed, inevitable.[4]

[2] On the widespread adherence among Elizabethan Protestants to the doctrine of election see Charles H. and Katherine George, *The Protestant Mind of the English Reformation: 1570-1640* (Princeton, 1961). The Georges argue that it is very hard to distinguish "Anglicans" from "Puritans" and that all English Protestants before the period dominated by Archbishop Laud were essentially Calvinists (p. 71).

[3] The terms "communal" and "random" belong to Bernard Beckerman, whose *Dynamics of Drama: Theory and Method of Analysis* (New York, 1970) contains a useful theoretical analysis of the relationship between audience and play.

[4] For a more general theory of the presence of topical moral issues in pop-

My third premise is that whenever plot and character play a primary role in narrative or dramatic literature, the reader or spectator enters into a special kind of relationship with the protagonist. We relate differently to the protagonist than to other characters, and this relationship fulfills a deeply rooted need of some kind. Young children, in my experience, prefer stories with clearly defined protagonists to those without them. So, I suspect, do adult audiences, although our ability to adjust to the absence of a protagonist is greater than a child's. When literature is performed rather than read, this relationship is more complex yet also more direct, for the actor's physical presence gives his role a semblance of "reality." Yet because the actor does assume "a local habitation and a name," he is also clearly different, or separate, from the spectator. For the Elizabethans, as for subsequent generations of audiences, this special relationship involves an element of engagement, that identification or fellow-feeling with and emotional attachment to the protagonist which the spectator feels during part or all of the play. It also involves a certain amount of detachment, the ability to judge the protagonist dispassionately and critically from a remove, which may at times become outright repudiation, particularly when to identify would implicate the spectator in a dangerous rebellion against accepted norms.

In the chapters to come, I shall be proposing a dialectical framework within which to describe the sixteenth-century spectator's relationship with the protagonist. The Elizabethan Protestants' conviction that all mankind is divided into the

---

ular drama, see J.S.R. Goodlad, *A Sociology of Popular Drama* (London, 1971). Goodlad proposes the following theory: that popular drama in any age deals with "the area of social living in which members of a community find it most difficult to comply with the moral requirements necessary for the survival of the prevailing social structure" (p. 9). Arguing for a topical approach to the drama which preceded the emergence of Elizabethan tragedy, David Bevington asserts that "during the formative midcentury years, religious politics was virtually the whole substance of drama. . . ." *Tudor Drama and Politics: A Critical Approach to the Topical Meaning* (Cambridge, Mass., 1968), p. 3. As Bevington demonstrates, this tradition of topical commentary played an important role in the development of secular drama.

saved and the damned reveals a fundamental dualism in their way of thinking, which is significantly different from our twentieth-century relativism. We employ a multiplicity of categories to define another human being: ethnic or religious background, political leanings, economic status, place of origin, level of intelligence or education, professional or avocational interests. For the Elizabethans these factors may have been of interest, but there were only two categories that truly mattered, and any person, no matter how complex, ultimately belonged in one or the other. To judge another person, one applied a series of antitheses, for all traits could be reduced to goodness or wickedness. Moreover, every judgment invited an implicit comparison with one's own state of election. Self-definition in contrast to others was an ongoing process, ending only when one made one's final peace with God.

Although the extent to which the Elizabethans brought their religious convictions to the theatre will always remain debatable, the dualism I have just described went beyond consciously adhered to religious belief. Indeed, it was so basic to the Elizabethans' way of perceiving reality that it became a lens through which they viewed themselves and everyone around them. In discussing the earliest experiments in Elizabethan tragedy, I plan to show how the playwrights used this dualism to direct their audience's response, and how the inclination to divide people into the saved and the damned gradually yielded to the discovery that more complex discriminations were needed.[5] In proposing the paradigms of saved

[5] The influence of Puritanism on the emergence of Elizabethan tragedy has received surprising little attention from scholars. Notable exceptions are Alfred Harbage, who observed in *Shakespeare and the Rival Traditions* (1952; rpt., Bloomington, Indiana, 1970), that "To an extent that has never been recognized, the popular drama at its height expressed many of the attitudes we associate with Puritanism, and its period of hardiest growth had been synchronous with that of the bitterest and most sustained attacks by the clergy" (p. 27), and Robert G. Hunter in *Shakespeare and the Mystery of God's Judgments* (Athens, Georgia, 1976), which starts from the premise "that a necessary (though far from sufficient) cause for the ability of the Elizabethans to write great tragedy was the impact on their minds of some of the more strik-

INTRODUCTION

and damned as a context for looking once again at these oft-discussed plays, I have borne in mind that this is one possible approach among many—for just as there is no poetics of tragedy, but only tragedies, as Morris Weitz reminds us at the end of *Hamlet and the Philosophy of Literary Criticism*, so there is no single explanation for the emergence of Elizabethan tragedy.[6]

Since I began working on this topic ten years ago, a growing number of scholars in the field of Renaissance drama have begun to look at the play at least partly in terms of audience response. Taken together, they constitute a critical approach heralded by Norman Rabkin in his collection of English Institute essays of 1968, entitled *Reinterpretations of Elizabethan Drama*. Rabkin saw in the essays he chose a new paradigm for the study of Renaissance drama, concerned with the play as it impinges upon the audience. His call for more work in this area was echoed by Robert Weimann, in *Shakespeare and the Popular Tradition in the Theatre*. Weimann spoke of the mutual influence of "the sensibilities and receptivity of the audience and the consciousness and artistry of the drama" and invited "increased awareness of the dialectics of this interdependence" on the part of critics and scholars.[7]

Rabkin's collection contained Stephen Booth's detailed study of the manipulation of audience response in *Hamlet*, which employs a critical approach subsequently used by E.A.J. Ho-

---

ing ideas of the Protestant Reformation" (p. 1). George C. Herndl, in *The High Design: English Renaissance Tragedy and the Natural Law* (Lexington, Kentucky, 1970) looks at the influence of Calvin on Jacobean tragedy. Herndl uses Harbage's distinction between popular and coterie drama and is primarily concerned with the latter.

[6] Morris Weitz, *Hamlet and the Philosophy of Literary Criticism* (Chicago, 1964), p. 307; cf. the recent caveats against comprehensive explanations by Richard Levin in *New Readings vs. Old Plays: Recent Trends in the Reinterpretation of English Renaissance Drama* (Chicago, 1979) and Norman Rabkin in *Shakespeare and the Problem of Meaning* (Chicago, 1981).

[7] Robert Weimann, *Shakespeare and the Popular Tradition in the Theater: Studies in the Social Dimension of Dramatic Form*, trans. and ed. Robert Schwartz (Baltimore, 1978), p. xii.

8

nigmann in *Shakespeare: Seven Tragedies: The Dramatist's Manipulation of Response* and Larry Champion in *Shakespeare's Tragic
Perspective*, among others. Other scholars who have recently
recognized the importance of the audience in a variety of ways
include Patrick Cruttwell in *The Shakespearean Moment*, Juliet
Dusinberre in *Shakespeare and the Nature of Women*, Alan Dessen in *The Viewer's Eye*, Michael Goldman in *The Actor's Freedom*, Terence Hawkes in *Shakespeare's Talking Animals*, G. K.
Hunter in his preface to the essays collected as *Dramatic Identities and Cultural Tradition*, Emrys Jones in *The Origins of
Shakespeare*, Michael Manheim in *The Weak King Dilemma in
The Shakespearean History Play*, Robert Y. Turner in *Shake-
speare's Apprenticeship*, Judith Weil in *Christopher Marlowe:
Merlin's Prophet*, John Weld in *Meaning in Comedy*, Joel Alt-
man in *The Tudor Play of Mind*, and, perhaps most obviously,
Ann Cook in *The Privileged Playgoers of Shakespeare's London*,
the first full-scale study of the Elizabethan audience since Alfred
Harbage's *Shakespeare's Audience*.

For all of these scholars, Stanley Fish's pronouncement in
his influential essay "Literature in the Reader" might be said
to be an operating assumption. Fish declared that "the information an utterance gives, its message, is a constituent of, but
certainly not to be identified with, its meaning. It is the experience of an utterance . . . that *is* its meaning."[8] For Fish, as
for most of the "reader-response" critics, the reader or spectator whose experience or response is the subject of criticism
can belong to any time and place; little effort is made to distinguish between the original audience and subsequent ones.
One objective of this book is to bring together an audience-
oriented approach to literature and some of the extensive material on sixteenth-century religious attitudes available to the
student of the period. In speculating about the original audience's images of themselves and how the plays were affected

[8] Stanley Fish, *Self-Consuming Artifacts: The Experience of Seventeenth-Century Literature* (Berkeley, 1972), p. 393.

by those images, I hope to reconstruct an important element in the Elizabethan response to tragedy.

This kind of imaginative reconstruction is an essentially interdisciplinary undertaking and, as such, it has benefited greatly from the increasing willingness on the part of literary critics to look to other disciplines for fresh insights and approaches. Much of the best work on Elizabethan literature has resulted from the critic's creative use of the historian's tools and insights. The fields of linguistics and anthropology, more recently, have helped us to view drama as an integral part of its surrounding culture, linked to it through the verbal and visual symbol systems which the community shares and through which its essential values are expressed. As Stephen Greenblatt observes in *Renaissance Self-Fashioning*, the goal of cultural or anthropological literary criticism is to become a "poetics of culture," one which approaches literature in terms of "the social presence *to* the world of the literary text and the social presence of the world *in* the literary text" (my emphasis). Or, as Terence Hawkes puts it, drama is by definition "a communal art by whose means a community 'talks' to itself. A good play 'utters' (or 'outers') the inward and formative presuppositions of its audience, confronts it with, and so potentially resolves, its own essential and defining tensions."[9]

[9] Stephen Greenblatt, *Renaissance Self-Fashioning from More to Shakespeare* (Chicago, 1980), p. 5; Terence Hawkes, *Shakespeare's Talking Animals: Language and Drama in Society* (London, 1973), p. 1. An earlier statement of the influence of a writer's culture on the drama was formulated by Madeleine Doran, who observed in *Endeavors of Art: A Study of Form in Elizabethan Drama* (Madison, Wisconsin, 1954) that the culture supplies the writer with formal possibilities and formal restraints that affect the shape of the work by restricting his conscious choices (pp. 3-19). The relationship between the literary critic and the historian is explored in the opening chapter of Wilbur Sanders' *The Dramatist and the Received Idea: Studies in the Plays of Marlowe and Shakespeare* (Cambridge, 1968). Sanders employs a synthesis of historical and literary methodologies to grasp the "interaction of the personal and social in the creative act," that is, the artist's "creative assimilation" of the "received ideas" his culture offers him. Hence Sanders proposes that an Elizabethan play constitutes "*prima facie* evidence for the state of mind of the audience to which it is addressed" (pp. 17, 40). I am also indebted to William

10

The defining tensions in Elizabethan England were social, political, economic, and, above all, religious. M. C. Bradbrook once said that "in an age of religious tension, all social and political problems tend to formulate themselves in religious terms."[10] The doctrines of election and justification by faith provided the Elizabethans with a particularly apt framework for articulating the tensions of a highly mobile and rapidly changing society. Although Calvinism emphasized man's innate depravity, its corresponding emphasis on God's omnipotence led circuitously, as J.F.H. New observes, to an intensified conviction of human regeneracy. The result was a new dignity afforded to man as a consequence of the exaltation of God's power to grant faith.[11] The implications of Calvinism were as much social and political as they were theological. Lawrence Stone concludes in *The Crisis of the Aristocracy* that the exaltation of private conscience associated with Puritanism "erected a second, independent, hierarchy of spiritual grace alongside that of temporal authority and dignity," and thus contributed to the aristocracy's deeply felt loss of power and influence.[12] As the aristocracy's confidence decreased, that of other classes increased, particularly the mercantile class for whom the doctrine of election provided the assertive self-confidence necessary for survival in a time of economic fluctuation. Because the only true sign of election was inner assurance, Calvinism inadvertently both demanded and encouraged a general self-confidence in people who had until then been told to believe that God rewards humility, subservience and resignation.[13]

Haller's *The Rise of Puritanism: Or, the Way to the New Jerusalem as Set Forth in Pulpit and Press from Thomas Cartwright to John Lilburne and John Milton, 1570-1643* (1938; rpt., New York, 1957).

[10] Muriel C. Bradbrook, *The Rise of the Common Player* (London, 1962), p. 33.

[11] J.F.H. New, *Anglican and Puritan: The Basis of Their Opposition 1558-1640* (Stanford, 1964), pp. 20-21.

[12] Lawrence Stone, *The Crisis of the Aristocracy 1558-1641* (Oxford, 1965), p. 743.

[13] This is a recurring argument of Christopher Hill's in his many studies of the intellectual and economic implications of English Puritanism. In *Change*

But if the doctrine of election offered Elizabethans a way of dealing with the tension posed by social change, it also contributed to those tensions. Implicit in the believer's religious experience was the coexistence of an intense consciousness of natural sinfulness and a belief in the efficacy of God's grace; in Luther's words, "A Christian man is both righteous and a sinner, holy and profane, an enemy of God and yet a childe of God. . . ."[14] This unresolved tension between two utterly opposed self-perceptions was, as scholars frequently observe, the central paradox of Protestantism, and it created an undercurrent of uncertainty and anxiety that could easily lead to despair in even the most confident member of the elect. Two recent studies of Protestant poetics in the sixteenth and seventeenth centuries emphasize the extent to which this aspect of religious experience informed the structures of literature. Both Andrew Weiner and Barbara Lewalski show how the range of emotional states which marked the believer's inner life are reflected in the meditative poem, a form which provided the writer with a way of defining himself.[15]

---

and Continuity in Seventeenth-Century England (Cambridge, Massachusetts, 1975), a collection of essays, Hill stresses the point that "the elect were those who felt themselves to be elect. . . ." The self-confidence that Calvinism encouraged coincided with and spurred the commercial successes that gave rise to capitalism and increased productivity ("Protestantism and the Rise of Capitalism," pp. 92, 102). Hill's work grows out of the Weber-Tawney tradition, which links the emergence of a thriving capitalistic economy in seventeenth-century England with the confidence and self-assurance encouraged by the Puritan ethic. R. H. Tawney, for example, eloquently describes the Puritan as "a spiritual aristocrat" who "drew from his idealization of personal responsibility a theory of individual rights, which, secularized and generalized, was to be among the most potent explosives that the world has known. . . . For, since conduct and action, though availing nothing to attain the free gift of salvation, are a proof that the gift has been accorded, what is rejected as a means is resumed as a consequence, and the Puritan flings himself into practical activity with the daemonic energy of one who, all doubts allayed, is conscious that he is a sealed and chosen vessel." Religion and the Rise of Capitalism (1926; rpt., New York, 1947), p. 191.

[14] Quoted by Barbara K. Lewalski, in Protestant Poetics and the Seventeenth-Century Religious Lyric (Princeton, 1979), p. 17.

[15] Lewalski, and Andrew Weiner, Sir Philip Sidney and the Poetics of Protestantism (Minneapolis, 1978).

The notion that fictional characters can also serve as exercises in self-definition is hardly new; in recent years, it has received increased support from the contributions of psychology to literary criticism. Applying psychoanalytic theory to textual analysis, Constance Brown Kuriyama shows how Marlowe's protagonists reflect the playwright's own search for an ideal self that would fully meet his own requirements, or society's, or both. In the "wavering treatment of the protagonist" which other Marlowe critics have also observed, Kuriyama sees signs of Marlowe's own confrontation with the choice between a negative and positive identity. She uses Erik Erikson's concept of "negative identity," a composite of roles perceived as dangerous and desirable embodying an "evil self."[16] In much the same way, Kai Erikson identifies one of the essential characteristics of Puritanism—that impulse to define oneself in terms of what one is not. This impulse, I shall argue, is at the heart of the Elizabethans' interpretation of the doctrine of election.[17] Stephen Greenblatt posits a similar process in his description of "self-fashioning" in the work of selected Renaissance writers: ". . . self-fashioning is achieved in relation to something perceived as alien, strange or hostile. This threatening Other—heretic, savage, witch, adulteress, traitor, Anti-Christ—must be discovered or invented in order to be attacked and destroyed."[18] The tragic protagonist was, from one point of view, just such a discovery or invention.

Like the literature it explicates, every piece of criticism is part of the dialogue of its age. None is self-sufficient; none is all-explanatory. My approach to the emergence of Elizabethan tragedy builds on the work of many other scholars. Wherever possible, I have tried not to retrace their steps. Having chosen to focus on how the development of a genre reflects the atti-

[16] Constance Brown Kuriyama, *Hammer or Anvil: Psychological Patterns in Christopher Marlowe's Plays* (New Brunswick, New Jersey, 1980), pp. 108, 127. Kuriyama places a good deal of emphasis on Marlowe's alleged homosexuality in her discussion of negative identities.

[17] Kai Erikson, *Wayward Puritans: A Study in the Sociology of Deviance* (New York, 1966), p. 64.

[18] Greenblatt, *Renaissance Self-Fashioning*, p. 9.

tudes of its audience, I have consciously devoted little attention to the playwrights themselves. They undoubtedly had reasons for writing their plays that were unrelated to the audience's demands. Nevertheless, from what we know about the playwright's profession in the sixteenth century, their primary concern was to give their public what it wanted to see, and to prosper in the process. They did not expect their work to outlast marble and the gilded monuments of time, and could never have anticipated the critical attention that has been lavished upon them. If, like Chaucer's Troilus, they are looking down upon us from heaven and laughing at our follies, I beg their indulgence for still another attempt to reconstruct the complex web of circumstances from which their plays emerged.

CHAPTER I

Play and Audience

I. The Overlapping Audience

The medium through which the doctrine of election helped to shape the emergence of the tragic protagonist was the spoken word. In the London of the 1570s, 1580s, and 1590s, both the players and the preachers were attracting increasingly large audiences, and in both cases what they offered was a mixture of instruction and entertainment presented with considerable verbal artistry. Although there were pious sermongoers who shunned the theatres and, conversely, pleasure-loving theatre-goers who attended sermons only when compelled to do so, the two audiences undoubtedly overlapped. The fact that preachers and moralists frequently expressed their hostility to the playhouses is the best evidence that they did; just as the adult companies fought to keep their audiences from defecting to the boy companies, using plays as their weapons, so the preachers and London authorities used sermons, tracts, and public proclamations in their battle to discredit the theatres. These efforts were not limited to Puritans; as Chambers points out, the writings against the stage, especially during the critical period from 1576 to 1583, are of a very heterogeneous character.[1]

Evidence that the audiences overlapped abounds in the sermons and tracts of the 1570s and 1580s. The authors of the Marprelate tracts, for example, continually used theatrical jokes and allusions, assuming that their readers knew and enjoyed the plays. Neither they nor John Foxe, the celebrated author of *The Actes and Monuments*, better known as *The Book of Martyrs*, saw an innate antagonism between plays and religious zeal; as Foxe noted of one of the bishops, "He thwarteth and

---

[1] E. K. Chambers, *The Elizabethan Stage* (Oxford, 1923), I, 253.

wrangleth much against players, printers, preachers. And no marvel why; for he seeth these three things to be set up of God, as a triple bulwark against the triple crown of the Pope to bring him down; as, God be praised, they have done meetly well already." There are verbal echoes of the plays in the sermons that suggest both an attempt on the part of the preachers to enter into competition with the playwrights and a pervasive influence of sermon rhetoric upon the playwrights.[2] Still more evidence that the audiences overlapped can be found in the diary of John Manningham, a young gentleman law student at the Middle Temple in 1602-1603. Manningham's account of a performance of *Twelfth Night*, for which the diary is known to Shakespeare scholars, is juxtaposed with several summaries of sermons. For him, the sermon seems to have been a form of intellectual exercise, worth recording for its ideas and rhetorical presentation. He attended sermons delivered from pulpits throughout the city of London, by preachers as unlike one another as the Anglican Lancelot Andrewes and the Puritan Stephen Egerton. The interspersal of the summaries with jests and aphorisms, lines of verse and snatches of conversation, suggests that Manningham's interest was as much literary and rhetorical as it was pious.[3]

Manningham is typical of the privileged playgoers Ann Cook describes in her recent study of the London theatre audience. Estimating that the "privileged" constituted 10 percent of the permanent population of London and 15 percent of the London populace when visitors are taken into account, Cook hy-

---

[2] Chambers, p. 242n.; see also Lawrence A. Sasek, *The Literary Temper of the English Puritans* (Baton Rouge, La., 1961) and Margot Heinemann, *Puritanism and Theatre: Thomas Middleton and Opposition Drama under the Early Stuarts* (Cambridge, 1980), for evidence that the opposition to the theatre was shared by High Anglicans during the Elizabethan and Jacobean periods and that their condemnations shared the same terms as the Puritans'. For echoes of sermon rhetoric in the plays, see Peter Milward, *Shakespeare's Religious Background* (Bloomington, 1973), which focuses on parallels between the 1593 edition of Henry Smith's collected sermons and Shakespeare's plays.

[3] *The Diary of John Manningham of the Middle Temple: 1602-1603*, ed. Robert Parker Sorlien (Hanover, N.H., 1976).

16

pothesizes that they accounted for at least half of the audience at public and private theatres alike. Cook defines the "privileged" broadly enough to include London merchants, schoolmasters, clerics, soldiers, lawyers, writers, artists, students, well-born apprentices, and the upwardly mobile yeomen and tradesmen who were acquiring wealth, land, and coats of arms in unprecedented numbers during the 1580s and 1590s. Not all the privileged were wealthy, but most were fairly well educated. Unlike most servants, laborers, and craftsmen, they had the leisure time to attend a play in the middle of the day. For the most wealthy and idle among them, attending a play may simply have been a way of passing the time; for the others, it was an experience as instructive as it was entertaining.[4]

In the early years of the reform movement in England, the privileged were also the mainstay of the sermon audiences. They were intelligent, articulate, impatient with the laxness of the older, non-preaching clergy, and willing to support preachers out of their own pockets. The increased emphasis on preaching in Elizabeth's reign was a logical consequence of humanism, with its emphasis on learning, and of Puritanism, a movement led by the religious intellectuals of the day. These were men of education and advanced ideas who shared with their opponents the cultural legacy of the Renaissance.[5] The fact that seventeenth-century Puritanism opposed the monarchy and espoused radical egalitarian political positions has sometimes led to the conclusion that Puritanism began as a popular mass movement. Elizabethan Puritanism was, in fact, an intellectual movement with a relatively small lay base, which attracted the patronage of many of the most important peers of the realm.[6] William Cartwright, whose expulsion from

---

[4] Ann Jennalie Cook, *The Privileged Playgoers of Shakespeare's London 1576-1642* (Princeton, 1981), passim.

[5] For discussion of Puritanism as an intellectual movement, see Horton Davies, *Worship and Theology in England; Vol. I: From Cranmer to Hooker: 1534-1603* (Princeton, 1970), pp. 55, 285; and Michael Walzer, *The Revolution of the Saints* (Princeton, 1970).

[6] Elliot Rose, *Cases of Conscience: Alternatives Open to Recusants and Puri-*

17

Cambridge in 1570 is regarded by many as the first major event in the rise of Puritanism, was, as A. F. Scott Pearson observes, ". . . the mirror of the movement. He enjoyed the special patronage of statesmen like Leicester, Walsingham, Davison, etc., was regarded with sympathy by Burghley, and counted among his friends many of the leading gentry and parliamentarians. . . . His well-wishers were scholars, ministers, and men of social influence, and it was such who were the mainstay of Puritanism."[7] The Puritan nobility were particularly influential in enabling Puritanism to gain a foothold in the universities. Lawrence Stone calculates that "between 1565 and 1575 Cambridge produced no fewer than 228 Puritan ministers and schoolmasters to say nothing of the hundreds of young gentlemen who went out into the world with a firm belief in the need for a Puritan reformation of the Anglican Church."[8] Noblemen like Leicester, Bedford, Huntingdon, Warwick, and Rich were sufficiently powerful to insure Puritan spokesmen access to publication and to protect them from being silenced. Hence a highly verbal minority emerged, composed primarily of preachers and patrons, its influence vastly disproportionate to its lay base. They were united not so much by a desire to change the form of church government or a common theological doctrine; rather, they were united by their conviction that preaching was, as Archbishop Grindal told the Queen, "the only mean and instrument of the salvation of mankind."[9]

---

tans Under Elizabeth I and James I (Cambridge, 1975), p. 213. Rose adds that many of the patrons of Puritan preachers were not themselves Puritans.

[7] A. F. Scott Pearson, *Thomas Cartwright and Elizabethan Puritanism: 1535-1603* (Cambridge, 1925), p. 411. See also Patrick Collinson in *The Elizabethan Puritan Movement* (Berkeley, 1967).

[8] Lawrence Stone, *The Crisis of the Aristocracy: 1558-1641* (Oxford, 1965), p. 735.

[9] Quoted by Christopher Hill in *Society and Puritanism in Pre-Revolutionary England*, 2nd ed. (New York, 1967), p. 31. The debate about the appropriateness of the term "Puritan" to describe this group shows no signs of abating. As Patrick Collinson observes, the term "Anglican" is applied anachronistically to this period, and the ideological differences between those we call

Thousands of sermons were preached in London in the 1570s and 1580s. There were 123 parish churches in London and its immediate suburbs, many filled to overflowing, according to Manningham, by crowds eager to hear sermons. In London, the percentage of regular parish clergy who preached rose from 27 percent to 88 percent between 1561 and 1601. Independent lectureships, approximately a third of which were held by Puritans, produced still more sermons; by 1600, lecturers were preaching 100 sermons a week.[10] Like the theatres, the churches were meeting places, where business and social transactions took place, and where people gathered to talk and exchange news. According to contemporary accounts, sermons were disrupted by jests, laughter, and the showing off of new clothes, just as the plays were. Preachers whose

---

Puritans and Anglicans was one of degree, not fundamental principle (pp. 26-27). Andrew Weiner argues in *Sir Philip Sidney and the Poetics of Protestantism* (Minneapolis, 1978) that the term "Puritan" is used anachronistically also, since those to whom it was applied did not accept it as a positive apellation until well into the seventeenth century. He prefers the term "godly" for the reformers of the 1560s, 1570s, and 1580s (p. 6). Lawrence Stone notes that for long periods most of the men now referred to as Puritans were full members of the established Church, agitating change from within (p. 725).

[10] The lectureship was an essential element in Puritan proselytizing and education, and one which had long belonged to the English religious tradition. Begun by the medieval preaching friars, the endowed town lecture survived the Henrician and Edwardian reformations and became a vehicle for religious protest with the return of the Marian exiles, many of whom could not get preferments but could attract a constituency eager to hear sermons. The London lectureships were conducted within the parishes for the local congregations; some were endowed (usually by members of the business community), but many were initiated and financed by the parishioners themselves. The lecturer was therefore directly responsible to the congregation and could be dismissed at will; hence he had to be sure to please his audience in very much the same way as an acting company did. While the lectureship was not a strictly Puritan institution, the number of Puritans who came to London as lecturers reflected the extent of the demand for their style of preaching, particularly since, as Seaver notes, by the 1590s there were enough properly licensed Anglicans to answer the City's need. Puritans were more likely than Anglicans to hold a lectureship more than once, and their mobility contributed to the rise of a common rhetoric. Hill, p. 60; Paul S. Seaver, *The Puritan Lectureships: The Politics of Religious Dissent: 1560-1662* (Stanford, 1970), pp. 124, 180.

19

sermons did not please were known to have been pulled from the pulpit, or, at the very least, harassed by coughing and heckling. The growing popularity of preaching, like that of playing, accounted for a dramatic increase in the number of publications during the 1570s and 1580s. The publication of printed sermons rose from nine volumes in the decade of the 1560s to 113 in the decade of the 1580s.[11] Through pulpit and press, the attitudes of the preachers and the language that attached to those attitudes passed into the culture and became the common possession of playwrights and audiences alike. Whether or not these attitudes were consciously endorsed by the people exposed to them is unimportant; what matters is that their widespread influence gradually began to affect the way the plays were written and received.

The importance of the overlapping audience as a link between the pulpit and the stage predates the rise of Puritanism. An earlier wave of popular preaching, inaugurated by the friars of the thirteenth and fourteenth centuries, coincided with the emergence of the mystery cycles. G. R. Owst has speculated that the sermons, preached in the vernacular on outdoor scaffolds, helped bring about the "secularization" of the Latin liturgical drama which until then had been confined to the churches. The sermons contained "*every* variety of expression to be found in the plays—canonical and uncanonical, serious and humorous, satiric and tragic"—presented with a dramatic intensity that made them a truer antecedent of the medieval drama than the formal liturgical recitations of the priest. Responding to their audience's tastes, the preachers gradually incorporated more satire and comic *exempla* into their sermons. These corresponded to the comic interludes in the plays—they were designed "to plesen the puple," but with an eye to their ultimate edification.[12]

---

[11] Alan Fager Herr, *The Elizabethan Sermon: A Survey and a Bibliography* (Philadelphia, 1940), pp. 32-33; 27. For more information on Elizabethan preaching, see J. W. Blench, *Preaching in England in the Late Fifteenth and Sixteenth Centuries* (New York, 1964).

[12] G. R. Owst, *Literature and Pulpit in Medieval England* (Cambridge, 1933), pp. 473-90, 527-28.

What began as a process of mutual influence soon became a rivalry, as preachers and players competed for the same audiences. By the last decades of the sixteenth century, this rivalry was intense and frequently virulent, despite—or perhaps because of—the immense popularity of both forms of public entertainment. Threatened by the success of the plays, the preachers met "every attempt to justify players on didactic grounds . . . by the retort that plays were the devil's sermons—a hideous mockery or antitype of true instruction."[13] The efforts of the preachers, however, had no apparent effect on theatre attendance. Anthony Munday, who wrote *A second and third blast of retrait from plaies and Theaters* pseudonymously, probably at the commission of the City of London, complained that although preachers denounced plays "daie by daie in al places of greatest resort," it was nevertheless the case that "infinite thousands of Christians doe dailie abide at the showes of vnseemlie things." So great was the appeal of the players that on feast days "the temple is despised, to run unto Theaters, the Church is emptied, the yeard is filled; wee leaue the sacrament, to feede our adulterous eies with the impure. . . ." Munday represents theatre attendance as a hellish inversion or antithesis of church attendance. "How saie we that wee worship God in his Church, which serue the Diuel alwaies at plaies, and that wittinglie, and willinglie?" The theatre is "the destruction of our hope, and saluation," a despising of the Lord's table, the sin which replaces godliness, an uncleanness opposed to repentance, a filthiness opposed to purity of life.[14]

The neat parallelisms of Munday's tract suggest the extent to which the theatre was perceived as an alternative to the formal worship of God. Ironically, the reformers drove their audiences to seek in the theatre what the Church no longer

[13] Muriel C. Bradbrook, *The Rise of the Common Player* (London, 1962), p. 40.

[14] W. C. Hazlitt, ed., *The English Drama and Stage under the Tudor and Stuart Princes 1543-1664* (London, 1869), pp. 101-19. See Sasek for other examples of tracts which opposed the theatres because they offered alternative gathering places to sermon attendance.

21

provided. In their contempt for prelates as "stage players" engaged in "popish pageants,"[15] they had rejected the need for ritual and ceremony, for the incarnation of abstract beliefs in physical gesture, adornment, and symbolic objects, which is to be found in every culture. When the English Church ceased to fulfill this need, the drama began to take its place. Marlowe, who is reported in the Baines note to have said "That if there be any god or any good religion, then it is in the Papists' because the service of god is performed with more ceremonies . . . ," was among the first secular Elizabethan playwrights to recognize instinctively the existence of an audience whose need for dramatized ritual the Church could no longer satisfy. In *Doctor Faustus*, and again in subsequent Elizabethan tragedies, the ceremony of the mass is spectacularly, indeed blasphemously, transformed into secular drama.[16] In a similar way, the controversy over vestments, certainly one of the defining tensions of Elizabeth's reign, is imaginatively mirrored in so many plays' preoccupation with clothing and its significance, and in the process of assuming and putting off robes which come to stand for identities in plays from *Tamburlaine* to *Richard II* to *Macbeth*.

But if the drama provided Elizabethan audiences with the theatricality that the reformers had banished from religious observance, it also provided them with a searching examination of character for which the popular tradition of preaching had helped to create a demand. The preachers spoke directly to their audiences' need for "physicians of the soul." William Haller describes their method in *The Rise of Puritanism*:

For centuries preachers had been analyzing the moral life into such categories as pride, envy, lust, avarice and their

[15] Cf. Jonas Barish's two very suggestive essays on anti-theatrical prejudice: "Exhibitionism and the Anti-theatrical Prejudice," *ELH* XXXVI, 1 (March, 1969), 1-29; "The Antitheatrical Prejudice," *Critical Quarterly* 66, 329-48.

[16] C. L. Barber, "The form of Faustus' fortunes good or bad," *Tulane Drama Review*, 84 (Summer, 1964), 96 ff. Barber explores the idea of religious ritual in *Faustus* in a daring application of Freudian theory to the images of eating and drinking in the play.

opposites. They diagnosed spiritual morbidity by identifying the species of sin with which the soul might be infected. Their method was to make war on wickedness by attacking its several varieties. They treated sinners by showing them how to detect each sin in the abstract under the infinite disguises which evil knew but too well how to assume. . . . This often led the preacher—in the sixteenth and the seventeenth, as in the fourteenth, centuries—to more or less realistic description of actual manners and morals as well as to elaborate systematic allegorization of moral abstractions. . . . Thus he came to depict the miser or the hypocrite instead of, or in addition to, defining or allegorizing the sins they embodied.

The Puritan preachers and lecturers, competing with the depictions of sin and folly offered by the players and confronted with audiences who "longed to know what they must do to be saved," produced sermons that spoke eloquently to their listeners' needs:

> So they set out to describe the warfare of the spirit, to portray the drama of the inner life, to expound the psychology of sin and redemption. This, they found, was what the people would come to hear, and the more actively they responded to ever-increasing audiences the more they gave up abstractions in order to mirror the individual consciousness of spiritual stress, to convince the individual of sin in order to persuade him of grace, to make him feel worse in order to make him feel better, to inspire pity and fear in order to purge him of those passions.

"Had they but known it or been capable of admitting it," Haller adds, "precisely such a mirror was being held up to nature in the theatres, though not with quite the same intention or effect."[17]

The notion that the drama and the sermon spoke to the same need felt by the Elizabethan audience receives support

[17] William Haller, *The Rise of Puritanism* (1938; rpt., N.Y., 1957), pp. 31-33.

from no less a critic of the theatre than Stephen Gosson. Although he inveighs against the amorous scenes in the comedies, Gosson grudgingly admits that "nowe are the abuses of the worlde revealed, every man in a play may see his owne faultes, and learne by this glasse, to amende his manners." Indeed, while the declared purpose of *The Schoole of Abuse* was to be a criticism of poets, Gosson reveals himself to be just as preoccupied with gamblers and bearbaiters and other such characters. His main complaint against the plays seems to have been less concerned with their content than with the behavior of the audience: he speaks at great length of "suche heaving, and shoouing, such ytching and shouldring, too sitte by women . . . such ticking, such toying, such smiling, such winking," in sum, such activity that the playhouse resembled "a generall Market of Bawdrie."[18] His outrage implies that the innocent and well-intentioned were indeed present among the spectators, and could become corrupted by their environment.

The writings of Gosson and others indicate that the effort to subvert the theatres in sixteenth-century London was largely caused by an anxiety about the effects of assemblies in a compact and volatile community. Gosson accused the players of being instruments of the devil because they brought together multitudes of people. Ironically, Elizabeth regarded preaching in much the same way; the devil of sedition, she feared, was present wherever crowds were allowed to gather.[19] Indeed, the complaints about playing and preaching in the sixteenth century sound remarkably alike, and are, as the following examples suggest, somewhat at cross purposes with one another. In the Lord Mayor's protest to the Archbishop of Canterbury in 1592, he complained that "the youth is greatly corrupted and their manners infected by the wanton and profane devices represented on the stages; prentices and servants withdrawn

18 Stephen Gosson, *The s[c]hoole of abuse, conteining a pleasaunt invective against poets* (London, 1579), STC #12097, sig. C2ᵛ, B5⁴. (For this and all other sixteenth- and seventeenth-century works reproduced on microfilm, I have given the Short Title Catalogue [STC] number.)

19 Douglas Bush, *English Literature in the Earlier Seventeenth Century 1600-1660* (Oxford, 1962), p. 312.

from their work; and all sorts in general from their daily resort to sermons and other godly exercise, to the great hindrance of the trades and traders of the City and the profanation of religion." Interestingly, the same argument had been used against preaching back in the 1550s; allegedly, Chancellor Rich had objected to the practice of preaching on working days on the grounds that it might "increase the people's idleness." By the 1580s, "gadding to sermons" had inspired more vehement complaints. One observer noted that William Dyke, a popular Puritan preacher, attracted "many of this gadding people [who] came from far and went home late, both young men and young women together." And another noted that at outdoor preaching exercises followed by formal "repetitions" or debates, "these discussions were often wont, as it was said, to produce quarrels and fights."[20]

If the plays and sermons had produced nothing more serious than quarrels and fights, many of the important changes we associate with the Renaissance might never have occurred. Obviously, their influence was more far-reaching. In analogous ways, the preachers and players diverted their audiences from occupations presided over by traditional and vested sources of authority, substituting a new and threatening appeal to the intellect and the emotions. In messages that were diverse and frequently conflicting, the preachers and players presented vivid and uncompromising evidence that human existence was at once more fraught with possibilities and less predictable than it had been in the past.

II. THE TRAGIC RESPONSE

In "An Apologie for Poetry" Sir Philip Sidney defended comedy and tragedy through the following analogy: "Now, as in Geometry the oblique must bee knowne as wel as the right, and in Arithmetick the odde as well as the euen, so in

[20] G. B. Harrison, *An Elizabethan Journal* (New York, 1929), pp. 111-12; Patrick Collinson, *The Elizabethan Puritan Movement* (Berkeley, 1967), pp. 373-74.

the actions of our life who seeth not the filthines of euil want-eth a great foile to perceiue the beauty of vertue." Sidney presents his readers with a basic epistemological premise: we learn to recognize virtue by contrasting it with its opposite. The spectator responds to a play, he argues, by becoming as different as possible from the characters whose follies are exhibited therein. Hence comedy imitates "the common errors of our life . . . in the most ridiculous and scornefull sort that may be; so as it is impossible that any beholder can be content to be such a one." But underlying this rejection on the part of the beholder is a recognition of likeness without which the play would not have the desired effect: ". . . nothing can more open his eyes then to finde his own actions contemptibly set forth." "High and excellent Tragedy" performs the same function on a more exalted level: it "maketh Kinges feare to be Tyrants, and Tyrants manifest their tirannicall humors; that, with sturring the affects of admiration and commiseration, teacheth the vncertainety of this world, and vpon how weake foundations guilden roofes are builded."[21] The "affects of admiration and commiseration" became, in Shakespeare's words, the "woe or wonder" evoked by the spectacle which greeted Fortinbras, an audience within a play, when he came onstage in the final moments of *Hamlet*. Horatio offers to recreate the tragic events for Fortinbras, "lest more mischance/ On plots and errors happen"; like Sidney, he believes that tragedy can make kings fear to be tyrants.

Sidney's underlying assumption is a common one: things are defined by what they are not; that is, human reason relies

---

[21] Sir Philip Sidney, "An Apologie for Poetry," *Elizabethan Critical Essays*, ed. G. Gregory Smith (Oxford, 1904), I, 177 ff. Walter Kauffman notes that Elizabethan theories of literature constitute a "passive poetics," one which focuses on the audience rather than the author. *Tragedy and Philosophy* (New York, 1969), p. 100. His observation reinforces what Kenneth Burke says about the form of classical and Elizabethan tragedy: when a play is telling a story the audience is likely to know, as both classical and Elizabethan tragedy did, it is more concerned with "eloquence" than "sequence," and its form will be determined by the psychology of the audience rather than by the psychology of the hero. *Counter-Statement* (Chicago, 1931), pp. 31 ff.

on comparisons in order to comprehend whatever is subject to moral judgment. Nowhere was this more evident than in the Elizabethans' preoccupation with salvation and damnation. For the believer beset with doubts about his state of election, one means of achieving assurance was to measure himself against the examples of the damned with which his culture provided him. These figures, whether hypothetical or real, displayed characteristics that were the opposite of those he hoped to find in himself. Kai Erikson describes this process in his analysis of American Puritanism:

> One of the surest ways to confirm an identity, for communities as well as for individuals, is to find some way of measuring what one is *not*. And as the settlers began to take stock of themselves in this new and uncertain land, they learned to study the shapes in which the Devil appeared to them with special care—for he had always loomed in Puritan imagery as a dark adversary against which people could test the edge of their own sainthood.[22]

The Jungian psychologist M. Esther Harding suggests that the Protestants' preoccupation with the damned was directly related to their rejection of the old religion. She explains that

> ... the Protestant movement that made such strenuous efforts to cleanse the Church of "idol worship" succeeded only in destroying a form in which psychological elements could be housed. Because no more appropriate "house" was found for them they escaped into the world, so that an even darker era of superstition supervened, with witch-burnings, blue laws, and so on. For the evil of the unconscious was now projected not to images or idols but to *persons*.[23]

[22] Kai Erikson, in *Wayward Puritans: A Study in the Sociology of Deviance* (New York, 1966), p. 64; Larzar Ziff also, in discussing the concept of religious sect among New England Puritans, stresses the sectarians' consciousness of being different from others as the basis for their fellowship. See *Puritanism in America* (New York, 1973), p. 78.

[23] M. Esther Harding, *The I and the Not-I: A Study in the Development of Consciousness*, Bollingen Series LXXIX (Princeton, 1965), p. 206.

These persons represent that inescapable shadow self who embodies all the qualities perceived as undesirable in a given culture. By projecting them onto another (i.e., an "other") the individual can be convinced of his own rectitude, while the person to whom the shadow qualities are attached will seem to be the devil incarnate.

Variously called "the alien," "the outsider," or "the stranger," the "other" is a borderline figure, sometimes a hero, more often a villain, who marks "the limits of the human," customarily from the farther side, though never without some ambiguity. So theorizes Leslie Fiedler, in *The Stranger in Shakespeare*, a provocative book which argues that Shakespeare presents Jews, women (e.g., woman as witch), blacks, and savages as strangers or "others" at various times in the plays, and that these figures threaten destruction rather than offer hope of salvation.[24] In a time of uncertainty and change, the "other" functioned as an exercise in negative definition, draw-

[24] Leslie Fiedler, *The Stranger in Shakespeare* (New York, 1972), p. 15. I have encountered the term "the other" in psychological, anthropological, philosophical, and theological contexts. In most usages, the "other" is the "not-self," as in Emerson's distinction between the "me" and "not-me." This does not necessarily carry any implications of value—the "not-me" need not be better or worse than the "me," simply different. Sometimes the difference plays on fundamental dichotomies—for Simone de Beauvoir, woman is the "other" from the perspective of man and vice versa. For a recent application of de Beauvoir's concept to Shakespeare's plays, see Linda Bamber, *Comic Women, Tragic Men: A Study of Gender and Genre in Shakespeare* (Stanford, 1982). Elsewhere, the difference depends wholly on context. As Giles Gunn demonstrates in *The Interpretation of Otherness: Literature, Religion, and the American Imagination* (Oxford, 1979), American literature is rich in dramatizations of the relationship between self and other—Ahab and Moby Dick represent one form, Whitman's sense of the "other" as comrade is another. Robinson Jeffers' sense of the "other" as the opposite of the self who holds absolute dominion over the self is still another (p. 183). Gunn returns to a paradigm set forth originally by Perry Miller: man defines or redefines himself in response to an ideal "other," which he may confront in various human or non-human forms. From this process of encountering the "other" emerges a new understanding of the self.

My paradigm is not inconsistent with Miller's and Gunn's, but it is more specific to the Calvinist dichotomy of saved and damned, which I see as a

ing attention to the bonds which hold the community together by transgressing them. We can speculate that this process of self-affirmation lies behind the Elizabethans' fascination with the behavior of such "others" as devils, witches, spirits, heretics, and criminals, not to mention Moors, Turks, Jews, and other infidels. As their writings indicate, the Elizabethans found examples of the "other" all around them. There were the papists, whose cruel persecutions of true Protestants during Mary's reign were vividly recounted in Foxe's *Book of Martyrs*, the Pope, popularly regarded and reviled as Antichrist, and especially the Spanish, against whom the English perceived themselves as the Elect Nation, God's chosen people. One of the most obvious versions of the "other" was the Machiavel, whose monstrous self-interest and the malevolent world in which it was permitted to flourish were the antithesis of the ideal commonwealth and its inhabitants. The caricaturing of the Machiavel became an act of exorcism, a way of dealing with the moral cynicism and political opportunism which seemed to threaten traditional values.[25]

Although we may not share the Elizabethans' beliefs about what constitutes the "other," our conception of character in the drama will never entirely cease to be "a matter of moral partisanship," to use Harbage's phrase. Observing that our

---

central factor in the Elizabethans' frame of reference. While the self-other paradigm can be perceived vertically (i.e., Man-God or Man-Devil), it is more frequently perceived horizontally within the human realm (saved-damned). For the Elizabethans, the "me" or self was always ultimately a member of the elect, while the "other" represented the damned and what it meant to be damned. The "other" is thus a negation or opposite of the self, and not simply an alien. Moreover, it is a negation in a clearly moral sense. The "understanding" of which Miller speaks I would call instead an affirmation of oneself, of one's value, one's rightness, and one's identity as a child of God. I will thus be using the term "other" throughout this book to refer to the attributes Elizabethans associated with the reprobate, imaginatively embodied in fictional form. These attributes are the opposite of those which the Elizabethans used to define themselves.

[25] Robert Ornstein, *The Moral Vision of Jacobean Tragedy* (Madison, 1960), pp. 27 ff.

29

moral responses to characters are inextricably joined with one another (we disdain Polonius because Hamlet does, and because Claudius trusts him), Harbage maintains that the distinctions among characters in the plays will always be "predicated upon a preexisting distinction between good and evil in the minds of the spectators."[26]

These distinctions, while they never disappear, begin to play a different role as didactic drama gives way to tragedy. What Sidney described in 1583 seems quite remote from what would soon become a much more complex relationship between the spectator and the tragic protagonist. For Sidney, the drama is still essentially didactic, just as it had been since the first English plays were performed some two centuries earlier. Didactic drama seeks to convert identification into repudiation; if the spectator recognizes any resemblance between himself and an erring character, he resolves to become the opposite of what he sees. Unless the play concludes with the reformation of the character and his reconciliation with the forces of good, such repudiation is a necessary part of the spectator's experience. As he witnesses the character's punishment or destruction, he dissociates himself and regards what he has seen as a cautionary tale, a mirror of what could happen to him if he is not careful.[27] Any enjoyment he feels is a function of vicarious, or utterly different, experience—through the "other" on the stage he experiences a release from the strictures of ordinary morality and the perpetual anxiety about election without any personal guilt or fear of the consequences. Any sympathy he feels for the protagonist is contained within limits set by his own clearly defined sense of right and wrong. The structure of di-

---

[26] Alfred Harbage, *As They Liked It* (1947; rpt., Philadelphia, 1972), pp. 20, 59-61.

[27] In *Shakespearean Tragedy: Its Art and Its Christian Premises* (Bloomington, 1969) Roy Battenhouse argues that the unhappiness with which tragedy ends could take the form of "a soul lost in damnable error." So, for example, Battenhouse suggests that many members of Shakespeare's audience might have seen in Hamlet "a profane fool and ignorant scourge—and might thereupon have confessed, 'There but for the grace of God, go I.' " One need not agree entirely with Battenhouse to see this as one element of many in the Elizabethan spectator's response (p. 155).

dactic drama continually reinforces this sense of right and wrong: for example, in the fifteenth- and sixteenth-century didactic dramas based on the Christian myth, the virtuous are always rewarded, if not in life, then after death. Evil is always contained and ultimately punished, for it is never more powerful than good.

In its most fundamental form, the Christian myth had none of the tragic possibilities of the Greek myths. The playwrights and audiences of antiquity recognized that tragedy poses moral dilemmas which resist simple solution. Like those audiences, we continue to respond imaginatively to the great tragic protagonists of every age, knowing that we cannot judge them easily or with any conviction that our judgment is valid. We may feel that we would not have acted as Oedipus or Othello did, yet we do not know how, in their circumstances, we could have approached their nobility and greatness of spirit. So powerful is their hold over our imaginations that we cannot repudiate them; yet, at the same time, their tragedy is so absolute, so terrible, that we cannot identify with them either. In effect, the identification and repudiation that are separate and successive responses in the audience's experience of didactic drama intermingle in tragedy to become a complex synthesis that can never be wholly reduced to either.

The notion that tragedy somehow brings together the contrary responses of engagement and detachment has a long history. Shakespeare critics, in particular, speak of the double vision that Shakespeare creates and sustains in his audience, provoking us, as Larry Champion tells us, "simultaneously to participation in the protagonist's spiritual anguish and to judgment on the decisions and actions that destroy him as well as those he loves." Certain characters, Faustus and Macbeth, for instance, can only be understood in terms of this double response. It also helps to explain the aesthetic pleasure that the spectator feels in the presence of terrible suffering, which is surely one of the most mysterious aspects of the tragic response.[28]

[28] Larry Champion, *Shakespeare's Tragic Perspective* (Athens, Georgia, 1973),

The first critical treatise to look at the audience's response in this way was Aristotle's *Poetics*, a work derived from its author's observations of the audience's response to Greek tragedy. The protagonist, Aristotle said, must be a man "like ourselves," not eminently good and just, nor utterly villainous, but brought to misfortune primarily through some error or frailty. But he is also unlike most of us, inasmuch as he is highly renowned and prosperous, and inasmuch as character and circumstance have conspired to create an uncommon sequence of events leading to his downfall. The playwright will have succeeded in combining these likenesses and unlikenesses if the audience feels both pity and fear for the protagonist he has created.[29] The passage in which Aristotle states that tragedy must contain or consist of "incidents arousing pity and fear, wherewith to accomplish its katharsis of such emotions" is one of the most debated in the *Poetics*.[30] The words "pity"

---

p. 3. C.f. E.A.J. Honigmann, who says of the "poetic assent" that the audience gives to Macbeth's crime that "We approve in a no-man's land between moral engagement and aesthetic detachment, which may be called psychological assent," *Shakespeare: Seven Tragedies: The Dramatist's Manipulation of Response* (London, 1976), p. 19. Other critics who have discussed the double response in Macbeth include R. S. Crane in *The Languages of Criticism*; Wilbur Sanders in *The Dramatist and the Received Idea*; and Richard Waswo in "Damnation, Protestant Style: Macbeth, Faustus and Christian Tragedy," *Journal of Medieval and Renaissance Studies*, IV (1974), 63-99. Sir Kenneth Clark has suggested that the dual vision, or double response, characterizes other art forms as well: he says of Titian that "he could maintain that balance between intense participation and absolute detachment which distinguishes art from other forms of human activity" (quoted by Maynard Mack in "Engagement and Detachment in Shakespeare's Plays," *Essays on Shakespeare and Elizabethan Drama in Honor of Hardin Craig*, ed. Richard Hosley [Columbia, Missouri, 1962], p. 275).

[29] *On Poetry and Music*, trans. S. H. Butcher, ed. Milton C. Nahm (Indianapolis, Library of Liberal Arts, 1948), sec. XIII, p. 16.

[30] *On Poetry and Music*, sec. VI, p. 9. Gerald Else, whose translation I have also used, renders this phrase differently: ". . . through a course of pity and fear completing the purification of tragic acts which have those emotional characteristics." *Poetics* (Ann Arbor, 1967), p. 25. Else's controversial reading seems to place less emphasis on katharsis as an effect on the audience than does Butcher's. Still another theory of katharsis, which completely divorces

and "fear" are always linked throughout the work, and Aristotle distinguishes between them only once: pity, he says is aroused by unmerited misfortune, fear, by the misfortune of a man like ourselves.[31] More extended definitions appear in the *Rhetoric*, as part of a catalogue of the emotions to which a speaker may appeal in order to persuade his audience. Pity is defined as "a sense of pain at what we take to be . . . an evil of a destructive or painful kind, which befalls one who does not deserve it, which we think we ourselves or some one allied to us might likewise suffer. . . ." Those whom we pity may be like us "in age, or character, or habits of mind, or social standing, or birth and blood"; but if they are too closely allied to us, we will feel alarm, not pity, as if we ourselves were threatened. Pity is thus distinguished from fear in respect to its object: "whatever men fear for themselves will arouse their pity when it happens to others."[32] The element of nearness or likeness which pity involves thus seems to be an artistic one, arising from illusion, not actual identification:

> . . . it is when suffering *seems* [my emphasis] near to them that men pity. . . . Accordingly, the speaker will be more successful in arousing pity if he heightens the effect of his description with fitting attitudes, tones, and dress—in a word, with dramatic action; for he thus makes the evil seem close at hand—puts it before our eyes as a thing that is on the point of occurring or has just occurred.

Aristotle apparently distinguishes between two levels of identification, or likeness. One is a complete identification—if we

the work from the audience, is that of Kenneth Telford, who believes that katharsis is the final cause of tragedy and that pity and fear are functional properties of dramatic action, not emotional effects on the audience. (*Aristotle's Poetics: Translation and Analysis* [Chicago, 1961], p. 23.)

[31] *On Poetry and Music*, sec. XIII, p. 16.

[32] Lane Cooper, *The Rhetoric of Aristotle: An Expanded Translation with Supplementary Examples for Students of Composition and Public Speaking* (New York, 1932; rpt., 1960), pp. 120-22 (sec. 2.8). Aristotle formally defines fear as "a pain or disturbance arising from a mental image of impending evil of a destructive or painful sort," p. 107 (sec. 2.5).

fear for ourselves, then the fear which belongs to tragedy must arise from a strong and complete identification with the protagonist. The second level of identification, causing pity, is based on a likeness which can be rationally analyzed as one of age, or birth, and so forth. Furthermore, it is a picture of suffering which we see,[33] not a feeling which we endure, and our detachment stems from that very awareness that this is another in whom we can see some resemblance to ourselves.

If indeed the definitions in the *Rhetoric* may be applied to the *Poetics*, Aristotle's consistent pairing of the two words might be interpreted as a recognition that the audience's pleasurable participation in dramatic tragedy depends primarily on a balance between their inclination to identify with the tragic protagonist and their sense of detachment from him. Too much of the first would destroy the dramatic illusion; too much of the second would undermine their awareness that the tragic protagonist, though similar, remains essentially different from themselves, and that his fate could never be their own. The essence of the tragic response, then, as Aristotle envisioned it, is an ability to view the character from two different perspectives at the same time. When the spectator experiences the double response of engagement and detachment, he will feel intensely involved with the tragic character, yet he will be able to accept that character's downfall and death. Like the Greeks, the audiences who watched Shakespeare's plays had the ability to experience a dual response, despite the fact that, only two or three decades earlier, the only drama they knew was primarily didactic. Scholars have attempted to account for this ability in various ways. S. L. Bethell, for instance, has suggested that the Elizabethan audience was capable of "multiconsciousness," that is, "the ability to keep simultaneously in mind two opposite aspects of a situation." He attributed this "dual mode of attention" to the mixture of conventionalism and naturalism in Elizabethan stage technique, a mixture which enabled the playwrights to create characters who elicited two

[33] *Rhetoric*, pp. 122-23 (sec. 2.8).

very different kinds of response. For example, an Elizabethan audience would find Falstaff both amusing and morally repre-hensible; they would applaud his wit, but approve his final dismissal. In their recognition that the "play world" is just that—an unreal and impossible fabrication constructed from conventions upon which they and the playwright have tacitly agreed—they could enjoy Falstaff and his antics, just as they had enjoyed the comic devils of the morality and mystery plays. But their assent to the values of the "real world," which also informed their response to the play, prompted them to reject Falstaff, as Hal would utimately have to do.[34]

The same "dual awareness of play-world and real world," to use Bethell's words, underlies the audience's response to a tragic protagonist. Their sense of kinship with the protagonist stems from feelings appropriate to the real world; they admire him for his endurance of suffering and feel sad because of his inevitable destruction. But juxtaposed with these feelings is relief that the tragedy is contained within the "play world." This relief results from the audience's ability to detach them-selves from what they see, an ability first described by Lucre-tius in the famous passage in *De Rerum Natura* which begins by exulting in the joy that comes from gazing "from the shore at the heavy stress some other man is enduring!"[35] Like the spectator who watches from a safe remove the storm at sea or the field of battle, the spectator at the play is always aware of the distance that separates him from what he observes, and of his identity as *spectator*, not participant.

Stage techniques alone do not account for the Elizabethan audience's ability to remain simultaneously engaged with and detached from the tragic protagonist. It has frequently been suggested that tragedy comes into existence during ages of

[34] S. L. Bethell, *Shakespeare and the Popular Dramatic Tradition* (Durham, N.C., 1944), pp. 26-29. For another approach to the role of stage techniques in producing engagement and detachment, see Mack, "Engagement and De-tachment."

[35] Lucretius, *On the Nature of the Universe*, trans. R. E. Latham (London, 1951), p. 60.

transition, and that the most profoundly tragic characters of such an age embody the uncertainties and conflicts as well as the ideals and aspirations of their time. According to the Hegelian view, the great heroes of history are tragic because they embody the new idea, and are destroyed in the last assertive effort of the old ways which, sensing the danger to their survival, attack the representative of the new. Hence the hero is a victim, sacrificed that the new may succeed the old.[36] Elizabethan England was clearly a time of transition; in the words of Hiram Hadyn, it was an age of "intellectual and cultural reorientation," in which the Reformation played a central role in breaking apart the "comprehensive and interlocking world order" formed by the Scholastics and the humanists.[37] This view is similar to Herbert Weisinger's, who reminds us that both fifth-century Athens and Elizabethan England were profoundly religious, yet in both eras skepticism and new doctrines challenged old ones. For Weisinger, tragedy questions the accepted order of things, but ultimately yields a sense of assurance achieved through suffering.[38] For other thinkers, the tragic vision is much more pessimistic, and offers no hope for the individual who, because he lives in a time of crisis and social flux, is separated from mankind, forced to gamble on his own salvation, and ultimately condemned as a heretic.[39] Recently, Charles and Elaine Hallett have suggested that Elizabethan revenge tragedy be viewed as the consequence of a shift from a stable culture which imparts a sense of coherence to the lives of its inhabitants, to a culture in which the myths that made suffering meaningful have crumbled and existence begins to seem absurd.[40]

[36] Karl Jaspers, "Tragedy is not Enough," reprinted in *Tragedy: Modern Essays in Criticism*, ed. Lawrence Michel and Richard B. Sewall (Englewood Cliffs, N.J., 1963).

[37] Hiram Hadyn, *The Counter-Renaissance* (New York, 1950), p. xiv.

[38] Herbert Weisinger, *Tragedy and the Paradox of the Fortunate Fall* (London, 1953), p. 267.

[39] See, for example, Lucien Goldmann's theories about seventeenth-century French tragedy and Jean Duvignaud, *Sociologie du Théâtre: Essai sur les Ombres Collectives* (Paris, 1965).

[40] Charles A. and Elaine S. Hallett, *The Revenger's Madness* (Lincoln, Ne-

Perhaps because they lived in a time of changing values, the Elizabethans possessed the willingness to accept ambiguity and unresolved contradictions which Norman Rabkin has seen at the heart of the tragic response. Tragedy insists that its audience accept values and choices that exclude one another and yet are equally valid when viewed from different perspectives, and assent to the play's refusal to present a single, all-encompassing answer to the questions it raises. Rabkin has recently suggested that the way Shakespeare's plays were rewritten after his death demonstrates that it was not within the power of every age to respond in this way to tragedy. The Restoration and eighteenth-century redactors of Shakespeare's tragedies sought to resolve the tensions between opposing views that are so central to the plays' meanings. In *Antony and Cleopatra* for example, Antony is faced with a choice between two worlds, two value systems, two modes of existence, neither of which the audience can with any certainty identify as "right." When Dryden rewrote the play, he turned it into a clear and unequivocal statement about the superiority of a life committed to reason, responsibility, and domestic order, a life in which the passions are kept firmly under control.[41] For Dryden and his audience, tragedy had come to serve a function much closer to the didactic one described by Sidney.

The plays written in the years after Sidney's *Apologie* appeared offer the best possible evidence that, though didacticism did not utterly disappear from the drama, the Elizabethan audience did not remain content with the simple didactic response that Sidney had described. As the playwrights themselves began to create an audience for tragedy, they drew upon those elements in their own upbringing and their audience's that encouraged a dual mode of vision. One of these elements, Joel Altman has suggested, was the rhetorical education which secondary and university students received. Trained in the rhetorical theories of the classical writers, students were taught

---

braska, 1980), pp. 107-113. The Halletts are strongly influenced by the theories of Eric Voegelin, as set forth in *From Enlightenment to Revolution*.

[41] Norman Rabkin, *Shakespeare and the Problem of Meaning* (Chicago, 1980), pp. 67-69.

to argue both sides of every question, in order to, as Aristotle put it, "see clearly what the facts are." Such training produced a mind that instinctively sought out multiplicity and revelled in contradictions. Plays like *The Spanish Tragedy*, *Tamburlaine*, or *Hamlet*, therefore, "functioned as media of intellectual and emotional exploration for minds that were accustomed to examine the many sides of a given theme, to entertain opposing ideals, and by so exercising the understanding, to move toward some fuller apprehension of truth that could be discerned only through the total action of the drama."[42] The audience was an active participant in this exploration, and as participant, was ultimately responsible for judging among the conflicting truths embodied in the characters and situations of the play. To this dialectical process the Elizabethans brought the ability to see themselves and others from two opposing perspectives that had been conferred upon them by their Christian inheritance. Viewed one way, all men and women were descendants of Adam and Eve, destined for a life of pain and constant struggle against the temptations of the flesh. Viewed another way, they were the noblest of God's creatures, upon whom He had bestowed a rich and abundant world, with the promise of an eternal life in heaven. Under the growing impact of the Reformation, the tension between these opposing images became increasingly acute. Caught up in another form of exploration, the object of which was to determine their own state of election, the Elizabethans came to the theatres with a searching interest in the complexities of human character and motives. This interest enabled them to scrutinize the tragic protagonists with the same intensity with which they examined their own souls. Like their own actions, those of the tragic protagonists were susceptible to multiple interpretations; like their own lives, those of the tragic protagonists were never free of ambiguity.

[42] Joel Altman, *The Tudor Play of Mind: Rhetorical Inquiry and the Development of Elizabethan Drama* (Berkeley, 1978), pp. 6, 39, and passim. Some of Altman's ideas were anticipated by Emrys Jones in *The Origins of Shakespeare* (Oxford, 1977), p. 14.

The tragic protagonist, then, is from one perspective a version of the "other," but from another perspective a version of the "self." In the early years of Elizabethan tragedy, the elements of the "other" frequently predominated, perhaps because the playwrights sensed that their audiences would be better able to accept the downfall of a character whom they could view with more detachment than engagement. To identify with a character who embodies qualities or values which one's culture rejects was, after all, a form of moral risk-taking for which the Elizabethans were unprepared. As Shakespeare and his contemporaries started to invite an increasingly complex sympathy for protagonists such as Faustus, Edward II, Richard III, and Richard II, they drew upon an innate ambivalence in their culture toward certain kinds of behavior. Their tragic figures began assuming what Michael Goldman calls the "simultaneously appalling and appealing stance," acting out "some version of a half-allowed, blasphemous and sacred freedom characteristic of the era in which the play was written." The tragic protagonist, thus conceived, combines two conflicting ideas, that of the norm and that of its violation,[43] although what constituted the norm in 1590 was increasingly subject to debate.

By the end of the century, the emergence of Elizabethan tragedy was complete. Shakespeare's great tragic protagonists from Hamlet onward are much more than versions of the "other"; they are singular human beings whose power to move the audience far transcends the moral categories and topical concerns the audience brings with them to the theatre. The

---

[43] Michael Goldman, *The Actor's Freedom: Toward a Theory of Drama* (New York, 1975), pp. 37, 55. This idea has been expressed elsewhere by L. S. Vygotsky, in *The Psychology of Art* (Cambridge, Mass., 1971). According to Vygotsky, ". . . the protagonist of a drama is therefore . . . a character who combines two conflicting affects, that of the norm and that of its violation; this is why we perceive him dynamically, not as an object but as a process (p. 231). Cf. Judah Stampfer, *The Tragic Engagement: A Study of Shakespeare's Classical Tragedies* (New York, 1968). Stampfer sees tragedy as "an encounter of a man with an inhuman image of himself, what is and is not himself" (p. 14).

presence of whatever we perceive as the "other" never utterly disappears from tragedy, however, though it may cease to be embodied in the protagonist. Speaking of tragedy in any age, George Steiner has observed: "Tragic drama tells us that the spheres of reason, order, and justice are terribly limited. . . . Outside and within man is l'autre, the 'otherness' of the world . . . a hidden or malevolent God, blind fate, the solicitations of hell, or the brute fury of our animal blood."[44]

[44] George Steiner, *The Death of Tragedy* (New York, 1961), pp. 8-9.

CHAPTER II

The Rhetoric of the Elect

I. ELIZABETHAN ASSURANCE

One of the most important and popular public events in Elizabethan England was the sermon preached at Paul's Cross. A wooden structure located in the churchyard of the great cathedral, the Cross served as the locus for the most prestigious and best-attended sermons of the age, as well as for official proclamations, state processions, and public penances. On a fair day, the audience numbered in the thousands, consisting of people from throughout the city, not to mention foreign travelers and visitors from the country who flocked to London on matters of business and pleasure. The sermons lasted as much as two hours, and, not unlike the actors at the public theatres, the preacher had to hold his audience's attention if he wanted to be invited to preach at the Cross again. Part of the spectacle at Paul's Cross consisted of the ritual of public penance imposed on a sinner, who provided the preacher with a topic and served as a warning to the assembled crowd. Wearing a white sheet and bearing a taper or faggot, the sinner stood on a platform level with the preacher for the duration of the sermon, sometimes enduring the jeers of the more raucous members of the audience and blows from the "rod of correction" wielded by the preacher himself. In this drama, the penitent was a visible embodiment of the "other," whose public humiliation confirmed the abiding strength of the social norms and the religious values which the community had gathered to celebrate. Disgraced and outcast, the penitent was the antithesis of the preacher and the audience themselves. Hence, by scorning and rejecting him, the audience strengthened their identification with the preacher and the way of life he espoused.[1]

[1] Alan Fager Herr, *The Elizabethan Sermon* (Philadelphia, 1940), pp. 11-

The preachers at Paul's Cross represented almost the entire spectrum of doctrinal difference in Protestant England. Typically, their sermons were addressed to a mixed audience, and emphasized "amendment of life" and the "saving knowledge" of the gospel. In this respect they were consistent with the Puritan theory and style of preaching.[2] Puritan sermons were seldom devoted to speculative theology; more often, they were functional, designed to provoke the listener to improve his behavior and to take responsibility for his own spiritual life. The sermons were at once carefully ordered and intensely analytical, yet filled with lively topical references and dramatic rhetorical appeals. In style they were generally plain, uncluttered by decorative flourishes or elaborate allegories, although the preachers were not above employing humor and satire to make a point. In order to watch their audiences and to react extemporaneously, if need be, to their responses, the Puritan preachers delivered their sermons from memory, accompanying their words with gestures. At Paul's Cross and elsewhere, many of Elizabethan London's most popular preachers were Puritans. Stephen Egerton, at St. Anne's Blackfriars, had a large following consisting mostly of women; Henry Smith, the most popular of all Elizabethan preachers, held forth at St. Clement Danes; others, like Richard Greenham, lectured from a number of London pulpits to eager followers who took down their sermons and circulated copies.[3]

These men, and others like them, attempted to lead their listeners to discover the signs of salvation within themselves, and hence to the attainment of assurance. The doctrine of assurance took its theological justification from the first epistle of John, repeatedly cited by Puritan writers and preachers.

24. Herr notes that audiences at Paul's Cross were often as large as 6,000. Cf. Millar Maclure, *The Paul's Cross Sermons* (Toronto, 1958), pp. 7-15.

[2] Maclure, *The Paul's Cross Sermons*, p. 145.

[3] Horton Davies, *Worship and Theology in England*, Vol. I: From Cranmer to Hooker: 1534-1603 (Princeton, 1970), pp. 227, 365; Herr, p. 27; William Haller, *The Rise of Puritanism* (New York, 1938; rpt., 1957), p. 27. John Manningham's *Diary* contains valuable examples of sermon summaries recorded by members of the audience.

William Perkins, the most influential and prolific of sixteenth-century Puritans, told his readers that "every faithful man must beleeve that he is elected. It is Gods commandment that we should believe in Christ. John 1:23. Now to beleeve in Christ is not only to beleeve that we are adopted, justified, and redeemed by him, but also in him elected from eternity." Perkins rendered the entire epistle in dialogue form, in a tract intended to show "How a man may know whether he be the childe of God, or no." He urges his readers to allow nothing, not daily slips or weakness of faith or even "hainous crimes" like David's adultery or Peter's threefold denial, to undermine their certainty of election. "We are," he says, "set apart from the common sort of man," and "appertaine no longer to the world, but to that citie which is above."[4]

Assurance, not works or outward behavior, thus became the sign of salvation, a sign which only the believer himself could recognize. As Arthur Dent told his readers in an oft-printed tract called *The Plaine Mans Path-way to Heaven: Wherein every man may clearly see, whether he shall be saved or damned*: "For, he, that knoweth not in this life that he shall be saved, shall never be saved after this life." To help his readers achieve this assurance, Dent lists three sets of signs of salvation, in order of increasing significance. The first set contains qualities like Sobrietie, Industrie, Humility; the second set, Faith, Virtue, Godlinesse; and the third, "the Spirit of adoption," "Assured faith in the promises," "Inward peace," and "Sound Regeneration, and Sanctification." This third group is the most reliable since, Dent warns, some of the unregenerate can surpass the saved in such external virtues as temperance, prudence, patience, and the like. Dent warns that some of God's children may be "clogged with some master sin"; and this, he says, is "their wound, their griefe and their hart-smart." And yet, he repeatedly urges, we *can* know that we are saved, for the conscience will not lie. He supports his claim with 1 John 2:3:

[4] William Perkins, *A Golden Chaine*, p. 104; *A Case of Conscience, the greatest that ever was; How a man may know whether he be the childe of God, or no.* (London, 1595), STC #19667, pp. 34, 26.

"Hereby we are sure we know him; If we keepe his Commandments." He glosses this as follows: ". . . that if we do unfeignedly endevour to obey God, there is in us the true knowledge and feare of God: and consequently, we are sure we shall be saved."[5]

This sureness, however, was sustained with the greatest difficulty. The fundamental paradox of Puritan belief was "he that never doubted, never believed." "The more grace we have," Dent advised his readers, "the more quicke are we in the feeling of corruption," for the certainty of election must coexist with the image we have of ourselves as "lumps of sin."[6] Such paradoxes are at the very core of Puritan psychology, as the sermons frequently reveal. In a series of sermons "wherein everie man may learne, whether he be Gods childe or no," George Gifford instructs his audience "to bee out of doubt, and surely resolved in our selves, not by fantasied opinions, but by sure and substantial proofe, that we be chosen of God, and therefore cannot perish." And yet this proof cannot be externally validated or confirmed. "We fetch our warrant," he told them, neither from revelation nor "the counsels of god," but "from within our selves." "From hence it cometh, that looke how muche more a man feeleth in him selfe the increase of knowledge, the increase of vertues and heavenly desires, so muche more sure hee is, that hee is the childe of God. . . ."[7] While certainty comes from within ourselves, our election does not derive from any "stableness in our selves or in our workes." Rather, our certainty should be based on knowledge that "the fruites of Gods spirit" are within us. Those who lacked certainty were doubtful, unsure, and convinced that they had evil

---

[5] Arthur Dent, *The Plaine Mans Path-way to Heaven: Wherein every man may cleerely see, whether he shall be saved or damned* (London, 1607), STC #6629 (this copy was from the ninth impression; the first edition was published in 1601), pp. 235, 232, 21, 240, 236.

[6] Dent, *The Plaine Man's Path-way*, STC #6629, pp. 242, 245.

[7] George Gifford, *Four Sermons upon the seven chiefe vertues or principal effectes of faith, and the doctrine of election: wherein everie man may learne, whether he be Gods childe or no.* (London, 1528), STC #11858, sig. E7ᵛ, E8ʳ, E8ᵛ.

consciences. Such feelings were inconsistent with assurance, and yet they often served as a prelude to the attainment thereof. The Puritans believed that repentance was an essential part of the process of achieving faith, and repentance, according to Gifford, followed from a recognition that "all corruption is of our selves, not comming from any outward cause." The believer was thus doubly responsible: first, for his own corruption, and, second, for attaining assurance.[8]

Faced with these paradoxes, the Puritan preachers urged their audiences onward by employing rhetorical strategies which blurred the distinction between recognizing one's election and acting to bring it about. When William Burton, in a series of sermons entitled *Davids Evidence, or the Assurance of Gods Love*, tells his audience that "Peter bids us make our election sure," or Lawrence Chaderton says that he speaks not to discourage, but to "stir us al up to a more diligent care in working our salvation," they imply that the believer can actually take part in deciding who shall be saved.[9] Encouraging his readers to strive for assurance, William Perkins goes so far as to say that

[8] Gifford, *Four Sermons*, STC #11858, sig. E8ᵛ, C1ʳ, F5ʳ, B3ᵛ. The paradoxes which I have been illustrating have been recognized recently by other scholars, most notably Christopher Hill, who observes in *Change and Continuity in Seventeenth Century England* (Cambridge, Mass., 1975) that "the paradox of protestantism is that it eternally strives to fulfill a law which it knows to be unfulfillable" and adds that the simultaneous conviction of depravity and righteousness made the Calvinists unattractive characters but also energetic and productive capitalists (p. 102). Similarly, Kai Erikson, in *Wayward Puritans: A Study in the Sociology of Deviance* (New York, 1966), sees the Puritan approach to life as "a fabric woven almost entirely out of paradoxes." Among these are: the medieval preoccupation with sin which coexists with a protest against the past; the Puritan's unrelenting shifts between conviction and uncertainty; his respect for individual freedom and yet his need for external discipline; and his reliance on self-assertion coupled with a belief in what Erikson calls "erratic fate," although surely no Elizabethan Puritan would have called it that (pp. 50-53).

[9] William Burton, *Davids Evidence or the Assurance of Gods Love* (London, 1592), STC #4170, p. 8; Lawrence Chaderton, *An Excellent and godly sermon, most needful for this time* (London, 1578), STC #4924, sig. G6ʳ. Cf. 2 Peter 1:10: "Give diligence to make your calling and election sure."

"the Evangelicall promises are indefinite, and do exclude no man, unlesse peradventure any man do exclude himself." In support of this, Perkins cites Matthew 11:28: "Come unto me, all ye that are weary . . ." and John 3:15 "That whosoever beleeveth in him should not perish . . . ," neither of which suggests quite so active a role for man. Nevertheless, Perkins also goes to great lengths to dispute the principle propounded by the Church of Rome, that "Man is neither by necessitie nor chance saved or condemned but voluntarily." On the contrary, Perkins says, "God in electing us did not regard anything out of himselfe. . . . Election is only of Gods mercy." However, God's mercy is infinite, and "If there be a willing mind, every one is accepted for the grace which he hath, not for that which he hath not."[10]

Like many other Elizabethan Puritans, Perkins recognized the pessimism inherent in Calvinist doctrine, and sought to soften and temper it. Calvin's view of human existence could be called tragic: he saw man in his natural state as solitary and powerless, alienated from both God and society, and unable to choose rightly, using his reason alone. "Men have no fixed dwelling and no clear line of work," he wrote. They "wander about in uncertainty all their days," assaulted by an "extreme anxiety and dread" from which only grace can deliver them.[11] Compounding this dilemma was a persistent paradox: man has absolutely no role in effecting his salvation, yet his whole spiritual life must be given over to the attainment of assurance.

To combat the despair to which such a dilemma might lead, the English Protestants began to equate faith with the certainty of salvation.[12] Preachers encouraged their listeners to

[10] Perkins, *A Golden Chaine*, pp. 86-98.

[11] Quoted in Michael Walzer, *The Revolution of the Saints: A Study in the Origins of Radical Politics* (Cambridge, Mass., 1965), p. 34.

[12] Perry Miller, *The New England Mind: The Seventeenth Century* (1939, rpt., Boston, 1961), p. 50. Cf. Charles and Katherine George's discussion of the inherent contradiction between the intense proselytizing of early Protestantism and strict predestinarian doctrine in *The Protestant Mind of the English Reformation* (Princeton, 1961), p. 58.

develop a zeal they sometimes called "boldness," the strength of character that enables the believer to withstand the doubts which work against assurance. Gifford ends his first sermon by urging every man to look to his thoughts, that "hee may boldly say, I have a newe hearte, and there is a right spirite renued in mee, I have repented. . . ." Burton proposes to show his audience "how carefull, how constant, how bold, and how holy we should be in praysing of God," and encourages them to believe that with God keeping watch at "the doore of our lippes . . . the toung doth boldly confesse ye truth." And Perkins, in his dialogue between Satan and a strong Christian, has his Christian reply as follows to Satan's efforts to undermine his certainty:

> For me thinkes I am as certaine of my salvation, as though my name were registred in the Scriptures (as Davids and Pauls are) to be an elect vessel of God: and this is the testimonie of the holy spirit of Iesus Christ, assuring me inwardly of my adoption, and making me with boldnesse and confidence in Christ, to pray unto God the Father.[13]

This is the boldness of an idealistic group of reformers convinced of the importance of their cause, but it is also a characteristically Elizabethan attribute. Like the Marlovian protagonist's boldness, it manifests itself in sweeping rhetorical phrases filled with a sense of the self's unlimited abilities. In a triumphant exhortation typical of the kind with which the Puritan sermon so often ends, Burton urges his audience as follows:

> Let us then diligently and carefully use these meanes, and then shall we be effectually assured of Gods love and favour in Christ Jesus, and being once assured of that, we may boldly cast downe the gantlet & bid defiance to hell and all the devils in hell, and make that chalenge which the Apostle Paule doth make in the behalfe of all Gods children, "Who shall separate us from the love of Christ?"

[13] Gifford, *Four Sermons*, STC #11858, sig. B5ʳ; Burton, *David's Evidence*, STC #4170, pp. 164, 161; Perkins, *A Golden Chaine*, p. 406. Cf. Ephesians 3:11-12.

Interestingly, this boldness is directed not only against the devils of hell, but also toward God himself; according to Burton, "so may we be bold to aske any thing of God our heavenly father that is good for us, when we be sure that he loveth us."[14]

Burton's language suggests that the preachers themselves displayed through their rhetoric the very boldness that they were encouraging their listeners to feel. To instill confidence they projected confidence, using striking images and rising cumulative sequences composed of one stirring phrase after another. Here, for example, is the final sentence of Dent's famous *Sermon of Repentaunce*, first published in 1583 and reprinted many times during the next two decades:

> Wherefore in conclusion, let us with godlie Ezechias bee afrayde of Gods threatenings, sorrow aforehand, stand in awe of GOD, examine our conscience, mourne for our sinnes & lament inwardlie, that when the wicked which have swimmed in plaisures here belowe, shal enter into their eternall paynes, we may then, I say there, have everlasting peace and reste, that when Jesus Christ shall appeare from heaven with all his holie Angels, we may have crownes of glory, and victorie clapped on our heades, and raigne with our God, and our Savior his Sonne, and all his Sainctes and Aungels in the middest of all ioye, in the heavens for ever-more.

Like so many of the sermons themselves, the sentence begins with warnings and instructions and then transcends them with a triumphant vision of the "everlasting peace and reste" which awaits the elect. Even bolder, if anything, is this declaration from Dent's *The Plaine Mans Path-way:*

> . . . hee [God] grudgeth us nothing; he thinketh nothing too much for us. Hee loveth us most dearely: he is most charie and tender over us: hee cannot endure the winde shoulde blow uppon us: hee will have us want nothing that

14 Burton, *David's Evidence*, STC #4170, pp. 70, 7.

48

is good for us. .... For Heaven is ours, Earth is ours, God is ours, Christ is ours, all is ours.[15]

This verbal boldness—the rhetoric of assurance—came to express the confidence which the elect were supposed to feel. Calvin, in the *Institutes*, places particular emphasis on confidence: "No man is a believer," he proclaimed, "except him who, leaning upon the assurance of his salvation, confidently triumphs over the devil and death." He goes on to say that man can never have complete confidence in his own righteousness, but that he can nevertheless have perfect confidence and assurance through faith. He observes with approval that "the saints quite often strengthen themselves and are comforted by remembering their own innocence and uprightness, and they do not even refrain at times from proclaiming it."[16]

To proclaim their uprightness without seeming to boast or succumb to self-admiration, and to encourage their audiences to feel the confidence which would signify their election, the preachers usually referred to the elect as "we." The most distinctive characteristic of the rhetoric of assurance, this usage effectively took for granted the election of all present. Although Puritan preachers occasionally address their audiences as "you," the "I—you" distinction is consistently deemphasized; instead, the audience is drawn into the community of the elect and made to feel no different from the preacher. Such diction appears as early as 1570, in John Foxe's *Sermon of Christ Crucified*, the only extant sermon by the author of the *Acts and Monuments*. Foxe dwells upon the process of regeneration, representing damnation and election as consecutive states, not mutually exclusive ones: ". . . now all is turned, our fear to hope; death to life: damnation to salvation: hell to heaven. . . ." This pattern carries over to the use of pronouns:

---

[15] Arthur Dent, *A Sermon of Repentaunce* (London, 1583), STC #6650, sig. D8ᵛ; Dent, *The Plaine Mans Path-way*, STC #6629, p. 115.

[16] John Calvin, *Institutes of the Christian Religion*, trans. Ford Lewis Battles, ed. John T. McNeil, The Library of Christian Classics, Vols. XX and XXI (Philadelphia, 1960), XX, 557 ff., XXI, 784.

the audience is often referred to as "you" in the early parts of
the sermon, but by the end Foxe can assure them: "Whatsoever therefore shall betyde us in thys worlde, and though we
be corrected here for our sinnes (as happeneth most comonly
to the elect) let us not measure the state of our election thereby,
nor thinke therefore to be cast out of favour. . . ."[17]

Foxe's parenthetical "as happeneth most comonly to the elect"
casually assumes the election of an audience still seeking assurance. Subsequent preachers were equally skillful at identifying the "we" of the assembled congregation with the elect,
despite the doctrinal contradictions inherent in such an assumption. The Puritan preacher could simultaneously believe
that only a tiny fraction of mankind had been chosen by God
before time began, and yet assure his audience that "it hath
pleased him to pick us out of so many."[18] Like Foxe, they
often emphasize repentance, in order to persuade their listeners that nothing in their past or present behavior necessarily disqualifies them from election. A necessary corollary to
strict predestinarian doctrine, this strategy prevented potential
believers from losing hope that they might eventually achieve
assurance, their sins notwithstanding. As John Dod told a
congregation that could possibly have included Marlowe (Dod,
"the chief holy man of the spiritual brotherhood," as Haller
calls him, was University Preacher at Cambridge during Marlowe's early years there), "the Lord is ready to pardon all, and
all manner of iniquities." And he ends his first sermon with
the stirring declaration that "whatsoever we have beene, or
whatsoever our sinnes have beene, if we can bring confession
and reformation, we shall find mercy: God will pitty us, and
have compassion on us."[19]

[17] John Foxe, *A Sermon of Christ crucified, preached at Paules Crosse the Friday before Easter* (London, 1570), STC #11242, pp. 10ʳ, 24ᵛ.

[18] John Knewstub, "Lectures upon the 20th chapter of Exodus and Certain
other Places of Scripture" (1578), *Elizabethan Puritanism*, ed. Leonard J.
Trinterud (Oxford, 1971), pp. 323-24.

[19] John Dod and R. Cleaver, *Ten Sermons tending chiefly to the fitting of men
for the worthy receiving of the Lords Supper* (London, 1634), STC #6949, pp.
41, 15; Haller, *The Rise of Puritanism*, p. 56.

Indeed, so great was the sixteenth-century Puritan preachers' apparent confidence in the power of repentance that even papists were not irrevocably damned. The highly unorthodox possibility of a reversal of God's predestined and eternal judgment would seem to underlie John Keltridge's *Two Godlie and Learned Sermons, appointed, and Preached, before Jesuites, Seminaries, and other Adversaries to the Gospell of Christ in the Tower of London*. Although he addresses the papists as "reprobate Silver, which God hath reiected," Keltridge affirms that a "returne" is yet possible: "And be you assured, that . . . the heavie judgment of the Lord God approacheth, yea, it is at hand, if you returne not. . . ."[20] William Fulke, in a sermon also preached at the Tower "in the hearing of such obstinate Papistes as then were prisoners there," is even more encouraging—he employs the rhetoric of assurance in linking the assembled "we" with the elect:

> Therefor it is only his goodnesse and mercy to disclose, those secret hidden mysteries of his kingdome unto his elect and chosen children . . . that wee may knowe the worde of God by his spirite, and his spirite by his word. Now seeing the Lord God hath opened his holie mouth to speak unto us. . . .[21]

This, then, is another fundamental paradox of Puritan thought: predestined election was unchanging and arbitrary, yet education, "reformation," and repentance were urged upon the believer as capable of effecting salvation. The preachers made no attempt to resolve this paradox, for, as H. C. Porter so succinctly observes, "however Calvinist in the study, the preacher must be Arminian in the pulpit." The early Puritans could not afford to discourage potential converts in their effort to gather enough strength to reform the Church. Hence

[20] John Keltridge, *Two Godlie and learned Sermons, appointed, and Preached before the Jesuites, Seminaries, and other Adversaries to the Gospell of Christ in the Tower of London* (London, 1581), STC #14921, p. 126.

[21] William Fulke, *A Sermon Preached upon Sunday, being the twelfth of March Anno 1581 within the Tower of London: In the hearing of such obstinate Papistes as then were prisoners there* (London, 1581), STC #11455, sig. C2ᵛ.

they deliberately extended the hope of salvation to all who came to hear them, and were careful to imply that the believer could assist God in bringing about his own redemption.[22] They were in a very real sense actors, actors who sought to please and hold their audiences, and who exerted an enormous power through their skill with words.

If only we knew how often the playwrights heard the performances of their natural rivals, the Puritan preachers! Although it is impossible to prove that Kyd and Marlowe and Shakespeare were directly influenced by the preachers, or, for that matter, that the preachers were directly influenced by the verbal bravado of sixteenth-century stage characters, comic or tragic, we can safely assume that the Elizabethan audience included large numbers of people who were familiar with the rhetoric of the pulpits. These people brought with them to the theatres feelings about assurance which other audiences in other ages would not have, and saw those feelings reflected in the rhetoric of the stage. Characters in search of some form of assurance, like Hamlet, or very much in possession of it, like Tamburlaine, were not, of course, exhibiting the specifically religious assurance of which the preachers spoke. But a kinship clearly exists between assurance and a number of related attitudes, such as self-confidence, self-assertion, arrogance (the conviction of the rightness of one's judgment) or, to use the language of plays and sermons alike, attitudes such as pride, presumption, and that most Elizabethan of mental states, aspiration. The presence of these attitudes is inseparable from the public and political events in which the English nation, as a whole, was engaged. As Philip Edwards observes, England as a Protestant nation was asserting its election and boldly defying its enemies just as the elect individual was urged to do: "self-defence, which is also defence of the true faith, merges easily with self-assertion, which is also the spread of

[22] Harry Culverwell Porter, *Reformation and Reaction in Tudor Cambridge* (Cambridge, England, 1958), p. 310; William Haller emphasizes this aspect of Elizabethan Puritanism in *Foxe's Book of Martyrs and the Elect Nation* (London, 1963), pp. 75 ff.

the new faith."[23] Bold, assertive, confident, and assured, the Elizabethan hero simply reflected to an exaggerated degree some of the most deeply rooted characteristics of the culture that created him.

II. THE PROUD AND PRESUMPTUOUS "OTHER"

Although the preachers acted upon the assumption that their audiences consisted entirely of the elect, the damned frequently played a significant role in the Puritan sermon. The existence of the damned served an important rhetorical purpose in helping to distinguish the elect. Calvin described two ways in which the saints proclaimed their innocence and uprightness. First, by "comparing their good cause with the evil cause of the wicked, they thence derive confidence of victory, not so much by the commendation of their own righteousness as by the just and deserved condemnation of their adversaries."[24] The other way is through self-examination, one of the defining characteristics of Puritanism. Lawrence Chaderton, one of the most prominent sixteenth-century Puritans, combined these two processes when he told the audience in his Paul's Cross sermon of 1578 that the whole study of a Puritan believer was to "looke into our selves, into our hearts, consciences, & whole maner of our life, that we may see & know in all our actions, wherein we differ from the wicked. . . ." The incessant desire to be certain that he indeed differed from the wicked caused perpetual anxiety in the Puritan, an anxiety which spurred the growth of assurance by creating such a need for it. To assuage this anxiety, the preachers relied heavily upon definition by antithesis, although they rarely actually used the words "damned" or "reprobate." Thus Chaderton, after explaining a point of doctrine, encouraged the audience to "applie it unto our selves, that we maye the better know whether

[23] Philip Edwards, *Threshold of a Nation: A Study in English and Irish Drama* (Cambridge, 1979), p. 73.
[24] Calvin, *Institutes*, XXI, 785.

we be the doers of the worde, and not onely hearers, which can have no hope and assurance of salvation." Later in the sermon he offers yet another distinction, between "the workers of iniquitie" who are "out of the Church" and the saints and elect of God, who are "in and of the Church," and who include every member of his audience. His final prayer confidently assures them: "that we being all, most perfectly by the holie Ghost, and fayth, united and incorporated into Christe (as the members of the body into the head) might be partakers of the fellowshippe of his glorie, together with his and our Father, and al the holy companie of Angels, in the heavenly kingdome of all happynesse and felicitie."[25]

In this sermon Chaderton has identified the reprobates as "Atheistes and infidels . . . , Jewes . . . , Libertines, Catholicks and carnall Protestants," categories in which his auditors would be unlikely to place themselves. Arthur Dent's list is composed of three groups: the most obvious reprobates are atheists, heretics, and papists; the second category, called "vicious and notorious evill livers," includes "Swearers, Drunkards, Whoremongers, Worldlings, Deceivers, Coseners, Proud men, Rioters, Gamesters, and all the prophane multitude." The third, which might have caused the ordinary Elizabethan most anxiety, consisted of "Hypocrites, carnall Protestants, vaine Professors, Backsliders, Decliners, and cold Christians."[26]

Although catalogues of this kind existed for the purpose of definition, it would be inaccurate to give the impression that the sixteenth-century Puritan sermon was excessively concerned with depicting the reprobate. Designed as they were to encourage the audience to believe in their election, the sermons seldom mentioned the damned except as "others" against whom the ordinary believer could contrast himself in his effort to achieve assurance. Descriptions of the damned are deliberately unrealistic, designed to present the most obvious

[25] Lawrence Chaderton, *An Excellent and godly sermon, most needful for this time* (London, 1578), STC #4924, sig. G5ᵛ, E4ʳ, H2ᵛ.

[26] Chaderton, *An Excellent and godly Sermon*, STC #4924, sig. E4ʳ; Dent, *The Plaine Mans Path-way*, STC #6629, p. 259.

differences between the reprobate and the elect. Gifford, for example, gives an exceptionally lurid description of the damned as:

> . . . beastly Epicures, folowing their own fleshly mind, let-ting lose the raines, and giving the swing unto the raging lustes of the fleshe, despising the knowledge of Gods will, . . . devising al the colours and shifts they can to maintain sin, inventing al the slanders that may be to discredite the godly conversation of such as folow the way here pre-scribed.

Acute psychologist that he was, Gifford is less interested in describing the "raging lustes of the flesh" than in the repro-bates' compulsive need to defend, or "maintaine" sin by slan-dering the godly; like the elect, they define themselves by dis-crediting what they are not. Gifford also finds the reprobates' characteristic vices of arrogance and pride far more interesting and dangerous than their bodily lusts. In the second of his four sermons, Gifford warns his audience against the arro-gance of the damned, telling them to "take heed of flattering our selves as some other doe, which having gotten some skil . . . they do excuse them selves after this sort, I thanke God, I am not of the ignorant sorte, nor of the meanest iudgement. . . ." With the instinct of a dramatist, he evokes a terrifying and potentially tragic image of those who are "meerie . . . and thinke themselves best, when they are least dealt withall . . . their myrth is nothing els, but a madde laughter, even in the middest of fearefull and horrible destruction." And he warns his audience to be well armed when we "have to do with those which are abused and grosse . . . [to hear] their spiteful rayl-inges, and fleering mockes, which they will use; their bolde abusing of Gods worde, their arrogant presumption, which causeth them to prattle very fast, even they know not what. . . ."27

This last passage is especially interesting, inasmuch as it em-

---

27 Gifford, *Four Sermons*, STC #11858, sig. F6r, C3r, C4r, C6v.

ploys the word "bold" in a negative sense to describe the "presumption" of the reprobate. The same consciousness of the dangers inherent in boldness is evident in Burton's sermons. In the same sermon quoted earlier, which advocates boldly casting down the gauntlet, bidding defiance to hell, and asking "any thing of God our heavenly father that is good for us," Burton advocates humility and self-abasement as a part of self-definition by antithesis:

> If then thy enemy be vaine glorious be not thou so too, but be lowly giving glory to God, if he be puffed up with pride, be thou of an humble spirite, if he boast himselfe, abase thou thy selfe; if he curse, blesse thou, if he be hoate, be thou cold, if he blaspheme, doe not ye so. . . .

Later in this sermon, Burton paraphrases Psalm 52 as follows:

> Why doest thou boast thy selfe in thy wickednesse, O man of power? . . . thou thinkest thy selfe a iolly fellow, and takest pride in thy wickednes, as though thou were a great man of power and shouldest never come downe, and because God doth suffer thee from day to day waiting for thy repentaunce, thou thinkest, either that he cannot, or dare not, or that he will not meddle with thee, but now see thy selfe in thy colours, and then iudge what cause thou hast to bragge it out as thou doest against all the world. . . .[28]

Burton's sermon dramatizes still another paradox in sixteenth-century Puritanism, elsewhere neatly articulated by James I, who complained in his *Basilikon* (1599) of "the preposterous humility of one of the proud Puritans . . . [who says] 'We are but vile worm, and yet will judge and give law to our King, but will be judged or controlled by none.' Surely there is more pride under such a one's black bonnet, than under Alexander the Great his diadem!"[29] Pride was the most troublesome and threatening of the Seven Deadly Sins for the Elizabethan Pu-

[28] Burton, *Davids Evidence*, STC #4170, pp. 89, 104.
[29] Quoted in Erikson, *Wayward Puritans*, p. 51.

ritans, torn as they were between humbly acknowledging their unworthiness and indebtedness to God and boldly affirming and asserting their election. It is the sin most often attributed to them by their critics, and one to which they themselves, in their most honest moments, acknowledge their susceptibility. Hence it is not surprising that Dent's list of the reprobate includes "proud men," and that the sermons and tracts return again and again to the dangers inherent in pride and arrogance.

According to an anonymous tract entitled *The Anatomie of Sinne*, pride is the most dangerous of the Seven Sins, for unlike the others, it proceeds from good and virtuous qualities— its roots are riches, nobility, fame, knowledge, strength. Here, as so often in sixteenth-century literature, it is characterized as "a puffing up" of the heart and mind. The author of the *Anatomie* identifies nine branches of pride: presumption, obstinacy, hypocrisy, boasting, ingratitude, contempt of others, disobedience, ambition, and curiosity. Presumption, perhaps the most characteristic sin of the Elizabethan tragic figure, takes three forms. The presumptuous man might undertake something above his skill or calling, or he might think himself better than others, or he might reject reproof but consider himself safe against retribution. The boastful man of the *Anatomie*, proud and arrogant, driven by vainglory, and the ambitious man, ruled by an inordinate desire for honor and dignity, not for their own sake, but to satisfy private appetite— both are potentially tragic.

The Anatomie of Sinne was evidently not written by a Puritan, since the author defines "curiosity," another form of pride, as the pursuit of learning instead of the Book of God, which is to say, interpreting the Bible on one's own, and searching into the secrets of God, rather than following the ancient fathers of the Church. Nevertheless, it formulates attitudes toward pride and presumption which were commonplace throughout Elizabethan England. Indeed, they were not restricted to England. For example, the de Florio translation of Montaigne's "Apology of Raymond Sebond" states that "all sinnes derive from selfe-overweening."[30] The characters in Dent's *The Plaine Mans Path-Way to Heaven* agree that pride was never so pronounced a characteristic as in Elizabethan England. They see signs of it, for instance, in the way people dress, and they long for the simplicity and modesty of former ages. Yet they also recognize that pride is directly related to the strengths and virtues of their contemporaries: "men will be proud, because they are wise, learned, godly, patient, humble" and so forth. They conclude that "humilitie in sinne, is better than pride in well doing."[31]

One of the most frequently used phrases of the drama and sermons of the 1580s and 1590s is "proud and presumptuous." It had a rolling alliterative sound which appealed to the Elizabethans, as this piece of invective from the Marprelate tracts suggests: "Therefore our Bishops and proud, popish, presumptuous, profane, paltry, pestilent and pernicious Prelates, Bishop of Hereford and all, are first usurpers, to begin the matter withal."[32] Actually, the phrase continued to be used well into the seventeenth-century—for example, in Milton's *Comus*, the Elder Brother, speaking of the power of the Lady's chastity, says that "she may pass on with unblenched majesty/ Be it not done in pride or in presumption." A typical homiletic use of the phrase "pride and presumption" occurs in Lawrence Humphrey's *A View of the Romish Hydra confuted in seven sermons*, in a sermon on Saul, David, Abishai, and the question of lawful regicide. Humphrey sees in the regicide qualities very much like those which Elizabethan audiences would soon be seeing in the tragic protagonists on the stage, such as "an insatiable desire of honor, principality, & sover-

[30] Anon., *The Anatomie of Sinne, Briefly discovering the braunches thereof, with a short method how to detect and avoid it* (London, 1603), STC #565, sig. B4ʳ ff.; Michel de Montaigne, *Essays*, II, 186, quoted in J. Leeds Barroll, *Artificial Persons: The formation of character in the tragedies of Shakespeare* (Columbia, S.C., 1974), p. 44.

[31] Dent, *The Plaine Mans Path-way*, STC #6629, pp. 33-38.

[32] William Pierce, ed., *The Marprelate Tracts, 1588, 1589* (London, 1911), p. 25.

aignty." The example he gives is of Julius Caesar, who, "imagining or rather dreaming of such a thing, for a kingdom & a Monarchy brake the laws of God & man. This is pride and presumption when men will not be content with David to tary their time, but wil adventure by hook or crook, by right by wrong surmount." At the end of this sermon Humphrey uses another expression which could easily describe the Elizabethan hero when he characterizes the predecessors and successors of Abishai as "ambition aspiring."[33]

Ironically, Humphrey's sermons are dedicated to Robert Dudley, Earl of Leicester, whose character and career displayed the exciting, half-allowed, half-blasphemous freedoms characteristic of the tragic hero. The most powerful of Elizabeth's favorites, Leicester was thought to have committed crimes worthy of an Italianate stage villain, such as poisoning the husband of the women he subsequently married, and then killing her (she apparently died after falling down a flight of stairs). These accusations were given wide publicity in a tract entitled *The Copie of a Leter* (1584), which described Leicester as one "of so extreme ambition, pride, falshood and trecherie," and "suffered so manie years wythout check to aspire to tyrannie by moste manifest wayes . . . that nothing wanteth to him but onlie his pleasure." Comparing Leicester to his father, John Dudley, the author laments that in his "outragious ambition and desire of reigne, he is not inferior to his father, or to anie other aspiring spirit in the world, but far more insolent, cruel, vindictive, expert, potent, subtile, fine, and fox-like than ever he was. . . ."[34] Leicester's supporters were given as much to hyperbole as his critics: he was as extravagantly praised in works such as Spenser's *Faerie Queene* as he was damned in *The Copie of a Leter*. Nor was he the only prominent Elizabethan courtier to be condemned for his pride. According to a letter concerning Raleigh which Burghley re-

[33] Lawrence Humphrey, *A View of the Romish hydra confuted in seven sermons* (Oxford, 1588), STC #13966, pp. 8, 26.

[34] Anon., *The copie of a letter wryten by a Master of Art of Cambridge to his friend in London* . . . (London, 1584), STC #1031, pp. 16 ff.

ceived from a correspondent, "no man is more hated . . . his pride is intolerable, without regard for any. . . ."[35] Yet Raleigh was also one of the greatest of Elizabethan heroes. Poet, courtier, soldier, explorer, he was the embodiment of the Renaissance man. That the behavior of men like Leicester and Raleigh could be simultaneously praised and despised tells us something about the ambivalence inherent in the Elizabethan's attitude toward pride, presumption, boldness, aspiration, ambitiousness, and similar characteristics. This ambivalence contributed to the Elizabethans' receptivity to tragedy by enabling the stage characters who possessed these qualities to evoke a mixture of sympathy, admiration, and repudiation.

Perhaps the clearest indication of this ambivalence was the preachers' recognition that the presumptuous man could conceivably be one of the elect. In *Two Sermons upon the History of P·ters denying Christ*, John Udall attributes Peter's fall to his presumption, observing that he was "blinded with the consideration of his owne power" and "carried away with a preposterous zeale to follow him [Christ]." Moreover, he "thought he was strong inough to be a Martyr, when indeede he had scarce learned the principles of hys faith, nor that whyche is most necessary for all men to knowe: namely, his own power and hability. . . ." From Peter's case Udall leads his auditors to an awareness of "the pryde of mans hearte, and confidence that fleshe and bloud conceiveth of him selfe."[36] Udall was particularly concerned about the Elizabethan susceptibility to pride. In a sermon delivered in 1589 he laments:

> Whereupon it commeth that we see the whole world so carried away in pride and presumption, that every man swelleth in his owne conceit, seeking to disgrace al other men in respect to himself, and liketh of nothing, be it never so good, holy, or wisely done or said, but that which is forged in his owne imagination. . . .

[35] Milton Waldman, *Sir Walter Raleigh* (London, 1928), p. 51.
[36] John Udall, *Two Sermons upon the Historie of Peters denying Christ* (London, 1584), STC #24503, sig. B2ʳ-B7ᵛ.

And he adds: "For of all sinnes, I am perswaded that the best and godliest can most hardly avoide this, to doe any thing that is good, and not be proud of it."[37]

Udall has articulated some of the gravest difficulties inherent in the doctrine of election. The saint must maintain his assurance of election without falling into confidence and self-congratulation, and he must strive to be virtuous without taking credit for his virtue. Ten years earlier Chaderton, too, had recognized that the evils of pride and arrogance could originate in the very self-scrutiny and assurance which the Puritan clergy so repeatedly encouraged:

> I can see no other roote whence these rotten and stincking bowes should spring, then this high and lofty minde whereby men do presume to think of them selves, and of the treasure of grace which they have, more than they ought to doe.

Chaderton has elsewhere declared his purpose as preacher to be, among other things, to terrify proud and presumptuous believers. He sees in the Puritan a potential for "pride, selfe-love, vaine glory, arrogancie and ambition" and he invokes a "humbling [of] our proude heartes, and working in our mindes a sound iudgement" by the sweet grace of God. His accusations could easily have been directed at Tamburlaine himself, as he rebukes his Elizabethan audience for the pride and ambition which make them discontented with their callings and concludes that we must rid ourselves of our "unquiet aspiring minds."[38]

[37] John Udall, *The Combate between Christe and the Devill: Four Sermons upon the temptations of Christ in the wildernes by Sathan: wherein are to be seene the subtile sleights that the tempter useth against the Children of God* (London, 1589), STC #24493, sig. F2ʳ, F3ʳ.

[38] Lawrence Chaderton, *A Fruitfull Sermon upon the 3.4.5.6.7.8. verses of the 12 Chapiter of the Epistle of S. Paul to the Romanes* (London, 1584), STC #4926, pp. 24, 21. Several decades later, Puritans evidently continued to see the dangers of presumption and boldness in England. The Puritan John Rogers, in 1627, prayed for God to be merciful to England, ". . . for it is a presumptuous nation, and a bold, and that without any warrant from God. They think most in England shall be saved. It is the voice of ministers and

Chaderton's use of the phrase "aspiring mind" in this context points to an important connection between the presumptuous man's pride in his abilities, or accomplishments, and his desire to extend or transcend them. Many such presumptuous men could be found in the political, economic, and social spheres of Elizabethan London, and their presumption, no doubt, was fundamentally concerned with the things of this world.[39] But there was also another form of presumption characteristic of the period—this was the presumption of the intellect, the Faustian aspiration for unlimited knowledge. The preachers warned their audiences about this kind of presumption, and set forth guidelines for the godly to follow. In a catechism entitled *A Pastime for Parents*, written in the form of a dialogue between a father and child, Dent has the Father ask the Child to describe the difference "betwixt the knowledge of the elect and the reprobate." The Child answers:

The knowledge of the reprobate doth puffe up.
The knowledge of the elect doth humble.
The knowledge of the reprobate is generall and confused.
The knowledge of the elect is particular and certaine.
The knowledge of the reprobates is onely literall; and
    historicall.
The knowledge of the elect is spirituall, and experimentall.
The knowledge of the reprobate is speculative.
The knowledge of the elect is practive, that is, ioyned with
    obedience.[40]

The association between right and wrong knowledge and humility and pride appears also in a sixteenth-century translation of St. Augustine, entitled *The glass of vaine-glorie* ("speculum

people." Quoted from *The Doctrine of Faith* by Larzar Ziff, in *Puritanism in America* (New York, 1973), p. 30.

[39] Cf. Anthony Esler, *The Aspiring Minds of the Elizabethan Younger Generation* (Durham, North Carolina, 1966).

[40] Arthur Dent, *A pastime for Parents: or A recreation to passe away the time; contayning the most principall grounds of Christian Religion* (London, 1606), STC #6622, sig. C6ᵛ.

peccatoris"), an instructive mirror held up to nature, designed to make "loose livers" fruitful in the knowledge of themselves. The anonymous translator, W.P., inveighs against the pursuit of secular knowledge, which is allied with all of the characteristics of the reprobate.

> Now let verie shame it self procure the proude hautie & unhappie sinner to blushe though blinded with ambition, inflamed with wrath, polluted with impatience, and hoven up with knowledge, who liketh better of Aristotles philosophie, than of the testimonie of all the apostles, and of the workes of Plato, than of the word of God. . . .[41]

Even more threatening to the Puritans, however, was pursuit of knowledge pertaining to God's purposes and intents. Calvin, in the *Institutes*, had warned his readers of "how exceedingly presumptuous it is only to inquire into the causes of the Divine will," and Perkins, likewise, told his readers to think or speak of God's works and judgment "with modesty and sobriety, with admiration and reverence, not daring to search into the reason of them. . . ."[42]

These prohibitions certainly must have been in the Elizabethan audience's minds as they watched Faustus assault the stronghold of God's incomprehensibility. And yet, as Perry Miller has observed, Calvin could not have wholly disparaged man's reason, for in doing so he would have conceded to the Catholic doctrine of fideism, which denied man's ability to interpret scripture. Calvin does, in fact, say that we have been endowed with reason and understanding in order that we may lead holy lives and achieve immortality. In the section of the *Institutes* devoted to Christian freedom (which in the original 1536 edition composed about one-fifth of the whole work) Calvin emphasized the believer's freedom from the law, an-

---

[41] St. Augustine, *The glasse of vaine-glorie*, trans., W. P. *Doctor of the Lawes* (London, 1585), STC #929, p. 29.

[42] Calvin's *Institutes*, III, xxiii, 2. Quoted by George Herndl in *The High Design: English Renaissance Tragedy and the Natural Law* (Lexington, Ky., 1970), p. 127; Perkins, *A Golden Chaine*, p. 723.

nouncing that the conscience is "set free" and that we are "released from the power of all men." Accordingly, he urged those in search of assurance to "rise above and advance beyond the law, forgetting all law righteousness." In the section which treats of Christian freedom in respect to things indifferent, or "adiaphora," he declares that "we should use God's gifts for the purpose for which he gave them to us, with no scruple of conscience, no trouble of mind." "Surely," he adds, "ivory and gold and riches are good creations of God, permitted, indeed appointed, for men's use by God's providence."[43] These freedoms were undoubtedly exploited by presumptuous and aspiring Elizabethans who saw in Calvinist doctrine justification for their actions, however questionable, in the secular realm. It must have been difficult at times to distinguish the believer exercising his Christian freedom from a reprobate "other" who was "ambition aspiring," just as it was difficult, as one of the characters in *The Plaine Mans Path-Way* recognized, to distinguish assurance from presumption: "Is it not meere presumption, and an overmuch trusting to our selves, to bee perswaded of our salvation?" Ambiguities and contradictions of this kind were intensified by limits inherent in the Puritan vocabulary. Chaderton, for instance, uses the word "secure" in series with "proud" and "presumptuous" in speaking of over-confident Protestants, while Dent uses it as a synonym for "good assurance." How, finally, one wonders, were Elizabethan sermongoers to distinguish between proud, secure, and presumptuous Protestants and the Christian who responds to the assaults of the devil by proclaiming as Perkins advises: "I assuredly beleeve that I shal not be condemned, but that I am elected, and justified in Christ, & am out of all doubt that my sins are pardoned"?[44]

---

[43] Perry Miller, *The New England Mind: The Seventeenth Century* (1939; rpt., Boston, 1961), p. 71; Calvin, *Institutes*, XX, 242, XXI, 834-46.

[44] Dent, *The Plaine Mans Path-way*, STC #6629, p. 244; Chaderton, *An Excellent and godly Sermon*, STC #4924, sig. G6ʳ; Perkins, *A Golden Chaine*, p. 87.

III. THE SCRUTINY OF THE SELF

One of the most frequently cited characteristics of English and American Puritanism was a preoccupation with the self. In the seventeenth century, the Puritan's penchant for self-scrutiny manifested itself in the lengthy and popular spiritual autobiographies which served the dual function of articulating the soul's own spiritual struggle to attain assurance and of serving as an example to others. Fortunately one sixteenth-century counterpart of the autobiographies exists in the Puritan preacher Richard Rogers' personal diary, a private record of the self-examination which the godly were urged to undergo by the spiritual guidebooks of the age. For Rogers and his contemporaries, self-examination served as a substitute for auricular confession, but was more analytical.[45] Taking their warrant from Paul's injunction to the Corinthians, "Examine yourselves whether ye be in the faith," the godly probed their actions and thoughts, searching for hidden weaknesses and signs of grace. Self-scrutiny was a continual process and, as Joan Webber has pointed out, a temporal one. The believer would repeatedly ask himself "How have I progressed (or regressed) from day to day?" rather than, "What am I like as a human being?"[46] Underlying this process was an inescapable anxiety about the pattern of one's experience and how it corresponded to the proper or ideal pattern set forth in the handbooks and sermons.[47]

The beneficent effects of self-scrutiny were repeatedly stressed by the more positive and encouraging of the sixteenth-century

[45] For a more extended discussion of the spiritual autobiography and its resemblance to auricular confession, see Haller, *The Rise of Puritanism*, pp. 38 ff.

[46] Owen Watkins, *The Puritan Experience: Studies in Spiritual Autobiography* (New York, 1972), p. 10; Joan Webber, *The Eloquent "I,"* p. 8, cited in Watkins, p. 228.

[47] John Dod, for example, provides such a pattern in his *Ten Sermons*. It takes the form of a checklist which moves methodically through the ten commandments, to be used by believers as they "search themselves" to detect corruption.

Puritan preachers. In his *Sermon of Repentaunce*, Arthur Dent describes the role played by self-scrutiny in the early stages of repentance. He tells his listeners that they will "feel a chaunge and alternation in the bottome of your heart" and that by rigorous probing "[you will] prove unto your consciences the forgivenesse of your Sinnes." Using a judicial metaphor, he speaks of a "clearing of our selves, that is, discharging of our selves, when sinne doeth accuse us."[48] The benefits of self-scrutiny are not gained without a good deal of emotional suffering and internal strife, however. Even so optimistic a Puritan as Perkins describes the "diligent examination of a man's own selfe" in the following way:

> If so be it, that after examination a man cannot find out his sinnes (as no man shall find out all his sinnes, for the heart of man is a vast gulf of sinne, without either bottome or banke, and hath infinite and hidden corruptions in it) then he must in a godly jealousie, suspect himself of his unknowne sinnes. . . ."[49]

Perkins' "godly jealousie" is part of the warfare of the soul, a form of ambivalence and inner conflict depicted through the language of military combat. The "auto-machia," as George Godwin called it in his book of that name published in 1607, employs the metaphor of the civil war to describe this conflict. The antagonists are the "self" and an "I" that is coextensive with the godly spirit in man and that undertakes the task of curbing or disciplining the "self." The vocabulary used by Puritan writers reveals a proliferation of "self" compounds, many of them colorfully metaphorical. They spoke of such things as self-trial, self-deceit, self-flattery, self-corruption, self-lust, self-affectation, self-lying, and self-theft.[50] Whether the "self" was the object or initiator of these actions or emotions varied from one usage to the next. What emerges, however, is a preoccu-

---

[48] Dent, *A Sermon of Repentaunce*, STC #6650, sig. B4ᵛ.

[49] Perkins, *A Golden Chaine*, p. 364.

[50] M. Van Beek, *An Enquiry into Puritan Vocabulary* (Groningen, 1969), p. 68.

pation with negative aspects of the self and a desire to reject or suppress them. Sacvan Bercovitch has suggested, in this context, that "self-examination serves not to liberate but to constrict; selfhood appears as a state to be overcome, obliterated; and identity is asserted through an act of submission to a transcendent absolute."[51] The believer, in order to turn toward God, must turn away from the self; hence self-abasement is good, self-esteem bad.[52] Imitation of Christ, not individual selfhood, is his goal. And yet in this very process of self-obliteration or submission, the Puritan continues to define and affirm his own identity. Because the rhetorical self-confidence necessary for the attainment of assurance is accompanied by a psychic uncertainty which incessantly undermines it, "self-fashioning," to use Greenblatt's terms, consists simultaneously of self-suppression and self-assertion.

This situation is vividly illustrated in Richard Rogers' diary, which offers a detailed depiction of the relationship of the "I" to the "self."[53] Rogers reports in his diary that "For the times have been when I was not sooner risen from bedde and board but I was immed [iately] with the lord in med [itation] about my self. . . ." He sought "to know mine owne hart better, where I know that much is to be gotten in understanding of it, and to be acquainted with the diverse corners of it and what sin I am most in danger of and what dilig [ence] and meanes I use against any sin and how I goe under any afflic [tion]." In his struggle to achieve assurance Rogers is aware of the paradoxical implications of the words "security" and "boldness": "I felt the rebellion ariseinge, so that I see not how one may safely grow secure and bolde but one daunger

---

[51] Sacvan Berckovitch, *The Puritan Origins of the American Self* (New Haven, 1975), p. 13.

[52] Van Beek speaks of a vertical scale in his analysis of the safeguards against spiritual pride. The dangers of confidence are expressed in words such as over-esteem and over-valuation; on the other hand, spiritual depression, or absence of assurance is spoken of as downcasting, diseasement, p. 60 and passim.

[53] For a discussion of the confessional diary as a Puritan form of expression, see Watkins, *The Puritan Experience*, Chapter 2.

or other may holde him from it. . . ." And he worries generally about the ungodly confidence implicit in godly assurance, fearing that "we shall rest our selves too much in the meanes by which we are made godly."[54]

The word "self" dominates the Rogers diary. Within the space of a couple of pages, which cover a bleak period from April to October of 1588, Rogers speaks of being unable "to recover my self," because of a "want of continuance by my self in one place without hindraunce," of being engaged in "foolish busyinge my selfe in the world," of feeling "my self brought low" and unable to "stirre up . . . either our selves or the soldiars," of having "solace[d] my self with trash" and of giving "my self to contrary considerations" in an effort to renounce that solace. In all of these examples the words "my" and "self" function in an essentially reflexive sense, like the modern English "myself." Just as frequently, however, what appears grammatically to be the same reflexive formation reveals a distinction between the "I" and the "self" which draws attention to the warring impulses in the spiritual life of the godly. For example, in August 1587, Rogers worries about the fact that "I cannot yet setle my selfe to my study" and hopes to "look more diligently to my selfe then I have done and weane my selfe from some lawful profites and pleasures" and unlawful ones as well. In various other entries he speaks of having given liberty to his self, of having roused and stayed and shamed and made promises to his self, and of having found in the self "declineings . . . from that staidnes in a godly life" which the "I" had determined to continue.[55]

Similar to the self in Puritan writings is the heart, which often seems to occupy the same position in respect to the "I." Like the self, it is often represented as a pupil or a child or even as an animal which needs to be bridled and trained. Rogers speaks of desiring to know his own heart better, of the

[54] Marshall Mason Knappen, ed., *Two Elizabethan Puritan Diaries* (Chicago, 1933), pp. 56, 57, 62, 67, 72.

[55] Knappen, *Two Elizabethan Puritan Diaries*, pp. 62-63 and passim.

love of worldly things which "cleaveth so neer to my hart" and must be purged, and of having "well seasoned our hartes" so that they will be able to tolerate the infinite number of troubles "incident to our lives."[56] Sometimes, however, the self and the heart can become so riddled with sin that they pose a serious threat to the "I," and, as the preachers talk about them, they seem to assume some of the qualities associated with the reprobate. Consider, for example, the dire warning offered by Henry Smith in his second sermon on the Lord's Supper, which stresses the self-examination that prepares the believer to be a participant. Smith insists that "a man must be jealous of himselfe and take himself for a liar, a flatterer, for a dissembler, untill he be throughlie acquainted with himselfe, for no man is so often beguiled as by himself, by trusting his double heart."[57]

Language like this suggests a distinction between an "I" charged with the responsibility of exercising discipline and control, and a self or heart which represents all other aspects of the human being. This is clearly a more complex dichotomy than the traditional Christian distinction between the soul and the body, for the self, as Rogers and other Puritans use the word, consists of body, soul, mind—everything except the critical faculty which is capable of self-examination. Dent employs this dichotomy in one of many Puritan formulas for distinguishing the regenerate from the unregenerate. One sign of the regenerate mind, he says, is "Deniall of our selves": the corresponding sign of the unregenerate is "Trusting to our selves."[58] The denial of self that signifies election can be so

[56] Knappen, *Two Elizabethan Puritan Diaries*, pp. 62-66.

[57] Henry Smith, *Sermons* (London, 1593), STC #22719, p. 135; Perkins (*A Golden Chaine*, p. 375) must have also been thinking of a "double heart" when he explained that when the godly are tempted to sin, "there is a fight between the heart . . . and it selfe" (here the heart seems more like Rogers' "I"). Like Smith, he represents the process of self-examination in terms of jealousy and suspicion; interestingly, however, he distinguishes the inner struggle of the godly from that of the wicked, in whom the fight "is only between the heart and the conscience."

[58] Dent, *The Plaine Mans Path-way*, STC #6629, p. 30.

intense an experience that it can lead to what Perkins calls "holy desperation." Holy desperation occurs when a man is "wholly out of hope" of attaining salvation and thinks and speaks more vilely of himself than any other. Although traditionally desperation was viewed as a characteristic of the unregenerate (one thinks for instance of Doctor Faustus), for Perkins it is a sign of true humility.[59]

Even more extreme than denial of self and holy desperation is the self-punishment inflicted by the true believer referred to as "revenge," frequently described in Puritan tracts as the last of the seven stages of repentance (cf. II Cor. 7:11). Dent, for example, speaks of the penitent person as being "so offended, with the sinne he hath committed, that hee will bee revenged of himselfe for it" in the *Sermon of Repentaunce*. Egerton, in a lecture preached at Blackfriars in 1589, illustrates the "holy revenge" which accompanies repentance with the famous story of Bishop Cramner, who thrust into the fire the right hand with which he had signed his recantation.[60] Revenge of this kind was a legitimate action which could be performed in the service of God, one to which the ordinary believer might have the occasion to resort. We can speculate that one reason the earliest revenge plays appealed to Elizabethan audiences was that they enabled the relationship between the "I" and the erring "self" to be imaginatively projected into a fictional realm. In this realm a physical embodiment of the "I," with whom the audience could identify, took revenge upon an "other" who exhibited to an exaggerated degree all of the most negative characteristics of the "self" or "heart." Or, as Muriel Bradbrook has suggested in *The Rise of the Common Player*, revenge plays acted out the punitive aspects of religion, allowing "the

[59] Perkins does not think of desperation as a sin against the Holy Ghost, because "desperation may arise through ignorance of a mans owne estate: through horrour of conscience for sinne; through the overdeepe consideration of a mans own unworthinesse" (p. 378).

[60] Dent, *A Sermon of Repentaunce*, STC #6650, sig. B8ʳ; Stephen Egerton, *A Lecture preached by Maister Egerton, at the Blacke-friers, 1589* (London, 1603), STC #7539, p. 27.

projection of deep fears, and the exorcism of guilt which the actors and audience shared." Bradbrook further speculates that when the revenger takes God's role upon himself, the playwright is in effect reducing a frightful and terrifying God "to dimensions merely human, and show [ing] him in the end as falling to death's mace himself. . . . [This] must have given sweet if unrecognized relief to fear."[61]

In their anxiety to define themselves in antithesis to that "other," the Elizabethans repeatedly sought out occasions to contrast themselves with those who were not among the elect. Linaker, for example, leads his reader through a reassuring exercise in self-assurance after a discussion of the sins of Mary Magdalene. In the process he raises an interesting problem inherent in self-scrutiny: how are self-denial and self-revenge to be distinguished from self-slander?

> Now let mee reason a little with you, concerning this woman: can you when you have strained out your sinnes to the uttermost, make your selfe as bad as this woman? No, you cannot, you may not, you dare not. For how dare you slaunder your owne selfe, when it is not any way lawful to slaunder another? and if you bee bound to tender the good name of your brother as well as your owne, then it must needes follow, you are by nature most bound to tender your owne.[62]

The example of Mary Magdalene serves a similar function to that attributed to God's punishment of sinners, as described by Dent. These punishments serve for the instruction or "advertisement" of the godly, "as it were looking glasses, wherein every man may see his owne face" and compare it with others.[63]

[61] Muriel C. Bradbrook, *The Rise of the Common Player: A Study of Actor and Society in Shakespeare's England* (London, 1962), pp. 128-133.

[62] R. Linaker, *A Comfortable Treatise, for the reliefe of such as are afflicted in Conscience* (London, 1607; first edition, 1590), STC #15640, p. 30.

[63] Dent, *The Plaine Mans Path-way*, STC #6629, sig. A3ᵛ; Barroll notes, in *Artificial Persons*, that every system of thought contains polarities which are defined as opposites and which cannot be understood except in terms of the

This ability to "looke unto him selfe," or engage in self-examination, is precisely what the reprobate is incapable of doing. As Perkins describes him, "the reprobate may goe further in the profession of religion" than the elect for a time, and may seem to believe God's promises and precepts, but "he cannot apply them to him selfe." Perkins depicts the dilemma of the reprobate as painful and, indeed, tragic. God is at first patient with them, and "useth many means to winne them. . . ." After a while, however, "God in his just judgment hardneth their hearts, blindeth the eyes of their minds, he maketh their heads giddy with a spiritual drunkenness. . . ." When the reprobate "committeth a sinne, hee sorroweth and repenteth . . . when he repenteth, he cannot come unto God. . . . Hee is very like a man upon a racke, who cryeth and roareth out for very paine, yet cannot desire his tormentor to ease him of his paine."[64] Eventually, Perkins observes elsewhere, the sinner is driven to hardness of heart and madness. Reading this vivid characterization, one thinks of Faustus and, later, Macbeth.

Because the tragic downfalls of reprobate sinners played an important part in the instruction of the elect, their presence on the stage was acknowledged by the Puritans to serve a useful purpose. Despite his violent invective against the playhouses, Stephen Gosson, for example, praised such plays as "The Iew and Ptolome, showne at the Bull, the one representing the greedinesse of worldly chusers, and bloody mindes of usurers; the other very liuely discrybing howe seditious estates, with their owne deuises, false friendes, with their owne swoordes, & rebellious commons in their owne snares are ouerthrowne."[65] For such "others" to emerge as dramatic

---

other. The "hero" and the "villain" are opposites according to the terms of the system that polarizes them, he suggests (pp. 106-107). The polarities of the saved and the damned served this kind of function in Elizabethan England, I would argue, and contributed significantly to the corresponding secular polarities of hero and villain.

[64] Perkins, *The Golden Chaine*, pp. 357-60.

[65] Stephen Gosson, *The S[c]hoole of abuse, conteining a pleasant invective against poets* (London, 1579), STC #12097, sig. C6ᵛ.

characters in the early years of tragedy seems a logical consequence of the Elizabethans' curiosity about the types of people they hoped *not* to be. And for those "others" to become increasing realistic characters is in turn a consequence of the audience's growing sensitivity to human psychology. This sensitivity—and the playwrights' willingness to draw upon it—was not altogether new; audiences had seen dramatized versions of the inner workings of the soul in the early morality plays based on the concept of the *psychomachia*. By the 1570s and 1580s, their interest in the complexities of human motivation had received a tremendous impetus from the analyses of behavior which issued from the pulpits and the presses. Hence as audiences became more receptive to complex characterization, the playwrights were encouraged to probe more and more deeply into the sources of their characters' action.

In Rogers' diary, as elsewhere, the use of self-examination as a substitute for confession points to an increasing recognition in the society as a whole of man's own responsibility for the state of his soul and for the choices he makes. This aspect of Protestantism became one of the defining characteristics of modern consciousness. It also provides one of the essential preconditions for tragedy. The tragic protagonist, as Herbert Weisinger describes him, is free to choose and indeed, is forced to choose: "Oedipus . . . between demands of his own reason and those of the gods; Hamlet . . . between taking justice into his own hands . . . and God's own way of establishing justice; Adam . . . between his own will and that of God. In each case the protagonist is left free and, in each case, he chooses wrongly. . . ." The result, Weisinger concludes, is "our own escape and our enlightenment," for "only the symbolic sacrifice of one who is like us can make possible our atonement. . . ." [66] The tragic protagonist is sufficiently like us to arouse our sympathy and take our place; ultimately, however, he remains in some sense the "other," because he has made the wrong choice.

[66] Herbert Weisinger, *Tragedy and the Paradox of the Fortunate Fall* (London, 1953), p. 268.

CHAPTER III

Morality Play Protagonists

Any art form created by and for mixed popular audiences is by nature conservative, if only because the habitual expectations of the audience themselves are inclined to resist change. Emrys Jones has suggested that popular drama "to succeed in performance . . . must establish a more or less instantly recognizable relation to traditional expected forms; however innovative in detail, it must in essence work through a modification of what is already known. No more than the entire system of a spoken language can the development of dramatic form tolerate large hiatuses."[1] To understand how Elizabethan tragedy came into being, we must view it as a modification of what was already known to Elizabethan audiences, as a form which grew along with the society for which it was written, while remaining to a remarkable degree deeply rooted in the traditional expected forms of the popular religious drama. The dominant form of popular drama in the sixteenth century was the morality play, a form heavily dependent on allegorical characterization and overt didacticism.[2] Originally, the mo-

[1] Emrys Jones, *The Origins of Shakespeare* (Oxford, 1977), p. 33. Cf. A. P. Rossiter, *English Drama From Early Times to the Elizabethans* (London, 1950). Rossiter describes the audience as "a representative of the mind-of-the-times, [which] provides the *continuum* between past and present" (p. 11).

[2] Scholars frequently use the term "moral interlude" to distinguish the sixteenth-century allegorical plays from the "full-scope" moralities of the fifteenth century. I will be using the term "morality" to include the interludes which seem clearly to be based on morality play conventions. As Robert Potter points out in *The English Morality Play* (London, 1975), the morality tradition mingled with comic traditions derived from native and humanistic sources, to provide various comic transformations and adaptations of the morality form, which are corrective in spirit and indebted to the didactic dramaturgy of the earliest morality plays (p. 109). Discussions of such plays will be included in this chapter.

rality play acted out the pattern of temptation, fall, and repentance in the life of a human protagonist, whose ordinariness and universality were commonly expressed by his name: Everyman, Mankind, Youth. The spectator was thus presented with a character "like himself" in whom his own spiritual state was mirrored so that he, too, would reform and repent. The protagonist was surrounded by a group of characters who were allegorical embodiments of moral qualities bearing the relationship to him of either tempter or redeemer. Insofar as these characters represented aspects or potential aspects of the protagonist, they served to illuminate his character and create a semblance of the indecision and internal struggle—indeed, of the psychological complexity—which would later characterize the tragic protagonist. As the protagonist underwent the process of experience and correction that led to his reformation, he underwent a recognition which was a specifically religious version of the Aristotelian *anagnoresis*. Contained within its essentially comic structure, therefore, the morality play harbored one of the key ingredients of tragedy.

Elizabethan tragedy was also influenced by the mystery cycles (which continued to be performed in England until the 1570s), but to a lesser degree. Whereas the predicaments of the Mankind figures foreshadowed the tragic choices and tragic responsibilities later protagonists would experience, the characters in the mysteries enacted well-known roles that had remained fixed for centuries. The mythic structure of the mysteries placed its primary emphasis on the institution of the Church, while the allegorical structure of the moralities focused on the individual believer. This difference corresponds to the changes in religious attitudes that led to the English Reformation and the rise of Puritanism. Instead of the salvation conferred vicariously by Christ's sacrifice, the moralities dramatized the salvation which follows from the believer's own act of repentance.

How a drama devoted primarily to providing positive and negative models to be imitated or shunned could evolve into or, at the very least, contribute to what we think of as tragedy

75

has been an underlying question in a number of studies of the origins of English tragedy. J.M.R. Margeson, for example, ends his discussion of morality plays by asking: "Was it necessary for the didactic to be eliminated before tragedy could emerge?" The answer, surely, is no, for didacticism never altogether disappeared from the drama during Shakespeare's lifetime. Perhaps recognizing this, Margeson redefines his terms somewhat and concludes that tragedy did not become possible until "the nature and intensity of human experience became a matter of greater concern in the drama than the moral idea."[3] The plays to be discussed in this chapter span a century or more, and the modifications which they reflect gradually brought the morality form closer to tragedy by replacing "the moral idea" with several less absolute moral ideas, not all of which could be reconciled with one another. Potentially tragic situations began to result from the complex interplay of these moral ideas, in plays which raised issues relating to human experience that the preachers were also discussing. Unlike the mysteries, which were confined by the shape of the biblical myths they celebrated, the moralities explored topical issues and engaged in social satire and religious polemics. As the playwrights discovered new subjects, the morality form began to change, particularly toward the end of its existence, in the 1560s and 1570s. Many of these changes reflect the impact of

---

[3] J.M.R. Margeson, *The Origins of English Tragedy* (Oxford, 1967), p. 58. The whole issue of the relationship of didacticism to tragedy is also addressed by Willard Farnham in *The Medieval Heritage of Elizabethan Tragedy* (Berkeley, 1936). He notes that while the tragic spirit remained undeveloped in the essentially affirmative medieval mystery and miracle plays, "we may find a tragic spirit definitely developing" in the morality play because it takes place "in that moral world of stresses and strains between good and evil where humanity by reason of its freedom of choice shapes character" (p. 177). Farnham's argument that the English morality was essential preparation for Elizabethan tragedy has been widely accepted by subsequent scholars. Farnham emphasizes, however, that the "abstracting and allegorizing" employed by the didactic playwrights of the fifteenth century needed to give way to the creation of "authentic human individuality" before tragedy could emerge (p. 212). This is also the basic assumption of Potter and of Margeson.

Calvinism, which was affecting other literary forms as well.[4] When it had evolved to the point that its traditional comic ending was no longer inevitable, the morality play had ceased to fulfill its original function of reassuring its audience. At this point, its didactic motive could give way to something else. What followed was the emergence of tragedy.

I. THE FIFTEENTH-CENTURY MORALITY PLAYS

No one knows how many morality plays there were in the fifteenth century or how and where they were performed. Unlike the mysteries, they seem to have involved professional rather than amateur companies. A few records of payments to *homines ludentes* exist, but it is not known how clear a distinction was made between the activity of actors and that of minstrels who performed songs and dances.[5] Apart from the fragmentary *The Pride of Life* (late fourteenth century) and the well-known *Everyman* (1495), possibly of Dutch origin, the only plays from the fifteenth century to survive are the three Macro plays: *The Castle of Perseverance* (1405-1420), *Mind, Will and Understanding*, or *The Wisdom That is Christ* (1450-1500), and *Mankind* (c. 1465). Edmund Creeth has recently speculated that a number of plays existed throughout England in the fifteenth century which employed the same basic patterns as *The Pride of Life* and the Macro plays, and that these

---

[4] The influence of the mystery plays on English tragedy, while different in character than that of the morality plays, should not be overlooked. Both Jones and Margeson devote chapters to this subject. See also Eleanor Prosser's *Drama and Religion in the English Mystery Plays* (Stanford, 1961) and Glynne Wickham, *Shakespeare's Dramatic Heritage* (London, 1969). For discussions of the topicality of the morality play see Norman Sanders, Richard Southern, T. W. Craik, and Lois Potter, *The Revels History of Drama in English*, Vol. II (London, 1980), chapter 1, and David Bevington, *Tudor Drama and Politics* (Cambridge, Mass., 1968). On the morality form's ability to change and to reflect change, see Robert Weimann, *Shakespeare and the Popular Tradition in the Theatre* (Baltimore, 1978), pp. 98 ff.

[5] Stanley J. Kahrl, *Traditions of Medieval English Drama* (Pittsburgh, 1974), pp. 16, 100-101 and passim.

four survivors could conceivably represent *"states* of plays" performed into the sixteenth century, though "varying somewhat according to time and place." He offers as evidence, among other things, the fact that the plot of *The Castle of Perseverance* does not entirely agree with the summary of it given in the Proclamation which precedes the play. Creeth proposes the possibility that Shakespeare knew plays similar in design to these fifteenth-century moralities, which would account for the remarkable kinship he sees between *The Pride of Life, Mind, Will and Understanding, The Castle of Perseverance*, and *King Lear, Othello*, and *Macbeth* respectively.[6]

The potential for tragedy in the early morality plays was largely a function of the protagonist's innate human weakness and the threat of damnation that was thus never wholly absent. The prominent position given to characters representing divine mercy, however, prevented tragedy from actually occurring. For example, at the end of *The Castle of Perseverance*, Mankind, who has been tempted, converted, and then captured in battle by Covetousness, is finally rescued from Belial by Mercy, whose claim on his Soul triumphs over the contrary claims presented by her sisters Truth and Righteousness. God, who presides over the debate among Mercy, Peace, Truth, and Righteousness, proclaims that his judgment is not based on deserving, for "misericordia Domini plena est terra."[7] Reflecting on this pattern of events, Willard Farnham has observed that as long as "a universal law of justice, under which man lives and engages himself with his destiny, is dominated by the force of mercy, [the audience's] recognition of tragedy must necessarily be small."[8] Small though it may be, even the superior claim afforded to Mercy cannot altogether cancel out the tragic implications of the human condition. In his final exhortation to the protagonist of *Mankind*, the clerical char-

[6] Edmund Creeth, *Mankynde in Shakespeare* (Athens, Georgia, 1976), pp. 10 and passim.

[7] *The Macro Plays: The Castle of Perseverance, Wisdom, Mankind*, ed. Mark Eccles (London, Early English Text Society, 1969), p. 108.

[8] Farnham, *The Medieval Heritage of Elizabethan Tragedy*, p. 193.

acter Mercy, who has persuaded Mankind to believe that God's mercy supersedes His justice, nevertheless warns him that of his three ghostly enemies—the World, the Flesh, and the Fell, or devil—he remains always susceptible to the flesh. "Your body ys your enmy," he stresses, conveying a bleak vision of the human condition, one which sees no end to the inner conflict between the soul and the body. This conflict is dramatized even more visibly in the third of the Macro plays, *Mind, Will and Understanding*. Instead of a single Mankind figure, the play contains a maiden named Anima, and three allegorical faculties, Mind, Will, and Understanding, who succumb to Lucifer's temptations, with the result that Anima is literally rendered "fowlere than a fende."[9] As in the relationships among the "I" and the "self" or "heart" discussed in the last chapter, human susceptibility to the devil is perceived as the consequence of internal divisiveness and of the weakness of those aspects of consciousness and volition which the Puritans called the "self."

The best known of the extant fifteenth-century morality plays, *Everyman*, is based on the idea of the journey, a journey toward death and the grave. Unlike other morality plays, *Everyman* is concerned only with the very final moments of the protagonist's life span. It is also atypical in that it lacks a temptation sequence and the comic business usually associated with it. In place of Mercy, *Everyman* emphasizes good deeds as the key to repentance, which might seem to ally it with orthodox Catholicism unaffected by the reforming impulse that informs even the earliest morality plays. *Everyman*'s effectiveness as drama is due primarily to the fact that it focuses more intensely on its protagonist and the process of recognition than any of the Macro plays. As a result, it draws the spectators into a closer and closer involvement with Everyman as his friends and relatives and external attributes successively abandon him.

The emotional engagement or identification which the

[9] *The Macro Plays*, p. 143.

spectators are made to feel for a protagonist like Everyman was essential to the morality play's success as didactic literature. Significantly, it was a relationship which had no real counterpart in the mystery cycles. As Michael Goldman has suggested in *The Actor's Freedom*, the distance between the actor and the character he played was greater in the English mystery cycles than in any other phase of Western drama. The amateur actor, the audience felt, was one of us; the character, a sacred personage, one of them. The spectator thus felt a distance between himself and the play reinforced by a powerful awareness of the presumption, the risk of blasphemy, involved in the actor's undertaking such a role. Hence, Goldman suggests, acknowledging his indebtedness to V. A. Kolve's *The Play Called Corpus Christi*, the insistence on the play as play, game, or jest, as a form of protection from this sense of blasphemy.[10] In the morality play, however, the distance between the actor and the role he assumed in the play was less pronounced, both because the characters were mostly inventions of the playwright, with no independent existence in scripture, and because of the professional status of the actor. To make explicit the play's didactic intent, the playwrights overtly invited audience identification with the Mankind figure.[11] In the Banns which introduce *The Castle of Perseverance*, for instance, the second vexillator, or flagbearer, proclaims that every man may in himself find "the case of our comynge," or the argument of the play. As they briefly describe the events

[10] Michael Goldman, *The Actor's Freedom: Toward a Theory of Drama* (New York, 1975), p. 78. V. A. Kolve's study of the mystery cycles, *The Play Called Corpus Christi* (Stanford, 1966), explores meanings of the word "play" originally discussed in Huizinga's *Homo Ludens*.

[11] Anne Righter emphasizes the morality playwright's efforts to get the audience to identify with the Mankind figure in *Shakespeare and the Idea of the Play* (London, 1962). She notes, though, that the "Mankind in the audience" was granted "a measure of enlightenment denied his counterpart on the stage." The spectators thus stood "in the very centre of the drama and, at the same time, a little outside" (pp. 25-27). What Righter describes is an early version of the mixture of identification and detachment the Elizabethan audience would come to feel for the tragic protagonist.

to come, the flagbearers speak interchangeably of man in general and the Mankind who is the protagonist of the play. Mercy, who serves a similarly introductory role in *Mankind*, speaks of "our dysobedyenc" for which Jesus died, and begs the audience to rectify their conditions. He offers himself as the means for their restitution and warns them of their "gostly enmy," urging them not to put their felicity in things transitory. Thus he places them in the very position in respect to himself and the events of the play which the character Mankind will shortly assume. Similarly, the Messenger who begins *Everyman* tells his audience that the play will show how transitory our lives are, then adds "Man, in the beginning/ Look well, and take good head to the ending,/ Be you never so gay!"[12] The use of direct address here, as in *Mankind*, has the effect of dissolving the boundaries between stage and audience and drawing the spectator into the action of the play. By the time the play arrived at its redemptive ending the fifteenth-century audience's identification with the Mankind figure had become a projected acting-out of their own salvation. Hence their emotional engagement with the protagonist served an important spiritual and psychological purpose.

This emotional engagement was a strong enough element in the audience's response to the character they perceived as the protagonist that it did not disappear once the didactic motive no longer existed. In plays as late as *Othello* and *King Lear* something very like the morality play structure persists, through the conflicting claims of virtuous and vicious characters on a central protagonist.[13] Such a structure encouraged the identification the audience had once felt for a generalized Mankind figure even after the protagonist had become a more individualized and less universal character. This is not to say

---

[12] *Everyman and Medieval Miracle Plays*, ed. A. C. Cawley (New York, 1959), p. 207.

[13] For a discussion of morality play elements in *Othello*, see Bernard Spivack's *Shakespeare and the Allegory of Evil* (New York, 1958). Alvin Kernan discusses the morality play elements in *King Lear* in *The Playwright as Magician* (New Haven, 1979).

that the Elizabethan audience felt as strong and unmixed an identification with Lear or Othello as they did with Mankind or Everyman. Had they done so, the play's tragic ending would have been emotionally unsupportable. As the morality play began to change in the course of the sixteenth century, the spectator would cease to see his own moral condition so closely reflected in that of a single central protagonist. This increasing sense of detachment from the protagonist helped to prepare audiences to accept the tragic protagonist's downfall even as they continued to feel a profound sympathy for him.

II. THE EDUCATION-OF-YOUTH PLAYS

With its reliance on humor and spectacle, and its ability to make visible the allegorical concepts so frequently employed by the preachers, the morality play was an obvious vehicle for educating the young. From *Mundus et Infans*, written early in the sixteenth century, to W. Wager's markedly Calvinist *The Longer Thou Livest the More Fool Thou Art*, written sometime between 1559 and 1568, the popular education-of-youth plays served as vivid illustrations of the temptations to which youths were susceptible.[14] These plays were limited in their potential for tragedy, since the didactic motive is uppermost and, except for *The Longer Thou Livest*, they present an essentially reassuring picture of the internal and external guides to reformation which are capable of overcoming human weakness. They do, however, represent a first step in the breakdown of the dramatic structure centered around the Mankind figure, a break-

[14] The education-of-youth plays' concern with education attracted humanist playwrights from the circle of Sir Thomas More, including John Rastell, whose play *The Four Elements* (1517) depicts the student Humanity abandoning Studious Desire to follow Sensual Appetite. Similarly, John Redford's *Wit and Science* (1539) revolves around a young man named Wit, the beloved of Reason's daughter Science, who rebels against his tutor Instruction. Another learned play of this period, the Latin prodigal son play *Acolastus* (1529; translated 1539) introduced classical variants on the morality motif. Later examples of the prodigal son play are Thomas England's *The Disobedient Child* (1560) and the school play *Misogonus* (1570).

down which would eventually lead to the creation of morally complex tragic protagonists who contained within them aspects of both the "other" and the "self."

The earliest popular "youth" plays, *Mundus et Infans* (1508) and *The Interlude of Youth* (1520), are short and relatively simple plays designed for the limited attention span of youthful spectators. Both plays encourage the spectators to identify with their fun-loving protagonists, who enact an outrageous rebellion against the moral norms the play is intended to reinforce. This rebellion, however, takes place in a spirit less of hardened sin than of harmless and temporary release in which the audience can participate vicariously. The sins of the child are small and hardly mortal, as Infans illustrates:

> Aha wanton is my name
> I can many a quaynte game
> Lo my toppe I dryve in same
> Se it torneth rounde
> I can with my scorge stycke
> My felowe upon the heed hytte
> And wyghtly from hym make a skyppe
> And blere on hym my tonge
> If brother or sister do me chyde
> I wyll scratche and also byte
> I can crye and also kyke
> And mocke them all berewe
> If fader or mother wyll me smyte
> I wyll wrynge with my lyppe
> And lyghtly from hym make a skyppe
> And call my dame shrewe.[15]

Both plays contain straightforward preaching by the virtues at the beginning and the end, and a middle section filled with songs, jests, and horseplay. The virtues represent latent qualities in the youth figure posing as stern yet kind tutors. These

[15] Anon., *The worlde and the childe, other wyse called Mundus et Infans* (1522; facsimile rpt., London: Tudor Facsimile Texts, 1909), sig. A2ᵛ.

83

tutors oppose the inducements of the vices and convince the youth figure to reform, using arguments very much like those in the didactic dialogues of Perkins and others. In *The Interlude of Youth*, Charity speaks eloquently of Christ's sacrifice for man to youth, whose irreverent posture is displayed in the arrogant assertion:

> I wot not what He hath bought for me,
> And He bought anything of mine,
> I will give Him a quart of win
> The next time I Him meet.[16]

By describing man's bondage to the devil and God's act of redemption, Charity finally persuades Youth to forsake his sins by literally taking leave of Riot and Pride. The play ends with Youth promising to give good counsel to others like himself.

Roughly contemporary with *Mundus et Infans* and *The Interlude of Youth*, *Hickscorner* (1513) represents a departure from the single-protagonist youth play in that its cast consists of three virtues and three erring youths. The anonymous playwright implies the damnation of one of the youth figures by omitting him from the repentance scene. Perseverance and Contemplation succeed in converting Freewill and Imagination, who have been engaged in wickedness among the thieves and prostitutes of the London underworld; however, Hickscorner, the most corrupt of the three, disappears in mid-play and is not mentioned again. David Bevington has suggested that the limitations imposed by the number of actors may have necessitated this: the play was evidently cast for four actors, leaving Pity and Hickscorner offstage for the repentance sequence, which occupies roughly the last third of the play.[17] We cannot know whether the sixteenth-century audience would have inferred the damnation of Hickscorner; since no mention is made of him by the other characters, it would seem that the author did not want to be explicit about the consequences of

[16] *English Morality Plays and Moral Interludes*, ed. Edgar T. Schell and J. D. Schuchter (New York, 1969), p. 162.

[17] David M. Bevington, *From Mankind to Marlowe: Growth of Structure in the Popular Drama of Tudor England* (Cambridge, Mass., 1962), pp. 138-39.

his failure to repent. In later plays, more strongly influenced by Calvinist doctrine, such a contrast between a saved Mankind figure and a damned one would be a central feature of the play.

The allegorical schemes of the early sixteenth-century youth plays, in contrast to the Macro plays, are no longer likely to contain characters such as God, Christ, Death, the Devil, Mercy, or Justice; instead, the characters are more frequently allegorical projections of the protagonist himself. Conscience and Perseverance in *Mundus et Infans*; Humility in *Youth*; and Pity, Perseverance, and Contemplation in *Hickscorner* all imply by their presence that salvation is no longer largely the result of mercy given freely without, as in *The Castle of Perseverance* or *Mankind*. Rather, man is saved by acts of contemplation or self-examination, by the inner probing of conscience, and by perseverance in faith. In effect, what would eventually become the Puritan emphasis on man's own burden of responsibility for his attainment of grace through prayer and inner conviction, unaided by priestly intercession, has started to appear in these early sixteenth-century morality plays. As later playwrights were to realize, this burden was a potentially tragic one.

During the reign of Edward VI, the education-of-youth play again became a useful vehicle for public instruction, though in a more serious, less playful way. Two plays written in 1550, *Lusty Juventus* by R. Wever and the anonymous *Nice Wanton*, reflect in interesting ways the influence of Protestant doctrine upon the content and structure of the moral interlude. The tutelary virtues of *Lusty Juventus*, Knowledge and Good Counsel, are not so much allegorical characters who stand for specific virtues as they are stern and businesslike preachers who engage Juventus in the long catechistical dialogues so characteristic of later Puritan tracts. Unlike the impudent youth figures of the earlier plays, Juventus participates willingly and eagerly in these dialogues before his temptation by Hypocrisy, and even delivers instructive speeches directly to the audience. When he is eventually rescued from despair by God's Merciful Promises (i.e., assurance of salvation), he delivers a long speech

85

of repentance and exhortation to "you that be young" in the audience. The protagonist of *The Interlude of Youth*, by contrast, had delivered a mere four or five perfunctory lines to Charity and Humility, who, like most morality play virtues, dominated the final scene. The explicit Protestant didacticism of *Lusty Juventus* seems to be responsible for the expansion of the protagonist's role in the serious sections of the play. Moreover, though it has the effect of making him a stronger and less passive figure than his predecessors, it also suggests that he is flawed and hence potentially tragic. Despite the happy ending, Juventus is told that he receives mercy not according to his deserts, which are vile, but solely because of God's goodness.

In *Nice Wanton*, the education-of-youth play undergoes significant variation, as the single protagonist is replaced by a family of four. This play reveals the increasing tendency of the sixteenth-century interlude to treat youthful misbehavior as a social problem as well as a moral one—a problem that implicates the parents along with the children.[18] It also represents an important departure from the allegorical formula which tends to focus upon a single and generalized representative of mankind. *Nice Wanton* creates a lively domestic situation; the indulgent and permissive mother, Zantipe, scorns her worthy and pious son Barnabas, while defending her wanton children, Ismael and Dalila, against the warnings and scoldings of her upright neighbor Eulalia. The radical telescoping of time so common in the moral interlude deemphasizes the temptation section of the play, in which the vice Iniquity leads Ismael to the scaffold and Dalila to her death in the stews. Xantipe hears the news from Worldly Shame and is prevented from killing herself in despair by Barnabas, who informs her that his brother and sister repented before their deaths and that Dalila was even persuaded to believe that God's mercy would save her. *Nice Wanton* illustrates several potentially tragic characteristics of the mid-sixteenth-century morality. The offstage salvation

---

[18] Potter, *The English Morality Play*, p. 107.

of the erring characters comes almost as an afterthought, after the impact of their downfall has been fully felt. Furthermore, the play presents its audience with characters who are more human and more limited in what they stand for than the allegorical abstractions of earlier plays. As Robert Potter has observed in *The English Morality Play*, the "logical possibility of tragedy" would not occur until the central figure of the morality play ceased to represent all mankind, and became individualized, qualified, or multiplied.[19]

The education-of-youth play undergoes still further variation in *The Longer Thou Livest the More Fool Thou Art* by the Protestant playwright W. Wager. Nothing is known of Wager except that he is also the author of *Enough is as Good as a Feast*, but his two plays clearly indicate his sympathies with Reformation doctrine. In *The Longer Thou Livest*, he inverts the traditional morality form by presenting a single protagonist who, unlike Ismael and Dalila, is irrevocably damned and incapable of repentance. In the final scene of the play, Moros is *not* saved; rather, he is carried offstage by Confusion, his destination "eternall fyre/ Due for fooles that be impenitent."[20] At first, however, Moros is in many ways a typical youth play protagonist—witty, imaginative, and mischievous. As in the early youth plays, his wickedness is often more apparent in the accusing speeches of Discipline than in his own behavior. Moros does very little in the course of the play that is actively wicked. Unlike other morality play sinners, he indulges in no acts of lechery, gluttony, or exploitation of the poor—he even refuses to engage in a fight until the very end of his life, when he appears as a "furious" old man. His sin is that of unbelief, a sin which cannot be rectified, and it is dramatically rendered through blasphemy, irreverence, and refusal to receive religious instructions. The prologue overturns

[19] Potter, *The English Morality Play*, p. 117; see also Farnham, *The Medieval Heritage of Elizabethan Tragedy*, p. 247.

[20] W. Wager, *The longer thou liuest, the more foole thou art*, ed. John S. Farmer (c. 1568; facsimile rpt., London: Tudor Facsimile Texts, 1910), sig. G2^v.

the fundamental premise of the youth play that education can effect salvation:

> For neither councell, learninge nor sapience,
> Can an euill nature to honest manners allure:
> Do we not see at these daies so many past cure,
> That nothing can their crokednes rectifie,
> Till they haue destroied them utterly:
> The Image of such persons we shall introduce,
> Represented by one whom *Moros* we do call.[21]

The "we" of the prologue clearly disassociates itself from the "other" being described, a representative of "such persons" as are presumably not present in the audience. Wager implies that the highly valued virtues of Piety, Discipline, and "Exercitation" (i.e., exercise of vocation) are helpless against predestined reprobation. Yet he recommends them to his audience, thus implying that they are members of the elect. Because Wager offers no admirable figure to be imitated, he impresses upon the members of his audience the irremediable differences, rather than the similarities, between them and his play's human character. Notwithstanding the obvious Protestant temper of the play, the didactic link between stage and pulpit has, paradoxically enough, been broken—the purpose of the morality play as a provider of models is abandoned. *The Longer Thou Livest* does not even offer the kind of negative models contained in *A Mirror for Magistrates*, because the logic of the doctrine of election undermines the basic didactic principle that one can learn by example. Thus freed from its instructive duties, this play anticipates the development of a tragic drama which is seldom amoral but is no longer primarily didactic.

III. THE DUAL-PROTAGONIST PLAYS

The Longer Thou Livest was not the last of the education-of-youth plays, but in a very real sense it carried the form as far

---

[21] Wager, *The longer thou liuest*, sig. A2ᵛ.

as it could go. As a dramatization of the doctrine of election, it subverted the most basic purpose of the morality form, that of providing positive models and redemptive endings. Wager solved the problem posed by Moros' damnation in his second play, *Enough is as Good as a Feast*, which offers its audience two protagonists, one saved and one damned. He was not the only playwright to adopt this formula; it can be found in two French dual-protagonist moralities, *Bien-Avise, Mal-Avise* (1439) and *L'Homme juste et l'Homme mondain* (1476), as well as the English plays to be discussed here. The dual-protagonist scheme lent itself naturally to highly structured closet drama, an example of which survives in George Gascoigne's Terentian education-of-youth play *The Glasse of Government*. Dramatically, the dual-protagonist play is a less satisfactory form than the single-protagonist play; theologically, it resolves the Calvinist's dilemma by permitting him directly to contrast the saved and the damned.

The emergence of the dual-protagonist play is a good example of the way in which changes in doctrine affect literary forms. Because the morality play in its original form could not accommodate the logic of Calvinism, the form would eventually have to change if the drama was to continue to serve as an extension of the pulpit. It was difficult to reconcile the concept of prior election with the youth play's emphasis on education; hence something else, called "ill inclination" in the school play *Jacob and Esau*, would have to be invoked to explain youthful wickedness. The authors of *Jacob and Esau* found in the biblical story a much-needed precedent and justification for consigning a human character to damnation in a genre which was designed to work by positive, rather than negative, reinforcement. As the neighbors observing the two boys' behavior explain, ill inclination, not education, is responsible for Esau's wildness, because both were brought up "under one tuition." The prologue announces the doctrine of election to the audience:

> As the prophete Malachie and Paule witnesse beare
> Iacob was chosen, Esau reprobate:

Iacob I loue (sayde God) and Esau I hate
For it is not (sayth Paule) in mans renning or will,
But in Gods mercy who choseth whome he will.[22]

Jacob and Esau is not a typical moral interlude. There are no allegorical virtues and vices, and the play's didactic impact stems mainly from its biblical authority. The dramatic expectations of an audience accustomed to the morality ending would have been unfulfilled, for the author's source prevented him from displaying either the deserved death of the reprobate protagonist or his repentance and reformation: the play ends with Esau promising to slake his anger but vowing in an aside to act otherwise. A potentially tragic situation is thus initiated but not carried out. Instead, the play is essentially comic, replete with several comic servants for whom the author was indebted to Roman comedy.

More conventional morality play trappings are employed by Wager, whose paired protagonists in *Enough is as Good as a Feast* are Heavenly Man and Worldly Man, and by the anonymous author of *The Trial of Treasure*, whose protagonists are named Just and Lust.[23] All four characters appear surrounded by the usual complement of vices and virtues. The plot structures of both plays use the old morality temptation-redemption formula, but rearrange it so that the redemption phase represented by the unswerving goodness of the saved protagonist occurs simultaneously with the temptation and indul-

[22] Anon., *Iacob and Esau*, ed. John S. Farmer (1568; facsimile rpt., London: Tudor Facsimile Texts, 1980), sig. A4^r, A1^v.

[23] W. Wager, *Inough is as good as a feast*, ed. Seymour de Ricci (c. 1565; facsimile rpt., New York, Henry E. Huntington Facsimile Reprint, 1920); Anon., *The Triall of Treasure*, ed. John S. Farmer (1567; facsimile rpt., London: Tudor Facsimile Texts, 1908). These two plays have some seventy-four lines in common, of which forty-six have variants and six are variant lines (introduction to modern spelling edition of *Enough Is as Good as a Feast* by R. Mark Benbow [Lincoln, Nebraska, 1967], p. ix ff.). *Trial* was published in 1567 and *Enough* has been variously dated by Harbage at 1560 in *Annals of English Drama*, by de Ricci at c. 1565, and by Benbow at 1570. For an extensive discussion of *Enough*, see T. W. Craik, *The Tudor Interlude: Stage, Costume and Acting* (Leicester, 1958), pp. 100-110.

gence-in-vice phase, rather than succeeding it as in the single protagonist morality play. The thwarting and dismissal of the vices, which traditionally occur in the final scene, are now accompanied by the punishment and death of the damned protagonist. The conclusion gives equal emphasis to the rewards accorded to the saved protagonist, who is explicitly called a member of the elect. Thus the Elizabethan theatre embarked upon its first experiments in parallel plot and sub-plot, involving, as one might expect, a certain dramatic neglect of the saved protagonist, whose situation is such that very little development or advancement is possible. Indeed Heavenly Man appears only in the first and last scenes of *Enough*; elsewhere his role seems usurped by Enough, a curious allegorical character who embodies the proverb which gives the play its title. *The Trial of Treasure* does better in this regard, by presenting a love match between Just and the virtuous maiden Trust to parallel Lust's disastrous alliance with the temptress Treasure. The playwright also intertwines the plot and sub-plot by bringing Just and the Vice Natural Inclination together in two symbolic scenes in which Just literally bridles Natural Inclination. Such an incorporation of wordplay in allegorical *action* (as distinct from the essentially static allegorical characterization of the earlier plays) reveals the increasing sophistication and complexity of the morality play form.

The two plays also reveal an increasing complexity and subtlety in the treatment of the traditional morality play virtues and vices. Wager takes up the theme of avarice or covetousness, which was becoming a favorite subject for satirical treatment. His understanding of the psychology of those susceptible to vice goes beyond the traditional notion of temptation brought on by the weakness of the flesh. Instead of Envy or Lechery his vices are called Temerity, Inconsideration, and Precipitation. Their strategy, as outlined by the chief Vice Covetous, is to "get into his [Worldly Man's] habitation," in order to make him weary of "Inough and contentation." Rather than enticing him directly with the objects of covetousness, they plan to weaken his ability to think "of things to come or of things past" so that he will of his own volition "run hedling into the pit."[24] They thus begin a transferral to the protagonist himself of the kinds of weaknesses that would ultimately distinguish the tragic protagonist. Long before the allegorical externalizations of vice were dropped altogether, playwrights like Wager were creating more complex and culpable protagonists whose temptations came primarily from within.

The author of *The Trial of Treasure* also presents human susceptibility to temptation in a new way. Among his vices is a character called Elation, whose function is as follows:

> Elation shal puffe him hie
> For to aspier above the skie.

Aspiration, of course, would become one of the most important characteristics of the Elizabethan tragic protagonist. Sapience, one of the virtuous characters, describes the psychology of moral weakness in terms of an inability to "battle & combate/ Against the cogitations that inwardly spring"—what Rogers might have called the failure of the "I" to exert authority over the wayward "self." Because of this, Sapience continues:

> men are so ambitious
> And so foolishe led by the luste of their braine,
> Sometime to covet, sometime to be vicious,
> Sometime the councell of the wyse to disdaine,
> Sometime to clime till they fall downe againe.[25]

Here the inward source of temptation is the lust of the brain, not of the senses or the emotions. Wager's vices use similar techniques when they disguise themselves in order to subvert Worldly Man. They assume forms which appeal directly to man's intellect, and which reflect the new secular "virtues" in the ascendant in Elizabethan England—Reason, Agility, Ready Wit, and Policy. Worldly Man succumbs to their temptations

[24] Wager, *Inough is as good as a feast*, sig. C2ʳ, C2ᵛ.
[25] *The Triall of Treasure*, sig. B4ʳ, C1ʳ.

and, with Covetous as his steward, cruelly exploits a trio of victim figures, a poor servant, an Old Tenant whose rents have been doubled, and an unpaid Hireling. These actions distinguish him from earlier morality protagonists, whose descent into wickedness hurts no one but themselves. *Enough* departs even more significantly from its predecessors in the complete absence of mercy at the end of the play. Worldly Man is visited by God's Plagues, dies a slow and painful death, and is unable to pronounce the word "God" while attempting to dictate his will. His damnation is more explicit than anything which had yet appeared in the morality play, including *The Trial of Treasure*, in which Lust is merely led offstage by Time at the end of the play to an indeterminate punishment. This represents a considerable change in the attitude of the playwright and audience toward the protagonist, notwithstanding the contrary example offered by Heavenly Man, for Wager has presented the moment of death onstage, without leaving any opening for a last-minute repentance. Such a sight must have been capable of exciting great horror in the audience. This horror was prevented from dominating the theatrical experience, however, for the audience could view the reprobate protagonist as an "other" without relinquishing that identification with the saved Mankind or Everyman figure which had long served as a source of comfort and encouragement.

The dual protagonist play contributed to the evolution of Elizabethan tragedy in two important ways. As an exercise in double plotting, it anticipated the development of complex plot structures in which contrasting secondary characters help to define the audience's response to the main character. More important, the audience's opposite responses to the saved and damned protagonist provided the discrete elements from which a more complex synthesis could eventually be forged. This synthesis was already taking place in the minds of the audience, due to the doubling parts, as David Bevington has pointed out: when one actor played two utterly different characters, he indirectly invited a blurring of the audience's separate responses. In a similar way, opposite qualities embodied in their most absolute forms in the saved and the damned protagonist would soon begin to merge in the multiple aspects of a single protagonist, a character in whom the coexistence of apparent opposites encouraged a double response.[26]

IV. THE ASCENDANCY OF THE VICE

Both *Enough* and *Trial* illustrate another advance in morality play technique which is distinctively Elizabethan: the emergence of the Vice as an increasingly prominent and complex character. The origins of the Vice are not altogether clear; a character named Merry-Report is termed "the vyce" in the list of players which precedes the text of John Heywood's *Play of the Wether* (1528), a secular interlude which owes more to Roman comedy than to the indigenous morality play. Early morality plays such as *Mankind* or *The Interlude of Youth* ordinarily had three allegorical vices, among whom no leader was clearly evident. In Bale's *King Johan* Sedition emerges as a leader of the vices, and Iniquity, the solitary tempter of *Nice Wanton*, to whom Prince Hal may have been referring when he called Falstaff "that reverend Vice, that grey Iniquity," seems to be an early type of the Vice although not named as such by the playwright. Elizabethan morality plays frequently contain both a chief Vice and three attendant vices who obey and acknowledge the Vice as their master. Such is the case in *Enough* and *Trial*, in which Covetous and Inclination are specifically identified as the Vice in their respective lists of players. These lists also specify the doubling of parts, and it is significant that of eighteen parts to be played by seven players, only Covetous and Worldly Man are not doubled at all in *Enough*, whereas of fifteen parts to be played by five players in *Trial*, Inclination

[26] John Lawlor, in *The Tragic Sense in Shakespeare* (New York, 1960), suggests that this duality of vision allows the spectator to be both involved in and removed from the action, both "detached" and committed. He sees this balance of sympathy and detachment in Aristotelian terms as part of the tragic experience and tragic pleasure of the audience (pp. 10-11).

alone is not doubled. Thus the center of the morality play has begun to shift away from the Mankind figure to the Vice, a shift which eliminates the Mankind figure altogether in some of the plays of this period. Although the Vice is nominally an allegorical figure, he can, unlike his attendant vices, step out of his role in the *psychomachia* and interact with non-allegorical characters. For example, in the last part of *Enough* Temerity, Precipitation, and Inconsideration disappear, and the actors who had played their parts reappear as the Hireling, the Tenant, and the Servant.[27] The Vice remains, however, as steward to Worldly Man in his role as landlord, just as he will remain in later plays after the rest of the virtues and vices have been replaced by more realistic characters.

The Vice Inclination in *The Trial of Treasure* displays a different and more important kind of flexibility. He engineers the complete downfall of Lust, which culminates in Lust's liaison with Treasure and her brother Pleasure, but he does so in the spirit of contempt for tempters and tempted alike, using the effective stage device of the aside to the audience, which is then repeated in changed form to the gulled character whom it concerns:

Luste.   Truly of him I would faine haue a sight,
         For because in pleasure I haue marueilous delight
Inclina. Then honestie and profite you may bidde good
         night
Luste.   What saiest thou?
Inclina. I saie he will shortly appeare in sight.

The significance of this device lies not in the trickery and wordplay it employs, but in the keen moral sense which the Vice seems to have. Some years later, Richard III, likening himself to the "formal Vice Iniquity," was to call this form of wordplay moralizing two meanings with one word:

[27] In fact, Wager's doubling chart does not provide for the doubling of Hireling and Temerity although it easily could have, since Temerity does not appear again.

Inclina. Loue, yes they loue you in deede
        without doubte,
        Which shutteth some of them Gods
        kingdome without:
        They loue you so well that their
        God they do hate,
        As time hath declared to us euen
        of late,
        But he that on such thinges his
        study doth caste,
        Shalbe sure to be deciued at the
        laste,
Luste. What doest thou saie.
Inclina. Of treasure forsoth ye must euer
        holde fast,
        For if you should chaunce to lose
        lady Treasure,
        Then fare well in post this gentleman Pleasure.[28]

In Inclination, for the first time, we find a wicked character whose heightened awareness enables him to recognize and understand the implications of his own wickedness. In this respect Inclination prepares the way not only for Richard III and Barabas but for tragic protagonists like Hamlet and Macbeth, who perceive more clearly than anyone else the evil that is taking place around or within them.

By the 1560s, the Vice had become a more interesting character than the Mankind figure, largely because of the duality which attached to his role. Both the object of and spokesman for the play's satirical vision, a Vice like Inclination at once represented and reprehended the sins the play was meant to illustrate. Disarming the audience with his antics and festive, playful manner, he was nevertheless an embodiment of evil and therefore allied with the forces of hell.[29] After the breaking up of the single protagonist form, the Vice's popularity

---

[28] *The Triall of Treasure*, sig. C3ᵛ, D4ᵛ.

[29] For more on these aspects of the Vice, see Weimann, *Shakespeare and the Popular Tradition*, pp. 153-54.

led to a series of dramatic experiments in which he was the protagonist. In these plays the temptation-redemption sequence occupies a small part in the overall action, and the old structure is replaced by a theatrical approach rather like that of a music hall revue, which strings together several unconnected situations and sets of characters. The first of these plays, *Like Will to Like Quoth the Devil to the Collier* (1568), presents a rogues' gallery of comic types, with names like Rafe Roister and Pierce Pickpurse, who fall somewhere between the attendant vices and the damned protagonist among the traditional morality character types, but bear a passing resemblance to the rogues of Nashe and Greene as well. They enter one or two at a time, to be encouraged in their pre-existing wicked ways, rather than actually tempted, by Nichol Newfangle the Vice, who is onstage throughout. There is no plot development to speak of: the succession of repetitive scenes simply comes to an end when Newfangle, who possesses something of the moral sense observed in Inclination, turns his now-ruined victims over to Severity, the judge. A brief set piece of pious exhortation from Virtuous Life, Good Fame, God's Promise, and Honor follows, but its function in the morality structure has disappeared, for the play contains no repentant Mankind or Heavenly Man to be redeemed or rewarded. *Like Will to Like* ends as Newfangle is borne triumphantly from the scene on the back of his proud parent-figure, Lucifer.

This triumphant conclusion to the machinations of the Vice is similar to the ending in *Enough*, in which Covetous leaves unpunished to wreak further damage; it contrasts with that of *Nice Wanton* or *Trial*, in which the Vice is apprehended and punished by the forces of good. The survival of the Vice, when it does occur, suggests a partial breakdown of the original didactic intent of the morality play and the introduction of a tragic vision which refuses to believe that evil can be totally overcome. This is not to say that *Like Will to Like* is tragic in tone or mood, for the behavior of and response to a character like Newfangle is essentially comic. But by allowing an evil character to get off scot-free, such a play undermined the notion of poetic justice and thus helped to prepare Elizabethan audiences for subsequent experiments with tragedy. One can see the legacy of the Vice in Shakespeare's Aaron, who remains alive and unrepentant at the end of *Titus Andronicus*.

The Tide Tarrieth no Man (1576) is among the most explicitly concerned with religious reform of the extant late morality plays, and, like *Enough*, it also explores the abuses created by the economic upheaval of the late sixteenth century. In contrast to *Like Will to Like*, its Vice, Courage, is apprehended and punished in the concluding scene. Among a large cast of characters, the role which most closely approximates the traditional morality play protagonist is that of Christianity, who undergoes a reformation at the end of the play, encouraged by a character named Faithful Few. The cast also includes a young gentleman named Wastefulness, who is saved by Faithful Few from committing suicide under the influence of Despair and then undergoes a conversion, and a landlord named Greediness, who has been manipulated by Courage throughout and does commit suicide in the end. *The Tide Tarrieth no Man* thus successfully dramatizes the contrasting fates of the saved and damned without employing the strict parallelism of the dual protagonist scheme.

All for Money (1577), by T. Lupton, draws this contrast repeatedly in an even more episodic, revue-like arrangement. The play consists of five discrete episodes, without even a single Vice to unite them. Lupton presents Money as the ultimate source of damnation in an allegorical enactment of doctrine whereby Money vomits up Pleasure, Pleasure produces Sin in like fashion, and Sin produces Damnation, with various attendant vices acting as midwives for these births. The play also includes a debate among four characters representing various combinations of Money and Learning, from which Money without Learning emerges as the embodiment of avarice, Learning with Money as munificent nobility, and Learning without Money as a virtuous scholar. At the end of the fourth episode, Sin, with the perceptiveness which has come to characterize Vice figures, comments on the damnation which awaits all sinners. Lupton next presents two striking examples of the damned from the Bible: Judas and Dives, who each deliver speeches of remorse and self-accusation acknowledging their damnation and advising the audience that God will have mercy on those who ask for it. Damnation then enters and chides them both, using the third person pronouns characteristic of the Puritan preachers:

For the most part on the earth do live so wickedly
That they thinke there is no hell to punishe sinne truely.[30]

Damnation drives Judas and Dives offstage to Hell, and Godly Admonition, Virtue, Humility, and Charity enter to pronounce the final lesson and to pray for the Queen:

That she may raigne quietly according to Gods will:
Whereby she may suppresse vyce and set foorth Gods
    glorie and honour,
And as she hath begon godly, to so continue still.[31]

(The last line displays the reformers' anxiety about the Queen's unpredictable role in advancing their reforms.) Their final prayer is for the salvation of "all that be here present"; like the preachers, Lupton wishes to assume the election of his audience.

In these three plays we find a greater and greater preponderance of wicked and unredeemed human characters, in a setting which remains admonitory but has ceased to celebrate a universally embraced vision of order. Most strikingly absent is a single character who invites the audience's identification. Lacking such characters, these plays are in some respects more removed from tragedy than their fifteenth- and early-sixteenth-century predecessors. What they do contribute to the creation of an audience for tragedy, however, is the dramatized idea that evil cannot always be contained and that the effects of its influence do not always yield to the last-minute

[30] Thomas Lupton, *All for Money*, ed. John S. Farmer (1578; facsimile rpt., London: Tudor Facsimile Texts, 1910), sig. E3ʳ.
[31] Lupton, *All for Money*, sig. E3ᵛ.

intervention of mercy. In *All for Money*, the very presence of a character named Damnation as an allegorical embodiment of the opposite of mercy signals the willingness of the playwright to represent the Calvinist vision in all of its uncompromising bleakness. All that remained was for Damnation's victim to become a human character rather than an archetypal "other" like Judas or Dives.

V. PROTESTANT POLEMICS AND THE TRAGIC PROTAGONIST

The last two plays to be discussed in this chapter are unusual examples of the popular morality tradition inasmuch as they were inspired by historical events and shaped in significant ways by their sources. The use of historical material enlarged the sixteenth-century playwright's range considerably, for it enabled him to explore real and complex human characters within a generic framework that could be made to serve didactic ends without being limited by them. At the same time, it imposed a pre-existing pattern of events on the playwright that effectively prevented the strength of tradition from being the major determinant of plot. Historical sources led playwrights in new directions and gave them the authority and precedent to dramatize situations that departed from the reassuring morality structure. These situations, the playwrights discovered, could be presented as isolated tragedies within the larger context of human history without necessarily rejecting the essentially redemptive vision that the drama was supposed to uphold.

John Bale's *King Johan* (1538) is the first English history play and, as S. F. Johnson has observed, the first English play to present an isolated human protagonist whose downfall follows from his inherent virtue and nobility.[32] The play suc-

---

[32] S. F. Johnson, "The Tragic Hero in Early Elizabethan Drama," *Studies in the English Renaissance Drama in Memory of Karl Julius Holzknecht*, ed. Josephine W. Bennett, Oscar Cargill and Vernon Hall, Jr. (New York, 1959), p. 159. See also Barry B. Adams' introduction to his edition of *King Johan* (San Marino, California, 1969).

ceeds in being at once a redemptive morality and an embry-
onic tragedy of martyrdom, by juxtaposing the temptation-
redemption morality structure with the well-known story of
King John's refusal to succumb to the tyranny of the Pope.
Bale was one of several reformers from the 1530s onward
who used the stage to attack the Catholic Church and pro-
mote the new religion.[33] As an alternative to the Catholic
mystery cycles, Bale wrote his own cycle based on the life of
Christ, a series of plays in which preaching unfortunately
overshadows dramatic action. His *Comedy Concerning the Three
Laws*, a moral interlude in which the Law of Nature, the Law
of Moses, and the Law of Christ are corrupted by the Vice
Infidelity and two attendant vices, comes to a traditional morality play conclusion when God punishes the vices and re-
stores the three laws to their original condition.

King Johan retains this tripartite scheme: the role of the
morality play protagonist is assumed by Nobility, Clergy, and
Civil Order, who exhibit rebelliousness and succumb to the
temptations posed by Sedition the Vice. In contrast to these
figures King John occupies a role ordinarily reserved for alle-
gorically portrayed virtues (of which the play has one, Verity).
Unlike the traditional morality protagonist, who can be swayed
one way by vice and another by virtue, John remains firmly
committed to righteousness and dies a martyr's death, poi-
soned by Dissimulation. Yet if the pattern of John's career as
Bale presents it seems tragic, the play is nevertheless not a
tragedy; it ends in the traditional morality play manner with
the reformation of the erring Nobility, Clergy, and Civil Order, at the urging of Verity, and with formal forgiveness conferred by Imperial Majesty. Despite the restoration of order
with which the play ends (and with which many tragedies
would of course end), John's death remains an irreversible fact
of history. His death is tragic, but only in a qualified sense,

---

[33] Most of their works are lost; however, Bale made a catalogue of British
authors which gives the names of their plays. See *The Revels History of Drama
in English*, Vol. II, p. 178.

because his audience would have viewed him as a martyred saint like the characters in Foxe's *Book of Martyrs*, who are victorious in death.

Bale's King John is and is not a predecessor of later tragic protagonists. Significantly, he lacks the characteristic of the morality play protagonist most clearly retained by the Elizabethan tragic protagonist—the susceptibility to vice or error which brings about his fall. Although John seems to follow the morality play pattern when he agrees to give up his scepter and crown to the Cardinal over England's protests, Bale makes it clear that his actions are not due to moral weakness. Rather, John shows compassion for the people of England who will shed their blood in the threatened wars, and succumbs reluctantly, fully conscious of the implications of his actions. King John is thus noble and self-sacrificing precisely at the point at which the morality play protagonist is most weak. As a result, he is potentially tragic in stature and in the fact of his death, though not in the actions which leads to that death.

King John is not the only historical character in this play, which in so many ways constitutes a link between the moralities and the early history plays. Bale's handling of the traditional morality play vices in effect acts out the evolution of historical characters from allegorical ones. He exploits the extensive doubling of parts which the audience had come to expect, and so superimposes an historical role upon the role of the traditional vice. Usurped Power, for example, turns out to be the Pope in disguise. Sedition becomes Stephen Langton, a prelate who had been nominated to the see of Canterbury and was subsequently refused recognition by King John. This action precipitated an early Church-State quarrel which Bale made use of in order to represent John as a Protestant martyr. This ingenious device, anticipating Spenser's moral and historical senses of allegory in *The Faerie Queene*, portends the adaptability of the traditional virtues and vices to future history plays and tragedies.

The final step in the transformation of the morality play is accomplished through a return to a single central protagonist—a protagonist who is not inherently good but inherently evil, not saved but damned. Nathaniel Woodes' *The Conflict of Conscience*, the original version of which may have been written any time between 1570 and 1581, is based upon the history of a learned Italian Calvinist named Francis Spera, whose sensational recantation was much discussed on the continent and in England. The immediate source of *The Conflict of Conscience* was an account of Spera's denial of the Protestant faith commissioned by Calvin and written by Matthew Gribalde, supposedly an eyewitness to the events recorded. Gribalde's "notable and marvellous Epistle" was translated in or about 1570 by Edward Aglionby, and published in London with a preface by Calvin himself. The play is very closely based on the epistle, except that the morality-play elements of the Vice and his henchmen have of course been added by the playwright. Despite its morality structure, the play's characterization has clearly advanced beyond the boundaries of the morality form, and its allegorical machinery seems incongruous with the detailed and realistic portrayal of Spera, called Philologus to retain the Mankind or Everyman guise.[34]

The Conflict of Conscience begins with a prologue and preliminary speech by Satan, in which he pointedly arouses anti-Catholic feeling by calling the Pope "my darling dear" and "My eldest Boy." The audience then meets Philologus, in learned discussion with his colleague Mathetes; the discussion consists of much Biblical exegesis and typological analogy, leading to the conclusion "That God punnish His electt to keepe their faith in ure." Two lines later, the elect have become "us." The cause of God's punishment is further explained as being "to prove our constancy," that "we may/ Be

[34] In his discussion of *The Conflict of Conscience*, Spivack draws attention to Woodes' prologue, which observes that the play will stir the spectator more if the protagonist stands for a common human trait. The prologue explicitly invites the audience to identify with Philologus: "Philologi we are. And so by his deserved fault, we may in tyme beware." The most important departure from morality convention, Spivack adds, occurred when a typical human hero was replaced by a literal person and the literal events of his life. Woodes was not quite ready to admit to making this transition (*Shakespeare and the Allegory of Evil*, p. 237).

instruments in whom his might, God may abroad display."[35]
The tragedy of Philologus thus entails the audience's awareness that knows these crucial points of doctrine at the outset—
and yet disregards them. Brought before the Cardinal, a papal
legate, and urged to recant, Philologus engages in a lengthy
versified debate on matters of doctrine, until finally his resistance is broken down by his concern for the fate of his wife
and children. Since this is a negative, rather than a positive,
inclination, Woodes has the Vices Avarice and Sensual Suggestion offer Philologus a magic glass depicting wealth and
worldly joys. He instantly falls prey to this temptation, crying
out "Oh peerelesse pleasures! Oh ioyes unspeakable!" in the
most unconvincing manner. This incongruous scene simply
shows how little function remained to the externally tempting
vices of the *psychomachia* once the protagonist ceased to be
motivated by the traditional sins and developed a less easily
objectified internal motivation for his actions.

After recanting, Philologus remains no less a Calvinist. Like
Faustus, he puts off his good angel Conscience and follows
his bad angel Sensual Suggestion.[36] Finally, he is confronted
with Confusion and Horror-of-the-Mind, who bring him to
the ghastly realization that

> I am refused utterly; I quite from God am whorld.
> My name within the Booke of lyfe, had neuer residence:
> Christ prayed not, Christ suffered not, my sinnes to
> recompense:
> But only for the Lordes elect, of which sort I am none,
> I feele his iustice towardes me, his mercy all is gone.

[35] Nathaniell Woodes, *The Conflict of Conscience*, ed. John S. Farmer (1581,
2nd issue; facsimile rpt., London: Tudor Facsimile Texts, 1911), sig. B2^r.

[36] Lily B. Campbell was the first to point out the similarity between the
two plays. Doctor Faustus' uttermost sin is to yield to the counsels of despair
urged by Mephistophilis and the Bad Angel, rather than succumbing to worldly
pleasure. "*Doctor Faustus—A Case of Conscience*," PMLA, 67, No. 2 (March,
1952), 219-39.

The comforts of Biblical analogies are now lost to him; his friends plead with him to think of the lapses of Peter, or King David, but he replies, "King *David* alwaies, was elect, but I am reprobate."[37] Steadily, without raving, he discusses what he has done, and what the consequences will be. His is the calmest, most rational, kind of despair. And then, only twenty lines after his last exit, the play ends abruptly with the entrance of a Nuntius, who announces that Philologus has hanged himself.[38] This act makes him, from the point of view of the audience, the embodiment of the "other"—fascinating, terrifying, pitiable, and perhaps in some way admirable, but utterly and irredeemably different from their image of themselves. Such "otherness" signals a complete reversal in the relationship of morality play protagonist and audience, making it possible for them to feel the detachment which would be essential to the tragic response.

Philologus displays at once the self-awareness of the Vice, the sympathetic quality of the Mankind figure, and the utter reprobation of the sinner. By virtue of this synthesis he is perhaps the first Elizabethan tragic hero. Yet the play is without question a Puritan propaganda play, so much so that tragedy was sacrificed to exemplary didacticism in the second issue of 1581. An alternative ending was substituted for the original, providing for the reconversion and salvation of Philologus before his death. As Robert Hunter has suggested, the ending of the original play may have been perceived as insufficiently didactic, for the audience, rather than learning from Philologus's experience, might well have rebelled against the God of the play for creating such a terrifying prospect. With its substitute ending *The Conflict of Conscience* resembles a medieval miracle play of forgiveness, cast in a Calvinist framework, since it turns out that the protagonist was saved all

[37] Woodes, *The Conflict of Conscience*, sig. H3^r, I2^v.
[38] For the tragic ending of the first version of the play I have used the modern spelling edition contained in Schell and Schuchter, *English Morality Plays and Moral Interludes*.

along. It would be interesting to know whether pressure from censors caused Woodes to change the ending, or whether he was disturbed by the implications of the play in its original form.[39]

The second ending is of course an utter departure from the source, for no such happy ending was possible for the original Francis Spera. Gribalde's account is extremely dramatic, devoted mainly to the three days and nights preceding Spera's death, during which he lay in his bed convinced of his damnation while his friends gathered around him attempting to dissuade him from what they deemed so unnecessary a conviction:

> Doe not utterly dispaire of his pardon, and say not with a desperate minde, that God is against you, and that yee were reprobate and refused from the beginning. For no man can know, as long as he is in this mortall lyfe, whether he bee worthie the hatred or love of God . . . everie man that is borne (although he had committed all the sinnes of the whole worlde) ought yet to have some hope of the favour and mercy of God. . . .[40]

As in the play, the main issue is not recantation but despair of salvation. In the eyes of his friends, Spera's sin is his refusal to believe in himself and his salvation; such is the logic of the concept of assurance, that a man is reprobate only if he believes himself to be. To make sure that the reader recognized despair, not recantation, as the ultimate concern of the English translation, the epistle is followed by a prayer against desperation and "A Godlye and wholsome preservative against desperation"—a set of helpful prescriptions and advice.

[39] Robert G. Hunter, *Shakespeare and the Mysteries of God's Judgements* (Athens, Georgia, 1976), pp. 35-37.

[40] Matthewe Gribalde, *A notable and marvellous Epistle of the famous Doctour, Matthewe Gribalde, Professor of the Lawe, in the Universitie of Padua: concernyng the terrible iudgement of God, upon hym that for feare of men, denieth Christ and the knowne verritie: with a Preface of Doctor Calvine*, trans. Edward Aglionby (London, 1570?), STC #12366, sig. B4ʳ.

Calvin also seems to have felt that the sin of despair takes precedence over the sin of recantation. According to his preface, the purpose of the epistle is to offer a moral lesson to those who would "unreverently scorne religion," but Calvin adds that Spera "entangled hymself in many snares of desperation," a subsequent sin entailed by the first, for "the reprobate cease not to commit one mischief upon an other." He calls Spera a "reprobate" and describes him as "the vain fellowe puffed up with ambicious bragging, [who] would prophanely dispute and teache in the schole of Christ." This is a curious accusation, not at all borne out by the epistle and the morality play, both of which emphasize Spera's reluctance to recant and his persistent doctrinal orthodoxy.[41] It is also worth noting that Calvin refers to the incident as a "tragicall motion."[42] The great theologian of the reform movement may thus have inadvertently suggested to Nathaniel Woodes the possibility of rendering the epistle in dramatic form. As a result, Francis Spera became one of the last morality play protagonists and one of the first potentially tragic ones.

[41] Gribalde, *A notable and marvellous Epistle*, sig. A4r.
[42] Gribalde, *A notable and marvellous Epistle*, sig. A3v.

CHAPTER IV

The False Dawn of Tragedy

While the authors of the popular moralities were testing the limits to which the morality form could be pushed, other playwrights of the 1560s began to explore the dramatic possibilities inherent in stories drawn from history, legend, and other non-dramatic sources. The result was a decade of dramatic experimentation which has been called "the false dawn of tragedy" because it produced such plays as *Gorboduc, Cambises, Horestes, Appius and Virginia,* and *Gismond of Salerne.*[1] These five plays vary considerably in quality, and, though none is a fully realized tragedy, together they represent a breakthrough in the emergence of the tragic protagonist which was false only in the sense that it was followed by a period of relative inactivity during the 1570s and early 1580s. The playwrights who contributed to the false dawn of tragedy differed from the morality playwrights in that they seem to have recognized the limitations posed by allegorical characterization. Turning to other sources for plot and characters, they combined classical stories with the most popular features of the morality, producing what Bernard Spivack has called a hybrid play.[2] In the three classical hybrids, *Cambises, Appius and Virginia,* and *Horestes,* the Vice is retained as an embodiment of wickedness and a source of temptation, but the Mankind figure is replaced by an individual protagonist. Freed from the obligation to demonstrate the redemption of mankind in general, the play-

[1] I am indebted for this phrase to Philip Edwards, *Thomas Kyd and Early Elizabethan Tragedy* (London, 1966), pp. 5-6.

[2] Spivack defines the hybrid play as one which dramatizes a story from history or legend, replacing the mankind figure with an individual man or woman, but retaining the personifications of the mortality convention and reshaping the original story into a *psychomachia* (*Shakespeare and The Allegory of Evil* [New York, 1958], p. 254).

wright could dramatize the alternative to redemption. Tentatively and incompletely, *Cambises* and *Appius and Virginia* adumbrate the tragic struggle and downfall of characters whose inability to resist evil makes them "others" in the eyes of the audience. *Horestes*, in contrast, retains the typical morality's comic resolution, by superimposing a romance ending on the traditional legend. Nevertheless, like Cambises, Sisamnes, and Appius, Horestes is a precursor of what was to come, if only because he and his audience must confront the dubious morality of revenge.

During the same years, another approach to the legacy of classical literature was being taken by the students at the Inns of Court. Sackville and Norton's *Gorboduc*, traditionally regarded as the first English tragedy, was first staged in 1561 and is known to have been performed only twice; thus whatever influence it had on audiences and playwrights was exerted through printed texts. Much of the critical discussion of *Gorboduc* has revolved around the nature and extent of Senecan influence on the development of English tragedy. When J. W. Cunliffe published his collection of *Early English Classical Tragedies* in 1912, he concurred with Sidney that "the stately speeches and well-sounding Phrases, clyming to the height of Seneca his stile" were Sackville and Norton's main contribution to subsequent English tragedy. Twentieth-century critics of the play have mostly devoted themselves to disproving or qualifying Cunliffe's case for Senecan influence.[3] More inter-

[3] For discussion of the debate about Senecan influence on Elizabethan drama, see the following very useful bibliographical essays: Frederick Kiefer, "Seneca's Influence on Elizabethan Tragedy: An Annotated Bibliography," *Research Opportunities in Renaissance Drama*, XXI (1978), 17-34; and Anna Lydia Motto and John R. Clark, "Senecan Tragedy: A Critique of Scholarly Trends," *Renaissance Drama*, NS VI (1973), 219-36. The strongest argument against Cunliffe's emphasis on Senecan influence appears in Howard Baker's *Induction to Tragedy* (Baton Rouge, 1939). Baker proposes a greater role for non-dramatic poetry and especially medieval metrical tragedy in the development of Elizabethan tragedy. For an approach that mediates between Cunliffe and Baker, see G. K. Hunter's two essays on Seneca and Elizabethan tragedy reprinted in *Dramatic Identities and Cultural Tradition: Studies in*

esting, for our purposes, is the connection both Sackville and Norton had with the Elizabethan Puritan community, and the possible influence of attitudes associated with Puritanism on their conception of tragedy.[4] S. F. Johnson has argued that as tragedies, both *Gorboduc* and *King Johan* were "unanticipated consequences of the Reformation" because they presented the tragic falls of good kings without recourse to "explanations" in terms either of Fortune or retribution.[5] Because the reformers rejected the notion that Fortune was the cause of human actions, Bale and Sackville and Norton were disinclined to depict tragedy in traditional medieval terms. Nor did they wish to present tragedy as an instance of divine retribution against a wicked king, for one of their objectives was to provide instructive models to the reigning monarch. This is an instance of the didactic motive's unexpected contribution to the concept of the tragic protagonist. The falls of both Gorboduc and King Johan are more tragic, because they are less easily attributed to external causes, than the falls of other more conventional literary figures.

One of the most interesting plays of the 1560s is the Inns of Court drama *Gismond of Salerne*, which contributed to the false dawn of tragedy through its portrayal of the moral struggle and desperate end of a vengeful, irrational man who is nevertheless capable of inspiring some sympathy from the audience. This play looks forward to the revenge tragedies of the 1580s and 1590s in much the same way that *Cambises*

Shakespeare and his Contemporaries (New York, 1978). Like Hunter, Catherine Belsey also urges scholars to look at a confluence of many influences in assessing Elizabethan tragedy, and proposes an interaction between the morality play tradition and Senecan influences in "Senecan Vacillation and Elizabethan Deliberations: Influence or Confluence?" *Renaissance Drama*, NS VI (1973), 65-88.

[4] Norton was the translator of Calvin's *Institutes*, which was published by his wife's stepfather, Edward Whitchurch, a Puritan printer who was one of the initiators of *A Mirror for Magistrates*.

[5] S. F. Johnson, "The Tragic Hero in Early Elizabethan Drama," *Studies in the English Renaissance Drama in Memory of Karl Holzknecht*, ed. J. W. Bennett, Oscar Cargill, Vernon Hall (New York, 1959), p. 160.

anticipates subsequent developments in the conqueror play genre. More sophisticated dramatically than its contemporaries, *Gismond of Salerne* was sufficiently popular to be reissued as *Tancred and Gismond*, by R. Wilmot in 1594. Like the other products of its age, it is not a masterpiece, but it does hint at an increasing receptivity on the part of audiences and playwrights alike to new plots, character types, and dramatic situations, all of which were potentially tragic in nature. Significantly, *Gismond of Salerne* lacks the prominent Vice-like figure who serves as a source of temptation to one or more of the major characters in the four other plays of the period.[6] By omitting the externalized representation of evil, the authors of *Gismond of Salerne* take an important step in the direction of tragedy, for they isolate their protagonist and hold him directly responsible for his chosen course of action.

I. THE DOWNFALL OF KINGS: *Gorboduc* AND *Cambises*

Thomas Sackville and Thomas Norton wrote *Gorboduc* with the issue of audience response very much in mind; one of their objectives, as the play repeatedly emphasizes, was to present a warning to the Queen on the subjects of succession and the monarch's relationship with her counselors. Early in the play, the Chorus describes King Gorboduc as "a myrrour . . . to princes all/ To learne to shunne the cause of suche a fall" (I, ii, 23-24).[7] The notion that literature could serve as a mirror in an explicitly didactic sense was of course the underlying purpose of *A Mirror for Magistrates*, to which Sackville had contributed the Induction and the Complaint of Buckingham. The mirror metaphor has a long history,[8] but its use in this

[6] The role of Maegara, the embodiment of revenge, as a cause or prompter of the revenge action, will be discussed below.

[7] This and other quotations from *Gorboduc* are taken from *Chief Pre-Shakespearean Plays*, ed. Joseph Quincy Adams (Boston, 1924).

[8] For an overview of the way the mirror metaphor has been used in literary theory, see M. H. Abrams, *The Mirror and the Lamp: Romantic Theory and the Critical Tradition* (1953; rpt., New York, 1958), pp. 31 ff.

111

particular way makes an interesting point about the Elizabethans' conception of the relationship between the audience and the characters who serve as mirrors. A mirror image is both an exact likeness (compared, say, to a shadow or a picture, other terms used since Plato to describe the relationship of art to reality) and a reversal. The Elizabethans' use of the metaphor proposes, first, a likeness, whereby the spectator recognizes the similarity between his situation and the mirror image, and then a sense of otherness; for just as the mirror reverses the features of the person reflected, so the protagonist's fall will be the opposite of the spectator's reformed course of action. As a mirror image, King Gorboduc was intended to inspire a certain amount of identification on Elizabeth's part. Like her, he was a good and admirable monarch, whose wisdom and concern for his commonwealth are frequently commented upon.[9] But his initial error presents him as the reverse of the kind of monarch Elizabeth would be; enlightened by the play, *she* would heed the advice of her counselors and prepare wisely for the succession, or so at least the authors hoped.

In the opening scene of *Gorboduc*, Queen Videna angrily informs her elder son Ferrex of the King's decision to divide the kingdom between his two sons. It is significant that Gorboduc "hath firmely fixed his vnmoued minde" (I, i, 46) before the play begins; Sackville and Norton thus deliberately avoid the traditional morality pattern in which the protagonist is pulled one way and another by contrary forces. Perhaps Norton's Calvinist bias was responsible for this approach, for the dramatic situation implies a predestined doom that shapes the events of the play without relieving Gorboduc of ultimate responsibility for his action. For Gorboduc *is* clearly responsible, and in this respect he differs from the victims of Fortune's blows whose downfalls were chronicled in the medieval *de casibus* tradition, or from the Senecan protagonist bound

[9] S. F. Johnson gives a long list of such instances in the play ("The Tragic Hero," p. 165).

"to some horrific course of unwilled action."[10] The play's didactic motive requires that he be perceived as having chosen his course of action; yet the presentation of events shows him to be immoveably fixed in his error, like Philologus and other reprobate characters.

Gorboduc is thus an essentially static character, who undergoes no change or growth in the course of the play. Indeed, he views himself as a passive victim of Fate, a view the Chorus and the wise adviser Eubulus strongly contest. Although he is the play's protagonist for the purpose of serving as a mirror for Elizabeth, the real dramatic interest lies elsewhere, as Sackville and Norton implicitly acknowledged when they entitled the authorized edition of 1570 *The Tragedie of Ferrex and Porrex* rather than *The Tragedie of Gorboduc*, as it was called in the first, unauthorized edition. Gorboduc's original decision is important only inasmuch as it triggers a succession of tragic choices which are made onstage in the presence of the audience.[11] Sackville and Norton's real contribution to the emergence of tragedy stems from just this aspect of the play. They achieve a complex structure quite unlike that of the episodic morality by exploring the causal relationship among successive events, and the effect each character's choice has on other characters. Both Ferrex and Porrex are placed in the morality play situation of being torn between good and wicked counselors, but, unlike the typical morality protagonist, they are caught in a sequence of events not of their own making. The authors employ one of the most powerful sources of tragic irony: the well-meant action that releases forces of evil and anarchy, setting off an irreversible chain of events that leads ultimately to chaos and multiple deaths. This was a dramatic scheme which future playwrights, including Shakespeare, would

[10] Thus Willard Farnham characterizes Senecan tragedy in *The Medieval Heritage of Elizabethan Tragedy* (Berkeley, 1936), p. 355.

[11] For similar assessments, see Normand Berlin, *Thomas Sackville* (Twayne English Authors Series, New York, 1974), pp. 123 ff. and Irving Ribner, *The English History Play in the Age of Shakespeare* (Princeton, 1957), pp. 51-52.

use to good effect. The noble character who is backed into a tragic situation, not because of an arbitrary turn of Fate, but because of the specific and meditated action of another who is close to him, would acquire tragic dimensions in such plays as *Hamlet* and *King Lear*.

One of the many themes explored in *Gorboduc* is the potentially tragic parent-child relationship. The age-old idea that the parent's error leads to tragedy by recoiling upon the child is set forth by the Chorus at the end of the first act of *Gorboduc*:

> Oft tender minde, that leades the parciall eye
> Of erring parentes in their childrens loue,
> Destroyes the wrongly loued childe thereby.

The Chorus goes on to liken the erring parent's unwitting destruction of the child to the myth of Apollo and Phaeton, a favorite among Renaissance writers:

> This doth the proude sonne of Apollo proue,
> Who, rasshely set in chariot of his sire,
> Inflamed the parched earth with heauens fire.
>
> (I, Chorus, 13-18)

Phaeton is the classical embodiment of Elizabethan pride and aspiration; his desire literally to rise above human limitations is an emblem of the ambitions of Tamburlaine, Faustus, and a host of aspiring minds. Like the preachers with whose rhetoric they were undoubtedly familiar,[12] Sackville and Norton use the language of pride and aspiration to characterize the wayward soul who embarks on a desperate course of action that leads to destruction. Their seemingly inconsistent portrayal of Porrex reveals that, along with the most acute and thoughtful writers of their age, they recognized the morally ambiguous and psychologically complex features of the aspiring mind.

Porrex is initially described by his mother as the proud and

---

[12] See note 5, above.

ambitious aspirer: she speaks of his "growing pride" and "envious swelling heart" which is filled "with disdaine and with ambicious hope." Ferrex sensibly responds that "My brothers pride shall hurt him-selfe, not me," and refuses to succumb to his mother's inflammatory rhetoric (I, i, 31-44). Nevertheless, he refers to Porrex's "swelling pride" and "grudging harte" in Act II (scene i, 55, 62), only to be reproved by the wise counselor Dordan, who states

> I neuer saw him vtter liklie signe
> Whereby a man might see or once misdeme
> Such hate of you ne such unyelding pride.
> (II, i, 70-72)

At this point the audience has no way of knowing whether or not Porrex has been unjustly characterized.[13] When Porrex finally appears in Act II, scene ii, he is dramatically depicted reacting to the parasite Tyndar's account of Ferrex's preparations for war. The Porrex the audience meets is thus not the man they have heard described in the preceding scenes. Rather, he has been irrevocably altered by his brother's unwise decision to prepare secretly to withstand attack, the course of action proposed by his evil counselor. Ferrex's action, born of suspicion and mistrust, invites a corresponding mistrust from Porrex.[14] Porrex, though he is not as violently envious and ambitious a man as he has been accused of being, is clearly assertive and impulsive, two qualities frequently associated with pride and presumption. He utters short, emphatic bursts and aggressive rhetorical questions that enliven the iambic pentameter line and display some of the self-regarding boldness and self-confidence that would come to characterize Tamburlaine and his progeny:

[13] Berlin, in discussing this aspect of the play, confesses that he is "puzzled." This, I would argue, is exactly what the authors intended.

[14] This incident gives the play another dimension of political relevance, in what it says about the dangers inherent in military build-up for defensive purposes!

> Shall I abide, and treate, and send, and pray,
> And holde my yelden throate to traitours knife,
> While I, with valiant minde and conquering force,
> Might rid myselfe of foes and winne a realme?
>
> (II, ii, 59-62)

The Chorus sums up the act with laments about "growing pride," and the "greedy lust" which raises the "climbing mind," yet the play thus far is not exactly the tragedy of ambition they present it as being. On the contrary, the tragic action has had more to do with ironic misunderstanding and hasty conclusions than with simple, naked greed for power. Each time the wise counselors urging direct confrontation and discussion are ignored, the tragic ironies, as perceived by the audience, intensify.

Porrex continues to be inconsistently portrayed in the next two acts of the play. Offstage, he comes across as the reprobate "other," first as described by the messengers, who tell Gorboduc how brutally Porrex has invaded his brother's lands and slain Ferrex, and later as described by his mother. Videna's vivid description of Porrex in Act IV, scene i, employs all of the rhetoric associated with diabolical villainy: she speaks of his "murderous minde," his "hard hart of rocke and stonie flint," his "cruell tyrantes thought" and "gredie will." Yet when Porrex appears before his father in the next scene, he is overcome with remorse and speaks of inward griefs which Gorboduc cannot discern. His willingness to endure the torment of remorse and justly deserved death at his father's hands without asking for pardon hints at the other side of the proud aspiring mind—the greatness of spirit and readiness to accept suffering that will characterize later tragic protagonists. As Porrex describes how he came to kill his brother, Gorboduc's responses do not really acknowledge the depth of character the audience is permitted to see; they are simply conventional accusations and expressions of woe. The scene concludes with still another portrayal of Porrex, offered by the Lady Marcella, who in the manner of the classical *nuntius* recounts the Queen's

116

vengeful murder of her sleeping son. The Porrex she recalls was princely and valiant, the chivalrous knight in full armor with his mistress' sleeve on his helm. She describes how he awoke unsuspecting that his mother was the cause of his wound, and cried out to her for help as he bled to death. The audience is thus left with a sympathetic image of Porrex, despite the Chorus's reiterated comments about greedy lust, ambition, and divine vengeance.

Act V of *Gorboduc* seems dramatically superfluous, though it clearly applies most directly to the contemporary political situation that Sackville and Norton hoped to prevent. Rather than seeing the fifth act as evidence that Britain, not one of the human characters, is the play's real protagonist, as in the Catholic morality play *Respublica*,[15] I prefer to see it as a consequence of the playwrights' didactic intentions, which are somewhat at odds with their interest in the Gorboduc story's potential for tragedy. That the play operates on several levels is evident throughout; it is a political treatise on the subjects of primogeniture, the relationship of the monarch to the parliament, and the dangers of foreign invasion in the absence of a strong ruler.[16] It is also an exploration of the Senecan revenger, in its portrayal of Videna, and of the causal progression of events which the pervasive presence of revenge unleashes. Finally, and most important for the purposes of this study, *Gorboduc*, or the *Tragedie of Ferrex and Porrex*, is an early study of three types of tragic character: the King who unwisely relinquishes his authority and brings destruction upon his family and his kingdom, the essentially good and prudent man who is caught up in a sequence of events to which he unwittingly contributes, and the proud and self-confident as-

[15] This approach to the question of the protagonist of *Gorboduc* has been taken by Farnham, Baker, and Irving Ribner, among others (see Ribner, *The English History Play*, p. 49).

[16] For a discussion of these aspects of the play's purpose, see Joel Altman in *The Tudor Play of Mind* (Berkeley, 1978), pp. 250-58. Altman concludes that *Gorboduc* consists of two kinds of tragedies, a tragedy of moral error, and a tragedy of fate.

piring mind whose attractiveness and heroic qualities coexist uneasily with his resemblance to the reprobate "other." If we add to the principal characters Fergus, the Duke of Albany, a "Richard III in little," as Farnham refers to him, the play contains yet a fourth prototype of subsequent Elizabethan tragic protagonists.

Thomas Preston's *The Life of Cambises, King of Percia* (c. 1561) is far more indebted to popular tradition than *Gorboduc*; written for a professional troupe, it was performed for a variety of audiences, including, possibly, the Court. The play is a good example of the hybrid play, particularly in its juxtaposition of the historical scenes at Cambises' court with comic interludes involving the rustics. The link between the two classes is Ambidexter the Vice, who delivers a typical self-defining soliloquy on his first entrance. As an embodiment of the principle of playing with both hands, he articulates one of the most interesting features of the Vice, as illustrated in *The Trial of Treasure* and other late moralities—his dual role as tempter and moralizing critic of those he tempts. However crudely, Ambidexter serves as an illustration of the ambivalence that attaches to the "other" in Elizabethan England, if only because the characteristics that make him evil are closely akin to those which could, under the right circumstances, elicit admiration and respect. His shrewdness, his mastery over others, and his ability to offer the audience intelligent assessments of the characters around him are all qualities which make him appealing in spite of his role as agent of confusion.

Although the Vice and the comic interludes are his own invention, Preston closely followed his source, Richard Taverner's *The Garden of Wisdom* (1539), for the incidents concerning King Cambises. Following Taverner, he begins with the incident involving the unjust judge Sisamnes.[17] When Cambises appoints Sisamnes as his deputy to rule the kingdom while he is off on the field of battle, he gets conflicting

---

[17] For a more detailed discussion of Preston's indebtedness to Taverner, see Farnham, *The Medieval Heritage of Elizabethan Tragedy*, p. 264.

advice from his counselors in a manner reminiscent of *Gorboduc*. Although Council proffers Sisamnes, a Lord warns that he is known to be self-seeking, "one that favoureth much the world, and sets to much thereby" (68).[18] In a sense, Sisamnes is a more interesting character than Cambises himself; like Appius, another unjust judge, he struggles briefly with his evil impulses when tempted by the power delegated to him. The language of ascent he uses hints both at his aspiration and at his eventual downfall: he speaks of "erecting then my-selfe" and of having been "set up aloft" (79, 113). Left alone onstage, he delivers a soliloquy which is quite interesting in its mixture of attitudes. At first, his thoughts range from revelling in the prospect of material wealth to looking forward to abrogating the law and punishing anyone who offends him. He muses on the extent of his authority ("Now it doth lie all in my hand to leave, or els to take"), yet in an apparent reversal, concludes "No, truly—yet I do not meane the kings precepts to breake" (113-25). He is tempted to use his power unjustly, but held in check by some combination of conscience and fear of retribution. When Ambidexter tempts him to "play with both hands," Sisamnes responds eagerly that he has "inclined" to bribes. Dismissing a poor petitioner with insults, he causes Ambidexter to observe, in his role as moral commentary, that "Bribes hath corrupt him good lawes to polute" (338).

Before Sisamnes can develop further as a character, Cambises returns, becomes aware of the abuses through Commons Cry and Commons Complaint, and swiftly executes the judge before the eyes of his son and the audience. The play then proceeds to focus attention on Cambises, whose prominence in subsequent scenes looks forward to the role of protagonists such as Tamburlaine. Had Preston been more inclined to follow the morality structure, he might at this point have shown Cambises undergoing temptation and eventual corruption by

[18] This and other quotations from *Cambises* are taken from *Chief Pre-Shakespearean Plays*.

the Vice and hence becoming the violent and implacable tyrant that his subsequent actions show him to be. Instead, Preston uses an awkwardly interpolated report by Shame to inform the audience that Cambises has rejected the virtuous life and engages in lechery and drunkenness. Following Taverner, Preston then dramatizes the three criminal actions which earned Cambises his reputation. Interestingly, the first occurs without any provocation from Ambidexter, implying, possibly, that Cambises is inherently damned and inclined to evil, notwithstanding what Taverner regards as his one honest deed.

All three of the episodes involving Cambises pose the tyrant against a virtuous character. The first, the honest counselor Praxaspes, gently advises Cambises to refrain from drinking and is rewarded with a horrible spectacle intended to prove Cambises' ability to function while intoxicated. The onstage slaughter of Praxaspes' child, who is shot through the heart by the sadistic Cambises, is clearly reminiscent of the massacre of the innocents in the mystery cycles. The long and heart-rending lament of the child's mother is followed by a speech delivered to the audience by Ambidexter, who passes judgment on Cambises, calling him "the most evill-disposed person that ever was" (613). The fact that even the Vice is horrified by Cambises' actions surely affects the audience's feelings. In his utterly depraved wickedness, Cambises has left the realm over which comedy and its creations preside, and isolated himself from human and allegorical characters alike.

The tyrant's next victim is his virtuous younger brother, Smirdis, to whom Ambidexter appears as an adviser, warning him to live quietly and avoid criticizing his brother. In this episode Ambidexter does play with both hands; moments after he has left Smirdis, he tells Cambises that Smirdis has prayed for the tyrant's death so that he might reign. Cambises vows to have Smirdis murdered, and Ambidexter turns again to the audience, this time to boast of his duplicity. The Vice's inconsistency, perhaps even more than the tyrant's predictable villainy, vividly illustrates the moral chaos which seems to reign in the world of the play. After Smirdis is killed by Murder and Cruelty (two characters who invite comparison with the hired murderers in *Richard III* and *Macbeth*), Ambidexter appears once more in still another mood, weeping and grieving over Smirdis' death. Abruptly, his weeping turns to a kind of desperate laughter, and a prediction that "If the king use this geere still, he cannot long thrive"(753).

In the third major episode the tyrant opposes natural law by marrying his "cousin germane," whose nearness of blood prohibits the marriage. The audience is given a chance to witness and approve of the lady's virtue and gentleness; then she too is doomed to die at the hands of Murder and Cruelty. Like Smirdis and Praxaspes' child, she embodies the antithesis of reckless cruelty. She goes to her death singing a psalm to God in which she forgives the king for his deed; God, however, is less forgiving, for he finally avenges the death of Cambises' three victims in the final scene. Abruptly, with no preparation, Cambises enters, "a swoord thrust up into his side, bleeding" from an accident which occurred as he leaped upon his horse. In the last line he delivers before he dies, he acknowledges his death to be "A iust reward for my misdeeds" (1172). This single line hardly constitutes the moment of recognition so central to Aristotelian tragedy; indeed, the words, echoed a few lines later by one of the lords, are wholly inconsistent with the character of Cambises and far more appropriate to the Lord. Yet the fact that Preston gives his protagonist this insight, however fleeting and conventionally expressed, introduces an important element into the tragic protagonist's character which later playwrights would elaborate upon. Unlike Gorboduc, Cambises does not see his fall as the mysterious workings of Fate. Instead, he recognizes his responsibility for the shape of events, and, though he strives against death, he has also assented to its claim on him. As an experiment in tragedy, *Cambises* thus anticipates *Richard III* and *Macbeth*, though with much less attention to the psychology of the "other" as protagonist. Cambises himself is a crudely drawn and one-dimensional character, whom the audience sees only from a distance. As such, he is less interesting than the char-

121

acters in *Gorboduc* and the other plays of the 1560s. The play's main contribution to the emergence of tragedy is its structure, which repeatedly poses the protagonist against victim figures who help to define the audience's relationship with him. This structure appealed to the Elizabethan audience because of the dual response it invited: they could identify with Cambises' outrageous lawlessness, and then find satisfaction in the retribution visited upon him. The Vice Ambidexter, by confiding in the audience and inviting mixed reactions from them, encouraged this dual response, thus helping to create the complex and ambivalent relationship audiences would eventually enter into with tragic protagonists.[19]

Much of what has been written on Elizabethan and Jacobean revenge tragedy proceeds from the assumption that the Elizabethans were attracted to situations based on the act of revenge because of the opportunities they provided for violent, bloody action, and spectacular staging effects.[20] John Pikering's *A New Enterlude of Vice Conteyninge the Historye of Horestes* (1567), one of the first Elizabethan explorations of the revenge theme, provides evidence to the contrary. Like the morality plays from which it takes its basic structure, *Horestes* turns largely upon situations involving temptation and debate, with relatively little action of any kind. Comic inter-

[19] Cf. Edwards, p. 10. The Vice's role in shaping the audience's response is dealt with more fully in Robert C. Jones, "Dangerous Sport: The Audience's Engagement with the Vice in the Moral Interludes," *Renaissance Drama,* NS VI (1973), 45-64. According to Jones, the Vice involves the audience in the "dangerous sport" of experiencing the action from his point of view, while at the same time the playwright moves us from entertainment to judgment. This, I would suggest, leads to a recognition of the Vice's "otherness," and, in the case of *Cambises,* the protagonist's "otherness" as well. Looking forward to Shakespeare and Jonson, Jones concludes that the Vice's heirs among the villains and knaves of tragedy engage the audience even more dangerously because they do not "make us self-consciously act out our conspiratorial engagement . . . or our dissociations" with the embodiment of wickedness.

[20] For example, Fredson Bowers defines revenge tragedy as a species of the "tragedy of blood," so called because of its violence and bloodshed (*Elizabethan Revenge Tragedy: 1587-1642* [Princeton, 1940], p. 62).

ludes containing low characters interrupt the main action, giving the play a diffused and episodic structure characteristic of the late moral interludes. What the play does share with subsequent revenge tragedies, however, is an apparent interest in the moral ambivalence surrounding the issue of revenge, and in the conflicting claims on the protagonist's sense of duty which force him to choose a course of action. The story of Orestes was of course the archetypal expression of the revenger's dilemma: presented with the choice between father and mother, between one form of universal law and another, Orestes was, in the words of Charles and Elaine Hallett, "caught between two goods. Whichever way he turned, he was right—and yet wrong."[21]

Pikering dramatizes this conflict by presenting his protagonist as torn, in morality play fashion, between the virtue Nature and the vice Revenge, who uses the alias "Courage" to obscure his true identity. Horestes' first encounter with the Vice comes immediately after he has asked the gods to advise him. Revenge pretends to be a messenger from the gods, and, after listening to him, Horestes quickly feels a surge of courage and conviction where before he had felt doubtful and uncertain. Pikering then complicates the situation by having King Idumeus and the allegorical figure Councell, neither of whom are vices, approve of Horestes' decision to take revenge. Thus, when Horestes is confronted by Nature, who argues against revenge because of the natural bond between mother and son, he can respond that the law of gods and law of men support his choice. Like a medieval crusader convinced that his cause is just, Horestes mounts a military campaign against the walled

---

[21] Charles A. and Elaine Hallett's study of revenge, *The Revenger's Madness* (London, Nebraska, 1980), emphasizes this aspect of the revenger's dilemma. Their investigation of the appeal of the revenge theme leads them to conclude: "The revenger, seeking to comprehend the meaning of his situation and frustrated by the seeming injustice of it, became for the playwrights an emblem of Man himself." They also suggest that the psychological stress suffered by the character torn between two goods "provided a foundation for character delineation which is probably insurpassable" (pp. 5-6).

city occupied by Clytemnestra and Egistus. Again, Pikering complicates rather than simplifies the moral issues: Clytemnestra and Egistus are presented less as adulterous villains than as courteous lovers, and Clytemnestra invites audience sympathy by confessing to Horestes that she has offended and asking for pardon and mercy. Unmoved, Horestes responds that it is too late for her to repent. Citing Socrates and Juvenal as authorities, he offers a political and social justification for his actions: in a well-governed city, the public punishment of "wycked ones" restrains others from sin (875 ff.).[22] Although the Vice is present in these scenes, he does not have much to do, for Horestes does not waiver in his commitment to revenge. Once the lovers have been sent to their doom, however, Revenge reassumes the typical Vice's role, revelling in his entrapment of Horestes and posing the moral question to the audience: "And was it not yll/ His mother to kyll?" (1024-25.)

At this point the play is poised between tragedy and comedy. If Horestes were to discover that he had been duped by a Vice, rather than, as he still believes, commanded by the gods, there would be matter for a potential tragic recognition scene. But Pikering concludes the play quite differently. At a gathering of the kings of Greece, Menelaus, whom the Vice claims to have incited to revenge, argues that Horestes was wrong to kill his mother. Idumeus and Nestor support Horestes' decision, however, and the play ends happily, with a marriage between Horestes and Menelaus' daughter. Thus, the issue of whether Horestes was right or wrong is never fully dealt with, and the relationship between private revenge and the public duty to restore political order remains blurred.[23] The main source of ambiguity is the presence of the Vice; by

[22] John Pikering, *A New Enterlude of Vice Conteyninge the History of Horestes* (1567; ed. Daniel Seltzer, London: 1962).

[23] As Robert S. Knapp observes in "Horestes: The Uses of Revenge," *ELH*, XL, 2 (1973), 205-220, Horestes, like Hamlet, is more than a private person, and less than a magistrate; hence personal motives and passions tangle with public duty, creating a situation that is inherently complex.

linking revenge with vice, Pikering raises moral issues which he then declines to resolve. It is unclear to what extent the hybrid structure of the play is responsible for the apparent ambivalence concerning the morality of revenge, and to what extent Pikering deliberately juxtaposes morality play conventions with elements of comic romance in order to dramatize this ambivalence.

In another hybrid play which combines a classical story with morality play elements, the issue of revenge is given less ambiguous treatment. The anonymous "R. B.," author of *Appius and Virginia*, seems to equate revenge with divine justice.[24] At a crucial point in the plot a classical character named Rumour enters, calls upon the gods to take revenge, and sets in motion the events that lead to the downfall of the lascivious judge Appius. Appius is the main source of tragic interest in the play; he is an early study of the potentially good man who succumbs to the sway of passion after a struggle with his conscience and eventually dies in despair.[25] Described by its publisher as a "tragical comedy," the play is comic in its overtly didactic celebration of female chastity and familial devotion. The self-sacrificing Virginia, who prefers to die rather than submit to Appius, is a secular version of Foxe's martyred saints. She is more tragic but also more noble than the heroines of other "threatened chastity" plays which enjoyed a vogue during the 1560s and 1570s.[26] Virginius is also a tragic figure, inasmuch as he must choose between seeing his daughter dishonored and sacrificing her life, but a victorious one as well, for he and his daughter triumph in death over the evil perpetrated by Appius.

As in *Horestes* and *Cambises*, the most ambiguous figure in *Appius and Virginia* is the Vice Haphazard, who plays a prom-

---

[24] R. B., *A new tragical comedy of Appius and Virginia*, ed. John Farmer, *Early English Dramatists: Five Anonymous Plays* (1908, rpt., New York, 1966).

[25] Farnham first called attention to this aspect of *Appius and Virginia* in his discussion of the play (pp. 251-58).

[26] These include *The Most Virtuous and Godly Susanna* (1563) and Whetstone's *Promos and Cassandra* (1578).

inent role in both the main action and the scenes of low comic relief. Haphazard is the interesting result of the Vice's transferral from a Christian context to a classical one. He embodies the idea of blind fortune, reduced to the principle of "hazard," a kind of reckless risk-taking and refusal to regard actions in terms of their moral consequences. He demonstrates his methods by drawing three servants from their duties to indulge in a song; later, they report to him that by hap—that is, through a mixture of cleverness and good luck—they escaped punishment. Haphazard then comes to the aid of Appius, a once princely judge who describes his plight thus:

> I rule no more, but ruled am; I do not judge but am
>   judged;
> By beauty of Virginia my wisdom all is trudged.[27]

Haphazard urges Appius to summon Virginius and order him to deliver up Virginia, on the pretext that she was stolen by Virginius from her true parents. At this point Conscience and Justice enter and stand silently beside Appius. The author's departure from morality play practice here is revealing; rather than have the allegorical figures address Appius and attempt to win him from Haphazard, the author presents the conflict as an internalized one. Appius says to himself and the audience:

> But out, I am wounded; how am I divided!
> Two states of my life from me are now glided.[28]

Appius does not hesitate long, though, and Haphazard soon converts him to his own philosophy. Appius concludes that "hap as hap shall hit" and goes off determined to deflower the maiden "hap woe or wealth/ Hap blunt, hap sharp, hap life, hap death" (pp. 21-22)—he will risk anything and everything. His attitude reveals a careless fatalism that in a curious way

---

[27] *Appius and Virginia*, p. 17.

[28] *Appius and Virginia*, p. 21; cf. Spivack's discussion of the significance of this scene (*Shakespeare and the Allegory of Evil*, p. 271).

prefigures the next generation of protagonists' assumption that life is capricious and unpredictable—a belief expressed in the reckless courage of characters like Faustus or Richard III.

When Virginia hears of Appius' intentions, she begs her father to kill her and present the judge with her head. Virginius tearfully agrees, performs the beheading onstage, and after receiving encouragement from Comfort, bears the head to Appius. The judge angrily calls on Justice and Reward to punish Virginius; instead, they pronounce judgment on Appius himself. The rest of the play is devoted mainly to Haphazard's unsuccessful efforts to talk his way out of being punished, in keeping with the traditional ending of many morality plays. Unfortunately, the scene that takes place offstage, as reported by Virginius, is the potentially tragic one. The author's didactic intent prevents him from focusing the attention on Appius, which would give him tragic stature, yet even so, the judge's offstage despair and suicide make him the precursor, however distant, of a tragic figure like Othello. Had the author's early tentative steps in the direction of character development been carried further, the once highly regarded judge could have become a complex version of the "other" in whom the audience saw aspects of themselves. But, like Pikering, the author avoids the exploration of tragic emotions and ends instead with comic assurances from Justice, Reward, and Fame and a moralizing epilogue advising the audience to follow the examples set by Virginia and her father.

The dramatic experiment of the 1560s that comes closest to tragedy, particularly in its treatment of the potentially tragic villain and the destructive effects of revenge, is the Inns of Court drama *Gismond of Salerne* (1567). *Gismond of Salerne* is important in the history of Elizabethan drama for at least two reasons: it is the first known English tragedy based on an Italian novella, and the first love tragedy to have survived.[29] The text of the play is accompanied by three sonnets and the "argument" of the play, which are printed after the text in one

---

[29] Cunliffe, *Early English Classical Tragedies*, p. lxxxvii.

of the two surviving manuscripts. It would be interesting to know who wrote the argument and when it was written, for it leaves the reader with a considerably different impression of the play than the text proper. Significantly, the argument is presented almost entirely from the point of view of Tancred, the nature and depth of whose feelings are repeatedly emphasized. The argument begins:

> Tancrede, king of Naples and prince of Salerne gaue his onely daughter Gismonde (whome he most derely loued) in mariage to a forein Prynce: after whoes death she returned home to her father. Which, hauing felt grete grefe of her absence while her husband liued (so imeasurably he did esteme her) determined neuer to suffer any second marriage to take her from him.

The argument goes on to describe Gismond's secret love affair with the Counte Palurine (Guishard) and recounts the crucial incident of the play, in which Tancred accidentally sees the lovers together in Gismond's chamber. The argument is deliberately ambiguous about Tancred's reaction.

> There her father, espieng their secret loue, and he not espied of them, was vpon the sight striken with maruellous grefe. But, either for that the sodein despite had amased him and taken from him all vse of speche, or for that he reserued him self to more conuenient reuenge, he then spake nothing, but noted their returne into the vaut and secretely departed.[30]

Here, as in *Horestes*, the author experiments with the idea that the character can be seen in two different ways, as the scheming revenger, and as the parent (or son) moved by love and

---

[30] Cunliffe, *Early English Classical Tragedies*, p. 165. Compare this with Tancred's speech reporting the scene in Act IV, scene ii:

I thought euen in that pang the cortine to vnfolde,
and thonder at them bothe: but grefe did so withholde
my minde in traunslike maze, that, as a senselesse stone,
I neither wit nor tong could vse t'expresse my mone
(IV, ii, 71-74).

strong principles. Like subsequent playwrights, the author implies that his protagonist is an "other" only when viewed from one perspective, while from another he occupies the familiar role of the devoted father.[31]

The kind of duality hinted at in the argument is explored in various ways throughout the play itself. Cupid, the rather sinister figure who serves as the play's reigning deity, concludes his opening speech with the pronouncement that "Loue rules the world, Loue onely is the Lorde" (I, i, 68). Yet the Chorus actively preaches Stoic detachment and self-sufficiency; the one who "liues alone within his bounded rate" and "laughes to see the follie of mortal men," observing events from a Lucretian distance, is "surest of all" (I, iii, 56-59). This posture retreats from the involvements that lead to tragedy, and it is one which neither Tancred nor Gismond can attain, for they both need human love. Gismond's description of her efforts to conform to Tancred's will articulates the interior duality between the controlling "I" and the rebelling "self," much as Rogers' diary does:

> I can no more, but bend my self to finde
> meanes as I may to frame my yelden hart
> to serue his will, and as I may to driue
> the passions from my brest, that brede my smart,
> and diuersly distracting me do striue
> to hold my minde subdued in dayly paine:
> whome yet (I fere) I shall resist in vaine.
> (II, iii, 40-46)

[31] As with *Gorboduc*, Altman sees two plays here, one romantic, one moral. In the romantic play, Gismond and her lover engage our sympathy; in the moral play, they are sinners and cautionary exempla. A corresponding duality, I am suggesting, informs the audience's response to Tancred. Altman sees in this feature of the play evidence of the Elizabethans' "amazing ability to respond on very different levels to the same story. Evidently it did not matter to them that their emotional and moral allegiances might draw them in opposite directions" (*The Tudor Play of Mind*, p. 260). He attributes this ability to the sophistic tradition; I view it as a result of a complex web of factors, as described in Chapters I and II.

Other characters recognize similar kinds of conflicts. Tancred, when he confronts Gismond with her sin, says "I fight within my self" and goes on to describe how "iustices law enforced with furie" draws his mind one way while Nature "on th'other side doeth stiffly striue" (IV, iii, 33-41). Guishard, like Gismond, acknowledges his inability to control his "self" when he tells Tancred that love "hath larger reigne . . . than you vpon yor subiectes haue, or I/ vpon my self" (IV, iv, 36-39).

The complexity of character suggested by these speeches is wholly at odds with the role ascribed to Cupid, who attempts to take credit, both for having made Tancred refuse to let his daughter remarry and for having caused Gismond to "burne with raging lust." Like the increasingly unneccessary Vice in the last years of his existence, Cupid is an external representation of inner yearnings and impulses which the characters are beginning to reveal through their own words. Maegara, the goddess of revenge, who arises out of hell in Act IV to throw a stinging snake into the breasts of Gismond and her father, also seems to be an artificial imposition. A moralist advocating "chastenesse of life," she is the antithesis of Cupid, and as such embodies one of the two conflicting principles which war for possession of the characters' selves. The Chorus upholds Maegara's view, moralizing on the difference between unchaste love and the chaste love exhibited by Petrarch. The chaste lover, the Chorus declares, never feels the cruel pangs imposed by Cupid, the jealous dread, the suffering that comes of being torn "twixt ioy and care, betwixt vain hope and fere" (IV, iv, 19). (This notion, of course, is no more true of Petrarch than it is of any lovers interesting enough to be the makers or subjects of poetry.) Cupid, Maegara, and the Chorus each represent a single vision, a simplification of experience which no character in the play can adopt. And it is precisely because the characters evade narrow moral categorization that they can attain a very real nobility in the final scenes. Guishard's dying words express his concern for his lady and her grief; Gismond poisons herself because she cannot live without her beloved. But Gismond's suicide is also a form of revenge, for she realizes that Tancred "by my death shall haue more woe, than fire/ or flames with in his palace gates could bring" (V, ii, 80-81). The intermingling of love and hate in the father-daughter bond is perhaps the most moving aspect of the play, and it is sustained until the very end. Tancred and the dying Gismond have one final scene together, in which she appeals to his love for her and asks to be buried in one tomb with her beloved. In his final grief-stricken soliloquy, Tancred vows to fulfill her final request, and then to "wreke my wrathfull ire/ vpon my self" (V, iv, 30). In punishing the "self," he will gain mastery over the cause of his downfall, an excess of paternal love which tragically led to revenge.

The extent to which the authors of *Gismond of Salerne* anticipate subsequent developments in the emergence of tragedy becomes somewhat clearer when the play is compared with its source. In Boccaccio's rendition of the story, there is no Cupid or Maegara to represent the sway of passion which takes control of the "self," overcoming rational judgment and creating inner conflicts which the characters recognize but cannot resolve. In the first few paragraphs of the novella, the reader is told that Ghismunda realizes that Tancredi was "not concerned" about giving her in marriage again. She coolly decides to find a worthy lover, studies the available candidates, and settles on Guiscardo, a virtuous man of humble birth. The conflict between parent and child and the anguish that Gismond suffers during the first two and a half acts of the play thus have no counterparts in Boccaccio's novella. Absent from the source, also, is the important scene in which Gismond's aunt, at her request, urges Tancred to permit Gismond to marry again and tries to make him realize the implications of his actions. Tancred's insistence that his daughter remain with him, the audience realizes, invites tragedy. In both works, the father witnesses the lovers' tryst; he is grief-stricken and torn between love and righteous indignation. In Boccaccio's version, a large part of the ensuing dialogue between Tancredi and his daughter concerns the issue of Guiscardo's humble birth, which the authors of *Gismond of Salerne* omitted alto-

131

gether. Boccaccio gives Ghismunda the major role in this dialogue. With masterful self-possession, she presents a lengthy
defense of her choice, emphasizing the principle on which it
was based—intrinsic goodness, not birth or wealth, distinguishes one human being from another, and the true noble-
man is the man who lives virtuously. She challenges her father
to be cruel, in marked contrast to Gismond, whose "rutheful
teres/ do humbly craue" clemency, and who looks forward to
"frendly death" as an end to "this wretched life" (IV, iii, 55
ff.). The rest of Boccaccio's account dwells on Ghismunda's
eloquent reception of the goblet containing her lover's heart
and the final scene between father and daughter which serves
as the basis for scenes ii and iii of Act V. Altogether, Ghismunda dominates the novella, emerging as a proud, heroic
figure, who triumphs over her father by defiantly taking her
own life. The authors of *Gismond of Salerne* chose instead to
make Gismond an unhappy and much more passive figure,
and to give larger and more interesting roles to Tancred and
Guishard. The painful emotions endured by both Tancred and
Gismond are vividly evoked by the use of secondary characters
who listen to the laments of the principal characters and report offstage events. The result is the tragic depiction of a man
who, despite the efforts of those who would dissuade him,
defines his own happiness in terms that can only lead to his
daughter's disobedience and eventual death. He then succumbs to the self-defeating violence of revenge which, as he
recognizes in the end, recoils upon himself and causes him to
lose his "dearest ioy of all." The play ends with his planned
revenge upon himself, which has no counterpart in the novella
and which brings to tragic completion a sequence of events
that followed from his own choice. Finally, there is an epilogue, urging the women of Britain to "hold them vertuous
and chast" and "mainteine the vertues which we honor in yow
all."

The playwrights of the 1560s, to judge from the works that
survive, still believed firmly that the drama should serve as a
teaching device, and that the dramatist therefore has an obli-

gation to impose a didactic message upon his material, even if, as in *Horestes*, it requires some distortion of the original. This perception of the function of the drama was so firmly entrenched that it affected even the translations of Seneca which were prepared for presentation in the schools and universities. *Oedipus* (1563), translated by Alexander Neville (produced, probably, at Trinity College, Cambridge, where Neville was a student), transforms the protagonist into a mirror for magistrates; Seneca's victim of destiny becomes a self-accusing "wicked wight" who acknowledges that "the fault is all in mee" and accepts the gods' punishment for his "mischevous lyfe."[32] The impulse to pass judgment on the protagonist, so clearly a legacy of the morality tradition as well as the *de casibus* narrative and the preachers' exempla, continued to stand between audiences and the full experience of tragedy throughout the false dawn of the 1560s. Not until the 1580s, when Kyd and Marlowe declined to assume the moralist's role and presented audiences with protagonists who evaded, or at the very least straddled, the moral categories that playwrights and audiences had hitherto relied upon, did the age of Elizabethan tragedy truly begin.

[32] Bruce R. Smith, "Toward the Rediscovery of Tragedy: Productions of Seneca's Plays on the English Renaissance Stage," *Renaissance Drama*, NS IX (1978), 3-38.

CHAPTER V

The Conqueror Play

I. *Tamburlaine, Part I*

The First Part of Tamburlaine the Great, presented to London audiences by the Lord Admiral's Men in 1587, was an immediate and enormous popular success. Marlowe's bold and aspiring conqueror especially appealed to the audience of the 1580s, so much so that *I Tamburlaine* was followed by a succession of derivative conqueror plays during the next few years, beginning with Marlowe's own sequel.[1] *I Tamburlaine* represents a deliberate departure from the plays of Marlowe's predecessors. In the celebrated prologue with which the play begins, Marlowe rather arrogantly proclaimed his contempt for the dramatic techniques of his contemporaries: the "jigging veins of rhyming mother wits" and "such conceits as clownage keeps in pay." His setting is to be "the stately tent of War" and his protagonist, Tamburlaine, the Scythian shepherd, will threaten the world "with high astounding terms." The prologue ends by instructing the audience to

> View but his picture in this tragic glass,
> And then applaud his fortunes as you please.
>
> $(1-8)^2$

With this invitation Marlowe declares his independence from English dramatic tradition far more radically than in his open-

---

[1] After *II Tamburlaine* came Greene's *Alphonsus, King of Aragon* (1576-1588), Peele's *The Turkish Mahomet and Hiren the Fair Greek* (1588; lost), *I Tamar Cham* (1588; lost), *The Wars of Cyrus* (1588), Peele's *The Battle of Alcazar* (1589), Kyd's *Soliman and Perseda* (1590), *I Selimus* (1592), and *II Tamar Cham* (1592; lost), and possibly others which have completely disappeared.

[2] This and other quotations from the Tamburlaine plays are taken from the Revels edition of *Tamburlaine the Great*, ed. J. S. Cunningham (Manchester, 1981).

ing statement, by declining to assume the playwright's responsibility to judge and teach.[3] If Tamburlaine is to be judged,
Marlowe seems to say, he will be judged by an audience who
has looked into a mirror that reflects an image, however distorted, of themselves and the age in which they live. We can
only wonder whether the judgments in Marlowe's own age
were as various and conflicting as they are in ours.[4]

[3] In *The Rise of the Common Player* (London, 1962), Muriel Bradbrook
credits Marlowe with creating a new kind of Elizabethan audience. Unlike
his predecessors, he presents his characters almost without comment or intervention, leaving to the actors the task of establishing a direct relationship
with the audience. This amounts to a kind of abdication of the playwright's
traditional function, and it left the audience unable to "separate the actor
from the role." Bradbrook feels that this led to a greater involvement on the
audience's part; they were "completely carried away," and "lost themselves in
the action" (pp. 116-36). At the same time, however, they had to make for
themselves judgments which had hitherto been made for them. On this subject see also Robert Y. Turner in *Shakespeare's Apprenticeship* (Chicago, 1974).
Turner distinguishes between two kinds of audience-play relationships, the
didactic, from which the audience remains detached and unself-conscious, and
the mimetic, in which they must come to terms with the distortions latent in
their own perspective.

[4] Modern critical appraisals of Tamburlaine have assumed the same dialectical pattern which the most recent critics see in the play itself. The "romantic"
assessment of Tamburlaine, best represented by Una Ellis-Fermor, serves as
one extreme; Roy W. Battenhouse's moralistic assessment is its opposite.
Whereas Ellis-Fermor views Tamburlaine's language as a dazzling poetic display through which ". . . the audience is lifted from the plane on which judgments are given or withheld. . . . It is boasting which has no parallel in the
wise literature of gracious, civilised peoples" (*Christopher Marlowe* [1927; rpt.,
Hamden, Connecticut, 1967], p. 26), Battenhouse argues that the play is a
moralized history after the pattern of *A Mirror for Magistrates* and that Tamburlaine corresponds to the Renaissance idea of an evil man. Battenhouse
does admit a contradiction in the response of the Elizabethan audience, however: Elizabethan moralists may have disliked climbers and been horrified by
tyranny, but, on the stage, the audience loved tyrants. (*Marlowe's Tamburlaine: A Study in Renaissance Moral Philosophy* [Nashville, 1941; rpt., 1964],
pp. 176 ff.) In *Christopher Marlowe: A Study of his Thought, Learning, and
Character* (Chapel Hill, 1946), Paul H. Kocher proposes still another approach. For Kocher, Tamburlaine's self-praise justifies and invites audience
approval for his actions. Harry Levin accepts the assumptions of Kocher and
the "agnostic" school of Marlowe biographers that Marlowe "preached irre-

It is easy to see why Marlowe was attracted to the legendary Tamburlaine, who by the 1580s had taken his place "Amonge the illustrous Captaines Romaines, and Grecians, none of [whose] martiall acts, deserve to be proclaimed with more renown," as described in Marlowe's principal source, George Whetstone's *The English Myrror* (1586).[5] Marlowe no doubt

---

ligion wherever he went," in *The Overreacher: A Study of Christopher Marlowe* (Boston, 1952), an exuberant study which celebrates Marlowe's exaltation of the individual to heroic stature (p. 4).

As Clifford Leech observed in *Marlowe: A Collection of Critical Essays* (Englewood Cliffs, New Jersey, 1964), the dialectic in Marlowe criticism can be characterized as a conflict between the Christian and atheistic or agnostic views of the plays. Leech himself, as J. S. Cunningham notes in the new Revels edition of *Tamburlaine the Great*, was one of the first to attempt to resolve this conflict by recognizing the essentially ambivalent effect of the Tamburlaine plays. The dialectical approach to *Tamburlaine* and its effect on the audience could be said to begin with J. B. Steane's observation that there is a "to-and-fro movement in which the feelings alternately support and recoil from the protagonist" (*Marlowe: A Critical Study* [Cambridge, 1964], p. 62). A similar observation appeared at about the same time in Eugene Waith's *The Herculean Hero in Marlowe, Chapman, Shakespeare and Dryden* (London and New York, 1962). Waith comments on Marlowe's "essentially dialectical" method of constructing a dramatic portrait, balancing love against hate, cruelty against honor, against a background of parallels or contrasts (p. 70). Constance Kuriyama, following Steane's approach, argues that *Tamburlaine* represents experience as an oscillation between extremes, which serves as a symbolic working out of homosexual conflict (*Hammer or Anvil: Psychological Patterns in Christopher Marlowe's Plays* [New Brunswick, New Jersey, 1980]). Judith Weil likewise sees "great dialectical vigour" in the Tamburlaine plays (*Christopher Marlowe: Merlin's Prophet* [Cambridge, 1977], p. 117). In a much more qualified way than Battenhouse does, she views Marlowe as a moralist who makes his protagonist's folly a virtue as well as a vice. The dialectical approach also animates Joel Altman's reading of Tamburlaine. He concludes that Tamburlaine is an ambiguous hero, since "ultimately . . . we must locate the tragic in the hero's success" (*The Tudor Play of Mind*, p. 323).

[5] This and other quotations from Marlowe's sources are taken from the appendix in Cunningham, *Tamburlaine the Great*, pp. 318-29. For a discussion of Marlowe's use of his sources, see Leslie Spence, "The Influence of Marlowe's Source on *Tamburlaine I*," *Modern Philology* 24 (1926), 181-99. Spence argues that Marlowe was most inventive in areas he is frequently given least credit for, but that the play's chief characteristics, particularly its unifying hero, were the "unavoidable molding of history."

realized that Tamburlaine's career was an inversion of the traditional *de casibus* pattern, which cautioned against aspiration and upheld obedience to moral law. The *de casibus* pattern is conventionally depicted in the career of the emperor Bajazeth, whom Whetstone describes as "a notable example of the incertaintye of worldly fortunes . . . that in the morning was the mightiest Emperor on the earth, at night was driven to feed among the dogs. . . ." Expanding on this image, Marlowe presents Bajazeth's fall and subsequent humiliation in vivid detail, while drawing attention to his hero's immunity from the same uncertainties of fortune. In their litany of warnings and curses, Bajazeth and the rest of Tamburlaine's enemies repeatedly predict the retribution which never comes.[6]

In the first lines of his account, Whetstone presents Tamburlaine as a kind of folk hero, a poor shepherd elected king "in a merriment" by his fellow herdsmen, who commands his followers to condemn their mean estates and join him in robbing wealthy merchants, rather like the English Robin Hood. With the quick-wittedness and cleverness of a folk hero, Tamburlaine wins over the king of Persia's captain of one thousand horses, befriends and crowns the king's brother, and then, in a masterful reversal, deposes the new king, so "redeeming (by this industry and dexterity in armes) his countrey from the servitude of the *Sarizens* and Kinges of *Persia*." Whetstone depicts Tamburlaine as an aspiring mind, using the characteristically Elizabethan rhetoric of ascent: "even from his infancy

---

[6] In *The Medieval Heritage of Elizabethan Tragedy* (Berkeley, 1936), Willard Farnham observed that Tamburlaine was a "rebellious violation" of *de casibus* tragedy (p. 369). Cf. Stephen Greenblatt, in "Marlowe and Renaissance Self-Fashioning," *Two Renaissance Mythmakers: Selected Papers from the English Institute 1975-76*, New Series, no. 1, ed. Alvin Kernan (Baltimore, 1977), pp. 51-52; and Robert Kimbrough, "I Tamburlaine: A Speaking Picture in a Tragic Glass," *Renaissance Drama* VII (1964), 20-34. Kimbrough notes that the history of Tamburlaine was as well known as any that appeared in popular Elizabethan works and that Tamburlaine would thus have been a familiar figure to many playgoers. Kimbrough argues that Marlowe overturned the expectations of audiences accustomed to sermon *exempla* on the subject of ambition.

he had a reaching and an imaginative minde, the strength and comelinesse of his body, aunswered the hautines of his hart." This description reflects the contemporary attitude toward Tamburlaine; in at least half a dozen other European accounts, he is presented as a lowly peasant or shepherd whose high ambition elevated him to a position of power. The historians praise Tamburlaine for such positive qualities as heroic valor, military skill, wisdom, liberality, ability to discipline his troops, and an imposing appearance.[7] These qualities are coupled with other less attractive ones, however. As Perondinus describes him, Tamburlaine was "shrewd, savage, treacherous in mind, and lacking any scruples," capable of being "exceedingly brutal," seeking out "people enjoying complete freedom, so that he could impose on them a savage yoke." The Tamburlaine of the sources was thus a character who could be approached from two perspectives; he was at once the aspiring youth who becomes a great military hero, and the cruel and pitiless overreacher who escapes being overthrown. As such, Tamburlaine was already a potentially complex figure, one capable of eliciting a mixture of admiration and condemnation from the Elizabethan spectator.

It must have been Tamburlaine's status as scourge of God, however, that especially captured the imaginations of both Marlowe and his audience. Marlowe does not actually use the incident included in his sources, in which Tamburlaine announces to the merchant of Genoa that he is, in Whetstone's words, "the ire of God, and the destruction of the world." Instead, he seems to take Tamburlaine's role as scourge for granted. He also assumes that his audience is familiar with the concept of the scourge of God from the Book of Isaiah, where it is prophesied that the King of Assyria, whom God calls "the rod of mine anger," will wreak vengeance and destruction upon the hypocritical Israelites. The King will in turn be punished for his "stout heart," "high looks," and boastfulness (Isaiah

---

[7] Battenhouse gives examples of and quotations from these sources in *Marlowe's Tamburlaine*, pp. 134-41.

138

X:5-15). The scourge, clearly, was an archetypal "other," set apart from ordinary humanity by his divinely ordained role. As described by Renaissance writers, he displays the qualities associated with the proud and presumptuous reprobates of the sermons. Calvin, in his *Commentary Vpon the Prophecie of Isaiah*, viewed as scourges the tyrants who exercise their cruelty against the Church, and assured his readers that God, "hauing used them as his vassals to correct his people . . . will visit their pride and arrogancie." In adapting the conventional image of the scourge to the stage, Marlowe was especially interested in the scourge's characteristic boasts which, according to Calvin, are "so many bellowes (as it were) to kindle the wrath of God."[8]

In *Tamburlaine*, the boasts become the source of spectacular rhetorical effects that draw the audience into a realm where detached judgment becomes increasingly difficult. For example, when he first appears, Tamburlaine asserts that "sooner shall the sun fall from his sphere/ Than Tamburlaine be slain or overcome" (I, ii, 175-76). Through claims of this kind, Marlowe transforms the Biblical idea that the scourge serves God's purposes into an extreme form of the Elizabethan assurance of election. Not content to reign as consul of the earth, Tamburlaine intends to scale the heavens to become "immortal like the gods" (I, ii, 200).[9] Unlike other historical scourges, who remained unaware of their roles in God's providential design, he views himself as a member of a particularly exclusive elect; hence, his aspiration takes on the character of a sacred pursuit. This misplaced conviction of election, as we shall see, at times

[8] Calvin's *Commentary*, which appeared in Latin editions in 1551, 1559, 1570, and 1583, is quoted in Battenhouse, *Marlowe's Tamburlaine*, p. 109. The English translation was published in 1609.

[9] On this issue, Waith argues that Tamburlaine's "serene confidence . . . gives him the magnificence of the hero who transcends the merely human." In this respect he is like Hercules, and is "not so much the instrument as the embodiment of a divine purpose." Whether the Elizabethans would have perceived Tamburlaine in this light is somewhat doubtful. But, as Waith himself observes, "one may disapprove and yet, in [a] special sense, admire" (*The Herculean Hero*, pp. 67-70).

also possessed Elizabethan revengers, who believed themselves to be agents of God with special dispensations from heaven which justified their actions.[10] In both the scourge and the revenger, this trait reflects at once the Elizabethans' fascination with the dangers and uncertainties inherent in the doctrine of election, and the dual nature of the rhetoric of assurance, which can so easily become the arrogant overconfidence of the reprobate "other."

The scourge's role was fundamentally ambiguous, because it combined aspects of the images of the saved and the damned. As contemporary accounts and allusions indicate, this ambiguity permitted the Tamburlaine story to serve conflicting didactic ends. In Thomas Fortescue's *The Forest*, for example, Tamburlaine is cited in company with Cyrus, Darius, and Attila in a chapter designed to demonstrate "How for the most parte, cruel kings and bloody tirants are the Ministers of God, and how notwithstanding they continually end in state of most wretched and extreme misery." After describing Tamburlaine's announcement that he is the Ire of God, Fortescue interposes a moral commentary, observing that

> . . . whence we haue in fine to conclude, that all such cruel and incarnate deuils, are instruments wherwith God chastiseth sin, as also with the same approoueth and tryeth the iust, and yet they not withstanding are not hence held for iust, ne shall they escape the heuy iudgement of God. For necessary is it that example of it happen, but wo be vnto him by whom it happeneth.[11]

Tamburlaine is also held up as a minister of God in a published collection of sixteenth-century sermons. In his dedication to the Christian reader, the Puritan Edward Dering (or

---

[10] For a discussion of this aspect of the revenger's character, see Charles and Elaine S. Hallett, *The Revenger's Madness: A Study of Revenge Tragedy Motifs* (Lincoln, Nebraska, 1980), p. 77.

[11] Thomas Fortescue, *The Forest*, 2nd ed. (London, 1576), quoted in Battenhouse, *Marlowe's Tamburlaine*, p. 13.

possibly, the editor of his *Workes*), likens Tamburlaine to God's vengeance upon sinners. He warns that

> Surely, surely, if now it [salvation] be neglected, let vs not thinke too long to escape vnpunished. It will be too late the third day to intreate for mercie. Tamburlaine, Gods vengeaunce, when his blacke Tents are once vp, though we come out neuer so humbly with Laurell in our hands, be-clad in white garments, yet will he not be intreated, but by the selfe same sinnes whereby we haue offended, with the same we shall be punished.[12]

Interestingly, this allusion to the slaughter of the virgins of Damascus, unlike many of the historical accounts, lacks any implication that the objects of Tamburlaine's vengeance were innocent and helpless, or that the agent of "our" punishment will be punished himself in the end. For Marlowe, the ambiguity surrounding the scourge could serve as a source of dramatic complexity. Again and again, he seems deliberately to draw upon his audience's awareness of the dichotomy of saved and damned, alternately presenting Tamburlaine as an "other" to be shunned and judged and as a hero whose self-assurance and aspirations were wonderfully eloquent exaggerations of the feelings that the preachers encouraged in their elect audiences. Frequently, the speeches of other characters serve to direct the audience's shifting attitudes toward Tamburlaine. Thus in Act I, scene i, before his first appearance, he is characterized by Mycetes as a preying fox and lawless thief; yet because Mycetes' foolishness has been clearly established already, the audience presumably would not take these words very seriously. A more fitting description of Tamburlaine, mingling awe and admiration, comes from Theridamas when he first sees Tamburlaine in Act I, scene ii:

[12] Edward Dering, *M. Derings workes* (London, 1597), STC #6677, sig. A2ʳ. This dedication is followed by "M. Derings owne preface to her Maiestie," the explicit attribution whereof may suggest that the unattributed dedication from which this quotation comes was written by Dering's editor. This seems more likely, since Dering died in 1576.

His looks do menace heaven and dare the gods,
His fiery eyes are fixed upon the earth,
As if he now devised some stratagem,
Or meant to pierce Avernus' darksome vaults
And pull the triple-headed dog from hell.
(I, ii, 156-60)

Here, as so often in both parts of *Tamburlaine*, the imagery of heaven and hell is used to suggest the scope of Tamburlaine's aspirations and the moral implications thereof. The imagery of heaven largely predominates in Part I, creating the impression of a God-like, heroic figure. At the beginning of Act II, for example, Menaphon reports to Cosroe that Tamburlaine is

Of stature tall, and straightly fashioned,
Like his desire, lift upwards and divine. . . .

His eyes are

piercing instruments of sight,
Whose fiery circles bear encompassed
A heaven of heavenly bodies in their spheres,

And his hair is

Wrapped in curls, as fierce Achilles' was,
On which the breath of heaven delights to play. . . .
(II, i, 7-25)

Ortygius, a few lines later, calls him "the man ordained by heaven/ To further every action to the best" (II, i, 52-53).

The impression which Tamburlaine himself creates is more ambiguous, changing from one moment to the next. When he first appears in Act I, scene ii, his opening speech is filled with courtly assurances to Zenocrate, followed by a defense of his conquests which invokes his love of liberty and hatred of servitude. These are sentiments of which the audience would presumably approve, remembering, perhaps, that St. Paul urged those who were called, being servants, to choose freedom instead.[13] Tamburlaine's sense of calling quickly extends far beyond personal freedom, however; he "means to be a terror to the world," he tells Zenocrate, in his first allusion to his role as scourge of God. He also reveals ambitions which scorn earthly limitations; he will measure his empire "as Phoebus doth his course," and affect thoughts "coequal with the clouds" (I, ii, 38-40, 65). The stunning theatrical gesture whereby he strips away his shepherd's weeds to reveal glittering armor underneath, the audience discovers later in the scene, identifies him with Jove, who "sometimes masked in a shepherd's weed." Like a God, Tamburlaine imagines that he controls Fate and Fortune:

> I hold the Fates bound fast in iron chains,
> And with my hand turn Fortune's wheel about,
>
> (I, ii, 173-74)

This boast is part of a long persuasive speech directed at Theridamas, the Persian captain whom Tamburlaine enlists through the sheer force of his rhetoric. The speech is a parody, intentional or otherwise, of the rhetoric of assurance, with its appeal to the listener to embrace the life of the godly. Tamburlaine assures Theridamas that he is deserving and urges him to "Forsake thy king and do but join with me," just as the preacher might urge his listener to forsake the life of sin. Like a sermon, the speech ends with a triumphant apotheosis, but there is a startling difference. Tamburlaine invites Theridamas to join his following and sit, not with God, but "with Tamburlaine in all his majesty."

The appeal to Theridamas is a rhetorical set-piece, charging Tamburlaine's assertions with an energetic boldness that dazzles even as it shocks. It is the first of several speeches in which Tamburlaine's aspirations seem couched in terms very similar to those used by the godly in their pursuit of assurance. The famous monologue in Act II on "the thirst of reign and sweet-

---

[13] See Louis B. Wright, *Middle-Class Culture in Elizabethan England* (Chapel Hill, 1935), pp. 177 ff.

ness of a crown" is perhaps the best example. In this speech Tamburlaine cites Nature as the source and model of the "aspiring mind," and goes on to speak of the transcendent longings of the human soul,

> . . . whose faculties can comprehend
> The wondrous architecture of the world
> And measure every wand'ring planet's course,
> Still climbing after knowledge infinite
> And always moving as the restless spheres,
> Wills us to wear ourselves and never rest,
> Until we reach the ripest fruit of all,
> That perfect bliss and sole felicity. . . .

Until this moment the speech could be a description of the soul's aspiration toward a mystical union with God. Similarly, the "knowledge infinite" after which it climbs could be the perfect knowledge of God which awaits the elect in the afterlife. The last line of the speech, of course, comes as a complete reversal of the audience's expectations. It is hard to believe that Marlowe was not intentionally mocking the sermon rhetoric he heard all around him when he ended the speech's swelling upward movement by defining the perfect bliss and sole felicity as "the sweet fruition of an earthly crown" (II, vii, 12-29). Marlowe thus offers his audience an opportunity to see Tamburlaine's ambitions as a manifestation of their own aspirations to the heavenly crown reserved for the elect, until the very end of the speech, when the goal is revealed to be an earthly crown.[14]

---

[14] It has been frequently observed that the "earthly crown" is an inversion of the heavenly crown to which Christians are taught to aspire. Whereas Kocher uses this point to support his argument that Marlowe is challenging Christian orthodoxy (*Christopher Marlowe*, p. 77), Battenhouse and Levin agree that, in Levin's words, "an earthly crown is the notorious emblem of worldliness, heterodoxy, and pride of life" (*The Overreacher*, p. 39) and that the phrase would invite audience disapproval. Kuriyama attempts a resolution of these two approaches, suggesting that the speech "contains an element of aggression directed at a conventional audience," but that some of the aggres-

Faced with this distortion of the rhetoric of the godly, the Elizabethan audience might have viewed Tamburlaine as one of the damned, as depicted, for instance, in this sermon portrait of the wicked man confident that he is among the elect. Richard Greenham told his congregation that:

> . . . the wicked shew their wickedness in two waies. First on the right hand, the mercies of God doe worke in them such a wonderfull contention; but not such as causeth them to return the glorie vnto God, nay rather it is such as causeth them to take all glorie to themselves; for the graces of God doe puffe them up, and make them proude, and conceited in themselves.[15]

So boldly and completely has Tamburlaine taken all glory to himself that not only does he rely upon the precedent of Jove, but he directly challenges him as Jove challenged Ops. He tells Cosroe that with "bullets like Jove's dreadful thunderbolts" he and his followers "Shall threat the gods more than Cyclopian wars," and "chase the stars from heaven" (II, ii, 19-23). The audience might well ask with Cosroe, who is about to lose the crown so recently conferred upon him:

> What means this devilish shepherd, to aspire
> With such a giantly presumption,
> To cast up hills against the face of heaven,
> And dare the force of angry Jupiter?
> (II, vi, 1-4)

Cosroe depicts Tamburlaine as the kind of reprobate Udall spoke of in a sermon published in 1589, one whom the Devil has persuaded "that the world is his and he hath the bestowing of it at his pleasure. . . . They make no conscience of right or wrong; they neither feare God nor man, but (so they may

---

sion is directed at the hero as well, and that this is the first of many implicit criticisms of Tamburlaine's behavior (*Hammer or Anvil*, p. 36).

[15] Richard Greenham, *The Workes of the Reverent and Faithful Servant of Iesus Christ M. Richard Greenham*, 2nd ed., rev. and ed. H[enry] H[olland] (London, 1599), p. 97.

have their wils in pleasure, profite, or worldly estimation) they care for no further."[16]

Having allowed for the possibility that Tamburlaine's aspiration is a devilish parody of the behavior of the elect, Marlowe then returns to the ambiguities surrounding his hero suggested by his sources. The play's central episode, the defeat of Bajazeth, the Emperor of the Turks, is the key event in the Tamburlaine legend, and, because of it, Tamburlaine was regarded by Christian historians as a defender of Christendom. Marlowe draws attention to this aspect of Tamburlaine's role by linking his first explicit characterization of himself as scourge of God with a lengthy account of Turkish atrocities. Just before Tamburlaine confronts Bajazeth in Act III, scene iii, he speaks confidently of his "smiling stars [which] give him assured hope/ Of martial triumph . . ." and announces himself to Bajazeth's emissary as "the scourge and wrath of God,/ The only fear and terror of the world," who

> Will first subdue the Turk, and then enlarge
> Those Christian captives which you keep as slaves,
> Burdening their bodies with your heavy chains
> And feeding them with thin and slender fare
> That naked row about the Terrene sea;
> And when they chance to breath and rest a space
> Are punished with bastones so grievously
> That they lie panting on the galley's side
> And strive for life at every stroke they give:
> These are the cruel pirates of Argier,
> That damned train, the scum of Africa,
> Inhabited with straggling runagates,
> That make quick havoc of the Christian blood.
>
> (III, iii, 42-58)

This extended and vivid visual image of the torture of Christian captives was designed to arouse anti-Turkish sentiment in

[16] John Udall, *The Combate between Christe and the Devill: Foure Sermons* (London, 1589), STC #24493, sig. H7^r.

the audience and justify Tamburlaine's subsequent treatment
of Bajazeth. But the ensuing battle between the two generals
is essentially a verbal one, conducted on several levels; Bajazeth and Tamburlaine, Zabina and Zenocrate, and even their
maids exchange vaunts and insults. Bajazeth numbers among
his allies "Turks, Arabians, Moors and Jews/ Enough to cover
all Bithynia"—the entire spectrum of enemies of Christendom
(136-37). After he loses the offstage battle, he angrily predicts
that

> Now will the Christian miscreants be glad,
> Ringing with joy their superstitious bells. . . .

Tamburlaine responds to this with an imposing vow to "extend his puissant arm" from "the east unto the furthest west,"
beginning with the Venetian gulf where "pilling brigandines
. . . hover in the straits for Christians' wrack" and ranging
around the globe, "even from Persepolis to Mexico." The speech
concludes, significantly, with a promise to keep "in awe the
Bay of Portingale/ And all the ocean by the British shore" (III,
iii, 236-37, 246-59). This is a direct appeal to anti-Catholic
feeling, which will later be visually reinforced when Tamburlaine uses the defeated Bajazeth as his footstool. This gesture
was bound to strike a responsive chord in an audience accustomed to seeing, as Bradbrook relates, "In every parish church
of the land, a copy of Foxe's *Book of Martyrs* [which] displayed
the Pope riding in triumph, with kings at his stirrup; then
Henry VIII enthroned, and spurning the crown from the head
of the Pope, now his abject footstool."[17] In the year preceding
the defeat of the Armada, Tamburlaine is associated with contemporary English champions of Protestantism, aspiring minds
like Drake and Raleigh, whose confidence and bravado inspired similarly ambivalent feelings among the Elizabethans.

Tamburlaine resembles the well-known courtiers of Elizabethan England in another way, as the lover who uses all of

[17] Muriel C. Bradbrook, *English Dramatic Form: A History of its Development*
(London, 1965), p. 49.

his powers of persuasion to woo a fair lady. Marlowe's most significant addition to the story he received from his sources is the character of Zenocrate, whose name, a recent critic has suggested, was intended to remind the audience of the philosopher Zenocrates, an emblem of the virtuous man among the Renaissance thinkers.[18] Through Zenocrate, Marlowe subtly undermines the impression that Tamburlaine gives of being able to control the world he lives in. After the capture, Zenocrate resists Tamburlaine's offer to make her empress of the East, remaining silent after the impassioned speech in which he declares that her person is "more worth to Tamburlaine/ Than the possession of the Persian crown,/ Which gracious stars have promised at my birth" (I, ii, 90-92). Despite his extravagant offers of precious garments and an ivory sled to scale the mountaintops, she appears in this scene to be able to resist the power of words (unlike Theridamas, who is quickly won over). She alone remains unwilling to join Tamburlaine's following at the end of the scene, and her last line echoes mournfully as the stage is cleared: "I must be pleased perforce, wretched Zenocrate!" (259.)

Zenocrate does not appear onstage again until Act III, scene ii, when the audience learns that she has fallen in love with Tamburlaine and wants to be united to "his life and soul,/ That I may live and die with Tamburlaine" (III, ii, 23-24). The lover's union one might expect at this point does not occur, however; when Tamburlaine and Zenocrate appear onstage together in the next few scenes, it is to join in taunting Bajazeth and Zabina, both before and after the latters' capture. Then, in the midst of the rejoicing which follows the defeat of the Turks, Tamburlaine begins planning his conquest of the city of Damascus. Once again, Zenocrate is silently unhappy and withdrawn. In response to Tamburlaine's expression of concern,[19] she begs him to take pity on her

[18] W. L. Godshalk, *The Marlovian World Picture* (The Hague, 1974), p. 108.

[19] Cunningham's gloss of this speech is quite good: "The prose here is highly expressive—at once of Tamburlaine's chastened concern, meeting Ze-

homeland, but Tamburlaine refuses, boasting that "were Egypt Jove's own land,/ Yet would I with my sword make Jove to stoop" (IV, iv, 75-76). And so the siege of Damascus is mounted, with the legendary succession of white, red, and black tents culminating in the slaughter of the virgins sent to plead for mercy on the third day.

At this point Marlowe's reasons for adding Zenocrate to the story begin to emerge; faced with the loss of audience sympathy which this scene could be expected to provoke, Marlowe gives Tamburlaine an extraordinary soliloquy immediately after he orders the deaths of the virgins (V, i, 135-90). The speech begins with a hyperbolic description of "divine Zenocrate" in tears—tears which are likened to resolved pearls and sapphires, dropping from eyes that make light "the mantle of the richest night." These tears have caused an inner conflict in Tamburlaine, presented in terms of the *psychomachia*: his "tempted thoughts" find themselves in doubtful battle, under attack from angels who fight "For Egypt's freedom and the Soldan's life." That Zenocrate can lay siege unto his soul and trouble his senses more than Persian or Turk leads Tamburlaine to speculate about the nature of beauty. He concludes that no poet, no words, can completely express or capture its essence. Language is power, particularly for Tamburlaine, yet it is unequal to the elusiveness of Zenocrate. He then seems to dismiss as "thoughts effeminate and faint" all that he has been saying, only to return to an acceptance of beauty as the source of the "just applause" whose influence, or "instinct" touches the soul of man and beats on, or forges, the conceits of the warrior. The question "what is beauty" has evolved into another: what is the relationship between beauty and love, on the one hand, and virtue and nobility on the other? Tamburlaine concludes that the conqueror who loves fame, valor, and victory needs the inspiration which love of beauty provides, if he is to be fashioned of true nobility.[20]

---

nocrate's brooding silence, and of his attempt to persist with the taunting of Bajazeth" (p. 189).

[20] As Waith notes, the syntax here is treacherous, and it is virtually impos-

How the virtue and nobility that Tamburlaine aspires to can be reconciled with the slaughter of the virgins and the citizens of Damascus is a question the audience may very well ask. Marlowe seems to intend the audience to feel a sense of uneasiness here, for the soliloquy is immediately followed by the highly dramatic scene in which Bajazeth and Zabina violently kill themselves in the presence of the audience after uttering words of love and devotion to one another. Their speeches arouse a certain amount of sympathy, and irony as well, for they remind the audience of Tamburlaine's earlier association between love and nobility. Marlowe very clearly uses Zenocrate to direct the audience's response to these deaths. She comes onstage already wretched at having seen the streets of Damascus strewn with "disseevered joints of men" and the "sun-bright troop/ Of heavenly virgins and unspotted maids" hoisted up on horsemen's lances. How, she wonders, could Tamburlaine be the cause of all of this and yet call Zenocrate his dearest love? Horrified, she looks upon the bodies of Bajazeth and Zabina, whose deaths, her maid Anippe observes, were enforced by the "ruthless cruelty of Tamburlaine" (V, i, 320 ff.). A long speech follows, in the course of which Zenocrate presents a traditional *de casibus* interpretation of the deaths of Bajazeth and Zabina, as both an example of the fate which awaits those who "place their chiefest good in earthly pomp" and as a possible cause for divine vengeance against Tamburlaine. She then begs Jove and Mahomet to pardon Tamburlaine's "contempt/ Of earthly fortune and respect of pity," and to pardon her lack of "ruth" for the "Turk and hapless emperess" (365-71).

Zenocrate's act of repentance and explicit rejection of Tamburlaine's code of behavior functions rather like the moment

---

sible to be certain of Marlowe's meaning (*The Herculean Hero*, p. 73). It is important to recognize, however, that Tamburlaine does not dismiss love and beauty in preference for a Machiavellian *virtu*; rather, the virtue which is "the sum of glory" is an ability derived from and strengthened by the "conceiving" and then "subduing" of a love so strong that it has been known to stop the tempest of the gods.

of recognition generally reserved for the tragic protagonist, giving her a depth of character which she has lacked up to this point.[21] At this moment, she is most clearly Tamburlaine's opposite, and the values she upholds—pity, clemency, and a rejection of "earthly pomp"—are values which the Elizabethans would associate with the godly. Yet Marlowe does not ask his audience to choose between her and Tamburlaine; rather, he subverts the morality play overtones of this scene with a poignant encounter that further complicates the audience's sense of her tragic dilemma. A messenger interrupts her remorseful reflections on the bodies of Bajazeth and Zabina with the news that her father and the King of Arabia, to whom she was betrothed when the play began, have entered the field against Tamburlaine "as Turnus 'gainst Aeneas did." Filled

---

[21] Critics differ greatly about the significance of this part of the play. I am inclined to agree with J. W. Harper (ed., *Tamburlaine the Great*: New Mermaid edition [New York, 1971], pp. xiii-xv), who calls the dilemma of Zenocrate the "moral center of the play," a dilemma seemingly resolved by Tamburlaine's "league of honor" with the Soldan, but not without a disturbing and persistent moral ambivalence. Joel Altman likewise calls Zenocrate the play's "moral touchstone," inasmuch as her concern about Bajazeth and Zabina helps Marlowe "shift focus upon his characters" and "articulate our own growing malaise" about Tamburlaine (*The Tudor Play of Mind*, pp. 335-36). In contrast to Harper and Altman, most critics have tended to view Zenocrate as an essentially symbolic character, an embodiment of values which either Tamburlaine or the audience rejects. For Levin she is a sensuous ideal (*The Overreacher*, p. 41), for Battenhouse, a "Helen" devoid of religion or conscience (*Marlowe's Tamburlaine*, p. 167), for Steane, the spokeswoman for the "effeminate" values which Marlowe cynically belittles as a dishonor to manliness (*Marlowe: A Critical Study*, p. 82). In a recent essay on Tamburlaine as romance, Richard Martin interestingly characterizes Zenocrate as the representative of an antiromantic perspective which asks us to look at the tragic implications of conquest. He argues that this view fails to gather "rhetorical momentum" and is overcome by the romantic view which perceives Tamburlaine as heroic, for the play takes place in a world where "the standard judgment against worldliness fails." For an Elizabethan audience, however, that "standard judgment" could not have been set aside so easily, and, I would argue, remained an important element in the audience's complex response to the play and its protagonist. (See "Tamburlaine and the Language of Romance," *PMLA* 93:2 [March, 1978], p. 250.)

with sorrow, Zenocrate describes herself as "racked by duty from my cursed heart" and condemned and infamous for having shifted allegiance, though she pursues the messenger's analogy and likens herself to Lavinia, destined by the gods to become the wife of Aeneas. All she can hope for is a gentle victory for Tamburlaine and the safety of her father and Arabia as the "final issue to my griefs." At this point the stage directions indicate that "Tamburlaine enjoys the victory." Arabia enters wounded, cursing the "murdering hands/ Of this infamous tyrant's soldiers" and declaring his blood to be a witness of his love for Zenocrate. "Too dear a witness for such love, my lord," Zenocrate sadly responds, adding:

> Behold Zenocrate, the cursed object
> Whose fortunes never mastered her griefs.
> Behold her wounded in conceit for thee,
> As much as thy fair body is for me.
> (V, i, 413-17)

Arabia delivers one last speech proclaiming his contentedness, dying as he does in the presence of divine Zenocrate, the sight of whom drives all sorrow from his fainting soul. Zenocrate's sorrow is not so easily dispelled, however, and her sense of being torn between two irreconcilable allegiances, and cursed and overmastered by grief, cannot but darken the otherwise triumphant conclusion of the play.

Zenocrate speaks again only twice: once, joyfully welcoming her father as he issues safely "From dangerous battle of my conquering love" (a line which conveys in brief her contradictory feelings for Tamburlaine, who is both a source of danger and yet beloved) and then at last to Tamburlaine, whom she has not addressed directly since she last pleaded unsuccessfully for a truce in Act IV, scene iv. To his announcement that he plans to invest her as his queen of Persia she at first says nothing. When prompted by him to "consent to satisfy us," she replies dutifully but seemingly without emotion: "Else should I much forget myself, my lord" (V, i, 443, 500-501). This was, of course, a conventional female response, and may not have signified any reluctance on her part to a sixteenth-century audience. Yet Marlowe has given a great deal of attention to Zenocrate's dilemma, and her fifth act remorse caused by Tamburlaine's cruel treatment of his victims is never resolved. Far from accepting Tamburlaine's values at the end of the play, as W. L. Godshalk has recently suggested she does,[22] Zenocrate acts as representative and confirmation of the audience's own hesitation to approve of Tamburlaine's actions. And because Tamburlaine so highly prizes her approval, her refusal to accept his values demonstrates his failure to achieve everything he aimed for, notwithstanding his attainment of the sweet fruition of many earthly crowns. In large measure because of Zenocrate, Tamburlaine thus remains an ambiguous character to the end, and his roles as scourge of God and courtly lover are only imperfectly reconciled. Although Zenocrate does love him despite his actions, his fated inability to possess her completely was clearly an important part of Marlowe's dramatic conception, for her death was to be the starting point of his next play.

II. *Tamburlaine, Part II*

The popularity of *I Tamburlaine* led Marlowe to write a sequel almost immediately. Although he had exhausted the Tamburlaine legend of his sources, he found incidents in other histories from which to construct another conqueror play. Part II lacks the unity and sustained effect of the original play; in many ways, it is closer to the episodic structure of the late morality plays, which lacked the strong central protagonist Marlowe had so effectively created in Part I. As in Part I, Marlowe begins his play with a scene set in the camp of Tamburlaine's enemies, the Turkish successors to Bajazeth, led by Orcanes, the King of Natolia. They speak repeatedly of "proud" Tamburlaine whom Fortune has made great, and whose conquests extend to "All Asia" and "All Affric" (I, i, 60-76). But

[22] Godshalk, *The Marlovian World Picture*, p. 113.

episodes involving secondary characters, such as the Christian Sigismond's betrayal of the Turk Orcanes, distract the audience's attention from Tamburlaine.[23]

When Tamburlaine finally does appear, it is not as a conqueror, but as the victim of events which elude his control. Tamburlaine is powerless to prevent the death of Zenocrate, which in a very real sense is the most significant event in the play. Unlike her husband, Zenocrate can acknowledge the inevitability of death; she knows that her death is "enforced and necessary" and looks forward to her second life in heaven.

---

[23] Sigismond breaks his sworn oath to Orcanes, justifying his action on the grounds that Christian oaths made to infidels are not binding. When Orcanes hears of the deception, he prays to Christ for revenge with the stirring words, "If there be Christ, we shall have victory" (II, ii, 64). Of course, he emerges victorious, vowing to honor Christ henceforth, though without doing injury to Mahomet. Interestingly, this story was used by Lawrence Humphrey in his seven sermons of 1588 as part of a series of examples of Catholic usurpations and treachery. Humphrey retells the story of Amurathes the Turk, similarly betrayed, who cried out to Christ that if he was a true god he should be revenged against the false Christian Hunniades. Christ heard him and Hunniades was defeated. (Lawrence Humphrey, *A view of the Romish hydra confuted in seven sermons* [Oxford, 1588], STC #13966, pp. 96 ff.) Marlowe's version of the story is somewhat more ambiguous. His Sigismond repents, acknowledging God's "thundered vengeance from on high,/ For my accursed and hateful perjury." He dies praying:

> O just and dreadful punisher of sin,
> Let the dishonor of the pains I feel
> In this my mortal well-deserved wound
> End all my penance in my sudden death!
> And let this death, wherein to sin I die,
> Conceive a second life in endless mercy!
> (II, iii, 2-9)

Orcanes then appears, and gives orders that Sigismond's body be made prey to beasts and fowl, predicting that his soul will be led through "Orcus' burning gulf,/ From pain to pain, whose change shall never end" (25-26). The Elizabethan audience would probably be more inclined to approve Sigismond's repentance and expectation of a heavenly afterlife than Orcanes' dismissal of him as a faithless miscreant destined for hell. Orcanes, after all, remains a pagan: although he claims to honor Christ, be believes that Mahomet's power was partly responsible for his victory.

154

Tamburlaine reacts to her death by lashing out in extravagant threats and commands: he orders his men to draw swords and wound the earth, to break the frame of heaven with cannon, and to batter the sun and shiver the starry firmament. A vivid embodiment of impotent rage, he describes himself as "Raving, impatient, desperate and mad," his mind dying for want of Zenocrate, now queen of heaven and Jove's consort. His final protest against irreversible fate is to burn the town where she died and set up a statue around which he will march "Drooping and pining for Zenocrate" (II, iv, 112, 142).

The depth of Tamburlaine's grief and the frustration he feels at the limits of his power strongly reinforce the audience's sense of Zenocrate's importance. She remains to the end the embodiment of an ideal beauty whose love served to inspire and reward him throughout his many conquests.[24] Once she is gone, Tamburlaine's fortunes will be affected, or so Marlowe implies when he opens Act III with a scene that deliberately parallels one of Tamburlaine's most triumphant moments in Part I. Orcanes, surrounded by kings, crowns the escaped Callapine (the son of Bajazeth, whom Tamburlaine had captured and imprisoned), and Callapine in turn promises to crown his keeper Almeda, who deserted Tamburlaine just as, long ago, Theridamas had deserted Cosroe. As they prepare for battle, they are confident that "proud Fortune . . . Will now retain her old inconstancy" and that Jove will scourge the pride of "cursed Tamburlaine."

This confidence contrasts sharply with the grief which Tamburlaine continues to express. Standing outside the burning town accompanied by Zenocrate's hearse, he vows to make the singed plains as black "As is the island where the Furies mask/ Compassed with Lethe, Styx, and Phlegethon."[25] These

---

[24] In *Threshold of a Nation: A Study in English and Irish Drama* (Cambridge, 1979), Philip Edwards suggests that the marriage of Tamburlaine is a symbolic union of Conquest and Beauty, and that Zenocrate's "presence sanctifies conquest and helps to make it beautiful" (p. 58). Without her sanctifying presence, it seems, his ability to achieve unlimited conquests is diminished.

[25] Battenhouse uses contemporary sources to demonstrate that Tambur-

images of death and destruction will continue to accompany Tamburlaine for the rest of the play. As Tamburlaine approaches Orcanes and the gathered kings, Usumcasane observes to him that "your presence makes them pale and wan./ Poor souls, they look as if their deaths were near." Tamburlaine responds darkly "Why, so he is, Casane, I am here" (III, v, 60-62). He is both death personified and yet vulnerable to death: he first likens himself to Hector challenging Achilles to combat (the combat in which Hector lost his life) and then to a scorpion. The scene ends anticipating a battle, but what follows is the scene in which Tamburlaine's indolent son Calyphas declines to take part in the fighting. Marlowe is deliberately ambiguous about Calyphas' refusal; the youth offers as his reasons both remorse of conscience and a Falstaffian pragmatism which favors card playing over risking his life. The battle is won offstage, but the pleasures of conquest are overcast by Tamburlaine's disappointment with Calyphas, whom he scorns as

> A form not meet to give that subject essence
> Whose matter is the flesh of Tamburlaine,
> Wherein an incorporeal spirit moves . . .
> (IV, i, 112-14)

With this he stabs his son and declares himself an enemy to Jove, for sending him such offspring. This deed, virtually Tamburlaine's first in a play filled with words and very little action, must have shocked its original audience, regardless of their familiarity with violence and death. In cold-bloodedly killing his own son, Tamburlaine clearly becomes a character with whom the audience cannot identify. He undermines whatever sympathy they had for him in the aftermath of Ze-

---

laine's behavior in this scene is a sign of his wickedness. He quotes from William Baldwin's *Treatise of Morall Phylosophye*: "Euyll menne by theyr bodely strength resyste theyr mysfortunes, but good men by virtue of the soule, suffer them paciently" (*Marlowe's Tamburlaine*, p. 163). The good-evil dichotomy is a variant of the saved-damned one.

nocrate's death, and intensifies his image as a terrible embodiment of destruction.

The audience's detachment from Tamburlaine becomes more pronounced as, increasingly, he is associated with references to hell and damnation. When Orcanes calls the murder of Calyphas "thy barbarous damned tyranny," Tamburlaine replies that these tyrannies are "war's justice" and that Jove has *not* made him "arch-monarch of the world . . . for deeds of bounty or nobility" (IV, i, 139, 147-52). Renouncing the nobility he had aspired to in Part I, he now intends to deal only "In war, in blood, in death, in cruelty" (156). As the body of Calyphas is carried from the stage, the king of Jerusalem calls Tamburlaine a "damned monster, nay, a fiend of hell," and the king of Soria speaks of "The cursed substance of that cruel heart" (169, 179). Although these are the words of Tamburlaine's enemies, the audiences may find that they, too, think of Tamburlaine as a damned and cursed "other." Tamburlaine's final speech in this scene again emphasizes his role as terror of the world, as he depicts the destruction he intends to wreak in vaster and more cataclysmic terms than ever before. He will "Incense the heavens and make the stars to melt" and make the meteors "Run tilting round about the firmament"—all, he concludes, "For honor of my wondrous victories" (196-206).

The word "honor" seems strangely out of place here, belonging as it does with the deeds of nobility that Tamburlaine had earlier eschewed. The honor which seems so alien to Tamburlaine has been displayed instead by Olympia, who nobly slays her son (III, iv, 11-30) and later kills herself rather than submit to Theridamas. This interpolated story, taken from an incident in *Orlando Furioso*, serves as a comment on the main plot in a number of ways. Whereas Tamburlaine kills his son out of rage and injured pride, Olympia kills hers to save him from disgrace and suffering. Theridamas' inability to preserve the thing he loves—indeed, his inadvertent destruction of Olympia, who tricks him into stabbing her with a pretended life-preserving ointment, recalls Tamburlaine's helplessness, despite his military prowess, in the face of Zenocrate's death.

Olympia's victory in death also contrasts sharply with Tamburlaine's worldly conquests, visually represented seconds later by his entrance in the chariot drawn by kings. This scene, condemned by some critics as an absurd literalizing of the bridling metaphor, might well have had for Marlowe's original audience meanings of which the modern audience is unaware. Harry Levin suggests that the audience would have recognized the well-known story of Sesostres of Egypt, which frequently served to illustrate the evils of pride and ambition. For example, the prologue to the tragedy *Jocasta* relates that Sesostres did "cause those Kinges whome he had so ouercome, to draw in his Chariote like Beastes and Oxen, thereby to content his vnbrideled ambitious desire."[26]

Tamburlaine is not simply an embodiment of ambition, however. Although to a lesser degree than in Part I, his desires are more complex than they might at first appear. Marlowe achieves this complexity by juxtaposing the pleasure Tamburlaine takes in torturing the kings and debasing their concubines with a long speech in which he sets forth his plans for the future in the most dazzling language, filled with images of heavenly brightness and opulence. The earthly chariot in which he made his entrance is imaginatively transformed into Jove's "shining chariot, gilt with fire,/ And drawn with princely eagles through the path/ Paved with bright crystal and enchased with stars . . ." (IV, iii, 126-28). Carried by this chariot, Tamburlaine will ascend into the heavens "Until my soul, dissevered from this flesh,/ Shall mount the milk-white way and meet him there" (131-32). Here Marlowe varies the rhetorical strategy used in the speech which culminated with "the sweet fruition of an earthly crown." Tamburlaine begins in the realm of worldly gain and conquest, and is swept aloft by the power of language to an exalted vision of union with God, although this time there is no ironic reversal in the final line.

[26] Levin, *The Overreacher*, p. 48.

Instead, the irony becomes evident in the next scene: Babylon is besieged and conquered, its governor hung in chains and shot onstage, while Tamburlaine, still accompanied by the bridled kings, gives orders for the drowning of all the residents: man, woman, and child. The heavenly vision and hellish reality are sharply at odds.

Tamburlaine's last act brings about what is perhaps Marlowe's greatest irony. Vowing obedience to the God whose scourge he is, Tamburlaine burns the books of Mahomet, whom, he says, men worship in vain. As he does so, he dares Mahomet to avenge the insult. When nothing happens, he concludes that Mahomet "remains in hell" and that there is in heaven only one God—"For he is God alone, and none but he" (V, i, 201). Once again, a long and eloquent speech ends with a declaration which could easily have been spoken by a preacher. Moments later, Tamburlaine feels suddenly distempered, though he confidently asserts that "Sickness or death can never conquer me" (221). The audience, of course, realizes that they will do so, just as they conquered Zenocrate against her will. Marlowe seems to imply a connection between the burning of the Alcoran and Tamburlaine's sickness, though to do so would be to dignify a religion and a god that the Elizabethans feared and condemned. Is the scourge of God finally being punished by a false god who is himself being used as a scourge of God? The alternative is to see Tamburlaine's sickness as accidental and without moral significance, defying all of the rules of *de casibus* tragedy (rules which Marlowe has pointedly disregarded in Part I). Or perhaps Tamburlaine is being punished, as Faustus was to be, for seeing God as "full of revenging wrath" unmixed with mercy. Marlowe does not say; he leaves the audience free to choose.

As Tamburlaine begins to weaken, his antagonist Callapine gains in strength. Callapine is confident that he will be "eternized" for conquering the tyrant of the world; he seems to have all the assurance that once belonged to Tamburlaine. This assurance is sharply contrasted with the futile rage expressed by Theridamas and Techelles, who ask the heavens to continue protecting Tamburlaine and threaten them with shame and disgrace if they fail to do so. Tamburlaine, too, rages against whatever daring god torments him, and defiantly urges a march against the heavens replete with black streamers, "To signify the slaughter of the gods" (V, iii, 50).[27] Yet, as he says this, he admits that he can no longer even stand—his vows are only "impatient words," and his demand that Apollo come down and cure him sounds desperately preposterous.

The final movement of the play begins as Tamburlaine returns from his last offstage battle neither victorious nor defeated, for Callapine has fled unharmed. Tamburlaine prepares for death, passing on his "spirit," his title, scourge (a physical prop?), crown, and chariot to his eldest son Amyras, who, in his grief, "only strives to die" (V, iii, 197). Tamburlaine reproaches him for his grief, and, interestingly, returns to the complex relationship among love, honor, and nobility that he had probed at the climax of Part I:

> Let not thy love exceed thine honour, son,
> Nor bar thy mind that magnanimity
> That nobly must admit necessity:
> (199-201)

Thus Tamburlaine advises Amyras to do what he himself could not do three acts earlier when faced with the inevitability of Zenocrate's death. But his words fall on deaf ears, and Amyras mounts the chariot, the symbol of Tamburlaine's dominance, with a broken heart and "damned spirit," a spirit very different from the one Tamburlaine had tried to give him. In this

---

[27] Tamburlaine's complex and contradictory attitude toward the gods, which is increasingly evident in Part II, has been discussed by Waith (p. 68) and more extensively, by Kuriyama, who emphasizes the rivalry with the gods. Kuriyama argues that Tamburlaine's mixed feelings about the gods reflect an uncertainty about power and potency, and can be viewed in terms of Marlowe's own homosexual conflict (*Hammer or Anvil*, p. 19). Marlowe's audience, I would argue, could see in these mixed feelings a reflection of *their* own anxiety about the election which was at once God's gift to give or withhold and the result of their own inner assurance.

moment, the audience might have sensed the tragic implications of the successful man's failure to shape and educate his sons in his own image. Significantly, the extended title which follows Marlowe's verse prologue draws attention to this aspect of the play: along with Tamburlaine's two most obvious defeats, "the death of his Lady and love" and "the manner of his own death" is included "his form of exhortation and discipline to his three sons," words which recall the education-of-youth morality plays and their effort to instill saving grace through teaching. Both Amyras' crippling grief and self-imposed "damnation" and Calyphas' apparent cowardice indicate how much they fall short of their father's imposing stature.

Tamburlaine's final speech to Amyras invokes the example of "Clymen's brain-sick son" Phaethon, to whom he had likened himself as a source of destruction back in Part I. This time, however, the analogy serves as a warning to be forceful and vigilant, for

> The nature of thy chariot will not bear
> A guide of baser temper than myself,
> More than heaven's coach the pride of Phaeton.
> (V, iii, 231, 242-44)

Like Icarus, Phaethon aspired literally upward, seeking freedom from mortal limitations by physically ascending into the heavens. This ascent, the Elizabethans knew, could be made only by the elect soul after death; to attempt it while still alive was forbidden and could lead only to failure. Tamburlaine's appropriation for himself of a place in heaven and his recurrent challenges and threats to dislodge Jove have revealed him to be a Phaethon figure from the beginning. Though his king-drawn chariot was clearly earthbound, his imagination was not. The conqueror who once urged Theridamas to aspire with him to a celestial throne is now in the power of "the monarch of the earth,/ And eyeless monster that torments my soul" (216-17). To relieve his torment, he looks forward to a heaven which is once again associated with Zenocrate: his eyes long to pierce through her coffin, now onstage, and "glut" themselves "with a heaven of joy" (227). This is the heaven he has aspired to all along, and the audience is left to decide for themselves whether he will, indeed, be united with her in death, or whether she will continue to be the elusive beauty that resists his conquering grasp.

Comparing *Tamburlaine* to Shakespeare's tragedies, M. M. Mahood observed that in *Tamburlaine* the hero's death constitutes the tragedy, whereas, for Shakespeare's heroes, death is a release from pain. Only in death does Tamburlaine recognize the limits set to his ambition; death is an impediment, not a release.[28] Shakespeare's heroes usually recognize their humanity and mortality much sooner, in the moment of *anagnoresis* on which so much of the audience's experience of tragic engagement depends. If Tamburlaine experiences this recognition, it is in his very last line, which acknowledges that "Tamburlaine, the scourge of God must die." With these words, he confronts the essential difference between the scourge and the God whose purposes he serves. In accepting the scourge's predestined punishment, he seems to have come to accept the "necessity" or destiny of which he spoke to Amyras. At this moment Tamburlaine is almost tragic, because he reflects that part of ourselves which is mortal and ruled by necessity.

Accustomed as they were to the moral judgment implicit in the final disposition of characters on the stage, the Elizabethans were probably less sympathetic. If they had suspected all along that God would punish Tamburlaine just as he had punished the Assyrian king, their sense of detachment would have prevailed over their sense of engagement at this point. If, on the other hand, they thought of the scourge as an agent of divine Providence who did not necessarily come to a bad end, they would have remained uncertain about how to regard Tamburlaine's death.[29] Neither attitude would have pre-

[28] M. M. Mahood, *Poetry and Humanism* (1950; rpt., Port Washington, 1967), p. 60.

[29] Harold Brooks argues that the Elizabethans lacked a clearly defined convention to define their response to the scourge, noting that Holinshed describes King John as a scourge, even though he does not fit the "wicked

vented them from enjoying a temporary identification with an "other" who acted out their fantasies of unlimited aspiration. But however much they admired Tamburlaine, they must have at least suspected that his blasphemous pride and presumption would in the end place him among the damned rather than the elect.

III. TAMBURLAINE'S PROGENY

The popularity of *Tamburlaine* inspired a number of other playwrights to write conqueror plays, replete with Turks and Moors, battle scenes and triumphant conquests, and, above all, the rhetoric of ambition and self-assurance. None of the plays which survive seriously rivals *Tamburlaine*, but for this very reason they reveal much about Marlowe's distinctive contribution to the development of Elizabethan tragedy. As David Riggs has pointed out, the derivative conqueror plays frequently resort to a conservative interpretation of Tamburlaine's claim that his nobility is based on his deeds rather than on his parentage. Although the rhetoric of aspiration emphasizes heroic deeds and personal prowess, the pressures of political orthodoxy frequently caused the playwrights to seek out subjects of a more traditional social status. Such is the case, for example, in Robert Greene's *The Comicall Historie of Alphonsus, King of Aragon*, one of the first attempts to capitalize on Tamburlaine's success. Greene wrote his play in 1587-1588, even as he was publicly condemning Marlowe for "daring God out of heaven with that Atheist *Tamburlan*."[30] Alphonsus is no bold aspirer without legitimate claim to the crown he pursues, but instead a rightful heir attempting to regain his kingdom from a usurper. Yet, as Riggs observes, when he "appro-

tyrant" stereotype. See "Marlowe and Early Shakespeare," in *Christopher Marlowe: Mermaid Critical Commentaries*, ed. Brian Morris (New York, 1968), p. 90.

[30] Irving Ribner, "Greene's Attack on Marlowe: Some Light on *Alphonsus* and *Selimus*," *Studies in Philology*, 52 (1955), p. 162. This phrase first appeared in Greene's *Perimedes* (1588).

priates Tamburlaine's more sensational speeches, Alphonsus does not express the outlook of a prince regaining his hereditary birthright, but rather that of a martial superman in pursuit of limitless conquest."[31]

In the play's first scene Alphonsus recalls his father Corinus' words, telling him how his own father had lost the throne to "this wicked wretch/ His yonger brother [who], with aspiring mind,/ By secret treason robd him of his life" (143-45).[32] Alphonsus sets out to recover the crown of Aragon by enlisting as a common soldier with Belinus, who is making war upon the usurper, and by securing Belinus' promise to give him whatever he gains in battle. As in *Tamburlaine*, crowns are important props in this play. No sooner has Alphonsus acquired the crown of Aragon, then he turns on Belinus and demands his homage. When Belinus and his followers accuse him of displaying a "presumptuous mind" (552), he vows to defeat Belinus, driving him to seek assistance from Amurack, the king of the Turks. A crowning scene follows, in which Alphonsus distributes crowns to his loyal followers, including even the crown of Aragon, since, as he confidently announces, "*Alphonsus* shall possesse the Diadem/ That *Amurack* now weares vpon his head" (837). Although Alphonsus clearly resembles Tamburlaine in some respects, Greene reserves certain characteristics for his villains: Alphonsus describes Belinus as one who "Did with his threatenings terrifie the Gods" (758), and in the next act Amurack describes himself as one "whose mightie force doth terrefie the Gods" (1609). Even Alphonsus, at one point, seems to usurp the power of the gods: in verbal combat with Amurack, he proclaims "I clap vp Fortune in a cage of

[31] David Riggs, *Shakespeare's Heroical Histories: Henry VI and Its Literary Tradition* (Cambridge, Massachusetts, 1971), p. 77. As I do, Riggs takes a sociological view of the "aspiring mind," viewing it as "a focus for the acute conflict between self-esteem and a fixed social hierarchy that pervaded Elizabethan London" (p. 72).

[32] This and all other quotations from *Alphonsus, King of Aragon* are taken from *The Life and Complete Works in Prose and Verse of Robert Greene*, ed. Alexander B. Grosart (London, 1881-1886; rpt., New York, 1964), Vol. XIII.

gold,/ To make her turne her wheele as I thinke best" (1620-21). Amurack responds by calling him blasphemous; and Alphonsus in turn calls him proud; as in *Tamburlaine*, the word "proud" is repeatedly hurled back and forth by all of the characters.

Despite the echoes of Marlovian rhetoric, Alphonsus lacks Tamburlaine's moral ambiguousness and emerges instead as an unqualified hero. This play is, after all, a "comicall romance," and Greene gives it a resoundingly romantic ending with none of the qualifications that Marlowe interjects. In Act V Alphonsus falls in love with Iphigina, the daughter of Amurack. Their marriage has been prophesied earlier in the play through the conjuring of an enchantress named Medea. When Alphonsus and Iphigina meet, she at first scorns him. Finally Alphonsus' old father Corinus appears, and succeeds in bringing about a reconciliation and eliciting her joyful assent. Amurack gives his daughter's hand to Alphonsus, and the play ends with preparations for a wedding to be presided over by Venus, who has been the ruling deity of the play throughout. If there is anything potentially tragic about Iphigina, it is the irony implicit in her name rather than anything she does or says, for she attains none of the complexity or individuality Zenocrate displays at the end of *I Tamburlaine*. Neither, finally, does Alphonsus, for Greene has borrowed only the superficial sources of Marlowe's success, superimposing them on the arbitrarily chosen Alphonsus V, whose actual history and character he entirely ignores. If, as Irving Ribner has suggested, Medea is the moral spokeswoman of the play, her advice to Amurack's wife, Fausta, is a clear rejection of the ethos of aspiration: "In vaine it is to striue against the streame;/ Fate must be followed, and the gods decree/ Must needs take place in euery kinde of cause" (1195-97).[33] Tamburlaine's attitude was quite the opposite, an attitude which might best be summed up by Montaigne, in whose third book of *Essais*, published in 1588, appeared the following description of the aspiring mind:

[33] Ribner, "Greene's Attack on Marlowe," p. 166.

It is a sign of failing powers or of weariness when the mind is content. No generous spirit stays within itself; it constantly aspires and rises above its own strength. It leaps beyond its attainments. If it does not advance, and push forward, if it does not strengthen itself, and struggle with itself, it is only half alive. Its pursuits have no bounds or rules; its food is wonder, search, and ambiguity.[34]

George Peele comes somewhat closer to capturing the essence of the aspiring mind in his conqueror play, written at approximately the same time as *Alphonsus*. Like *Alphonsus*, *The Battle of Alcazar* fails to rival the Tamburlaine plays, but for different reasons. As Shakespeare was about to discover when he began transforming chronicle into drama, striking and memorable figures seldom emerge in history to dominate their surroundings as Tamburlaine did. More often than not, the potential hero is simply one of many in a sequence of interlocking events. *The Battle of Alcazar* has at least three possible protagonists, all of whom are would-be conquerors. The title page of the 1594 edition states that the play was acted by the Lord Admiral's company and that the actor who played Tamburlaine, Edward Alleyn, had the role of the villainous Moor, Muly Mahamet. "The Moor," as he is generally called, represents only one side of Tamburlaine; the others are reflected in Sebastian, the young Portuguese king whose ambition is regarded as honorable because he is determined to "plant the christian fath in Affrica" (734),[35] and Captain Thomas Stukley, an English adventurer who had already captured the imagination of the English audience. Sebastian and Stukley have unwisely come to the Moor's aid in his effort to usurp the crown of Morocco from the rightful king Abdelmelec, his uncle. The rebellion culminates in the battle of Alcazar, which

[34] Michel de Montaigne, *Essays*, trans. and introd. J. M. Cohen (Harmondsworth, England, 1958), p. 348.

[35] This and other quotations from *The Battle of Alcazar* are taken from *The Dramatic Works of George Peele*, gen. ed. Charles Tyler Prouty, Vol. II, ed. John Yoklavich (New Haven, 1961).

is won by Abdelmelec's forces, though he himself dies of ill-ness in the middle of the play. Fought in 1578, this battle was important to the English because Sebastian's death at Alcazar left the Portuguese throne without an heir, with the result that Philip of Spain, Elizabeth's great rival for dominance in the Old and New Worlds, easily took control of the entire Iberian peninsula.

By the time Peele wrote his play, an enormous body of history and legend had gathered around the event, much of it recounting the colorful career of Stukley, who also died at Alcazar. Stukley was a privateer commissioned and subse-quently dismissed by Elizabeth; later, he became involved with the Irish nationalists. He was knighted in Spain by Philip, distinguished himself at the Battle of Lepanto, and eventually set sail with the Pope's blessing from Italy in 1578, with an armada and plans to conquer Ireland. Even though he had joined forces with England's enemies, the Elizabethans ad-mired Stukley's aspiring mind, and he is one of the most en-gaging conqueror-heroes to emerge in the popular literature of the time. Though the official English view reviled him as "a defamed person" and "a faithlesse beast rather than a man," the legend and plays depicted him as a brave gallant who had, in Heywood's words, "a spirit equal with a king."[36] Peele's Stukley shares Tamburlaine's love of crowns, and in the long set speech with which he introduces himself in Act II, a speech strongly reminiscent of Tamburlaine's "earthly crown" speech (though far more straightforward), he proclaims:

> There shall no action passe my hand or sword,
> That cannot make a step to gaine a crowne,
> No word shall passe the office of my tong,
> That sounds not of affection to a crowne,
> No thought have being in my lordly brest,
> That workes not everie waie to win a crowne,
> Deeds, wordes and thoughts shall all be as a kings,
> My chiefest companie shall be with kings,

[36] Yoklavich, Introduction, *The Dramatic Works of George Peele*, p. 269.

167

> And my deserts shall counterpoise a kings,
> Why should not I then looke to be a king?
> I am the marques now of Ireland made,
> And will be shortly king of Ireland,
> King of a mole-hill had I rather be,
> Than the richest subject of a monarchie,
> Huffe it brave minde, and never cease t'aspire,
> Before thou raigne sole king of thy desire.
>   (452-67)

Just as the assurance and aspiration to heaven permitted by God were markedly different, as perceived by the Elizabethan audience, from the arrogance and ambition of the damned, so Stukley is clearly in a different category from the Moor, whom one of his uncles describes as one "Whose pride doth swell to sway beyond his reach" (160). Abdelmelec, a few lines earlier, had called him a "damned wretch" on whom "The Gods shal poure down showers of sharp revenge" (140-41). Peele visually links the Moor with Tamburlaine by having him make his first entrance in a chariot, from which he delivers a bombastic speech that includes Tamburlaine in a list of gods (Neptune, Jove, Pluto, etc.) whose force is not strong enough to overcome him. Tamburlaine must die, he observes, as Philip and Caesar did. This, of course, is an echo of Tamburlaine's last line in Part II, and it has the ironic effect of reminding the audience of the Moor's own mortality. The Moor differs most obviously from Tamburlaine in the total absence of moral ambiguity in his portrayal. The cast includes a "presenter" who narrates events and explains dumb shows at the beginning of each act, thus serving as a figure of authority who relieves the audience of the responsibility for making moral judgments. He characterizes "this Moore" as a "tyrant king," ambitious, cruel, and "bloudie in his deeds," on whom Nemesis, the "high mistres of revenge," will eventually inflict vengeance (14, 32-35). The emphasis on revenge is pronounced in this play (Act II begins with three ghosts crying "Vindicta"), an indication, perhaps, that Peele was borrowing successful devices from other plays besides *Tamburlaine*.

The events leading up to the battle begin when Stukley arrives in Lisbon, en route to Ireland, and is persuaded by Sebastian to give up his attempt and join the expedition to Africa instead. Sebastian tells him that his proposed invasion is in vain, for "heavens and destinies/ Attend and wait upon her Majestie. . . ." He goes on to glorify Elizabeth at great length, affirming her right to rule Ireland (677 ff.). In the alliance between Stukley, Sebastian, and the Moor, Peele creates a composite which begins to approach the complexity of Tamburlaine; the Moor displays his cruelty and potential for tyranny and deception, Sebastian, his conviction that he upholds the will of heaven, and Stukley, his irrepressible aspiration and capacity for self-dramatization. The pieces fall apart at the end of the play, however. After the battle has been lost, Sebastian dies, realizing that he had been used and deceived, and Stukley is killed by his own Italian forces and goes willingly, after a long autobiographical speech, to the "bed of honor" where Sebastian lies. The Moor, in contrast, flees cursing the whole world—stars, fire, air, water, earth, and all—only to drown offstage as he attempts to escape. The universe thus takes revenge for all the curses, far more explicitly than at the end of *Tamburlaine*. The final words of the play are spoken by the new rightful king, Abdelmelec's younger brother, who declares that the death of the "damned wretch" his nephew will be a lesson to all the world. With this *The Battle of Alcazar* comes to a resoundingly moral conclusion, invoking the didacticism of the *de casibus* formula.

Despite its large cast and ambitious scope, *The Battle of Alcazar* is only 1,450 lines long; this text was abridged, apparently, to accommodate a touring company when the Admiral's men left London in 1591.[37] Even the longer original could not have been as dramatically effective as *Tamburlaine*, however, because it divided the audience's attention and emotional

[37] Yoklavich, Introduction, *The Dramatic Works of George Peele*, p. 221.

involvement among three potential protagonists, no one of whom dominates the play. Peele's play shares this weakness with most of the conqueror, revenge, and history plays which experimented with tragedy in one way or another during this period. Marlowe's are an exception: more than any of his contemporaries, Marlowe could isolate a single protagonist and make all of the other characters clearly subordinate to him. He realized that nothing, not even the author's desire to leave the audience with a moral lesson, must come between them and their involvement with the protagonist, although paradoxically, that involvement may contain a strong element of detachment. H.D.F. Kitto has observed that the emergence of the tragic protagonist and the disappearance of the didactic motive are strongly allied. In a discussion of Greek tragedy, he points out that only in the fourth century, when philosophy had become a form of discourse distinct from drama, could there be a tragic hero as we conceive him. His suggestion that the same thing happened at the end of the sixteenth century and the beginning of the seventeenth helps to explain why Marlowe's imitators, though they adopted some of *Tamburlaine*'s most obvious elements, failed to create a tragic protagonist.[38]

As still another derivative conqueror play demonstrates, the villainous conqueror did not have to die defeated at the end for the author's intended didacticism to assert itself. *The First part of the Tragicall raigne of Selimus* (1592?), written, it has been argued, by Greene, ends with its title character undefeated and anticipating more conquests in a projected second part, which, as far as is known, was never written. Selimus is the youngest of three sons of Bajazet, an adaptation of Marlowe's Turkish tyrant. He resembles not only Tamburlaine, but also Barabas and a host of cynical, self-congratulatory Machiavellian villains to come. His character is revealed at the

---

[38] On the hero as unifying principle, see Fredson Bowers, *Elizabethan Revenge Tragedy* (Princeton, 1940), p. 105; H.D.F. Kitto, "Damn the Tragic Hero," *Studies in Theatre and Drama: Essays in Honor of Hubert C. Heffner*, ed. Oscar G. Brockett (The Hague, 1972), pp. 46-47.

outset in a long set speech which rejects religion and its laws as "bug-beares to keepe the world in feare/ And make me quietly a yoake to beare." Selimus is above such laws:

> But we, whose minde in heauenly thoughts is clad,
> Whose bodie doth a glorious spirit beare,
> That hath no bounds, but flieth euery where;
> Why should we seeke to make that soule a slaue,
> To which dame Nature so large freedome gaue?
> (268-69, 281-85)[39]

He thus feels justified in deposing his father and his eldest brother Acomat, vowing to risk even hell to be emperor of the Turks. Rather like Faustus, he doubts the existence of heaven and hell, but as he tells his follower Sinam: "An Empire *Sinam*, is so sweete a thing,/ As I could be a diuell to be a King" (367-68). Interestingly, a large section of this long monologue was copied and circulated by Raleigh's enemies as "Certain hellish verses devysed by that traitor Ralegh." Evidently the rhetoric of a fictional "other" was readily transferable to a living one.

Despite these echoes of Tamburlaine, Selimus does not entirely dominate the play which bears his name. Much of the audience's attention is diverted to Bajazet, a king reminiscent of Gorboduc, in that he is torn between giving up his crown to Acomat and retaining it himself, as advised by his loyal followers and his virtuous middle son, Corcut. Bajazet is aware of Selimus' ambitions, and resigns himself to the fact that "Hee's born to be a scourge to me & mine" (410). Later, he reproaches Selimus for not having been "A scourge and terrour to mine enemies" (517). It is important to note that, although the author of *Selimus* follows Marlowe in using the word "scourge," the complex implications of the scourge's ambiguous status are never explored. Bajazet decides to remain Emperor about halfway through the play, at which point Acomat

---

[39] This and other quotations from *Selimus* are taken from Grosart, ed., *Works of Robert Greene*, Vol. XIV.

emerges as a villain figure determined, like his brother, to depose his father. Acomat begins by assaulting Natolia, where he defeats his nephew Mahomet, strangles Mahomet's sister Zonara after she calls him a monster to his face, and orders the slaughter of all the town's inhabitants. When Bajazet sends his follower Aga to protest, Acomat pulls out his eyes and cuts off his hands onstage, vowing to kill Bajazet just as brutally, in his unrelenting desire to become Emperor of the Turks. The brothers' cruel devices are virtually indistinguishable as the play progresses, and violent deaths by poisoning and strangling follow one another in rapid succession. Selimus, who is reconciled with his father, promptly seizes the crown and poisons Bajazet and Aga. He then captures his brother Corcut, strangles him, and finally captures Acomat and his Queen and has them strangled as well. At the end of the play Selimus reigns triumphant, his reign "tragicall" only in its effect on others. The detached horror which he and Acomet inspire is counter-balanced by the sympathy the audience feels for their deposed and heartbroken father, who with Aga inspires some of the pathos Shakespeare's Lear and Gloucester would arouse nearly two decades later. The audience also sympathizes with Corcut, whose role looks back to that of the Heavenly Man figures in the dual-protagonist plays. Corcut is a philosopher retired from worldly life who has just been converted to Christianity, as he tells Selimus in a long speech which expounds Christian doctrine. He stresses the anger with which God will reject those of us who neglect his warnings "And giue vs ouer to our wicked choyce" (2095).[40] Corcut thus serves to emphasize Selimus' resemblance to the reprobate "other" in explicitly Christian terms, as he summons up images of the torments of hell which await him "Where woe, and woe, and neuer ceasing woe/ Shall sound about thy euer-damned soule" (2112-13).

As Peele had done, the author of *Selimus* tried to outdo

[40] The Grosart text misnumbers lines from 2000 on. I have given correct line numbers here.

Marlowe by giving more than one character the role of the aspiring conqueror, with the result that the audience's response was diffused and their instinct to identify frustrated. But the absence of the single protagonist does not alone explain why *The Battle of Alcazar* and *Selimus* fall short of the Tamburlaine plays as effective drama and potential tragedy. Marlowe seems to have been alert to the aspirations and anxieties of his age to an extraordinary degree, and while his plays are less overtly moralistic than those of his contemporaries, they probe and make dramatic use of the age's preoccupation with salvation and damnation in startling and innovative ways. Marlowe's choice of Tamburlaine as his hero was both brilliant and lucky. In bringing to life a self-proclaimed scourge of God, he seized an opportunity to explore the psychology of the elect—in particular, the terrifying possibility that their assurance of election might turn out to be the presumptuousness of aspiring minds who fall prey to the error of confusing God's authority with their own. What Marlowe's imitators failed to understand was that because he views himself as God's scourge, Tamburlaine is both more and less than a villain ambitious for worldly power—more, because he blasphemously proclaims himself to be equal with God, less, because he believes he executes God's will. He displays at once the presumption of the devil and the equally mysterious and distant quality of God's avenging angel. Yet Tamburlaine is also a lover, which gives him the human vulnerability and love of beauty he would otherwise lack. Marlowe creates a powerful tension between Tamburlaine's ambiguous role as scourge and his sympathetic role as eloquent lover and bereaved husband. This tension, so essential to tragedy, is absent from the other conqueror plays; only Stukley, perhaps, shares something of Tamburlaine's quest for that elusive sum of glory which, tragically, can manifest itself only in earthly conquest.

CHAPTER VI

Revenge Tragedy

I. THE DUBIOUS MORALITY OF REVENGE

Like the conqueror plays, the revenge plays of the late 1580s and 1590s share certain similarities of plot, theatrical conventions, and character types. Structurally, however, the revenge play represents a major innovation, for it introduces the element of intrigue, which replaces the linear, episodic sequences of action characteristic of the conqueror play with elaborately plotted ones employing deception, suspense, and surprise revelations. In one sense, the protagonist of the revenge plot becomes a complex character purely by virtue of his position in the web of intrigue that surrounds him. Drawn into his role by another's crime, he is never a simple villain, for he does not initiate the events that lead to the acts of violence he eventually performs. However much he becomes enmired in evil, he has at some point in the play aroused a sense of engagement in spectators who pity his misfortunes and sympathize with his feelings of helplessness. This relationship becomes increasingly complicated as the play continues, and acts of violation begin leading to acts of revenge, causing the audience to alternate between sympathy and horror. In another sense, the protagonist is a complex character because of the audience's ambivalent feelings about revenge, feelings that color their response to him quite apart from anything he says or does. By devising a dramatic structure that turned upon a controversial topical issue with strong moral implications, the playwrights of the 1580s and 1590s were able to arouse the mixed emotions necessary for tragedy, even when, as in *The Jew of Malta*, their intentions seemed more comic than tragic.[1]

---

[1] Eleanor Prosser lists twenty-one revenge tragedies written between 1562 and 1607 in *Hamlet and Revenge* (Stanford, 1967). Fredson Bowers discusses

Just as we can speculate that Marlowe was attracted to the Tamburlaine story because he recognized an inherent ambiguity in the concept of the scourge of God, so it seems altogether probable that the first revenge tragedies were inspired by a similar recognition on the part of the playwrights. In Belleforest's *Histoires Tragiques*, the source of the early Hamlet play, which was well enough known in 1589 for Nashe to assume his readers' familiarity with its most famous line, the revenger is referred to in terms remarkably similar to the sixteenth-century references to Tamburlaine. As the English translation of Belleforest affirms in its opening argument, Hamlet is to be regarded as an agent of God, executing His revenge upon sinners:

> . . . if the iniquitie of a brother caused his brother to loose his life, yet that vengeance was not long after delayed; to the end that traitors may know, although the punishment of their trespasses committed be stayed for awhile, yet that they may assure themselves that, without all doubt, they shal never escape the puisant and revenging hand of God.[2]

At the end of Belleforest's account, Hamlet delivers a long oration to the Danish people as he presents them with the bodies of his uncle and his uncle's followers. In Belleforest's source, the pagan Scandinavian legend written down in the twelfth century by Saxo Grammaticus, this oration consists of the typical epic hero's boasts; in Belleforest's narrative, however, it serves as a provocative examination of the revenger's difficult role. Hamlet reminds the Danish people that: "It is I

---

later revenge tragedies as well in *Elizabethan Revenge Tragedy: 1587-1642* (Princeton, 1940), and notes that the mixed sympathy and disapproval audience's felt for the Kydian protagonist eventually changed to unqualified disapproval of the villain-protagonist. For the most recent treatment of the shared charactistics of revenge tragedies, see Charles A. and Elaine S. Hallett, *The Revenger's Madness* (Lincoln, Nebraska, 1980).

[2] Israel Gollancz, *The Sources of Hamlet* (1926; rpt., New York, 1967), p. 173. For a reconstruction of the "Ur-Hamlet" based on Belleforest and *Der Bestrafte Brudermord*, see Bowers, pp. 86 ff. Bowers assumes that Kyd was the author of the Ur-Hamlet, and that the play preceded *The Spanish Tragedy*.

alone, that have done this piece of worke, whereunto you ought to have lent me your handes, and therein have ayded and assisted me" (p. 271). These words place him in something very like the traditional scapegoat's role, isolated and burdened by a guilt assumed for the sake of the community at large. If he is to avoid being the outcast, Hamlet must have the support of the community:

> To you also it belongeth by dewty and reason commonly to defend and protect Hamlet, the minister and executor of just vengeance, who being jealous of your honour and your reputation, hath hazarded himself, hoping you will serve him for fathers, defenders, and tutors, and regarding him in pity, restore him to his goods and inheritances (p. 279).

This Hamlet is akin to the ritual hero who, in Holloway's terms, assumes "a curiously ambivalent role, part victim and part cynosure, splendid and yet in a sense almost abject at once, the role of one who is passing through what is both an ordeal or infliction, and a triumph."[3] The tone Hamlet adopts toward his own audience reflects his sense of their ambivalence, as he asks them to honor him as a hero but also to protect him from punishment. Shakespeare's Hamlet does not live to make this kind of speech, but his final words to Horatio are filled with an urgent desire to have it made by another, lest a "wounded name" live on behind him. It would be interesting to know whether the first Hamlet delivered a speech similar to the one Belleforest's Hamlet gave and whether the speech communicated any of this desire to win the support and understanding of the audience within the play.

To judge from Belleforest's treatment of the Hamlet story, sixteenth-century readers received the revenger as a particularly self-aware version of the scourge of God, who reluctantly takes on the morally dubious role of executing divine vengeance. The issue of the morality of revenge did not have to be

---

[3] John Holloway, *The Story of the Night: Studies in Shakespeare's Major Tragedies* (Lincoln, Nebraska, 1961), p. 179.

openly debated within the play to become part of the audience's theatrical experience; their uncertainty about whether and under what circumstances revenge was justified was something they brought with them to the theatre. Most scholars agree that on the matter of revenge the Elizabethans were caught between conflicting ethical systems.[4] Despite the Biblical injunction to leave revenge to God, there had been a long tradition of private revenge in England. The Germanic law of *wergeld* was still in effect until the thirteenth century, when it finally disappeared during the reign of Edward I, and private revenge did not become a crime against the state until well into the fourteenth century. Nevertheless, this did not inhibit individuals, especially among the nobility, from continuing to seek revenge upon one another through duels, plots, and open warfare, as any student of English history knows. The most justified form of revenge was blood revenge, and, in particular, the revenge of a father's death by a son. According to Bowers, many Elizabethans may have believed that civil law denied the father's inheritance to a son who did not revenge his father's death, although no such law ever existed. As long as revenge took the form of an open duel, Bowers argues, the Elizabethans would have been willing to approve; only when the revenger turned to Machiavellian intrigue would they pass judgment on him and cease to sympathize.[5]

In the years since *Elizabethan Revenge Tragedy* was published, the question of the morality of revenge has been intermittently reopened. Bowers' conclusions are most vigorously opposed by Eleanor Prosser, whose *Hamlet and Revenge* challenges his assumption that Elizabethan audiences would have brought to the theatre a predisposition to favor revenge, even

[4] Joel Altman has discussed this aspect of the revenge play in *The Tudor Play of Mind* (Berkeley, 1978), as have Robert Y. Turner in *Shakespeare's Apprenticeship* (Chicago, 1974), Stephen Booth in "On the Value of Hamlet," in *Reinterpretations of Elizabethan Drama*, ed. Norman Rabkin (New York, 1969), Eleanor Prosser, and the Halletts.

[5] Bowers, *Elizabethan Revenge Tragedy*, ch. 1 passim.

under Hamlet's special circumstances.[6] Prosser provides a great deal of evidence to demonstrate the condemnation of revenge widespread among Elizabethan moralists, though she acknowledges that "we cannot find the reality by defining the ideal." Accordingly, she begins her study of *Hamlet* and the issue of revenge with the premise that the average spectator at a revenge play was "probably trapped in an ethical dilemma—a dilemma, to put it most simply, between what he believed and what he felt." She thus proposes a "double response" whereby the spectator "could instinctively identify with the revenger and yet—either at the same time or later, when released from emotional involvement—judge him, too." Prosser's notion of the double response (mentioned only in a footnote) is in effect the pity and fear which Aristotle recognized in the fourth-century Greek audience.[7] Prosser surveys the thirteen plays written before *Hamlet* which deal with revenge and finds that in all of them "revenge itself is treated as unmistakably evil," even when revenge is undertaken by good men. Her book has prompted some subsequent research; Philip J. Ayres, for example, finds in popular Elizabethan fiction some examples of good revengers, and concludes that the Elizabethan audience could have approved of revenge in defiance of the attitudes projected in the tracts and sermons which Prosser cites.[8]

As a political act, revenge may have been less ambiguous and reprehensible than it was in the realm of private action.

[6] Prosser notes that "A few people may have mistakenly believed that a son had to seek legal punishment of his father's murder to ensure his inheritance, but I have found no evidence to indicate that Elizabethans believed the law required blood revenge" (*Hamlet and Revenge*, p. 18).

[7] Prosser, *Hamlet and Revenge*, pp. 24, 4, 34. In a recent article entitled "*Antonio's Revenge*: Marston's Play on Revenge Tragedy" (*Studies in English Literature* 23, 2 [Spring 1983], 277-94), Barbara J. Baines discusses the way Marston comments on the audience's mixed response to revenge tragedy, using Bethell's concept of the dual perspective.

[8] Prosser, *Hamlet and Revenge*, p. 63; Philip J. Ayres, "Degrees of Heresy: Justified Revenge and Elizabethan Narratives," *Studies in Philology* LXIX (1972), 461-74.

178

John Sibley has noted that the Elizabethan "Homily Against
Disobedience and Wilful Rebellion" prohibited rebellion against
"naturall and lawful princes," but not against usurping or il-
legitimate ones. To protect the Queen, a Bond of Association
written shortly after the Succession Act of 1571 specified that
subjects are obliged "to pursue . . . by force of arms as by all
other means of revenge," anyone who harms the rightful
monarch, and "to act the utmost revenge upon them."[9] Belleforest draws upon similar attitudes toward revenge in his
choice of Biblical and classical analogies to justify Hamlet's
actions. He cites David's dying instructions to Solomon not
to leave unpunished men who had done him injuries and ap-
pends the following comment: "where the prince or countrey
is interested, the desire of revenge cannot by any meanes (how
small soever) beare the title of condemnation, but is rather
commendable and worthy of praise." He gives further support
to this point by invoking the Athenian law which ordered the
erection of images in memory of those who, "revenging the
injuries of the commonwealth, boldly massacred tyrants" (p.
261). If these were conventional arguments with which the
Elizabethan audience was familiar, then they might have felt
that Hamlet's revenge against Claudius was justified even
though Shakespeare places much less emphasis than Saxo or
Belleforest on the usurper's abuse of power. Admittedly
Shakespeare achieves a high degree of ambiguity by having
Hamlet's motives for revenge seem more private than political; yet his diseased Denmark, like the settings of other revenge tragedies, reveals a social disorder in which the source
of violation and transgression is the figure who should have
represented order and authority.[10]

Another approach to the Elizabethans' perception of revenge as a political act proposes linking divine vengeance with
the Reformation. In Ronald Broude's reading of *The Spanish*

[9] John Sibley, "The Duty of Revenge in Tudor and Stuart Drama," *A Review of English Literature*, VIII, 3 (July, 1967), 46-54.
[10] Hallett and Hallett, *The Revenger's Madness*, p. 103.

Tragedy, Hieronimo becomes a Protestant martyr who is caught up in God's vengeance against the unrighteous through political corruption and destruction. In their confident belief that they were the elect nation, the Elizabethan Protestants saw themselves as the agents of God's vengeance (Broude mentions Drake's ship, the "Revenge") in much the same way that Hieronimo does. Moreover, they could find in Luther explicit justification for taking revenge: "Whoso sheddeth man's blood, by man shall his blood be shed."[11] Just as the conqueror assumed a curious resemblance to the elect man of God in the feverish Protestant atmosphere of the late 1580s, so the revenger could be viewed as God's chosen agent, whose duty it was to restore order to a fallen world. But if to do so meant risking damnation, then his dilemma was indeed a tragic manifestation of the inscrutable and arbitrary will of God who was Himself the supreme revenger. Predictably, what damns the revenger is his presumption; he takes God's role upon himself, employing the concealed stratagems, the sudden unveiling of purpose behind events, the patient biding of time, and the well-chosen punishments that typify God's control of human events.[12]

II. VICTIM, VILLAIN, VICE, HERO

The Elizabethan revenger is the consummate chameleon; at various points in his play, he assumes the characteristics of four different character types. Each type evokes a different

[11] Ronald Broude, "*Vindicta Filia Temporis*: Three English Forerunners of the Elizabethan Revenge Play," *JEGP*, LXXII (1973), 489-502.

[12] This comparison of the revenger's role and God's is explored by Muriel Bradbrook in *The Rise of the Common Player* (London, 1962). Bradbrook cites Thomas Beard's *Theatre of Gods Judgments* (1597) as evidence that the Elizabethans made this connection. Beard portrays God as "a revengeful Father Deity, not scrupling to use evil men [e.g., Tamburlaine] as instruments of his wrath and then destroy them." Bradbrook goes on to suggest that the revenge play served a valuable purpose by reducing "this frightful God to dimensions merely human, and show[ing] him in the end as falling to death's mace himself" (pp. 131-33).

response, and these responses, under the right circumstances, can combine to create an intensely tragic experience for the spectator. From one point of view, the revenger is a victim, persecuted by a tyrant and forced to suffer without cause. The parent whose child is slaughtered is a type inherited from the Herod plays in the mystery cycles, and the persistence of this motif from *Apius and Virginia* into the seventeenth century gives evidence of its potential for tragic treatment. In an age which glorified martyrdom, to survive was in a very real sense more tragic than to perish, and the true victims are not the slaughtered children, but the parents who remain alive, tormented by the knowledge of their loss and unable to understand why God has permitted the death of innocents. If they could endure being victims, they might, paradoxically, become victors, as Christ did. But they do not, for in its simplest form the revenge plot dramatizes the process by which a victim becomes a villain, thus turning another into the victim he had been.[13]

The relationship between a character's act of villainy and his role as victim differs considerably in the plays which explore the revenger's dilemma. While Titus acts villainously in the first scene of his play, ordering the slaughter of Tamora's son Alarbus and killing his own son, Hieronimo does not finally succumb to villainy until he cold-bloodedly kills the children of other parents in the last scene of his. Where, as in *Titus Andronicus*, the protagonist's act of violence precedes his transformation into a victim, the character becomes directly responsible for his tragedy. With characters as diverse as Barabas and Macbeth, who are partly or wholly the victims of their own villainy, the formula yields to further, often intensely ironic, variations. However it occurs, the protagonist's transformation reflects the most distinctive characteristics of the age; for it generally takes place only after a painful process

---

[13] For the victim-victor concept, see John Seldon Whale, *Victor and Victim* (Cambridge, 1960). For use of the terms villain and victim in reference to Elizabethan character types, see J.M.R. Margeson in *The Origins of English Tragedy* (Oxford, 1967).

involving self-scrutiny, moral or theological inquiry, and ag-onizing uncertainty, all dramatically rendered by the play-wright. In becoming a revenger, the protagonist redefines his character and his concept of meaning in life. What makes the revenger's transformation tragic is that it requires him to take on the characteristics of the villainous "others" whom he must destroy if he is to purge society of its evils.[14]

In *The Spanish Tragedy, Hamlet,* and many other revenge tragedies, the catalyst triggering the protagonist's transfor-mation is the appearance of a ghost. From one viewpoint, the ghost is a voice from another world, an apparent agent of authority who frees the revenger from mundane legal restric-tions and substitutes natural law in their place. Viewed from another perspective, the ghost represents the voice of passion, which plunges the revenger into madness and gradually trans-forms him from a good and respected man to an "other." The revenger's descent into hell is a terrifying reversal of the mo-rality play protagonist's regeneration. The delay that prolongs and heightens his descent can be viewed as a dramaturgical device to express indecision. This indecision is caused by the workings of conscience, which at first resists, but finally suc-cumbs, to madness. In its true Kydian form, it has been sug-gested, the delay motif produces a double response; the au-dience feels pity for the revenger's sufferings, joined with fear of the consequences of his actions.[15] Their double response is heightened because they recognize the significant difference between the victim-turned-villain and the play's conventional victims and villains. Characters like Lorenzo and Tamora or Belleforest's Fengon (i.e., Claudius) make the revenger seem

[14] For the psychological implications of the revenger's transformation, see Richard S. Hillman, "Meaning and Mortality in Some Renaissance Revenge Plays," *University of Toronto Quarterly* XLIX, 1 (Fall, 1979), 1-17. See also Ernest W. Talbert, *Elizabethan Drama and Shakespeare's Early Plays* (Chapel Hill, 1963), pp. 63 ff.

[15] For a more extended discussion of the relationships among madness, conscience and delay, see Hallett and Hallett, *The Revenger's Madness,* pp. 86 ff.

noble by comparison. Conversely, victims like Lavinia or Hieronimo's wife Isabella make him seem impatient and bloodthirsty, since they assume the traditional Christian martyr's role and endure the evil to which they are subjected without seeking direct revenge. Marlowe's Barabas, who is much more the villain than the victim, contrasts less sharply with the other villains in his play, and more sharply with Abigail, who resembles Virginia and other threatened virgins from the homiletic drama.

The revenger's duality as both villain and victim is reinforced by another source of duality—his resemblance to the morality play Vice. As Michael Goldman reminds us, the revenger is "above all things, a maker of plots," plots shaped by a "flow of aggression" which causes him to "try to take charge of the laws by which things move and change in his world."[16] In this respect he is the direct descendant of the Vice, that master manipulator and intriguer whose role in the morality plays largely consisted of plotting against his victims. Whenever a sixteenth-century character employs manipulation and scheming to achieve his ends, he is almost invariably using stage techniques which originated with the Vice. The verbal dissimulation which leads to entrapment in the final scenes of *Titus Andronicus* and *The Spanish Tragedy* are good examples, particularly since both Titus and Hieronimo invoke the spirit of play and festivity as they arrange the horribly transformed versions of the traditional banquet and masque with which comedy so often ends. Comic devices also appear in scenes where the Vice's techniques are employed by characters other than the revenger protagonist: for instance, when Lorenzo tricks Pedringano into laughing as he is hanged, or when Aaron lures Lavinia's two brothers into the hole he has dug for them. In both cases, the audience is tempted to laugh at the ironic misunderstandings and the comedy of physical gesture and confusion. Their mingled horror and laughter, like their mixed feelings in general, have an important effect. The evil they

<hr />

[16] Michael Goldman, *The Actor's Freedom* (New York, 1975), pp. 97-99.

confront becomes psychologically acceptable, hence protecting them from the unbearable (in Weimann's words, "Terror, playfully experienced, acts as a charm against real terror . . .)."[17]

Revengers and subsequent tragic protagonists inherit other qualities from the Vice as well. From his antic speech, which originates in earliest folk drama, comes the nonsense of the comic fool, but also the reason mixed with madness of a Hamlet or Hieronimo or Lear. The Vice's privileged and confidential relationship with the audience, physically acted out by his movements on the stage and, at times, among the audience, encouraged their identification even in the midst of moral disapproval. Both Barabas and Hamlet exhibit this quality, particularly through their use of asides and soliloquies in the opening scenes of their respective plays. But, in Hamlet, the Vice's craftiness merges with the qualities of the epic hero, the character Belleforest described as "hardie," "couragious," and "worthy of eternal comendation," a man of prudence, boldness, magnanimity, and wisdom.

The legacy of the morality play Vice received an infusion of energy from the popular perception of the Machiavel as an unscrupulous villain who employs "policy" in much the same way as the Vice used trickery or "gear." Arguing that the Elizabethans in fact understood the import of Machiavelli's theories better than we do, Bernard Spivack observes that the Machiavel stands for the antitheses of the traditional Christian values upheld by the homiletic drama: "the Machiavellian villain, through his egoism, his ruthless energy unhampered by pious restraints, his deliberate disavowal of any law higher than his own appetite, his penetrating and cynical awareness of the animal impulses composing man's lower nature, enacts the thrust of the new *realism* against the traditional Christian sanctities applicable to the life of this world."[18] The Machia-

---

[17] Robert Weimann, *Shakespeare and the Popular Tradition in the Theatre*, ed. Robert Schwartz (Baltimore, 1978), p. 72. See also Bernard Spivack's discussion of the Vice in *Shakespeare and the Allegory of Evil* (New York, 1958), Chapter V.

[18] Spivack, *Shakespeare and the Allegory of Evil*, p. 375.

vel's identity as an "other," a negation of publicly cherished values, is thus complicated by the fact that he is associated with realistic assessments of human nature and political necessities which the Elizabethans were increasingly inclined to accept in practice, if not in theory, and which were reinforced to some extent by the doctrine of election and the rhetoric of assurance. In Gabriel Harvey's catalogue of maxims for the successful man appear attributes which belong alike to the Machiavel and the elect man of God: "Boldness, eloquence, and winning manners lead to success . . . [also] Self-confidence. . . . Begin with resolution: & follow it thorowly for life."[19] When revengers like Barabas and Aaron display boldness, eloquence, resolution, and self-confidence, these otherwise admirable qualities are subordinated to the Vice's enjoyment of the sport of villainy and hence rendered evil. But the qualities *themselves*, as distinct from the purposes for which they are employed, remain inherently good and even potentially heroic.

The fourth of the revenger's identities, his role as hero, is the most problematic, for any audience would have difficulty regarding a character who is part victim, part villain, and part Vice with the awe that is the hero's due. The revenger shares with traditional heroes a sense of being set apart from the great mass of men. Isolated by a special vision which is also a burden, he sees more deeply than those around him into the nature of his society and its evils, and acts alone to overcome the obstacles that confront him at every turn. If, like Hieronimo, the revenger is initially distinguished by his uprightness and honesty, his dilemma is tragic, particularly when he is forced to abandon the justice in which he once believed. If, like Barabas, he is essentially unprincipled, he is heroic only in the sense that he is surrounded by villains who have none of his positive qualities. In either case, his heroic nature is

[19] Quoted in Hiram Haydn, *The Counter-Renaissance* (New York, 1950), p. 449, as part of a discussion of the individualistic naturalism of the age. Haydn also sees similarities between Machiavelli's philosophy and Calvinism, although in a more pessimistic and negative sense than I do.

defined in opposition to the "otherness" of his antagonists; he is a hero because he seeks to destroy an "other" who embodies evil in its most absolute form.

III. *The Spanish Tragedy*

The first character that the Elizabethan audience met at a performance of *The Spanish Tragedy* was an allegorical character named Revenge, who calls himself the chorus but more closely resembles the stage manager or director for the show that follows. Kyd does not rule out the possibility that Revenge is something of a Vice figure, who creates disorder without any motive. Though he has none of the comic qualities of the traditional Vice, Revenge takes satisfaction in his ability to torment all the characters in the play; he assures the ghost of Don Andreas that:

> I'll turn their friendship into fell despite,
> Their love to mortal hate, their day to night,
> Their hope into despair, their peace to war,
> Their joys to pain, their bliss to misery.
> (I, v, 6-9)[20]

The audience watches the play from the vantage point of Don Andreas and Revenge, who both remain onstage for the entire performance, although without sharing these two characters' unquestioning acceptance of the necessity for revenge. This gap between the audience's values and those of the mediating characters is bound to make them feel somewhat detached as they watch the events leading to the promised death of Balthazar. Machiavel's prologue in *The Jew of Malta* prompts a similar wariness in the audience; in both cases it is as if the playwright felt the need for a theatrical device to encourage

---

[20] This and all other quotations from *The Spanish Tragedy* are taken from the Revels edition, ed. Philip Edwards (Cambridge, Massachusetts, 1959).

the audience to feel detached from a protagonist who would eventually become an example of the "other."[21]

The distance thus established is at odds with a contrary tendency in the play, once Hieronimo emerges as the protagonist. Hieronimo has several soliloquies in the last scene of Act II and throughout Act III. These speeches draw the audience into his dilemma and permit them to experience the full intensity of his grief and outrage. The first soliloquy accompanies his discovery of Horatio's body in the garden, and begins with questions which draw attention to the difference between the audience's knowledge and his own: "Who calls Hieronimo?" and "what murd'rous spectacle is this?" (II, v, 4, 9.) The speech gathers in intensity, drawing protagonist and audience closer together, as Hieronimo asks questions which neither he nor they can answer. These questions challenge the moral order of a universe which permits such injustice:

> O heavens, why make you night to cover sin?
> By day this deed of darkness had not been.
> O earth, why didst thou not in time devour
> The vild profaner of this sacred bower?
> O poor Horatio, what hadst thou misdone,
> To leese thy life ere life was new begun?
>
> (II, v, 24-29)

In a dialogue with Isabella which follows, Hieronimo first makes the association between ease and revenge, a coupling that will recur at the end of the play, when he surveys the

---

[21] As Altman observes, Kyd's play has "a frame that points in one direction and an action that points in another. . . ." The play invites us to respond in several different ways, one of which is "to reflect upon the simplistic judgment of the frame as an aspect of [the protagonist's] problem" (pp. 270-71). Booth notes that the Ghost and Revenge act as a chorus, and "keep the audience safe from doubt, safely outside the action, looking in" ("On the Value of Hamlet," p. 152). See also Anne Righter, *Shakespeare and the Idea of a Play* (London, 1962), for the play-within-a-play idea and its effect on the audience's identification.

body-strewn stage and declares himself "Pleas'd with their deaths and eas'd with their revenge" (IV, iv, 190; note that the soothing sound of the pleased/eased rhyme will return a few years later in Richard II's final soliloquy). Hieronimo's anticipation of the joy that revenge will bring overmasters the impulse to seek comfort in suicide. While they must have sympathized with his grief, the Elizabethan audience might have found it difficult to accept either suicide or revenge as a source of ease or joy. Moreover, they listened to these lines with a certain ironic detachment, aware as they were of the cool and unmoved presence of Revenge, in whose scheme Hieronimo serves almost as a pawn.

The soliloquies of Act III all deal in one way or another with the issue of justice, which is so closely allied with that of revenge. Earlier, Isabella had comforted herself with the assurance that "the heavens are just," an attitude which seems confirmed by the resolution of the Portuguese subplot, in which misplaced justice is exposed and corrected and the false accuser justly punished.[22] Hieronimo wants desperately to share her belief; indeed, like Job, his trust in the heavens is the very grounds for his agony, since he presumes too far in his faith that heaven will act according to his prayer, not realizing that "the wisdom and justice of God cannot be measured by human wisdom and law."[23] This presumption leads him to challenge divine judgment directly: if Horatio's death passes unrevenged, he asks the heavens, "How should we term your dealings to be just,/ If you unjustly deal with those that in your justice trust?" (III, ii, 10-11.)

The "mass of public wrongs" that Hieronimo bewails continues to grow. Lorenzo, suspecting his servants Serberine and

[22] As the Halletts point out, Alexandro, the falsely accused victim in the subplot, serves as a touchstone for Hieronimo: "his action—the action of unshaken faith—is the action that would be taken in the face of gross injustice by a man who accepts his society's symbols" (*The Revengers Madness*, p. 135).

[23] D. J. Palmer, "Elizabethan Tragic Heroes," *Elizabethan Theatre*, Stratford-upon-Avon-Studies, IX (1966), ed. John Russell Brown and Bernard Harris, p. 18.

188

Pedringano, arranges deviously contrived deaths for them both, and, as a result, Hieronimo assumes his official role as Knight Marshall. The victim of injustice, he must enact justice. Clinging to his belief in the "justice of the heavens," he wonders when he shall come "To know the cause that may my cares allay?" (III, vi, 6-7.) Bel-Imperia's letter has accused Lorenzo and Balthazar of murdering Horatio, but Hieronimo needs further proof. Ironically, he receives it just after, and as a result of, the injustice he unwittingly commits in his role as Marshall. No sooner is the wrongly condemned Pedringano condemned and executed than a letter is found in his pocket which conclusively identifies the murderers. Confident that the crime is one which "heaven unpunish'd would not leave," Hieronimo's first impulse is to go and complain to the king, "And cry aloud for justice through the court." Only if this fails will he resort to "revenging threats" (III, vii, 56, 70, 73). But his cry is a futile gesture, as Kyd has prepared the audience to realize. Pedringano's empty box, G. K. Hunter has suggested, is the "cynical emblem of man's hope for justice."[24] The seeming indifference of the gods toward the comic servant prefigures their more terrible and inexplicable treatment of the man who sacrifices his humanity to become their instrument.

An important part of Hieronimo's tragedy is that he knowingly chooses a course which he associates with damnation. His melodramatic proclamation that "The ugly fiends do sally forth of hell,/ And frame my steps to unfrequented paths . . ." (III, ii, 16-17) reminds the audience both that revenge is damnable and that Hieronimo realizes he is being acted upon by powerful supernatural forces. Revenge's presence on the stage is a visual embodiment of these forces, one which strengthens the audience's sympathy for Hieronimo. As his frustration increases, Hieronimo views justice and revenge as equally inaccessible; they are lodged in heaven behind walls of

[24] G. K. Hunter, "Ironies of Justice in *The Spanish Tragedy*," *Dramatic Identities and Cultural Tradition* (New York, 1978), p. 225.

diamond against which his pleas beat in vain. But he still appeals for justice to the king, the traditional source of authority. By this point in the play, however, his descent into madness has begun, and his behavior at the court is frenzied and impulsive. The change that is taking place in him is dramatically rendered in the soliloquy which follows. Hieronimo begins by assuring himself "heaven will be reveng'd of every ill,/ Nor will they suffer murder unrepaid," and urges himself to stay and attend their will. Yet two lines later, after recalling Seneca's words "*Per scelus semper tutum est sceleribus iter*" ("The safest way for crime is always through crime"), he advises himself "Strike, and strike home, where wrong is offer'd thee,/ For evils unto ills conductors be." He comforts himself with the knowledge, again derived from Seneca, that destiny will either ease his miseries or bring him the death he continues to long for, but concludes, "I will revenge his death!" (III, xiii, 2-20.)

From "stay" to "strike" is an abrupt transition. Has Hieronimo abandoned Christian doctrine for a reckless dedication to revenge at any cost, inspired by his reading of Seneca, or has he somehow become convinced that the heavens have chosen him as their agent? In other words, has he rejected the principle of "*Vindicta mihi*, saith the Lord" which he invoked at the beginning of the speech, or, embracing it, has he accepted his role as God's instrument?[25] The speech offers no satisfactory answer. The series of aphoristic pronouncements delivered by Hieronimo takes up the problem of action vs. inaction (which Hamlet was later to confront) from several perspec-

[25] Nearly every critical interpretation of this play turns on its interpretation of this speech. Bowers believes that Hieronimo casts off heaven at this point and turns the audience against him; Prosser, similarly, believes that he rejects patience and determines "to wait no longer upon the will of Heaven" (*Hamlet and Revenge*, p. 50). Palmer, on the other hand, believes that Hieronimo presumes too far in his faith that heaven will act according to his prayer, but that the audience, in the end, views him as a righteous man who thinks that he is accomplishing the will of heaven ("Elizabethan Tragic Heroes," pp. 11 ff.).

tives, but does not reveal the logic by which he arrives at his conclusions. One wonders, for instance, whether Hieronimo is speaking out in bitter irony against patience when he says "For he that thinks with patience to contend/ To quiet life, his life shall easily end." This, coupled with the realization that "evils unto ills conductors be" and "Heaven covereth him that hath no burial," prompts the critical decision: action must finally replace passive endurance in a world where evil breeds more evil, and the "quiet life" is an illusion (6-19). The only rest to be found in "unrest" is that which dissembles quiet and patience in anticipation of the right moment for revenge. The audience's difficulty with the first part of this speech is directly related to the struggle taking place in Hieronimo's mind; the deliberateness of the second part, on the other hand, has some of the craftiness of the incipient Machiavel. As if to compound the audience's uncertainty about how they are supposed to regard Hieronimo, Kyd follows the soliloquy with an enounter which is clearly designed to arouse sympathy for him. A servant announces a group of petitioners, who, as they enter, remind the audience that "There's not any advocate in Spain/ That can prevail, or will take half the pain/ That he will, in pursuit of equity" (52-54). Among them is another father of a murdered son, whom Hieronimo describes as a mute old man, his "mournful eyes and hands to heaven uprear'd" (just as Hieronimo had been before his resolution to take revenge). Hieronimo's grief-stricken and generous identification with the old man inspires a parallel identification and generosity of feeling on the audience's part. But Kyd does not sustain this mood long, for when Hieronimo concludes that "on this earth justice will not be found" (108) and resolves to go down to hell, the Elizabethan audience must have shrunk from following him. Thus by pulling his audience first one way and then the other, Kyd, in this scene especially, achieved a mingling of engagement and detachment that looked forward to the great tragedies.

In the last act of *The Spanish Tragedy*, Hieronimo becomes the calculating revenger, bent upon executing his plot and

191

confident that all the saints in heaven "do sit soliciting/ For vengeance on those cursed murderers" (IV, i, 33-34). Unable to share the certainty with which he links heaven and revenge, the Elizabethan audience would begin to see him as an "other." Thus their detachment would allow them to enjoy the preparations for and performance of the masque which occupy most of the last act, just as they could enjoy the machinations of the Vice. In the final moments of the play their sympathy might even have shifted to the bereaved King and Viceroy, who now assume Hieronimo's role as father-figures whose children have been murdered. Hieronimo's final act, the murder of Castile, is an act of gratuitous and insane violence which seals the audience's final detachment from Hieronimo and permits them to take leave of him confirmed in their belief in his "otherness."[26] They have been through the experience of suffering, indecision, and resolution with him, but now they pity him in his madness from an emotional remove. Their sense of detachment is further strengthened by the final remarks of Don Andreas, who has become, in the course of four acts, so utterly obsessed with revenge that his gleeful pleasure at the conclusion of the play is rather chilling. The elaborate classical imagery of his final vision of the rewards and punishments that await the characters in the underworld reminds the audience that Christian values have no place in the world of the revenge play. Kyd ends with a curious pronouncement delivered by Revenge:

[26] Critics are also divided about how the audience feels about Hieronimo at the end of the play. Barry B. Adams reviews recent critical appraisals of the play in an effort to "define the complexity of an audience's response," particularly to the catastrophe. He suggests a distinction between the *aesthetic* response of the onstage audience consisting of the Ghost and Revenge, and the non-aesthetic response, the horror in the face of violence, of the rest of the onstage observers. The theatre audience, he suggests, shares the aesthetic response of pleasure in seeing their expectations realized. I would argue that the audience experiences a double response, combining the two Adams describes, but that their sense of horror is greater than their sense of pleasure. "The Audiences of *The Spanish Tragedy*," *JEGP*, 68 (1969), 221-36.

Then haste we down to meet thy friends and foes,
To place thy friends in ease, the rest in woes:
For here though death hath end their misery,
I'll there begin their endless tragedy.

Presumably the first "their" in the final couplet refers to the misery of the friends, while the second "their" to the punishments which await the foes. These punishments constitute their "tragedy," a word which a modern reader would be more likely to use in reference to Hieronimo and Bel-Imperia. In the rigid division between friends and foes, or saved and damned, which prevailed in the 1580s, tragedy is reserved for *them*, the "others"; it has yet to become something that happens to someone like ourselves.

IV. *Titus Andronicus*

Although *Titus Andronicus* was not published until 1594, it is probably one of the early experiments in tragedy written between 1589 and 1592, and a contemporary of *The Spanish Tragedy*,[27] which it resembles in a number of interesting ways. The relationship between the two plays is somewhat analogous to the relationship between *Tamburlaine* and the other conqueror plays; instead of one main revenge intrigue, Shakespeare gave his audience a proliferation of revengers and revenge actions. The events which trigger the revenges result from the errors in judgment of a noble man in a position of importance, errors which lead to rash acts of violence, culminating in Titus' onstage slaughter of his own son. Such actions can only alienate the sympathy of the audience to whom he was introduced as a wise and brave warrior. Except for his decision to uphold the principle of primogeniture, which causes

[27] Although a production of *Titus* by the Lord Sussex's Men is listed as a new play by Henslowe in January 1594, the play was probably new only to that acting company; a more probable date is 1589-1590, judging from stylistic evidence. See R. F. Hill, "The Composition of *Titus Andronicus*," *Shakespeare Survey*, 10 (1957), pp. 60-70.

the villainous Saturninus to become emperor, Titus' errors in judgment are inexplicable; unlike the tragic choices of Shakespeare's later protagonists, they do not seem to result from inborn character traits, but to stem from violent and self-destructive impulses.

Like Marlowe and other sixteenth-century playwrights, Shakespeare uses his large cast to define characters by antithesis. At first, Titus' cruelty is highlighted by the pathos that attaches to Tamora, the victimized parent of a slaughtered child whose dignified and eloquent plea for her son's life falls on deaf ears. But, moments later, Titus rises in the audience's estimation when contrasted with the proud and inconstant "other," Saturninus. As Saturninus and Tamora affirm their villainy and join forces against the Andronici, the latter begin to be perceived as virtuous victims. Within the family, further distinctions emerge. Titus' initial folly and later madness are contrasted with the wisdom and virtue of his brother Marcus, the play's only entirely admirable character. Titus and Marcus almost always appear on stage together (interestingly, Titus has very few moments alone with the audience, in contrast to Hieronimo). The audience is thus encouraged to respond to them as a pair, with the result that they are inclined to identify with Marcus, whose normalcy sharply contrasts with his brother's extremes of feeling and behavior, and experience a corresponding detachment from Titus. There are some powerful moments, to be sure, when Titus' grief and acute disillusionment with Rome and the seeming indifference of the heavens inspires pathos of the kind the audience feels for Hieronimo, but, too often, Marcus intervenes, preventing the direct engagement between spectator and protagonist essential to tragedy. For example, in the scene in which Titus and Marcus finally discover who violated Lavinia, Marcus urges "Mortal revenge upon these traitorous Goths." Titus, maddened with grief, responds in a way that anticipates Hamlet: his first impulse is to write down what he has heard; his second, to proceed by indirection, using his grandson to bear a cryptic message to Tamora. Titus, Lavinia, and the boy then leave the stage, and Marcus is left alone to direct the audience's response. He begins by posing the kind of question Hieronimo had repeatedly asked:

> O heavens, can you hear a good man groan
> And not relent, or not compassion him?
> Marcus, attend him in his ecstasy,
> That hath more scars of sorrow in his heart
> Than foemen's marks upon his batt'red shield,
> But yet so just that he will not revenge.
> Revenge the heavens for old Andronicus!
> (IV, i, 123-29)[28]

The last two lines of this speech are somewhat puzzling, for it has not been clear from the preceding dialogue that Titus has indeed rejected revenge. Rather, the audience has been given a confused sense of Titus' feelings, which are left to Marcus to explain and pass judgment upon.

The character who most obviously channels audience sympathy toward the Andronici is Aaron the Moor, whose self-proclaiming opening monologue (II, i) links him with the aspiring minds of the conqueror plays. Using the rhetoric of Tamburlaine, he scorns "slavish weeds" and vows to "mount aloft" by allying himself with Tamora, whom his description transforms into an archetypal "other," a siren who destroys men, an anti-goddess whose frown causes virtue to stop and tremble. Aaron is the source of much of the play's energy. Vice-like, he confides in the audience, sharing with them the sheer pleasure he takes in cunning stratagems and excellent pieces of villainy, as he manipulates accomplices and victims alike to serve his turn.[29] His is the agent of Tamora's revenges throughout the play, and the casualness of his indulgence in evil gives the play a comic tone that frequently enables the audience to remain detached from the grotesque sufferings of

---

[28] This and all other quotations from Shakespeare's plays are taken from *The Riverside Shakespeare*, ed. G. Blakemore Evans (Boston, 1974).

[29] Aaron's resemblance to the Vice is discussed at length by Spivack, *Shakespeare and the Allegory of Evil*, pp. 380-86.

his victims. The link between his passion for Tamora and his acts of aggression is reminiscent of Tamburlaine and Zenocrate. This love, which evolves into a poignant devotion to their child, gives him more humanity, at least momentarily, than the play's Goths and Romans.[30] On the other hand, Aaron's blackness is clearly meant to be a visual sign of his "otherness," particularly when he uses his Moorish traits to express the absoluteness of his evil: "My fleece of woolly hair that now uncurls,/ Even as an adder . . ." (II, iii, 34-35).[31] So do other characters, notably Lavinia and Bassianus, in the scene in which they taunt Tamora, firing her desire for revenge and thus bringing their doom upon themselves. One wonders how Shakespeare intended his audience to react to this scene: were they supposed to feel that the taunts were justified, or is this another instance of human errors in judgment which recoil upon their authors? Is Shakespeare partly rejecting the cruel stereotypes that his countrymen associated with Moors, as he would later do in *Othello*? But is he also using his Moor as the morality playwrights used their Vices, to comment on the decadent passivity of both Romans and Goths?

These questions are not easily answered, for too often neither characters nor strands of plot are fully developed in *Titus Andronicus*. Instead, the play explores some of the ideas that Kyd had dealt with, ideas that will recur in other Elizabethan and Jacobean revenge tragedies. Titus' suffering is as much metaphysical as emotional; he shares Hieronimo's quest for

[30] So, at least, argues Nicholas Brooke, in *Shakespeare's Early Tragedies* (London, 1968), p. 24.

[31] Leslie Fiedler sees Aaron as an "embodiment of . . . psychic blackness" and suggests that Shakespeare was "suiting the expectations of an audience to whom Moors seemed creatures more diabolical than human." *The Stranger in Shakespeare* (New York, 1972), p. 179. For another discussion of antiblack prejudice as used by Shakespeare, see G. K. Hunter's "Othello and Colour Prejudice," in *Dramatic Identities and Cultural Tradition*. He sees "careless assumptions about 'Moors' " being manipulated in *Othello* and suggests that the audience could abandon these prejudices because they knew that "the breach between the chosen and non-chosen could be closed by faith" (pp. 47-48).

justice, though he does not experience his terrible and pro-
longed uncertainty about the identity of his antagonist. Both
characters demonstrate their inherent virtue by trusting to the
heavens, and both are maddened by the heaven's inability or
refusal to right the wrongs they have endured. As in *The Spanish Tragedy*, the desire for revenge is associated with madness,
a form of "otherness" which in some ways is more terrifying
and alienating than the "otherness" of the calculating Machiavel or the inhuman Vice, because of the threat it poses to our
belief in rationality. At times, madness becomes a form of
living psychological hell, particularly since the audience is never
sure whether it is feigned or real. The crux of both Titus' and
Hieronimo's tragedies is their eventual inability to distinguish
justice from revenge, a point Shakespeare first presents obliquely
in an emblematic mad scene. Faced with the realization that
"*Terras Astraea reliquit*," Titus instructs his kinsmen to dig
beneath the earth to seek Justice from Pluto. Publius, to "feed
his humor," replies that Titus may have Revenge from hell if
he will, but that Justice is "employ'd" with Jove in heaven,
"So that perforce you must needs stay a time" (IV, iii, 4, 38-
42). Shakespeare seems to be saying that Justice cannot be
summoned, as the forces of evil can (one thinks of Faustus
and Mephostophilis). But the message that the injured man
must "stay," or wait for Providence to shape events, eludes
Titus, who insists on soliciting the gods with letters attached
to arrows which he gives Marcus and the others to shoot into
the air. The scene is at once pathetic and comic, a farcical act
of futility and "a mad gesture [of] protest against tragic life."[32]

If madness is terrifying to the audience, it can also be pu-
rifying and transforming for the character who endures it. In
his madness, Titus comes to realize that he has caused his own
misery. Addressing "ungrateful Rome," he says, "well, well, I
made thee miserable/ What time I threw the people's suf-

[32] Brooke, *Shakespeare's Early Tragedies*, p. 47. Richard T. Brucher in "Comic
Violence in *Titus Andronicus*," *Renaissance Drama N.S. X* (1979), 71-91, makes
a similar observation about the play's final scene, in which the audience experiences a tension between the tragic and the ludicrous (p. 87).

frages/ On him that thus doth tyrannize o'er me" (IV, iii, 4, 17-20). In this respect he anticipates the wisdom in madness of Lear, who was also preoccupied with injustice and ingratitude (later in this scene, when he mistakes the clown for Jupiter's messenger, he is even more Lear-like). This awareness of self helps to generate sympathy, as Robert Y. Turner observes, by giving him an inner life apart from his deeds. We still hold him responsible for his actions, yet we realize that judgment is inadequate and that, like the most complex dramatic characters, he eludes familiar moral categories.[33]

Events finally conspire to prompt Titus' revenge in the weird and unlikely scene in which Tamora comes to Titus disguised as Revenge. The language of hell and damnation which dominates her lines removes any doubt the audience may have had about the moral status of revenge. As in *Hamlet*, there is an ironic and accidental quality to the circumstances leading to revenge; Tamora, by pretending to be a temptation figure, does in fact become one, by offering Titus the opportunity to seize her two sons. The very elements that make this scene seem so contrived to a modern audience might have served as evidence to a sixteenth-century one that Providence was indeed intervening, turning Tamora into the agent of her own destruction and Titus into the instrument of revenging gods.[34] But that audience might also have recognized in the conventions of masque and disguise an allusion to the old morality play devils and vices, and realized that God was using Tamora, now metamorphosed into a wicked fiend, to try the elect or confirm the reprobation of the damned.[35] By succumbing to the temptation offered him, Titus completes his descent into a damnation which can only lead to death. He undergoes a

[33] Turner, *Shakespeare's Apprenticeship*, p. 238.

[34] Ronald Broude, "Roman and Goth in *Titus Andronicus*," *Shakespeare Studies* VI (1970), 27-34. See also A. C. Hamilton in *The Early Shakespeare* (San Marino, California, 1967) who notes that while others seek revenge, Titus seeks Justice, until Revenge quite literally comes to him (p. 85).

[35] Cf. the discussion of Gifford's *Discourse of the subtill Practises of Deuilles* in Chapter VII.

more tragic metamorphosis than Tamora, because it is accompanied by more extreme suffering, but, like her, he has transcended the limits of humanity by the end of the play.[36]

With Titus' death, and the deaths of nearly every other character in the play, the state is purged of evil, and can now be rebuilt by Lucius, who is proclaimed Emperor by the "common voice." As Lucius pauses over his father's body, the parent-child motif, so central to this play, is evoked for the last time. Lucius describes Titus to his young son as a paternal figure who danced his grandson on his knee and told him many a pretty tale. This is a man the audience never really knew. The image lingers as the play comes to an end, contrasting sharply with Aaron's unrepentant villainy and Lucius' final reference to "that ravenous tiger Tamora . . . [whose] life was beastly and devoid of pity." The audience is left feeling that Titus, a man at once noble yet flawed in judgment, has been drawn into a nightmarish world of evil and has himself become part of that world. He has become a revenger among revengers, murdering his own children and the children of others. The grotesque horrors he succumbs to are apalling, but their very extremeness has an important salutary effect: it confirms the audience in their own sense of election, by offering them a spectacle of the "other" utterly removed from the realm of experience they inhabit.

V. *The Jew of Malta*

The Jew of Malta also piles horror on horror to create a world which the audience can regard from a distance, a distance made even greater by Marlowe's comic treatment of his protagonist. Barabas is not, strictly speaking, a revenger in the

---

[36] For extended discussions of the theme of metamorphosis in *Titus Andronicus*, see Brooke's analysis in *Shakespeare's Early Tragedies* (pp. 21 ff.), and Eugene Waith's, in "Metamorphosis of Violence in *Titus Andronicus*," *Shakespeare Survey*, 10 (1957), 39-51. Waith argues that Shakespeare was strongly influenced by Ovid's ideas about metamorphosis, and that, like Ovid, he was more interested in psychic metamorphosis than physical.

manner of Hamlet, Hieronimo, and Titus, for he has lost neither a child nor a parent as the result of another's villainy. Indeed, Marlowe is concerned only in the most irreverent way with the morality of revenge, but much of the play's success in the early 1590s must have depended on the audience's tendency to regard the play in the light of the moral issues with which contemporary plays and sermons and tracts dealt more explicitly. Marlowe appears to observe the rules of revenge tragedy by providing Barabas with an excuse for revenge in the confiscation of his wealth by the corrupt and hypocritical Ferneze. But Barabas is no conventional victim, for the audience's attitude toward him has already been shaped by Machiavel's prologue, which presents thirty lines of maxims reflecting the sixteenth-century image of Machiavelli, followed by a declaration of kinship with the Jew "Who smiles to see how full his bags are crammed,/ Which money was not got without my means" (32-33).[37] Like the prologue to I Tamburlaine, Machiavel invites the audience to "grace him as he deserves," his use of the word "grace" a deliberate and ironic allusion to divine grace.

In the play's opening scene Barabas reveals himself to the audience through soliloquies and asides which employ the Vice's technique of sharing his tactics with the audience, concluding with a triumphant proclamation of his reigning principle: "Ego mihimet sum semper proximus." These soliloquies serve to isolate and establish the primacy of Barabas as protagonist, drawing the audience into a conspiratorial relationship with him. Like Faustus and Tamburlaine, he seduces the audience with the splendor of his imagination, as he speaks of the "Bags of fiery opals, sapphires, amethysts,/ Jacinths, hard topaz, grass-green emeralds,/ Beauteous rubies, sparkling diamonds" wherein consist his wealth (I, i, 25-27). This wealth is proof that he is a member of a specially favored elect who are enriched with

---

[37] This and other quotations from *The Jew of Malta* are taken from the Revels edition, ed. N. W. Bawcutt (Manchester, 1978).

"blessings promised to the Jews." Reflecting on his fortune, he muses:

> What more may heaven do for earthly men
> Than thus to pour out plenty in their laps,
> Ripping the bowels of the earth for them,
> Making the sea their servant, and the winds
> To drive their substance with successful blasts?
>
> (I, i, 106-110)

Viewed in the context of the doctrine of election, this violent vision of worldly wealth falls ironically short of the spiritual benefits earthly man receives from heaven. In an even more characteristically Marlovian soliloquy, Barabas tells the audience that "Barabas is born to better chance/ And framed of finer mould than common men,/ That measure naught but by the present time" (I, ii, 220-22). Like Tamburlaine's "earthly crown" speech, these lines use the techniques of ironic inversion, mocking the language of assurance and the bombast of the hero alike.

The Jews' state of election is defined quite differently by Ferneze, the Christian governor of Malta who must pay ten year's tribute to the Turks. He summons the Jews and tells them that "through our sufferance of your hateful lives,/ Who stand accursed in the sight of heaven,/ These taxes and afflictions are befallen" (I, ii, 63-65). The audience is thus given two diametrically opposite perspectives from which to view Barabas, neither of which they can wholeheartedly accept. Clearly he is neither the chosen man of God he believes himself to be nor the damned "other" Ferneze dismisses him as. The audience would easily see through the Christians' self-serving effort to cast Barabas in the role of the scapegoat, who must "want for a common good" and be "poor and scorned of all the world" in order to "save the ruin of a multitude," for no other reason than his "inherent sin" (98-110). As Wilbur Sanders suggests, this is a scathing parody of Christian self-righteousness, particularly in its equation of Christian zeal

201

with a desire for financial gain.[38] Even if, as Leslie Fiedler has suggested, the Elizabethan community demanded a Jewish scapegoat on the stage against whom to vent their wrath and anxiety about the scandal involving Elizabeth's Jewish physician, Ferneze's tactics are contemptible.[39]

Barabas is also viewed as a scapegoat by his fellow Jews, who liken him to Job. Their pious passivity makes his energetic unwillingness to accept defeat seem admirable by comparison. But Barabas is not the victim that he seems to be in the play's opening scenes, as the audience discovers once his fellow Jews leave the stage and he drops his guise of outraged innocence. Vice-like, he congratulates himself on his cleverness and foresight, and begins plotting to retrieve his hidden wealth. As Machiavel had implied in his prologue, Barabas has long embraced and initiated villainy for its own sake. The catalogue of activities presented in the boastful set speech of Act II, scene iii, includes every kind of offense:

> As for myself, I walk abroad o' nights,
> And kill sick people groaning under walls;
> Sometimes I go about and poison wells;
> And now and then, to cherish Christian thieves,
> I am content to lose some of my crowns . . .
> Being young, I studied physic and began
> To practice first upon the Italian . . .

[38] Wilbur Sanders, *The Dramatist and the Received Idea* (Cambridge, 1968), pp. 43 ff. Sanders, disturbed by the "hard, self-righteous timber" of Marlowe's laughter, notes that he seems to draw on contempt rather than engaging the audience's capacity for self-criticism. But, as N. W. Bawcutt suggests, *The Jew of Malta* can be viewed as a serious statement designed to make its audience aware of the absurdity of their pretensions to moral superiority in a way that could be viewed as corrective (Introduction, pp. 36-37).

[39] Fiedler, *The Stranger in Shakespeare*, p. 86. Fiedler notes the ambiguity inherent in the Jew's identity as "stranger" or "alien": "Christianity managed to make the New Testament its Scripture without surrendering the Old, and in the course of doing so, worked out ways of regarding the Jews simultaneously as the ultimate enemy, the killers of Christ, and the chosen people . . ." (p. 117).

> And after that I was an engineer . . .
> Then after that I was an usurer. . . .
>   (II, iii, 171 ff.)

This monologue, as Douglas Cole has pointed out, is deliberately unrealistic, for it represents Barabas as a self-proclaimed embodiment of all the evils of which the Jews were accused. As is characteristic of the Vice, the list of Barabas' exploits transcends the "mortal limitations of space and time,"[40] and the result is a compendium of forms of "otherness" which eludes dramatic representation (just as Faustus' aspirations do; in both plays the audience is asked to accept the stageable pranks and plots as substitutes for more far-reaching activities). Despite Ferneze's provocation one never feels that Barabas has been forced into villainy; to do evil is simply in his nature.

Marlowe's depiction of human evil in its most extreme form is balanced in a starkly dualistic scheme by his depiction of human goodness. Barabas' daughter Abigail is an interesting composite of traditional character types, and her undisputed identity as a member of the elect is clearly reflected in the plot. That Abigail can undergo a conversion distinguishes her from the other characters in the play, whose moral status remains constant throughout. She is a traditional female victim figure, but with a passing resemblance to a morality play protagonist who experiences conversion, though she does so without the guidance of virtuous allegorical figures. In her final scene, as she prays for her father's salvation with her dying words, she serves as a powerful comment on the villainy of all of the play's other characters. Her death is neither tragic, because she is so clearly better off in heaven, nor is it the source of another's tragedy, and thus it lacks the significance that it might have in a different play. Marlowe's total concentration of goodness in the figure of Abigail is one of the principal dif-

---

[40] Douglas Cole, *Suffering and Evil in the Plays of Christopher Marlowe* (Princeton, 1962), p. 140.

ferences between *The Jew of Malta* and the other revenge plays of the late 1580s. Good and evil are utterly polarized, and there is never any indication that goodness can be corrupted and transformed by evil. Since the tragic impact of the revenge situation derives from its effectiveness in dramatizing this transformation, Barabas, though he engages in revenge plots, can never be a revenger in the tragic sense of the word.

Barabas nevertheless remains a fascinating and morally ambiguous character when set against the world in which Marlowe has placed him. On the most basic level of the play he may be the devil incarnate, the anti-Christ whose name invokes the archetypal reprobate in one of Christendom's first legendary dualities—Christ and thief Barabbas. Critics have seen him as a monster, a spectacle of personified evil, the absolute "other" who embodies everything the Elizabethans regarded as alien.[41] But when juxtaposed with the rest of the play's cast, Barabas can also be viewed as the comic and clever persecutor of the degenerate papists who were as hated as Jews in the England of the 1580s and were certainly the more immediate threat.[42] Watching scenes such as the one in which Barabas plays off the corrupt friars against one another, exposing the greed which they attempt to disguise as religious zeal, the Elizabethan audience might have forgotten to disapprove of Barabas as they enjoyed his exposure and manipulation of papist hypocrisy. On this level, he is the play's most

[41] Harry Levin points out the allusion to Barabbas the thief in *The Overreacher* (Boston, 1952). For appraisals of Barabas as a monster and personification of evil, see Cole, in *Suffering and Evil*, and M. M. Mahood in *Poetry and Humanism* (London, 1950). For Barabas as "a serio-comic villain," see Charles G. Masinton, *Christopher Marlowe's Tragic Vision* (Athens, Ohio, 1972), p. 56. David Bevington discusses and rejects the idea that Barabas is a sympathetic character in the first two acts and a villain in the last three in his discussion of the legacy of the Vice in *From Mankin to Marlowe* (Cambridge, Massachusetts, 1962), pp. 220 ff.

[42] Alfred Harbage notes in "Innocent Barabas," *Tulane Drama Review* (Summer, 1964), that a disapproval of Catholicism could be "incorporated in an approved Christianity," for "to be simultaneously 'pro' and 'anti' in religious sentiment presented no difficulties to the Elizabethan mind" (p. 53).

admirable character, always excepting Abigail, whose suffering as she is forced to assist in contriving the deaths of her beloved and his rival might inspire a pity in the audience that undermines their admiration for Barabas's cunning. This pity falls short of sympathetic identification, though, for Abigail's saintly goodness, her willingness to be made a victim, links her to the passive Jews of Act I. One of the revenge play's most interesting and historically relevant features is its exploration of the conflicting merits of passive endurance and heroic, assertive resistance. One cannot help admiring Barabas as he fights back, not only against the Christians who seek to exploit him, but against his partner in crime, the crafty Turkish slave Ithamore, who joins with some underworld acquaintances to steal Barabas's wealth.

Despised by Christians and infidels alike, Barabas refuses to be a victim, despite everyone's repeated efforts to cast him in that role, efforts bolstered by the morally questionable justification that, as Ithamore puts it, "To undo a Jew is charity, and not sin" (IV, iv, 80). With these lines, Marlowe mocks self-serving moral distinctions just as, throughout the play, he exposes the prejudices of his audience by placing the rhetoric of assurance in the mouths of Christians and Jews alike, all of whom see themselves as elect by contrast with the damned "other." In their presumption, they take upon themselves God's role, consigning their enemies to damnation. Barabas, furious with the Christians who have seized his wealth, intones:

> I ban their souls to everlasting pains
> And extreme tortures of the fiery deep
> That thus have dealt with me in my distress.
> (II, ii, 167-69)

With equal authority, Friar Jacomo says to Barabas, "Thou has offended, therefore must be damned" (IV, i, 25). Even Katharine, the mother of Abigail's beloved, pulls her son away from Barabas, telling him "Converse not with him; he is cast off from heaven" (II, iii, 160). Marlowe undertakes his most sustained satire, however, in the character of Ferneze, who is an obvious caricature of the wicked man who believes himself to be of the elect. A pious man of policy who regards himself as God's agent on earth, Ferneze greets the news that Barabas and his accusers are dead with: "Wonder not at it, sir, the heavens are just" (V, i, 55). Moments later, when he is captured by Barabas, risen from the dead and now in league with Calymath, he tells his captor: "O villain, heaven will be revenged on thee" (V, ii, 25). Like the Christians of *II Tamburlaine*, Ferneze breaks his word, and the play ends more ironically than tragically—not only because Barabas dies in his own outrageous trap, but because Ferneze, after engineering the betrayal, sums up the entire proceeding with his final sanctimonious couplet:

> So, march away, and let due praise be given
> Neither to fate nor fortune, but to heaven.[43]
> (V, v, 122-23)

The moral simplicity of this couplet is hardly adequate as a reflection of the audience's feelings about Barabas at the end of the play. They have just witnessed his downfall, which is quite literally enacted as the floor of the upper stage gives way and he falls into a cauldron below. This fall is caused both by his own careless and strangely uncharacteristic trust in his old enemy Ferneze, and by the villainy of the Christians who have once again made him a scapegoat—quite literally, for the final image of Barabas in the cauldron almost suggests that he is about to be cooked and eaten in a diabolic parody of the ritual of the eucharist. The cauldron was a conventional medieval symbol of hell, where the wicked are punished by being boiled in oil, and it explicitly links Barabas with the damned.[44]

But as he dies cursing the "damn'd Christian dogs and Turkish infidels" who will survive him, the audience is re-

[43] Bevington notes that Marlowe has created villains out of the very persons whom the structure of the play has cast in the roles of agents of retribution, thus creating a deeply disturbing ambiguity.

[44] G. K. Hunter, "The Theology of Marlowe's *The Jew of Malta*," in *Dramatic Identities and Cultural Tradition*, p. 93.

minded that Barabas is only one damned soul among many in the play, and they withhold the full force of their condemnation. Like the Faustus of Act I, the dying Barabas urges himself to strive for resolution, a quality which belongs to the Machiavel and the elect alike. Like Hieronimo and Aaron, he boasts of his plots, and, like them, shows no sign of repentance or regret. Barabas's unregretted wickedness has defined him as an "other" all along, and his end is consistent with his beginning. In his pure enjoyment of villainy and aspiration toward ever more ambitious schemes and plots, he enters the sphere of pure fantasy which Tamburlaine and Faustus inhabited and which the audience, for a brief two hours, could inhabit as well. Through Barabas, they vicariously enact those revenges to which the frustrations of daily life tempt them but from which they abstain out of obedience to Christian doctrine and civil law.

Speculating about the audience's ability to identify with characters like Barabas or Richard III because of their daring and intelligence, yet get equal pleasure from seeing them overthrown, Muriel Bradbrook hypothesized that the disguise convention familiarized Elizabethans with rapid shifts of this sort, enabling them to think of one character as playing two parts (just as one actor often did).[45] In effect, the audience was able to enter into two different and even opposite relationships with a character, knowing that in the fictional world of the play these relationships need never come in conflict. The revenge play, it seems to me, made its most significant contribution to the emergence of tragedy by encouraging just this kind of dualism in the audience's relationship with the protagonist. By playing with the Elizabethan's perception of the protagonist as both villain and victim, the authors of the early revenge plays helped to create the ambivalence that later audiences would feel for tragic protagonists who did not degenerate into "others" in as obvious a sense. Moreover, the

[45] Muriel Bradbrook, *Themes and Conventions of Elizabethan Tragedy* (1935; rpt., Cambridge, 1964), p. 66.

villain and victim archetypes stand for two contrasting states, that of the actor and that of the acted upon. Since human existence is a combination of both, these archetypes each represent a kind of "otherness" which is essentially remote from human experience. As we have seen in *The Jew of Malta*, neither archetype inspires a simple response; if the victim invites sympathy and the villain a corresponding repudiation, it is also true that the bold and assertive man of action is more "like ourselves" as we wish to be viewed than the passive and helpless sufferer. In an age which equated heroism with bold action and viewed the elect as resolute and unyielding, the revenger's decision to take action was an ambiguous one indeed.

CHAPTER VII

Doctor Faustus

In *The Tragical History of the Life and Death of Doctor Faustus* Marlowe draws upon some of the oldest, most traditional elements from the morality play—The Good and Bad Angels, the Heavenly Man-Worldly Man dual-protagonist scheme unevenly embodied in the Old Man and Faustus, the spectacle of the Seven Deadly Sins, and the dragon, devils, and traditional gaping hell beneath the stage. Among these he placed a protagonist who seeks out damnation more explicitly than any morality play character had done, and who dies in a torment more terrible than anything the morality playwrights had dared to represent onstage. In the evolution of English drama, *Doctor Faustus* can be viewed as a final rejection of the original morality pattern, with its assurance that divine forgiveness remains always within reach. For a society that sought everywhere for signs of election, Faustus was the ultimate "other," deliberately embracing damnation in a blasphemous parody of Christ's sacrifice for man.

If *Doctor Faustus* were simply a didactic demonstration of the proud man's rebellion against God, it would lose much of its interest for scholars and audiences alike. What makes Marlowe's play so fascinating is its dramatic treatment of one of the most important issues of its day. At the core of the play is the same central paradox which defines Elizabethan Puritanism: predestined election to salvation or damnation determines the spiritual state of each soul at birth, yet repentance is everywhere and at all times possible and to be encouraged. Faustus is at once free to damn or redeem himself, yet he is constrained by a devil with whom he makes an irreversible pact. For the Elizabethans, the haunting fear that they were living a life predetermined to end in damnation—a fear of becoming the evil selves of their most terrible imaginings—

made Faustus' life a tragic reflection of what their own could be.[1] Repentance, before Calvin, had been the easy remedy for despair; by the 1580s and 1590s, it could be presented as the unattainable tragic ideal.[2] More than any other play of its age, *Doctor Faustus* confronts the essential question of man's freedom of choice, and the problematic relationship between free will and predetermined fate.

Marlowe also explores another related subject about which the Elizabethans were deeply ambivalent. Initially, much of Faustus' complexity as a character results from the audience's uncertainty about whether to enjoy or disapprove of his aspiration. A brilliant scholar, Faustus possesses the yearning for greatness that the Elizabethans admired. Spurred onward by a desire for knowledge, and the power that knowledge confers, he resembles some of the most admired aspiring minds of his age, men whose boldness and ambition could be signs either of damnation or election. He aims not downward at those things commonly associated with sin and wickedness, but upward at powers possessed by God and thus not at all wicked in themselves. Nor does he deny God's possession of them; like Tamburlaine, who styles himself the scourge of God, thereby implicitly acknowledging God's power and authority, Faustus aspires to godhead, thereby affirming God's omnipotence. Assuming God's uppermost position in the ordered hierarchy, both Tamburlaine and Faustus strive to acquire that position for themselves. In a sense, they are most blasphemous even as they are most orthodox, as Philologus was in *The Conflict of Conscience*. The fact that heroic striving was some-

[1] Cf. Robert G. Hunter in *Shakespeare and the Mystery of God's Judgments* (Athens, Georgia, 1976). Hunter believes that tragedy emerged from the fear that one is living a life predetermined by an apparently unjust God, a fear of hell. Whether this is a belief or just fear of a possibility, "it can be evoked as tragic terror and coped with through the familiar therapeutic process of tragedy" (p. 34). On our fear of becoming our evil selves as part of our response to *Doctor Faustus*, see Constance Brown Kuriyama in *Hammer and Anvil* (New Brunswick, New Jersey, 1980), p. 133.

[2] Robert Potter, *The English Morality Play* (London, 1975), p. 129.

times indistinguishable from blasphemous presumption made Faustus' dilemma a tragic one.

As in the case of the Tamburlaine plays, a fortunate discovery of a contemporary prose narrative gave Marlowe the basic outlines of his play. Faust, like Tamburlaine, was a legendary figure of more than human stature, around whom a body of material had begun to accumulate in the mid-sixteenth century, finally appearing in print in 1587 as the Spies *Faustbook*. The scholar, vagabond, and reputed magician named John Faust who lived and traveled in Germany in the early sixteenth century was, as the modern editors of the Faust material observe, "merely the lodestone about which gathered in time a mass of superstition which in turn is the deposit of centuries."[3] Accounts of earlier magicians, in particular the legends of Simon Magus and Theophilus, the first magus to enter into a compact with Satan, were widely known throughout the Middle Ages. These legends contributed specific elements to the Faust story, and, more important, created a set of conventional attitudes toward the Faust figure which Marlowe could use as he played upon his audience's expectations.

By the time it was formulated in the Spies *Faustbook*, the Faust legend had come to reflect the Lutheran condemnation of ungodly speculation, even as it continued to delight its readers with accounts of Faustus' exploits. The unidentified "P. F." translated the Spies *Faustbook* into English sometime before the end of 1592 (possibly before 1590), and it was this version of the legend that Marlowe used as his source.[4] *The*

[3] Philip Mason Palmer and Robert Pattison More, *The Sources of the Faust Tradition from Simon Magus to Lessing* (New York, 1936), p. 4.

[4] Palmer and More believe that a reference to Pope Sixtus in the present tense in the English *Faustbook* indicates that the translation was made before his death in August, 1590 (*The Sources of the Faust Tradition*, p. 177). An early date for the *Faustbook* would support the theory that *Doctor Faustus* was written right after *II Tamburlaine*, in 1588 or 1589. Paul H. Kocher is the major advocate for an early date for *Doctor Faustus*; his argument appears in "The English Faust Book and the Date of Marlowe's Faustus," *Modern Language Notes*, 55 (1940), 95-101. W. W. Greg is the major spokesman for the theory that *Doctor Faustus* was written in 1592; his argument appears in the

History of the damnable life and deserved death of Doctor John Faustus, as its title suggests, is markedly moralistic in bent, and the narrative voice comments freely and frequently on the doctrinal implications of Faustus' actions and the lessons learned therefrom. P. F. has no doubts about Faustus' state of election, as his observations at the end of the first chapter indicate:

> It is written, no man can serue two masters : and, thou shalt not tempt the Lord thy God : but *Faustus* threw all this in the winde, & made his soule of no estimation, regarding more his worldly pleasure than ye ioyes to come : therfore at ye day of iudgement there is no hope of his redemptio (p. 136).

Marlowe's counterpart to P. F.'s moralistic narrative voice is the chorus which frames the play with a prologue and an epilogue. Marlowe's prologue is deliberately evasive, characterizing the performance about to begin as "The form of Faustus' fortunes, good or bad" (Pro., 8).[5] Some fifteen lines later,

---

introduction to his parallel text edition of the play, *Marlowe's Doctor Faustus: 1604-1616* (Oxford, 1950), and has been accepted by a majority of recent critics and scholars. However, Samuel Schoenbaum, in his revision of Alfred Harbage's *Annals of English Drama: 975-1700*, states that the argument for the early date has been "recently urged again" (p. 56), suggesting that Greg's word is by no means the last. Both the 1604 and the 1616 texts of *Doctor Faustus* borrow freely from the *Faustbook*: for example, the details of the conjuring scene, the magic circle, the thunder and lightning, the spectacular appearance of Mephostophilis in the form of a dragon and then his reappearance as a friar—all these come from the *Faustbook*. So do the visit to the papal palace and the snatching of the Pope's meat and drink (but not the escape of Bruno) and the appearance of Alexander and his paramour at the request of the Emperor. Marlowe also borrowed the tricking of the sleeping knight and his attempted revenge, the incident of the detachable leg, the deception of the Horse-courser, the pregnant Duchess of Vanholt's request for grapes, and the appearance of the beautiful Helen (who quite explicitly becomes Faustus' "bedfellow" in the *Faustbook* and bears him a child).

[5] All quotations from *Doctor Faustus* are taken from *The Complete Plays of Christopher Marlowe*, ed. Irving Ribner (New York, 1963). For occasional distinctions between the 1604 text ("A text") and the 1616 text ("B text") I have used W. W. Greg's parallel text edition. I have tried to keep my critical

however, the audience is given an image of Faustus as an Icarus figure, one whose "waxen wings did mount above his reach,/ And melting, heavens conspired his overthrow" (21-22). The time sequence implied in these lines, as Max Bluestone has observed, is equivocal: did the heavens conspire, or bring about, Faustus' initial abjuration (the "mounting," or aspiration which preceded the "melting," and fall), or did the conspiracy occur only after and because of the failure of his aspirations?[6] Does the past tense of the verb "conspired" hint at predestined reprobation, and, if so, to what extent does Faustus cause his own overthrow? And, finally, does Faustus' overthrow or fall necessarily mean that, in P. F.'s words, there is no hope for his redemption at any point in the play? These are only some of the questions which the seemingly conventional prologue invites the audience to ask.

I. THE PURSUIT OF DAMNATION

In choosing Faustus as his protagonist, Marlowe gave his audience a character whose reprobation depended not merely on the subjective judgment of his condemners, but on a contract with the devil—an act performed onstage. This would necessarily create a relationship between audience and character which was quite different from the shifting sense of moral distance that the audience had felt for Tamburlaine. Even Philologus, the most explicitly damned morality play protag-

---

interpretation of the play free from textual arguments and based on passages shared by the two texts, following the advice of Constance Brown Kuriyama in "Dr. Greg and *Doctor Faustus*: The Supposed Originality of the 1616 Text," *ELR*, 5 (1975), 171-97. Kuriyama believes that it is likely that both texts are "bad" in very different ways, but is inclined to agree with Fredson Bowers that the 1616 text is closer to Marlowe's original. Bowers' arguments appear in "Marlowe's *Doctor Faustus*: The 1616 Additions," *Studies in Bibliography*, 26 (1973), 1-18.

[6] Max Bluestone, "*Libido Speculandi*: Doctrine and Dramaturgy in Contemporary Interpretations of Marlowe's *Doctor Faustus*," *Reinterpretations of Elizabethan Drama: Selected Papers from the English Institute*, ed. Norman Rabkin (New York, 1969), p. 35.

onist (in the original version), was not visibly and irrevocably damned, as Faustus seems to be after the completion of his contract with Mephostophilis. Indeed, Philologus' self-proclaimed reprobation was subject to all of the uncertainties and ambiguities characteristic of Puritan doctrine, as revealed, for instance, in this defense of Francis Spera by William Perkins:

> Yet they are much overseene that write of him as a damned creature. For first, who can tell whether he despaired finally or no? Secondly, in the very middest of his desperation, hee complaineth of the hardnesse of heart: and the feeling of corruption in the heart, is by some contrary grace; so that we may conveniently thinke, that he was not quite bereft of all goodnesse: though hee neither felt it then, nor shewed it to the beholders.[7]

The "who can tell" of Perkins' argument was an objection which could legitimately be lodged whenever a mortal presumed to pronounce upon the state of election of another mortal. Marlowe's audience knew this, and thus the theatrical effect of the contract signed in blood, with its implied parody of the communion ceremony, gave Faustus' transformation into the "other" a certainty and definition which never occurred in real life.

For the Elizabethan audience, Faustus' status as a reprobate depended not only on the scene in which his damnation is acted out literally in Act II; just as important are the preceding scenes in which he knowingly and deliberately seeks out damnation. Faustus embraces damnation not by blindly and impulsively committing a crime or succumbing to irresistible lusts, but, rather, as the result of a reasoned intellectual debate with himself. He begins by vowing to "live and die in Aristotle's works," but then impatiently rejects the art of logic because it affords "no greater miracle" than disputing well (I, i, 5, 9). The desire to effect miracles leads him to consider

---

[7] William Perkins, *A Golden Chaine* (London, 1635), p. 378.

medicine, but he is dissatisfied with his ability to cure desperate maladies, and wants instead to be able to resurrect the dead. He then rejects the study of law, which merely "fits a mercenary drudge/ Who aims at nothing but external trash" (34-35). As he reviews these forms of knowledge he is urged onward by the desire to transcend human limitations, to be more than "but Faustus and a man" (23). And so he arrives at what the audience would have regarded as the admirable conclusion that "When all is done, divinity is best" (37). But of course this is not a conclusion, for, with hardly a pause, Faustus advances still further, toward a rejection of the Christian belief in salvation. He does so not out of ignorance, as a Turk or a Jew might do, but by entering into precisely the same activity in which Protestant preachers and laymen alike were zealously engaged—the reading of scripture and the piecing together of arguments from well-known tags and phrases.

Faustus rejects divinity on the strength of a syllogism based upon two frequently used verses from the Bible, each taken out of context:

> Jerome's Bible, Faustus, view it well:
> *Stipendium peccati mors est.* Ha! *Stipendium*, etc.
> The reward of sin is death. That's hard.
> *Si peccasse negamus, fallimur*
> *Et nulla est in nobis veritas.*
> If we say that we have no sin,
> We deceive ourselves, and there's no truth in us.
> Why then belike we must sin,
> And so consequently die.
> Ay, we must die an everlasting death.
> What doctrine call you this? *Che, sera, sera*:
> What will be, shall be! Divinity, adieu!
> $\qquad\qquad\qquad$ (I, i, 38-49)

The passages in their entirety read as follows in the Revised Standard Version:

For the wages of sin is death; but the free gift of God is
eternal life in Christ Jesus our Lord.
(Romans 6:23)

If we say that we have no sin, we deceive ourselves, and the
truth is not in us.
If we confess our sins, he is faithful and just and will forgive
our sins, and cleanse us from all unrighteousness.
(I John 1:8, 9)

By omitting the corollary phrase of each text Faustus has entered into no daring and exotic apostasy such as Marlowe
himself was accused of in the Baines note, but rather has
stumbled in a familiar way by failing to consider the text as a
whole.[8] As Kocher notes, the two parts of the passage from I
John readily lent themselves to syllogistic treatment. In the
"Dialogue Between the Christian Knight and Satan," by
Thomas Becon, Satan accuses the Knight of not having kept
the Ten Commandments and uses the words that Faustus
quotes in an attempt to convince the Knight that he will be
damned forever. The Knight rejoins by posing the gospel
against the law, arguing that he can simultaneously acknowledge that he is a sinner "guilty of everlasting damnation," and
believe in Christ, "by . . . [which] faith all my sins are forgiven
me. . . ."[9] Whereas Becon's dialogue represents the dominant
strain in Elizabethan Protestantism, Faustus, it has been suggested, takes the extreme Calvinist position; his "we" includes
only the reprobate, and his fatalistic doctrine "What will be,
shall be" excludes the Semi-Pelagian view so frequently invoked to temper the bleakness of the doctrine of election (i.e.,
that the believer, through his own efforts, can help bring about
his salvation).[10]

[8] Faustus' failure to complete the text in his syllogism was first noted by
Helen Gardner in "Milton's 'Satan' and the Theme of Damnation in Eliza-
bethan Tragedy," *Essays and Studies*, I (1948), reprinted in *Elizabethan Drama:
Modern Essays in Criticism*, ed. Ralph J. Kaufmann (New York, 1961).

[9] Paul H. Kocher, *Christopher Marlowe: A Study of his Thought, Learning
and Character* (Chapel Hill, 1946), pp. 106-107.

[10] Hunter, *Shakespeare and the Mystery*, p. 48.

As he proceeds to gloss his text, Faustus advances by means of questions and exhortations through stages of knowledge to an acceptance of God's word—and beyond. But, instead of moving toward an understanding of the spirit behind the text, as a preacher would do, Faustus rejects the words of the Bible and seeks out their diabolical counterpart, the metaphysics of magicians and their "heavenly" necromantic books. These books, Faustus believes, will elevate him above emperors and kings, making him the ruler of a dominion that "Stretcheth as far as doth the mind of man," a dominion as unlimited as the ambitions of the Elizabethan aspiring mind. Faustus ends his speech with a conclusion based on another faulty syllogism: "A sound magician is a demi-god./ Here try thy brains to get a deity!" (I, i, 62-64.)

And so Faustus embarks on the "otherness" of damnation as a result of pursuing the "otherness" of Godhood; he descends to magic in hopes that it will get him a deity. Earlier in the speech Faustus had sought in physic the ability to "make men to live eternally,/ Or, being dead, raise them to live again" (I, i, 24-25), in a perhaps unconscious wishful identification with Christ (this curious identification reappears when Faustus completes his signing of the bond with Christ's words on the cross, "*Consummatum est*"). Though the audience would have recognized the presumption inherent in Faustus' desire for a deity, they would also have known that the other objects of his aspirations were, in themselves, neither wicked nor prohibited. The "world of profit and delight,/ Of power, of honor, of omnipotence" which he describes is not so very different from the promises which John Udall extends to the godly in *Two Sermons upon the Historie of Peters denying Christ* (1584):

> Solomon . . . sheweth what the word of GOD shal bryng unto the lovers thereof: namely honour, ryches, long life and such like: which indeede figureth unto us al ioyes whatsoever, whyche the Godlye shall have in the lyfe to come.[11]

---

[11] John Udall, *Two Sermons upon the Historie of Peters denying Christ* (London, 1584), STC #24503, sig. B6ʳ.

This figurative relationship between worldly accomplishments and the life to come was an important element in Protestantism, one which served to justify or legitimize the acquisition of wealth, among other things. That Faustus originally expresses such ambitions is not, therefore, a sign of damnation. It is even possible to see Faustus' discontent with his past achievements and his aspiration toward greater things as an analogue to the yearnings of the godly. What distinguishes Faustus from the godly, however, is the course of action on which he embarks to realize his ambition.[12]

The moment Faustus acts on his decision to reject divinity and pursue necromancy by sending for the the two magicians, his conscience, represented by the recurring dialogue between the good and bad angels, begins to resist. These two characters give voice to the concept of free will, the freedom to choose which Puritan theologians insisted upon despite its apparent inconsistency with the doctrine of election. As Perkins explained in a tract entitled "Of God's free grace and Man's free will": "Gods decree doth not abolish libertie, but only moderate and order it; by inclining the will in milde and easie manner with fit and convenient objects, and that according to the condition of the will."[13] The Good and Bad Angels do not speak *to* Faustus in the manner of the virtues and vices of the moralities. Rather, they articulate the inner vacillations that Faustus experiences at crucial moments in the play, without his conscious awareness of their presence on stage.[14] In a

[12] As Richard Waswo observes in "Damnation, Protestant Style: Macbeth, Faustus and Christian Tragedy," *Journal of Medieval and Renaissance Studies*, 4 (1974), a central tragic irony in *Doctor Faustus* is Faustus' loss of his finest quality, his ability to aspire (p. 81).

[13] Perkins, *A Golden Chaine*, p. 740.

[14] Joel Altman likewise sees a departure from morality play technique in Marlowe's use of the two angels: "In the early moralities, spiritual beings such as angels and devils had an objective reality quite external to the psyche of the protagonist, just as the personified vices and virtues were understood to exist within him. There was no tension between a personal, subjective consciousness and these forces. . . ." Marlowe, however, uses these forces ironically, since his protagonist is attempting at this moment to assert his psychic autonomy. *The Tudor Play of Mind* (Berkeley, 1978), p. 381.

sense, they are part of the ongoing dialogue or debate he has been engaged in from the beginning of the long opening monologue (in which he addresses himself by name seven times). Perhaps because Faustus is unable to imagine a merciful God who extends the possibility of salvation to all, his Good Angel's initial efforts to win him over contain no mention of God's mercy but only His "heavy wrath" (I, i, 73).[15] The Good Angel urges him to lay aside "that damned book" (i.e., damning book) and to read the Scriptures instead, as if to tell him that by reading on he would discover the fallacy of his syllogism. The Bad Angel offers promises rather than threats, and inclines Faustus' will in the direction of godhood: "Be thou on earth as Jove is in the sky,/ Lord and commander of these elements" (77-78).

The distinction that Marlowe makes between "Good" and "Bad" as embodied in the two angels is deceptively simple, and ironically at odds with the far subtler moral ambivalence that the audience feels toward the desire Faustus continues to describe after the angels exit. Of the list of extravagant commands he plans to give the spirits his magic will summon, the first is to "Resolve me of all ambiguities," a longing which many among his audience must have shared (81). He also wishes for gold and pearls (which recalls both the "external trash" of "mercenary drudge" he rejected earlier and the wealth

[15] There has been considerable critical disagreement about the Good Angel's posture in this speech. Kocher, for example, uses it to support his theory that Marlowe's anti-Christian bias led him to present God as a wrathful Jehovah rather than a loving father (*Christopher Marlowe*, p. 118). Robert Ornstein takes a similar position in "Marlowe and God: The Tragic Theory of *Doctor Faustus*," *PMLA* LXXXIII (1968); he feels that for Marlowe, the Godlike and the Christlike remain antithetical (p. 1385). I prefer the approach taken by Pauline Honderich in "John Calvin and Doctor Faustus," *Modern Language Review*, 68, 1 (Jan. 1973). She observes that "Marlowe calls up and sets against each other the images both of the benevolent God of the Catholic [or moderate Anglican] dispensation and of the harsh and revengeful God of Calvinist doctrine." There is an ongoing dramatic tension in the pitting of the two theological schemes against one another because we don't really know which one will win until the play ends (p. 12). This interpretation makes the play into a powerful and dialectical reflection of the range of possibilities open to the Elizabethans.

Udall views as a prefiguring of heavenly joys), but plans to use his wealth to levy soldiers to drive out the Prince of Parma, a Spanish governor of the Low Countries in the 1580s and hated enemy of the Elizabethan audience. The magicians whom Faustus summons for his instruction also appeal to the audience's anti-Spanish sentiments: Valdes says, "shall they [the spirits] drag huge argosies" from Venice, "And from America the golden fleece/ That yearly stuffs old Philip's treasury,/ If learned Faustus will be resolute" (I, i, 131-34).

To this Faustus replies: "Valdes, as resolute am I in this/ As thou to live . . ." (135-36). This phrase echoes ominously as the play continues: Faustus urges himself to be resolute again just before the signing of the deed in blood. Resolution was a quality he shared with the believers who remained firm in their conviction that they were among the elect. As William Burton told his listeners:

> . . . in Gods service we must neither doubt of that which we do, nor waver in the perfourming of our uowes, neither must we do it fainedly, but with ful consent of heart and mind. Resolution is the thing indeed that we are here taught. Resolution in Gods matters is very requisite, as it is for a souldier in the field.[16]

But Faustus' resolution parodies that of the elect, just as Tamburlaine's assurance does: in each case Marlowe gives his protagonist qualities which his audience admired, but directs them to blasphemous ends. This resolution, rather than a predestination over which he has no control, is what prevents Faustus from repenting. Marlowe thus presents his audience with a paradox which in itself is a parody of the religious paradoxes of his age: had Faustus been weaker, he might have been saved. It is worth noting that P. F.'s Faustus lacks this resoluteness in the chapters that correspond to the early scenes of *Doctor Faustus*. He hesitates to commit his soul to Lucifer according

---

[16] William Burton, *Davids Evidence or the Assurance of Gods Love* (London, 1592), STC 4170, p. 157.

to Mephostophilis' conditions, and, after the bargain is completed and he hears of the pain awaiting him in hell, he repeatedly becomes sorrowful and tries to repent. As M. M. Mahood points out, the *Faustbook* devils withhold Faustus from repentance by brute strength, whereas Marlowe's Faustus is always at liberty to repent.[17]

The resoluteness of Marlowe's Faustus is given even more emphasis by comparison with the remarkably human and hesitant Mephostophilis who appears as a result of his conjuring and blasphemy in Act I, scene iii. Using parts of three different discussions of hell in the *Faustbook*, Marlowe presents his audience with a tempter whose first act is an attempt to dissuade his prey from persisting in his pursuit of damnation. Marlowe ironically makes Mephostophilis more orthodox than Faustus in this scene: he speaks of the "Saviour Christ" and man's "glorious soul," while Faustus, in return, confounds "hell in Elysium" (I, iii, 48-49; 60). The questions which Faustus then proceeds to ask are a brilliantly transformed condensation of seven chapters in the *Faustbook*, which occur *after* the signing of the contract, rather than before.

Faustus begins by asking about Lucifer, whose fall from heaven because of his "aspiring pride and insolence" is being reenacted at this very moment by Faustus himself. Faustus then asks "And what are you that live with Lucifer?" The echoing effect of Mephostophilis' response summons up powerful, reverberating sensations of the eternal doom from which Mephostophilis is trying to avert the oblivious Faustus:

> Unhappy spirits that fell with Lucifer,
> Conspired against our God with Lucifer,
> And are for ever damned with Lucifer.
> (I, iii, 71-73)

Mephostophilis proceeds to give his famous description of hell as a state of mind rather than a place:

---

[17] M. M. Mahood, *Poetry and Humanism* (London, 1950), p. 70.

> Why this is hell, nor am I out of it.
> Think'st thou that I who saw the face of God
> And tasted the eternal joys of heaven
> Am not tormented with ten thousand hells
> In being deprived of everlasting bliss?
> O Faustus, leave these frivolous demands
> Which strike a terror to my fainting soul.[18]
>
> (I, iii, 76-82)

Marlowe has taken his cue from a didactic speech in his source, in which Mephostophilis tells Faustus that if he were a man, he would "humble my selfe vnto his Maiestie, indeuouring in all that I could to keepe his Commaundements, prayse him, glorifie him, that I might continue in his fauour, so were I sure to eniuy the eternall ioy and felicity of his kingdome" (p. 158). The *Faustbook* description of hell is a compendium of physical description, vividly evoking the suffering of the damned, but without any sense that Mephostophilis has himself experienced suffering. Marlowe transforms these moralistic pronouncements into a fascinating depiction of damnation as "an ongoing process to the ultimate destiny," reflecting the Protestant's emphasis on the immediacy of damnation. As Douglas Cole observes, never before in English drama had a devil acted in this way.[19]

Marlowe's daring characterization of Mephostophilis emphasizes the diabolical nature of Faustus' pursuit of knowledge. Like Dent's reprobate in *A Pastime for Parents*, whose knowledge "doth puffe up," Faustus is "swoll'n with cunning

---

[18] Interestingly, Marlowe borrows a phrase from the *Faustbook*, but transforms it utterly. In response to Faustus' demand to know the secrets of hell the Faustbook Mephostophilis boldly declares: "I will tell thee things to the terror of thy soule . . ." (p. 154). In *Doctor Faustus*, this becomes instead the terror of Mephostophilis' fainting soul.

[19] The phrase "an ongoing process to the ultimate destiny" is Richard Waswo's; as Waswo points out, this attitude toward damnation was a clear departure from the medieval concept of damnation, which emphasized punishment after death ("Damnation, Protestant Style," p. 71); Douglas Cole, *Suffering and Evil in the Plays of Christopher Marlowe* (Princeton, 1962), p. 205.

of a self-conceit" (prologue, 20). He shares this preoccupation with self, as we have seen, with some of the most pious men of his age, yet the distortion implied by the word "swoll'n" alerts the audience to the degree of excess involved. The imagery of swelling is related to the motif of gluttony and surfeit and engorgement which, as C. L. Barber and others have shown, runs through the play.[20] But while food and drink appear in the play at a number of points, the appetite which Faustus most longs to satisfy is a craving for knowledge. As soon as the bargain with Mephostophilis is sealed, he begins asking questions about hell. The only true knowledge Mephostophilis offers him is based on his own experience of hell, and it is a definition, significantly, that can only describe hell as the absence of heaven.

> Hell hath no limits, nor is circumscribed
> In one self place, but where we are is hell,
> And where hell is, there must we ever be.
> And, to be short, when all the world dissolves
> And every creature shall be purified,
> All places shall be hell that is not heaven.
> (II, i, 119-24)

Faustus contemptuously rejects the warning implicit in this definition, and henceforth he receives only what Dent would call the knowledge of the reprobate, which is "generall and confused" rather than the "particular and certain" knowledge reserved for the elect. The knowledge of the reprobate is contained in the book Mephostophilis gives him, which the audience would recognize as a substitute for the Bible cast aside in Act I, scene i (the book is an important prop in this play). The shallowness of Faustus' newly acquired knowledge becomes evident as his efforts to "reason of divine astrology" are met with elementary and unsatisfying responses. Faustus' final question, "who made the world," cannot be answered at all,

[20] C. L. Barber, " 'The form of Faustus' fortunes good or bad,' " *Tulane Drama Review*, VIII, 4 (Summer, 1964), pp. 106 ff.

for the knowledge that God made the world is, again in Dent's terms, "spirituall and practiue, that is ioyned with obedience," and thus inaccessible to the reprobate.[21]

One of the most ironic uses Marlowe makes of the morality tradition is his transformation of Mephostophilis into the tempter in reverse. The devil with a fainting soul was an unprecedented concept in Elizabethan England. By presenting Mephostophilis in this way, Marlowe reminds his audience that all devils are ultimately instruments of God, just as scourges are. As George Gifford told his readers in a tract published in 1587,

> . . . reprobat angels . . . be instruments of Gods vengauce [sic], and executioners of his wrath, they doe not exercise power and authoritie which is absolute, and at their owne will and appointment, but so farre as God letteth foorth the chaine to giue them scope. Touching the reprobat, which despise the waies of God and are disobedient, we are taught, that God in righteous vengeance giueth them ouer into their hands . . . therefore they come under the tirannie of wicked divels, which worke in them with power. . . .

Among the greatest and "general mischiefes" of the Devil, Gifford observes, is his ability to "hold men from turning unto God by repentance." Lucifer and Beelzebub, Marlowe's more conventional devils, and the Bad Angel assume this role.

As Gifford's tract on devils makes clear, the fact that Faustus comes under the influence of the devil does not mean that he is reprobate. Gifford notes that

> . . . these wicked fiends doe also set upon the faithful and elect people of God, for God useth them also as instruments for their triall, they tempt and trie them, they doe wrestle

[21] Arthur Dent, *A pastime for Parents: or A recreation, to passe away the time; contayning the most principall grounds of Christian Religion* (London, 1606), STC #6622, sig. C6ᵛ. The emphasis on the book is more pronounced in the A text; Faustus requests the book of astronomical knowledge from Mephostophilis, but when he receives it, and Mephostophilis turns the pages, he says to himself, "O thou art deceived."

224

and fight against them, they buffet them, every way seeking to annoy and molest them both in bodie and soule.[22]

In keeping with the spirit of Elizabethan Protestantism, the play withholds definitive evidence that Faustus is *not* of the elect. Just as the preachers urged their listeners to believe that no sin was too great for God's forgiveness, so Marlowe uses the Good Angel and the Old Man as signals to the audience that even the selling of one's soul can conceivably be overcome by repentance. Faustus thus remains both potentially elect and potentially damned until the final moments of the play, and, despite the fact that many members of the audience probably knew how the Faust story ended, they must have been caught up in the dramatic suspense. As they waited to see whether Faustus would repent before his twenty-four years ran out, they gave vent to some of their own anxieties about election.

II. REPENTANCE OR DESPAIR

Repentance and despair are the central theological issues in *Doctor Faustus*, and critics continue to debate about whether Faustus could have repented, and about the doctrinal implications of his inability to do so.[23] Faustus' opening soliloquy

[22] George Gifford, *A Discourse of the subtill Practises of Deuilles by witches and Sorcerers. By which men are and haue bin greatly deluded.* (London, 1587), STC #11852, sig. D2ʳ, H2ᵛ, D2ʳ.

[23] Kocher uses contemporary sources to show that Faustus could have repented and that he becomes one of those willful men who resist grace, a view also reflected in the *Faustbook*. This means that the audience is meant to view Faustus, *not* from the Calvinist perspective, according to which God hardens men's hearts, but from a more moderate Protestant perspective, according to which the initiative must come from man, who will not be damned unless he actively resists the grace God offers him (*Christopher Marlowe*, p. 110). Similarly, Lily B. Campbell sees Faustus as "one whose fate was not determined by his initial sin but rather as one who until the fatal eleventh hour might have been redeemed." See "*Doctor Faustus*: A Case of Conscience," *PMLA*, LXVII (1952), p. 239. Marlowe's insistence on ambiguity in respect to whether Faustus can or does repent is stressed by Susan Snyder in "Marlowe's *Doctor*

in Act II powerfully reveals how torn he is between the despair in God to which he is resolved and a lingering desire to repent:

> Now Faustus, must thou needs be damned,
> And canst thou not be saved.
> What boots it then to think on God or heaven?
> Away with such vain fancies, and despair;
> Despair in God, and trust in Beelzebub.
> Now go not backward; Faustus, be resolute.
> Why waver'st thou? O, something soundeth in mine ear:
> 'Abjure this magic; turn to God again.'
> Ay, and Faustus will turn to God again!
> To God? He loves thee not.
> The God thou serv'st is thine own appetite,
> Wherein is fixed the love of Beelzebub.
> To him I'll build an altar and a church,
> And offer lukewarm blood of new-born babes.
>
> (II, i, 1-14)

This soliloquy demonstrates the increasing skill at rendering the inner conflict of a morally and emotionally complex character that begins to appear in the tragedies of the 1580s and 1590s. In his dialogue between the "I" and the "thee," Faustus vacillates between his commitment to despair and its opposite, turning to God. The Elizabethan audience must have noticed the way Faustus aligns despair, trust in Beelzebub, and resolution against going "backward" toward God. This is the antithesis of repentance, which entails trust in God and a resolution to go forward. The speech rises to a peak of hope at its midpoint, with the repeated phrase "turn to God again," then falls downward, with Faustus' stark conclusion, "He loves

---

Faustus as an Inverted Saint's Life" *Studies in Philology*, 63 (1966). Snyder notes that the play exhibits two patterns simultaneously, that fallen man cannot initiate repentance, and that repentance is a constant possibility (p. 565). This approach is also discussed by Max Bluestone, who regards Faustus as "neither repentant nor reprobate" (*"Libido Speculandi,"* p. 79).

thee not." His blasphemous love of Beelzebub, false church and altar, and pagan rite of bloodshed will replace the God, Church, and communion ritual of the orthodox Christian, or so at least he tells himself.

Although the soliloquy expresses sentiments that few Elizabethans would admit to, Faustus' desperate state of mind may well have been a common one in Elizabethan England, to judge from the many manuals in print designed to soothe troubled consciences. R. Linaker's *A Comfortable Treatise, for the reliefe of such as are afflicted in Conscience*, published in 1590, seems to speak directly to a soul in Faustus' spiritual condition. Using David and Paul as examples, Linaker argues that the more one is persecuted by temptations and punishments the more certainly he is chosen by God. If you doubt you are among God's chosen, you do so, he says, because your conscience prompts you to, a sign that God's spirit is bringing you to effectual repentance. Linaker might very well have seen in Faustus' speech evidence that he was saved, though he had succumbed to the "temptation of Satan . . . [intended] to drive you to desperation." His remedy is as follows: "there is no cause why you shoulde believe him. First because hee is a lyar. Secondly because hee is your enemy, who meanes you no good at all." Linaker goes on to say that since Satan is a liar, you are to believe the opposite of what he tells you: if he says you are damned, be assured that you are saved.[24] He recommends that the sinner be aggressive with Satan and refuse to be browbeaten:

> And if, with his wily and uiolent temptations, hee [Satan] carrie you into anie sinne, let him be sure that he shal answere it, & not you: it shall be set on his score at the day of iudgement: because he was ye author of it & forced you against your wil as he did that holy man Job. . . .[25]

[24] R. Linaker, *A Comfortable Treatise, for the reliefe of such as are afflicted in Conscience* (London, 1607; first edition, 1590), STC #15640, pp. 9, 22, 23.
[25] Linaker, *A Comfortable Treatise*, p. 81.

How one makes sure that Satan answers for his temptations is not absolutely clear, however. As the audience undoubtedly knew, the cool reasonableness of Linaker's argument is seldom so easily accessible to the soul in torment.

Faustus' inability to shift the blame to Mephostophilis becomes clear in Act II, scene ii. The scene begins with Faustus repenting and cursing Mephostophilis, claiming that he has been deprived of the joys of heaven. To this Mephostophilis replies: "Twas thine owne seeking, Faustus; thank thyself" (II, ii, 4). Mephostophilis then quickly changes the subject, unlike his predecessor in the *Faustbook*, who, at the end of his account of what he would do if he were a man, reproaches Faustus at length:

> . . . yea wickedly thou hast applyed that excellent gift of thine vnderstanding, and giuen thy soule to the Diuell: therefore giue none the blame but thine owne selfe-will, thy proude and aspiring minde, which hath brought thee into the wrath of God and vtter damnation.

To Faustus' rejoinder that "it were time enough for me if I amended," the *Faustbook* Mephostophilis replies: "True . . . if it were not for thy great sinnes, which are so odious and detestable in the sight of God, that it is too late for thee, for the wrath of God resteth vpon thee" (pp. 158-59). One wonders what Linaker would have advised Faustus to say to so eloquent and moralistic a devil. Marlowe deliberately makes his Mephostophilis much less forceful on this point, confident, perhaps, that his audience did not have to be told that Faustus' self-will and aspiring mind has brought him to his present condition. Nor does he wish to be so definite about what Faustus' present condition *is*; like Linaker, he lets the audience believe that Faustus may yet successfully shift the blame and the punishment—to Mephostophilis. Not until the very end of the play does Marlowe finally resolve the dramatic suspense which surrounds Faustus' state of election.

Rather than preach to Faustus as does his predecessor, Marlowe's Mephostophilis tries to divert him from thoughts of repentance, using the same kind of deceptive logic Faustus himself had used in Act I. Heaven was made for man, he tells Faustus; therefore man is more excellent than heaven. But his argument misfires, and Faustus concludes from it: "If heaven was made for man, 'twas made for me./ I will renounce this magic and repent" (II, ii, 10-11). At the mention of the possibility of repentance, the angels reappear. The Good Angel speaks first, urging Faustus to repent and promising that God will pity him. Faustus holds up against the first assault of the Bad Angel, who tells him, "Thou art a spirit; God cannot pity thee," by responding "Be I a devil, yet God may pity me;/ Yea, God will pity me if I repent." The Bad Angel rejoins ominously, "Ay, but Faustus never shall repent," sounding a note of predestined doom. Faustus abruptly shifts direction, and agrees: "My heart is hardened; I cannot repent./ Scarce can I name salvation, faith, or heaven" (18-19). Thus the dialogue ends with Faustus hardened of heart and resolved not to repent. The same kind of rhythm, in reverse, can be observed in the sermons and tracts: the despairing believer, led step by step by the preacher, is brought to an assurance of his election.

After another round of astronomical questions and answers, Faustus again begins to waver in his allegiance to the powers of hell. When Mephostophilis brushes aside his question with: "Thou art damned. Think thou of hell," Faustus responds, addressing his errant self: "Think, Faustus, upon God that made the world." He repeats his accusation against Mephostophilis: " 'Tis thou hast damned distressed Faustus' soul./ Is't not too late?" The angels reenter, but, this time, the Bad Angel speaks first. "Too late," he echoes, to which the Good Angel responds, "Never too late, if Faustus will repent." Swept along by the Good Angel's assurance, Faustus reaches a conventional turning point in the process of redemption as he calls out, "O Christ, my Savior, my Savior,/ Help to save distressed Faustus' soul" (73-84).[26]

---

[26] Robert G. Hunter sees this moment as the *peripeteia* in *Doctor Faustus*;

This heart-rending cry brings not comfort, but instead Lucifer and a slightly clownish Beelzebub, who with ease extract from Faustus his vow never to look on heaven or name God. They reward him with the extraordinarily crude and unconvincing display of the Seven Deadly Sins, whose talk of wenches' smocks and gammons of bacon, raw mutton, and fried stockfish seems hardly capable of delighting the soul of the Faustus, who earlier in the scene had recalled the sweet pleasure of Homer and Amphion's songs. Even if the spectacle could divert Faustus from thoughts of God, it could hardly convince the audience to do likewise; as they watched—and maybe enjoyed—the procession, their thoughts might have lingered upon the falsity of Lucifer's pronouncement that "Christ cannot save thy soul, for he is just./ There's none but I have interest in the same" (II, ii, 85-86). Christ, they knew, was the champion of that mercy which transcended and, if need be, overruled justice. Faustus' immediate acquiescence here is as doctrinally misguided as his original reading of Scripture; had he persisted a little longer, defying Lucifer instead of deferring to him, Christ would indeed have come to his aid—or so Marlowe's audience might have been tempted to think.

The interchange between Faustus and Lucifer that leads up to this turning point could easily have been a deliberate parody of the instructive dialogues that the preachers were fond of writing. In 1586, Marlowe's last year at Corpus Christi College, William Perkins, who was also in Cambridge, published "A treatise tending vnto a declaration, whether a man be in the estate of damnation, or in the estate of grace: and if he be in the first, how he may in time come ovt of it: if in the second, how hee may discerne it, and persevere in the same to the end." This treatise contains a series of dialogues between Satan and Christians of varying degrees of strength, or

---

at this point, the play could become either "a comedy of forgiveness or a tragedy of God's judgment." Hunter notes that to the Calvinists in the audience, Faustus has been damned all along, while to the non-Calvinists, his contrition is not sufficient (*Shakespeare and the Mystery*, pp. 55-56).

resolution. Here is the beginning of "A dialogue containing the conflicts between Sathan and a Christian":

Sathan. Vile hell-hound, thou art my slave and my vassall, why then shakest thou off my yoake?

Christian. By nature I was thy vassal, but Christ hath redeemed me.

Sathan. Christ redeemeth no reprobates such as thou art.

Christian. I am no reprobate.

Sathan. Thou art a reprobate, for thou shalt be condemned.

Christian. Lucifer, to pronounce damnation belongs to God alone: thou art no judge, it is sufficient for thee to be an accuser.

Sathan. Though I cannot condemne thee, yet I know God will condemne thee.

Christian. Yea but God will not condemne me.

Satan goes on to list the Christian's sins in lurid detail, but the Christian "dares to presume" on God's mercy, and insists that his afflictions are a sign of his salvation. The dialogue ends when the Christian asserts with finality: "I have true saving grace."[27]

Faustus is a mirror image of Perkins' Christian; he is the elect man of God in reverse. Where the Christian is strong, Faustus is weak; his irresoluteness when confronted by Lucifer and Beelzebub is the opposite of the Christian's persistence in his belief. Despair, then, is the absence of resolution; but it is also a terrible kind of arrogance, a refusal to accept as a gift the salvation one cannot earn. Without falling into arrogance, the believer must possess two kinds of confidence, a confidence in self and a greater, all-encompassing confidence in God, if he is to attain the greatly sought-after assurance of election.

The comic procession of the Seven Deadly Sins effectively dissipates the tension building in the audience as they are

[27] Perkins, *A Golden Chaine*, pp. 405 ff.

brought face to face with their own anxiety about election. This, and the scenes of comic conjuring that follow, are remarkably different in tone from the play's first two acts, and the considerable differences between the 1604 and 1616 texts make it difficult to arrive at conclusions about their dramatic and thematic purposes. The Elizabethan audience presumably enjoyed watching Faustus mock the pride of the Pope; indeed, for a strongly anti-Catholic audience, the humiliation of the Pope may even have seemed admirable, although the practical jokes at the banquet are hardly the awe-inspiring triumphs of a hero. Yet Marlowe does not let the audience forget that Faustus is potentially damned even in the midst of the fun. As the invisible Faustus is snatching dishes and cups from the hands of the Pope at the feast, the Pope crosses himself in protection against what he thinks is a troublesome ghost. Injured by the gesture, as devilish spirits are, Faustus strikes back at him. The Pope responds with lines that constitute a formula some variant of which can be found in countless Elizabethan or Jacobean tragedies:

> O I am slain. Help me, my lords.
> O come and help to bear my body hence.
> Damned be his soul for ever for this deed.
> (III, ii, 90-92)

To call one's enemy "damned" is a conventional insult in the Elizabethan theatre, but, here, the stock phrase reverberates with meaning, for the curse is literally fulfilled within the play. The friars proceed with the Catholic exorcism ritual, and, as Faustus mocks them, he again reminds the audience of his self-willed damnation: "Bell, book, and candle, candle, book, and bell,/ Forward and backward, to curse Faustus to hell" (95-96). The irony here is that the friars are superfluous, for Faustus has already cursed himself.

The comic exploits of the servants play a similarly ironic role, paralleling and hence debasing Faustus' great achievements. Robin's adventures with the stolen "conjuring book" remind the audience that the knowledge for which Faustus sold his soul offers little beyond trickery and is available to whoever possesses the book. These scenes, beginning in Act I with Wagner's mockery of Faustus' survey of the disciplines, and his promise to turn Robin into "a dog, or a cat or a mouse, or a rat, or anything," provide the audience with a set of familiar character types with whom to take refuge from Faustus' "otherness." Wagner and the clowns, after all, remain alive and unscathed at the end, despite their experiments with conjuring. They belong to the normal, everyday world, where the devil is only a character in a costume frolicking on the morality play stage.

In the midst of the final comic episode, the horse-courser scene, Faustus speaks his first soliloquy since Act II:

> What art thou, Faustus, but a man condemned to die?
> Thy fatal time draws to a final end.
> Despair doth drive distrust into my thoughts.
> Confound these passions with a quiet sleep.
> Tush? Christ did call the thief upon the cross;
> Then rest thee, Faustus, quiet in conceit.
>   (IV, v, 33-38)

There is a deliberate echo here of the line "Yet are thou still but Faustus, and a man" from the long monologue of Act I, scene i: Faustus' pact with Mephostophilis, he recognizes, makes him no less subject to death than before. He comforts himself with a trust in divine providence which his audience would have known to be presumptuous, for they had been taught that those who despair of forgiveness and those who gamble on God's mercy, expecting last-minute forgiveness, are equally damnable.[28] This reflective moment over, Faustus returns to his conjuring and mischief, which culminates in the appearance of Helen to the scholars. Their awed reaction to her "heavenly beauty" and gratitude for "this blessed sight" (V, i, 32, 35) are ironic reminders of the death which, as Wagner

---

[28] Cf. the official Elizabethan homily "How daungerous a thing it is to fall from God," cited in Cole, *Suffering and Evil*, p. 218.

tells the audience in a prologue to the scene, rapidly approaches. Even more ironic are the first scholar's parting words of thanks: "Happy and blest be Faustus evermore" (36). The encounter with Helen, as Marlowe seems to suggest, makes Faustus momentarily happy, but damned forevermore.

At this point Marlowe introduces a new character, the Old Man, whose sudden and unprepared-for appearance is derived from the *Faustbook* incident in which Faustus dines with an old neighbor who tries to persuade him to repent. The Old Man is not of the same order of reality as the other human characters in the play; rather, he is an allegorical embodiment of divine love and mercy. He pleads with Faustus to turn away from magic, assuring him that his soul is still "amiable," or potentially elect, and that repentance is thus possible. Such is the Old Man's extra-human spiritual insight that he can see an angel hovering over Faustus' head, offering to pour a vial of grace into his soul (61 ff.). In a visual echo of the conflicting appeals of the Good and Bad Angels, the Old Man's presence onstage and his envisioned vial of grace are counterbalanced by Mephostophilis and the dagger, a symbol of despair, which he wordlessly offers Faustus. Torn between the two, Faustus resumes the dialogue with himself in which he had been engaged in Acts I and II. Hell strives with grace for conquest of Faustus, and hell wins. Accused by Mephostophilis of disobedience to "my sovereign Lord" (as distinct from *the* sovereign Lord), Faustus quickly inverts true repentance and "repents" having offended Lucifer. Moreover, he seeks pardon for his "unjust presumption." This phrase is pointedly ironic, for Faustus has not presumed enough, and in the proper way, upon God's ability to forgive. What Faustus calls presumption has been in fact the absence of the godly believers' boldness and assurance in the face of all temptation. Similarly, the unlawful aspiration to godhood with which he embarked upon damnation is in fact the source of his unjust presumption.

In the Good Friday sermon of 1570, John Foxe assured his audience thus: "Be you willing to be reconciled, and you shall speede: come and you shall be received, holde out your hand to take what he will geue, and you shall have."[29] Like Foxe, the Old Man has presented the availability of salvation in the most generous of terms, but he has made it clear that salvation must be actively, not passively, sought out. For a moment, Faustus "feels" the comfort which the Old Man's words have attempted to convey, but, instead of holding out his hand, he succumbs to despair, the ultimate source of defeat to the human spirit. The preachers knew how easily the impulse to repent could turn into despair and warned most urgently against the pitfalls of "over-sharpe sorrow." As Perkins explained:

> When the spirit hath made a man see his sins, he seeth further the curse of the Law, and so he finds himselfe to be in bondage under Satan, hell, death, and damnation: at which most terrible sight his heart is smitten with feare and trembling, through the consideration of his hellish and damnable estate. . . . All men must take heed, lest when they are touched for their sinnes, they besnare their owne consciences: for if the sorrow be somewhat over-sharpe, they shall see themselves even brought to the gates of hell, and to feele the pangs of death.[30]

Desperately intent on shunning the pangs of death, Faustus turns back to Mephostophilis and frantically offers to reconfirm his vow in blood, even though that vow, by its very nature, leads to certain death at the end of the twenty-four years. Marlowe has altered his source in a significant way here. In the *Faustbook*, the devil orders Faustus to "write another writing" (p. 215), whereas in the play Mephostophilis merely demands that Faustus "Revolt" (i.e., turn back—but the choice of words is ironic, reminding the audience as it does of the fallen angels who revolted against God).

Helen, who reappears at Faustus' request, represents Faus-

---

[29] John Foxe, *A Sermon of Christ Crucified* (London, 1570), STC #11242, p. 10.
[30] Perkins, *A Golden Chaine*, p. 364.

tus' last effort to achieve superhuman stature—embracing her, he will be made immortal. Faustus seeks in Helen's embrace the satisfaction of appetite (Marlowe draws attention to this with the words "crave" and "glut"), then an escape from "Those thoughts that do dissuade me from my vow" (V, i, 90, 91). He deludes himself into thinking that heaven is in her lips, but just as he says this, the Old Man returns (in the 1604 text only), and undermines the soaring poetry of Faustus' declaration of love with these words:

> Accursed Faustus, miserable man,
> That from thy soul exclud'st the grace of heaven
> And fliest the throne of his tribunal seat!
> Satan begins to sift me with his pride.
> As in this furnace God shall try my faith,
> My faith, vile hell, shall triumph over thee.
>   (122-27)

The Old Man's reappearance serves as an echo of the visual contrast of the preceding scene, in which the Old Man and Mephostophilis represented the alternatives of repentance and despair. Now the Old Man embodies salvation, and Helen, by contrast, can stand only for damnation. The Elizabethan audience certainly would have recognized that the final triumph of the scene, greatly overshadowing Faustus' delight in Helen, is the Old Man's, as he and the heavens laugh to scorn the proud Satan and ambitious fiends who torture him (the physical antithesis of Helen's embrace). As he flies unto God, the audience is perhaps reminded of the Icarus image as well as Faustus' flights in pursuit of knowledge and experience in Act III. To make the contrast explicit, Marlowe has the Old Man observe that Faustus has begun his doomed and inexorable descent to hell by flying *away* from "the throne of his [God's] tribunal seat."

The Old Man's exit is virtually an allegorical action; once he is gone, Faustus' damnation seems unavoidable. Yet, paradoxically, when Faustus takes his leave of the scholars, he is in many respects a more sympathetic character than he is at any other point in the play. Tragically, he understands with utter clarity the implications of his deed:

> And what wonders I have done, all Germany can witness—yea, all the world—for which Faustus hath lost both Germany and the world, yea heaven itself, heaven the seat of God, the throne of the blessed, the kingdom of joy, and must remain in hell for ever.   (V, ii, 46-49)

The scholars urge him to call on God and he does, but ineffectually: "Ah, my God, I would weep, but the devil draws in my tears" (54-55). And so, knowing that his time has come, he dismisses the scholars, with a concern for their safety that makes him seem almost noble.

In the 1616 text, this scene is followed by the final appearance of Mephostophilis and the Good and Bad Angels. Here, for the last time, the play probes the ambiguities inherent in the theological concepts of election and free will. Mephostophilis once again instructs Faustus to despair, and Faustus turns on him with the accusation: "O thou bewitching fiend, 'twas thy temptation/ Hath robbed me of eternal happiness" (V, ii, 87-88). Surprisingly, Mephostophilis agrees, though earlier, as we have seen, he had told Faustus to blame himself. Now the traditional devil, gloating in the destruction he has wrought, Mephostophilis boasts:

> 'Twas I, that when thou wert i'the way to heaven,
> Damned up thy passage. When thou took'st the book
> To view the Scriptures, then I turned to the leaves
> And led thine eye.
>   (90-93)

This speech has no counterpart in the *Faustbook*, unless one counts a very early speech of the *Faustbook* Mephostophilis in which he tells Faustus that when the devils saw him despise divinity and seek to know the secrets of hell "then did we enter into thee, giuing thee diuers foule and filthy cogitations, pricking thee forward in thine intent, and perswading thee that thou couldst neuer attaine to thy desire, vntill thou hast the help of some diuell" (p. 153). But Marlowe's Mephostophilis waits until his last speech to assume responsibility for Faustus' initial act of despising divinity. The renowned scholar thus is transformed into a puppet whose very act of reading is determined by the devil.

Critics have suggested that Mephostophilis' speech may not have been part of Marlowe's original design. W. W. Greg, for example, finds it hard to believe that Marlowe wrote this section, with "its piety and its frequent rimes," and concludes that the 1604 text, by omitting these speeches, "undoubtedly heightens the effect of the human tragedy." The 1616 text, on the other hand, keeps the action on "what can perhaps best be described as an allegorical plane" by including them. This plane is clearly inconsistent with the final tragic soliloquy. Greg suspects that the soliloquy in its present form was a second draft of an earlier, more conventional, speech, and that in the process of writing it Marlowe realized that the "morality" tone of the earlier section was inappropriate and that the dialogue with Mephostophilis and the Angels would have to be cut.[31] Certainly the tragic involvement Marlowe has cautiously reinforced in the farewell to the scholars is undermined by the reproaches of the two angels. Conventional pronouncements like "He that loves pleasure must for pleasure fall" (V, ii, 127) encourage the audience to see Faustus from a moral distance and judge him in simple and moralistic terms which do injustice to the complexity of his motives. The image of hell which the Bad Angel gleefully elaborates upon (accompanied, according to the stage direction, by a physical "hell" which "is discovered") is likewise extremely conventional in comparison to Mephostophilis' earlier arresting descriptions; this too suggests an earlier stage in the evolution of the play.

Finally the audience is left alone with Faustus, as they listen together to the clock strike eleven. The soliloquy that follows is the counterpart to the long speech with which the play began: once again, Faustus addresses himself, the "self" whom

---

[31] W. W. Greg, *Marlowe's Doctor Faustus: 1604-1616*, pp. 126-32.

twenty-four years ago he instructed to "Try thy brains to gain a deity." Now comes the inevitable corollary: "thou must be damned perpetually" (V, ii, 132). The speech derives much of its power and urgency from the passage of time. Both Faustus and the audience await the next striking of the clock; both know that, despite all his power, Faustus cannot, after all, command the spheres of heaven to stand still, "That time may cease." Struggling like a trapped animal against the inexorable passage of time, Faustus is confined by a kind of moral gravity as well. He tries to leap up to God, but finds himself pulled down; he asks to be drawn up into clouds which might "vomit" him forth into heaven, only to find himself still on earth and on the stage. Desperately, he thinks of rushing headlong into the earth, of hiding from God's wrath beneath mountains and hills, of disguising and obliterating himself through Pythagorean transformation or dissolution into "little water drops"— all to no avail. Faustus experiences a sensation of physical entrapment which his soul cannot escape through metempsychosis as he descends to an eternal hell to which "No end is limited." This experience brings to completion the flights, the comic transformations, and the sense of unlimited possibilities that he had enjoyed throughout the play. The Elizabethan audience would presumably appreciate the moral symmetry here, yet Marlowe has drawn them into the experience of Faustus' desperation and fear so effectively that their involvement in his agony is at least as great as their detached judgment of him. As Faustus cries out to God, breaking up the rhythm of the blank verse with one outburst after another, he becomes more real than he has been at any other point in the play. Yet, paradoxically, he is now more fully and entirely the "other" than ever before. By dramatizing their own fear of hell and instinct for survival, Marlowe has brought his audience to an extraordinary degree of emotional involvement with a soul whose damnation is certain, an involvement from which, under any other circumstances, they would seek to detach themselves as much as possible.

Although Faustus' fate is resolved in this final speech, the play's theological ambiguities are not. Faustus cries out to Christ and God, and receives in return not the grace Foxe promised to those willing to be reconciled but a vision of God's "ireful brows" and heavy wrath. Is it because Faustus still fails to repent that he sees the outstretched arm as a bearer of punishment and not forgiveness? Is he wrong to assume that God "wilt not have mercy on my soul" (163)? In what way does his cry "My God, my God, look not so fierce on me" (184) constitute a plea for mercy devoid of the accompanying willingness to repent? An Elizabethan audience might have asked these questions, but they might also have finally realized that the offers of salvation extended by the Good Angel were illusory. As William Perkins observed, God does give the commandment "Repent and believe" to those who lack the requisite grace to do so. He explains that

> . . . though in the intent of the Minister it have onely one end; namely, the salvation of all, yet in the intention & counsell of God, it hath diverse ends. In them which be ordained to eternall life, it is a precept of obedience: because God will enable them to doe that which he commandeth; in the rest it is a commandement of triall or conviction, that to unbeleevers their sinne might be discovered and all excuse cut off. Thus when the precept is given to beleeve, and not the grace of faith, God doth not delude, but reprove and convince men of unbeleefe, and that in his justice.[32]

Perhaps this cutting off of all excuse was the Good Angel's intent when he encouraged Faustus to repent. Yet this is a judgment that an audience could only make in retrospect; when the words were originally spoken, it would have been an act of ungodly cynicism to doubt their sincerity.

Even if Faustus' damnation was predestined, he remains subject to the central paradox of Puritanism, which declares him morally and intellectually responsible for his own fall.

---

[32] Perkins, *A Golden Chaine*, p. 724 (misnumbered 745).

Faustus acknowledges this in the final soliloquy, at least for a moment; after cursing his parents for engendering him, he corrects himself and says "No, Faustus, curse thyself." But in the next breath he adds "curse Lucifer/ That hath deprived thee of the joys of heaven" (178-79). Yet significantly, his last line contains still another reversal. With the final desperate offer to "burn my books" Faustus seems to recognize the causal link between his desire for knowledge and his damnation. His offer brings the play full circle to the very first words of the Good Angel: "O Faustus, lay that damned book aside." That "damned book" was laid aside only to be replaced by a still more damned one, which Faustus, at the end of Act II, scene ii, vowed to "keep as chary as my life" (171). Tragically, he failed to act upon his apparent disappointment with its contents when they fell short of the absolute and perfect knowledge he so desired. And just as tragically, he failed to realize that keeping the book meant relinquishing his life. That the final significance of this not be lost, Marlowe reminds his audience of Faustus' stature before the events of the play began. The final chorus, though it warns against his hellish fall, nevertheless pronounces Faustus to have been a learned man in whom "Apollo's laurel bough," the emblem of knowledge, once grew.

III. DOCTOR FAUSTUS AND THE DIDACTIC TRADITION

With its exhortation to the wise "Only to wonder at unlawful things" instead of practicing them, the chorus superimposes a traditional didactic ending on a play which has, in a sense, violated certain expectations its audience had brought to the theatre. As in *Tamburlaine*, Marlowe has taken a conventional literary form and inverted it: just as his audience might have expected Tamburlaine to undergo a well-deserved downfall, a sign of God's just retribution against the overreacher, so that same audience could have awaited Faustus' final repentance as a sign of God's infinite mercy to the most hardened sinner. In writing *Doctor Faustus*, Marlowe assumed his audience's acquaintance with the logical counterpart of the *de casibus* formula, the fall and reformation of the flawed but eventually redeemed Christian. This was the dominant pattern of the morality play, as we have seen, despite the variations which were introduced during the final years in which the genre flourished. It was also a recurring structure in the published didactic literature of the Elizabethan age, much of it inherently dramatic in character, and very likely influenced indirectly by the religious drama.

One literary form which *Doctor Faustus* inverts is the saint's life, with its pattern of fall and repentance. As Susan Snyder has pointed out, the parody of a saint's life in *Doctor Faustus* is too consistent to be accidental. Faustus is "converted" to the devil after an orthodox early life, seals his pact with a diabolical sacrament, is "tempted" by the Good Angel and his own conscience and then "rescued" by his "mentor" Mephostophilis, performs "miracles," experiences a "heavenly" vision, and is received at death by his "master," Lucifer.[33] Marlowe and his audience were undoubtedly familiar with any number of saint's lives, including possibly some cast in characteristically Puritan terms. A good example is the account of the fourth-century Church father Eusebius, which Perkins presents in dialogue form in his treatise "whether a man be in the estate of damnation or in the estate of grace . . ." (the source of the dialogue between Satan and the Christian quoted earlier). The story had long been popular among Protestant writers, evidently. Perkins' subtitle indicates that it was "gathered here and there out of the sweete and savourie writings of Master Tindall and Master Bradford."

The dialogue begins as Timotheus, the interlocutor, asks Eusebius to describe to him "how it pleased God to make you a true Christian, and a member of Christ Iesus, whom I see you serve continually with a fervent zeale?" Eusebius answers that:

[33] Snyder, "Marlowe's *Doctor Faustus*," p. 566.

The fall of Adam did make me the heire of vengeance and wrath of God, & heire of eternall damnation, and did bring me into captivity and bondage under the divell: & my governour, and my prince, yea, and my God. And my will was locked and knit faster unto the will of the divel, than could a hundred thousand chaines bind a man unto a post. Unto the divells will did I consent withal my heart, with all my minde, with all my might, power, strength, will, and life: so that the law and will of the divell was written as well in my heart, as in my members, and I ran headlong after the divell with full saile, & the whole swing of all the power I had; as a stone cast into the ayre commeth downe naturally of it selfe with all the violent swing of his owne waight. O with what a deadly and venemous heart did I hate mine enemies? With how great malice of mind inwardly did I slay and murther? With what violence and rage, yea with what fervent lust committed I adultery, fornication, and such like uncleannesse? With what pleasure and delectation like a glutton served I my belly? With what diligence deceived I? How busily sought I the things of the world? Whatsoever I did worke, imagine, or speake, was abominable in the sight of God, for I could referre nothing unto the honour of God: neither was his law or will written in my members, or in my heart, neither was there any more power in me to follow the will of God, then in a stone to ascend upward of it selfe.

Eusebius, like Faustus, has consented to the devil's will, although not explicitly out of aspiration to knowledge and godlike power. When the turn toward repentance first begins he resists it vigorously:

And besides that, I was asleepe in so deepe blindnes, that I could neither see nor feele in what miserie, thraldom, and wretchednesse I was in, till Moses came and awaked me and published the law. When I heard the law truely preached, how that I ought to love and honour God with all my

243

strength and might from the low bottome of the heart . . .
then began my conscience to rage against the law and against
God. No sea, be it never so great a tempest, was so unquiet,
for it was not possible for me a naturall man to consent to
the law that it should be good, or that God should bee
righteous that made the law: in as much as it was contrary
unto my nature, and damned me and all that I could doe,
and never shewed mee where to fetch helpe, nor preached
any mercie, but onely set mee at variance with God, and
provoked and stirred me to raile on God, and to blaspheme
him as a cruell tyrant.

The preaching of the law, Eusebius explains, was "the key that
bound and damned my conscience," but "the preaching of the
Gospel was another key that loosed me againe." First the law

. . . pulled me from all trust and confidence I had in my
selfe, and in mine owne workes, merits, deservings, and ceremonies, and robbed me of all my righteousnesse, and made
mee poore. It killed me in sending me downe to hell, and
bringing me almost to utter desperation, and prepared the
way of the Lord, as it is written of *Iohn Baptist*. For it was
not possible that Christ should come unto mee as long as I
trusted in my selfe, or in any worldly thing, or had any
righteousnesse of mine owne, or riches of holy wordes. Than
afterward came the Gospel a more gentle plaister, which
suppled and swaged the wounds of my conscience, and
brought me health: it brought the Spirit of God, which
loosed the bands of Satan, and coupled me to God and his
will through a strong faith and fervent love. Which bands
were too strong for the divell, the world, or any creature to
loose.

After listening to his long account, Timotheus protests that
"you doe too much condemne your selfe in respect of sinne."
But Eusebius responds that "my nature is to sinne as it is the
nature of a serpent to sting . . . we are of nature evill, there-

fore doe we evill, and thinke evill, to eternall damnation by the law. . . ."

Timotheus explains that his experience has been different: "As yet I never had such a feling of my sinnes as you have had, and although I would be loath to commit any sinne, yet the Law was never so terrible unto mee, condemning mee, pronouncing the sentence of death against mee. . . ." To this Eusebius answers: "A true saying it is, that the right way to go unto heaven, is to saile by hell, and there is no man living that feeles the power & vertue of the blood of Christ, which first hath not felt the paines of hell."

And he continues "But the Lord which bringeth forth even to the borders of hell his best beloved when they forget themselves; knoweth also how well to bring them backe againe." In response to further questioning from Timotheus about his earlier life Eusebius describes how "the divell himselfe (as I now perceive) did often perswade my secure conscience that I was the child of God, and should be saved as well as the best man in the world: and I yeelded to his perswasion, and did verily thinke it." This confidence then gave way to despair, as "the divell changed both his coate and his note, and in fearefull manner cryed in my eares, that I was reprobate, his child: that none of Gods children were as I am, that this griefe of my soule was the beginning of hell. And the greater was my paine, because I durst not open my minde unto any for feare they should have mocked mee, and have made a jest of it."

Finally he went to a godly learned preacher, and after two or three days received promises of mercy, shown to him in "the booke of God." Now, says Eusebius: "I have had some assurance (in spite of the divell) that I doe appertaine to the kingdome of heaven, and am now a member of Iesus Christ, and shall so continue for ever." Timotheus then asks: "How know you that God hath forgiven your sinne?" Eusebius answers: "Because I am a sinner, and he is both able and willing to forgive me." Timotheus' questions persist, but Eusebius stoutly maintains: "I am certainly perswaded of the favour of God, even to the salvation of my soule."[34]

I quote from this at such length because I feel that the character of Eusebius reveals much about the Elizabethan audience's response to Faustus. His account of his bondage to the devil has the same stubborn energy which Marlowe translates into a powerful drama, though Marlowe, following the legend he inherited from the *Faustbook*, makes it clear that Faustus' bondage to the devil is chosen, not inherited. Eusebius' subsequent disillusionment and bitter protest against the law of Moses corresponds to Faustus' rejection of Christianity after reading the two fragments from Jerome's Bible; this is perhaps Marlowe's most important addition to his source. The successive periods of confidence and despair which Eusebius experiences under the influence of the devil also have their counterparts in *Doctor Faustus*. Though Faustus never has the confidence of election that Eusebius had possessed, he is encouraged by Mephostophilis to feel a somewhat analogous sense of security at many points in the play. As in Eusebius' story, this encouragement ultimately changes to a bitter taunting. Faustus' despair is given far more emphasis than his security, and, significantly, it too derives in part from the kind of arrogance associated with unjustified confidence in election. Ironically, Faustus has a conviction of election in reverse: "The serpent that tempted Eve may be saved, but not Faustus" (V, ii, 42). It is this inverted assurance that prevents his final repentance, a repentance which some members of the audience might still have anticipated in the final moments of the play, accustomed as they were to accounts like Perkins' in which the protagonist is on the very brink of hell when the reversal takes place. Faustus' soliloquy frantically explores many forms of escape from the inevitable damnation that awaits him—but not repentance. And so, though like Eusebius he "lived as though there were neither heaven nor hell, neither God nor divell," Faustus dies a damned soul.

[34] Perkins, *A Golden Chaine*, pp. 381 ff.

246

CHAPTER VIII

From History to Tragedy

In 1528, William Tyndale compared the relative merits of tyrants and weak kings and came down squarely on the side of the bold, assertive tyrant, even though he recognized that the good would suffer:

> Yea, and it is better to have a tyrant unto thy king: than a shadow; a passive king that doth nought himself, but suffereth others to do with him what they will, and to lead him whither they list. For a tyrant, though he do wrong unto the good, yet he punisheth the evil, and maketh all men obey, neither suffereth any man to poll but himself only. A king that is as soft as silk and effeminate, that is to say, turned into the nature of a woman—what with his own lusts, which are the longing of a woman with child, so that he cannot resist them, and what with the wily tyranny of them that ever rule him—shall be much more grievous unto the realm than a right tyrant. Read the chronicles, and thou shalt find it ever so.[1]

These are sentiments the Elizabethans would have expected to find in Machiavelli, rather than in one of the earliest treatises of the English Reformation. Their presence in *The Obedience of a Christian Man* suggests that, once informed by worldly concerns, the standard dichotomy of good and evil became more complicated in the eyes of the reformers than the simple antithesis of piety versus impiety. Tyndale supported his observations by advising the skeptical to "read the chronicles," advice which would be taken by countless Elizabethans, among them the playwrights whose search for material in the 1580s

---

[1] *The Obedience of a Christian Man*, quoted by Irving Ribner in *The English History Play in the Age of Shakespeare* (Princeton, 1957), p. 158.

brought them closer and closer to their own age. Whereas the conqueror plays placed the tyrant at a safe historical remove, locating him in exotic faraway places and distant times, the English history plays examined the behavior of tyrants and weak kings in political situations that more nearly resembled their own. At first drawing heavily on the legacy of the morality play, with its tendency toward sharp contrasts, the playwrights soon discovered that Tyndale's two categories raised serious questions about the tragic implications of the public and private behavior of monarchs.

By the end of the 1580s England enjoyed a sense of national security and prominence as a world power, bolstered by the defeat of the Armada and the death of Mary, Queen of Scots. Elizabeth had entered her fourth decade of uninterrupted and prosperous rule; as a monarch, she was weak only in the sense that she belonged to the weaker sex. Yet it was by now clear that she would never marry and produce heirs, and the anxiety about the succession which would increase toward the end of the 1590s may have been making itself felt in the audience's receptivity to plays about chaotic reigns, weak kings, depositions, usurpations, and regicide.

These elements are all present in the Henry VI plays, which present the womanly softness of the weak king and his susceptibility to the wily tyranny of others as the main causes of the Wars of the Roses. Henry's weakness as a king corresponds directly with his weakness as a protagonist: in all three plays, he is overshadowed by large casts of characters, each cast containing several versions of the heroic conqueror, the aspiring upstart, or the villainous Machiavel so familiar to the audiences of the 1580s and so often reduplicated in plays based on chronicle material. Described by one of his own followers as base, fearful, despairing, and fainthearted (*3 Henry VI*: I, i, 178), Henry reveals himself to be the exact opposite of the Elizabethan aspiring mind: "Was never subject long'd to be a king/ As I do long and wish to be a subject" (*2 Henry VI*: IV, ix, 5-6). Henry is also the antithesis of the revengers of the 1580s; in a play filled with the deaths of fathers and sons, he suffers the loss of his own son just before he himself dies.

But, unlike Hieronimo and Titus, he has neither the time nor the temperament to be driven into a frenzied obsession with revenge by the loss he has suffered. Whereas the revenger thinks only of the past, Henry looks forward to the future as he assumes the prophetic voice of a martyred saint, predicting Richard's bloody progress to the throne. His dying words are the very antithesis of the revenger's: he tells Richard, who has just stabbed him, "O God forgive my sins, and pardon thee" (*3 Henry VI*: V, vi, 60). Henry thus emerges as a victim who triumphs over his persecutor by facing death nobly, much as Foxe's martyrs did. Shakespeare makes it clear that his weakness as a king is inextricably linked with his goodness as a man. In Act IV, just before he is taken to the Tower, he naively expresses his trust in his virtues' power to win the support of his people:

> My pity hath been balm to heal their wounds,
> My mildness hath allay'd their swelling griefs,
> My mercy dried their water-flowing tears;
> I have not been desirous of their wealth,
> Nor much oppress'd them with great subsidies,
> Nor forward of revenge, though they much err'd.
> Then why should they love Edward more than me?
> (IV, viii, 41-47)

If these qualities cannot save his life, they can save his soul, and though Richard tells his bleeding corpse "If any spark of life be yet remaining/ Down, down to hell, and say I sent thee thither" (V, vi, 66-67), the Elizabethan audience would almost certainly have felt that Henry was destined for heaven.[2]

---

[2] J. P. Brockbank has noted that Henry VI is a sacrificial victim and that Richard, as he himself boasts, is a Judas figure in *3 Henry VI*. See "The Frame of Disorder—Henry VI," rpt. in *Twentieth Century Views: Shakespeare: The Histories*, ed. Eugene Waith (Englewood Cliffs, New Jersey, 1965), pp. 55-65. Cf. Larry S. Champion in *Perspective in Shakespeare's English Histories* (Athens, Georgia, 1980), on Henry as an ambivalent figure: "On the one hand, the spectators despise him for his inability to govern the passions and the ambitions of those who surround him. On the other, they tend on occasion to admire him for a passivity provoked by religious concern (p. 33).

And so the weak king, understandably dreaded by Tyndale, emerges as the elect saint, in direct contrast to the diabolical tyrant, Richard, Duke of Gloucester. Richard is in many respects the most complete rendering of the protagonist as "other" in the plays of the late 1580s and early 1590s.[3] His "otherness" is physical as well as moral, and he revels in it just as the morality play Vices, from whom he is so clearly descended, revelled in theirs. *Richard III* employs a number of other morality play strategies, including the verbal manipulation at which Richard excels, the penitent recognition speeches delivered by Hastings and Buckingham, and the deliberately parallel treatment of Richmond as the saved protagonist and Richard as the damned one. The morality play structure invites the audience to look at Richard's tyranny from a quite different perspective from Tyndale's pragmatic one. The Christian premise that goodness is always stronger than evil leads to the conclusion that the tyrant's strength will fail him when he confronts the strength of the divinely ordained leader whose power comes from God.

Marlowe's *Edward II* expands upon the theme of the weak king whose status places him at the upper limit of human achievement when the play begins, and whose aspirations point downward, away from power and great renown and toward the anonymity, privacy, and repose that belongs to those in modest stations. This idea of inverse aspiration, which Shakespeare would employ in his portrait of Richard II and then in subsequent plays seriously questions the value of the traditional trappings of power and privilege. These trappings, as

[3] Richard's "otherness" was nicely formulated by Edward Dowden, who remarked that he "inverts the moral order of things, and tries to live in this inverted system." (Quoted by E.M.W. Tillyard in *Shakespeare's History Plays* [New York, 1946] p. 210.) More recently, Edward Berry has likened Richard's role to that of the Antichrist: ". . . he is not merely a figure of demonic evil who fulfills the will of God, an 'angel with horns,' but one who mocks, parodies, inverts all Christian values." He suggests that Shakespeare makes use of the "underlying cultural myth of the Apocalypse." *Patterns of Decay: Shakespeare's Early Histories* (Charlottesville, Va., 1975), pp. 93-94.

Richard II eventually realizes, are little more than physical properties external to the essential self. Edward and Richard begin at the point that conventional aspirers strive toward; both are youthful kings who have taken for granted what Tamburlaine and his progeny had to work to attain. Neither Edward nor Richard is as obvious a weak king as Henry VI, however, nor is either so unambiguously transformed into a martyred saint. Rather, both kings presume upon and misuse their powers even as they chafe against the responsibilities which power confers. At once victims and villains, divinely anointed kings and threats to public order, Edward and Richard combined elements of what the Elizabethans perceived as the "other" and admirable qualities with which they could identify. This mixture, particularly in *Richard II*, produced a more human and more tragic protagonist than any hitherto presented on the Elizabethan stage.

I. ASSURANCE AND DESPAIR IN *Richard III*

Richard III is a study in assurance coupled with unabashed villainy, an assurance akin to the theatrical bravura of the Vice, but depicted with a fearful and fascinating realism—for Richard, unlike the allegorical Vices, is a human being. Richard nevertheless deliberately repudiates his humanity, setting himself apart from mankind as a monster whose defining qualities are the opposites of the positive ones he will play upon in others: "And if King Edward be as true and just/ As I am subtle, false, and treacherous,/ This day should Clarence closely be mew'd up . . ." (I, i, 36-38). Richard's eagerness to celebrate his own villainy is at once alienating and appealing, alienating because he claims for himself the qualities reserved for reprobate "others," and appealing because he projects an absolute confidence in his ability to control events. His is the assurance of the consummate actor, who prevails over others through the sheer force of language. Watching him perform, as for example in the wooing scene, the audience is left with the feeling that anything is possible for those bold enough to believe against all odds in their own success.[4]

From the moment Richard steps onstage, Shakespeare emphasizes the physical deformities which Thomas More's account had made a permanent feature of the Crookback legend.[5] Richard's insistence upon his grotesqueness in the opening soliloquy allies him with the devil (all nature, even barking dogs, recoils against him). Yet, interestingly, his physical traits seem less the outward manifestation of evil in a well-ordered universe where appearance corresponds to essence, than pretexts for the villainy he deliberately embraces. In this respect Richard anticipates Edmund and Iago, two rationalists who, even as they attribute their villainy to the abuses of society,

[4] The audience's dual response to Richard has been discussed in various ways by a number of recent critics. Nicholas Brooke, for example, notes in *Shakespeare's Early Tragedies* (London, 1968) that "in the technical construction of the play, Richard is set apart from the other actors. . . . Everyone else is distanced from the audience, is in sense taking part in a play within a play of which Richard is the presenter." This alienates (in the Brechtian sense) the other characters, which makes it difficult for us to detach ourselves from Richard and sympathize with his victims (p. 57). A. P. Rossiter, in "Angel with Horns: The Unity of Richard III," in *Angel With Horns*, ed. Graham Storey (London, 1961), emphasizes Richard's "impish spirit" and delight in his craft which makes the audience forget to pity his victims and "urges us toward a positive reversal of Christian charity" (p. 78). Similarly, A. C. Hamilton, in *The Early Shakespeare* (San Marino, California, 1967), says that Richard "browbeats us into accepting him" by using tricks to provide the delight for which we come to the theatre. In a discussion of Anne's inexplicable yielding to Richard, Hamilton proposes that her "submission becomes ours: with her we recognize the reasons to curse Richard, yet we find our horror replaced by fascination" (p. 192). In all of these appraisals, the audience's attitude toward Richard is inextricably linked with their contrasting attitude toward other characters.

[5] For a discussion of the evolution of the Tudor portrait of Richard III, starting with Sir Thomas More's *History of King Richard III* (1557), see Geoffrey Bullough, *Narrative and Dramatic Sources of Shakespeare*, Vol. III (London, 1960). Shakespeare's main sources for *Richard III* were Hall's and Holinshed's reshaping of More's history. He may also have been familiar with two earlier plays, Thomas Legge's Latin play *Richardus Tertius* (1579-1580) and *The True Tragedy of Richard III* (1589?), both of which present Richard as a Senecan tyrant and emphasize the revenge motif.

also take complete credit for all of their actions.[6] By using Vice-like soliloquies to establish an intimacy between the audience and such characters, Shakespeare invites us to adopt their perspective. Yet he also contrasts this explanation for the origins of evil with another, antithetical one, particularly in *Richard III*, where a self-assertive, autonomous villain is posed against the traditional scourge of God.

From the point of view embodied in Margaret, a choral figure whose presence is intentionally ahistorical, Richard is the unwitting agent of God's vengeance upon the wicked. He is the scourge sent to punish and destroy the last generation of evildoers in the bloody succession of events that began when Henry Bullingbrook became king and will conclude with Richmond's restoration of order. Shakespeare thus ironically juxtaposes the Tudor myth with the depiction of a character who cannot be contained within its controlling vision.[7] If Richard is a scourge, he is also an honest, forthright creature who claims no motive other than pure self-interest. Because he lacks Tamburlaine's self-righteous conviction that he is the agent of divine punishment, his assurance is more human but also more damnable than Tamburlaine's.

Richard's own arrogant dismissal of religious sanctions and divine justice does not prevent him from exploiting the conventional beliefs of other characters in the play. His greatest moment occurs when he impersonates a humble believer reluctantly compelled to give up his otherworldly occupation for the sake of his country. Richard has all along shared with the audience his intention to "seem a saint, when most I play

---

[6] Richard's kinship with Iago and Edmund as Machiavels whose wickedness is ostensibly caused by the society they react against because of their resentment about their deformity, bastardy, or ill-usage is discussed by John F. Danby in *Shakespeare's Doctrine of Nature: A Study of King Lear* (London, 1948).

[7] The idea that Shakespeare has coupled two quite different myths with ironic effect is Rossiter's (*Angel with Horns*, p. 82). For extended descriptions of the Tudor myth and readings of the history plays as conventional expressions of the workings of divine providence see Tillyard, Ribner, and M. M. Reese in *The Cease of Majesty* (London, 1961).

the devil," clothing his "naked villainy" with "odd old ends
stol'n forth of holy writ" (I, iii, 335-37). The saint-devil antithesis is the basis for the scene in which he agrees to become
king. Richard enacts so broad a parody of Christian humility
that the spectator may have difficulty understanding how the
citizens could be taken in. Everything is carefully staged: after
a suitable preparatory dialogue between Buckingham and
Catesby describing the holy man on his knees in meditation
and prayer, Richard enters flanked by two bishops. The bishops are quite literally "Two props of virtue" in the theatrical
sense, just as the prayer book is a strategic ornament:

> Mayor: See where his Grace stands, 'tween two clergymen!
> Buck: Two props of virtue for a Christian prince,
>   To stay him from the fall of vanity;
>   And see, a book of prayer in his hand—
>   True ornaments to know a holy man.
>   (III, vii, 95-98)

Richard's disguise is a much verbal as visual: his characteristically sardonic speeches with their comic pragmatic asides are
replaced by a humorless formality. His long, ponderous response to the proffered crown brilliantly captures the accents
of those Puritans whose zealous commitment to a life of unswerving holiness was a form of pride. In a splendid caricature
of the rhetoric of the elect, Richard boasts that "so much is
my poverty of spirit,/ So mighty and so many my defects,/
That I would rather hide me from my greatness—" (III, vii,
159-61). He does, of course, reverse himself, in a mock recantation that seeks to excuse itself by invoking the still recalci-
trant conscience and soul; "Call them again, I am not made
of stones,/ But penetrable to your kind entreaties,/ Albeit against
my conscience and my soul" (224-26). We can speculate that
the Elizabethan audience would have enjoyed the joke at the
expense of the gullible audience of citizens onstage, and at the
same time regarded Richard's performance with a suitable degree of disapproval. They may have viewed this mockery of
religious zeal as blasphemy of the worst kind, while realizing
that because it occurred within the confines of the play it was

unlikely to constitute a serious threat to the precarious religious stability of their own time.

Richard's diabolical parody of the elect man of God is only one of several incidents where the contrast between the elect and the reprobate serves as a source of dramatic effect. Shakespeare prepares his audience for the final powerful comparison of Richard and Richmond with scenes that encourage the audience to think in terms of salvation and damnation as they pass judgment on secondary characters toward whom they feel little emotional engagement. In one of the most interesting of such scenes, the audience's own moral dilemmas in the face of temptation are vividly reflected in the dialogue between the two hired murderers sent by Richard to kill Clarence (I, iv, 84 ff.). Shakespeare creates an exchange that sounds remarkably like one of Perkins' instructive dialogues. The first murderer, whom we might call the Momentarily Conscience-Stricken Reprobate, deliberates with the second murderer, an example of the Weak but Repentant Christian, just as if they were personified attitudes in a tract designed to help readers to overcome their doubts of election and conviction of sin. The second murderer hesitates to stab Clarence as he sleeps, holding back from sin not through love of virtue but through fear of being damned. He finally achieves a Faustian inversion of resolution, defeating a few remaining "dregs of conscience" by recalling the purse which is the worldly counterpart of the reward that the saint seeks in heaven. Now the roles are reversed: the once unswerving first murderer, open to the power of suggestion, succumbs to the "blushing shame-fac'd spirit" conscience. When the second murderer exhorts him to "Take the devil in thy mind, and believe him not; he would insinuate with thee but to make thee sigh" the first murderer regains his resolution: "I am strong-fram'd, he cannot prevail with me."[8]

---

[8] For a discussion of this scene as a personification of the workings of conscience, see Wolfgang Clemen, *A Commentary on Shakespeare's Richard III*, trans. Jean Bonheim (London, 1968), pp. 83 ff. William B. Toole views the

Together they confront Clarence, who adopts the posture of a sainted martyr, attempting to save the souls of those who would kill him.

> I charge you, as you hope [to have redemption
> By Christ's dear blood shed for our grievous sins,]
> That you depart, and lay no hands on me.
> The deed you undertake is damnable.

He reminds the murderers that God "holds vengeance in his hand,/ To hurl upon their heads that break his law." The murderers in turn assume a tone of pious superiority toward Clarence, calling attention to past events which stand in the way of simple moral judgments:

> Second Mur. And that same vengeance doth he hurl on
> thee
> For false forswearing and for murther too.
> Thou didst receive the sacrament to fight
> In quarrel of the house of Lancaster.
> First Mur. And like a traitor to the name of God
> Didst break that vow, and with thy treacherous blade
> Unrip'st the bowels of thy sov'reign's son.

The first murderer concludes, "How canst thou urge God's dreadful law to us,/ When thou hast broke it in such dear degree?" Cruelly depicting Richard as a diabolical anti-God who "delivers you/ From this earth's thralldom" the murderers shatter Clarence's illusions about his brother. Shakespeare passes up this opportunity to explore Clarence's feelings, concentrating instead on the debate between the murderers and their victim. This debate centers upon some of the most problematic issues of the age, the conflict between obedience to a temporal superior and obedience to divine law, and the question

---

"conscience-created psychological separation" of the two murderers as a foreshadowing of the psychological division that occurs later in Richard, noting that Richard eventually follows the path of the first murderer rather than the second. "The Motif of Psychic Division in Richard III," *Shakespeare Survey*, XXVII (1974), pp. 28, 31.

of whether men are justified in becoming agents of God's vengeance against one who has sinned against God. This is a variation on the revenger's dilemma in little, although the two hired murderers lack the psychological complexity of a Hieronimo or a Hamlet. Clarence's repeated allusions to the Bible and the Book of Common Prayer intensify the religious implications of their dilemma, as the argument moves from legal and theological points to an appeal to human feeling.[9] Clarence, at this moment, possesses the stature and the persuasive power of the preacher; so formidable is his presence that the dialogue comes to an abrupt halt as the second murderer asks helplessly, "What shall we do?" Clarence intones: "Relent, and save your souls" (the substitute of "relent" for "repent" is obvious); to which the first murderer scornfully responds, "Relent? No, 'tis cowardly and womanish." Clarence appeals to the second murderer, in whose eye he spies some pity, but it is too late. The first murderer stabs Clarence and carts him off to the malmsey-butt, leaving the belatedly repentant second murderer to lament, "A bloody deed, and desperately dispatch'd!/ How fain, like Pilate, would I wash my hands/ Of this most grievous murther!" (I, iv, 84-273.) The second murderer confirms his repentance by refusing his share of the fee and sending a defiant message to Richard. Whether this act is sufficient to insure him a place in heaven— and, for that matter, whether the pious sounding though tainted Clarence is destined for heaven—remains unsaid, for the play is, after all, a play and not a tract.

Although the murderer of Clarence would seem to add nothing to the characterization of the play's protagonist, it reveals quite a lot about Shakespeare's willingness to learn how to construct dialogue from the non-dramatic sources that were familiar to his audience. Shakespeare was probably inspired

---

[9] Wilbur Sanders has an interesting discussion of the moral ambiguities in this scene: he notes that "Clarence has no right to live, the Murderers none to kill." *The Dramatist and the Received Idea* (Cambridge, 1968), pp. 78-79. Clemen discusses the issues of divine vengeance and justice in *A Commentary*, pp. 86-87.

by a brief, albeit very human, moment of hesitation experienced by the "two murtherous villaines that are resolute" which occurred just before the murder of the two young princes in *The True Tragedy of Richard III*.[10] Shakespeare may have decided to use the scene at the beginning of his play as a way of drawing attention to the effect that murder has on the murderer, both before and after the event. By exempting Richard from such momentary qualms, he is indirectly calling attention to the "otherness" that sets his protagonist apart from ordinary men. Shakespeare's conspicuous use of the instructive dialogue form to probe the workings of conscience and the logic men use with themselves and others suggests that at this point in his career as a playwright he was still feeling his way toward the complex and naturalistic characterization of the later plays.

Another episode involving a secondary character that reveals Shakespeare's receptivity to the concepts and character types being examined by the preachers occurs in Act III, scenes ii and iv, when Hastings undergoes his abrupt and ironic fall from grace.[11] This episode is reminiscent of a sermon exemplum, for the consequences of Hastings' blind assurance are, or should be, a direct warning to all of the other characters, including Richard himself. As Richard will later do, Hastings contemptuously dismisses the prophetic warning dream, secure in his conviction that he is favored by the "boar." Hastings is very like the bold and presumptuous sinners whom the preachers and chroniclers depict revelling in their prosperity and the downfall of their enemies, just before they them-

[10] Bullough, *Narrative and Dramatic Sources*, pp. 326 ff. Interestingly, the hesitant murderer, after being exhorted by his fellow, says, "now I am resolute"; like Faustus, his resolution leads him away from heaven rather than toward it.

[11] For a discussion of the idea of the Fall as a major theme in the history plays, see John Wilders, *The Lost Garden: Shakespeare's History Plays* (London, 1978). Wilders argues that, while Shakespeare was not a consciously theological writer, the doctrines of the Fall were part of the instinctive way he looked at history.

selves are suddenly struck down by the unrelenting hand of God. This is the presumption of the reprobate who mistakes himself for one of the elect. Succumbing to the sinner's false assurance that he is loved by God and understands God's ways, Hastings has fallen into the error of believing in appearances: "I know he loves me well," he confidently asserts, and "For by his face straight shall you know his heart . . ." (III, iv, 14, 53). This is in many respects an ironically comic moment, not only because of the audience's superior knowledge as they anticipate Hastings' fall, but also because the agent of retribution is not God but the playfully cruel Richard, who entraps the unsuspecting Hastings into pronouncing his own sentence. As in the morality plays and the *de casibus* chronicles, Hastings is given a final speech of recognition, in which he laments the "momentary grace of mortal men/ Which we more hunt for than the grace of God" (III, iv, 96-97). The contrast between More's account, where the narrator delivers the lesson ("O Lorde God the blyndenesse of our mortal nature . . ."), and Shakespeare's dramatization is revealing. Hastings couches his and other men's error in terms of aspiration rather than blindness, aspiration for the wrong kind of grace.[12]

Hastings' recognition that his death is the deserved outcome of his "too fond" actions will be echoed by Buckingham in Act V, scene i. In his moment of recognition, Buckingham recalls his vows to be true to Edward and his children which, providentially, have brought about his fall. Both Hastings' and Buckingham's speeches are clearly indebted to *A Mirror for Magistrates*, where lamenting ghosts look back on the events of their lives and describe their punishments for the enlightenment of others. Shakespeare will eventually explore the potentially tragic failure of such recognition scenes to constitute genuine acts of repentance, in Claudius' famous speech which acknowledges both the severity of his sin and his inability to seek divine forgiveness.

Although in *Richard III* Shakespeare is still relying heavily

[12] Hamilton, *The Early Shakespeare*, p. 196.

on the parallel circumstances of secondary characters to explore the moral and psychological implications of Richard's actions, the play does show early signs of the character development that will distinguish the later tragedies. Once Richard is king, the comic assurance of the Vice that had sustained him from one victory to the next begins to undergo a subtle change, giving way to the uneasy fear of losing control. His chilling treatment of Buckingham and the haunting recollections of a prophecy concerning Richmond in Act IV, scene ii, anticipate analogous moments in *Macbeth*, as do the cold-blooded arrangements with Tyrell for the murder of the princes. Shakespeare uses scenes which parallel earlier ones to emphasize the change taking place in Richard's character. The Richard who engages in logic chopping with Queen Elizabeth about her daughter has none of the bold wittiness of the Richard who wooed Lady Anne with such effortless audacity. The audience senses that the Queen has gained control of the exchange and is scoring rhetorical points, forcing Richard to intensify his vows and even call down curses on himself to prove his good intentions. It is not at all clear that Richard wins this debate; indeed, when the audience learns in the next scene that Elizabeth has promised her daughter to Richmond, they may feel that she evaded him quite skillfully.

In the final scenes Richard ceases to be the confiding clever Vice. The audience is encouraged to view him from a distance as the monstrous "other," the "wretched, bloody, and usurping boar" who spoils the fields and swills the blood of his hapless subjects (V, ii, 7-9). Shakespeare employs the morality play contrast of Worldly Man and Heavenly Man to reinforce the audience's sense of Richard's "otherness" in the highly symmetrical scene set in the two camps on the eve of battle. Like the morality Heavenly Man, Richmond is a one-dimensional figure whose every action and word makes him the antithesis of Richard. For example, when Richard sends Stanley a message bearing the threat that his son George Stanley will "fall/ Into the blind cave of eternal night" if Stanley's regiment fails to arrive, Richmond offers his stepfather "all comfort that the dark night can afford." While Richard calls for a bowl of wine to restore his wonted "alacrity of spirit" and "cheer of mind," Richmond prays to God: "Make us thy ministers of chastisement/ That we may praise thee in the victory." In the elaborately ritualized succession of visitations to the two sleeping generals, the ghosts of Richard's victims deliver their contrasting injunctions: to Richmond they say "Live and flourish," to Richard, "Despair and die" (V, iii, 120 ff.). The haunting repetition of the phrase "despair and die" fixes Richard's identity as a damned soul, doomed to suffer the spiritual torment of despair which is the opposite of assurance. Richmond, in contrast, receives repeated assurances that the next day's joyful victory will be accomplished with "good angels," external symbols of his election. Richmond is a member of the elect in the strictly Calvinist sense, not because of any intrinsic merit in himself but because God has chosen him to be His minister, the agent through whom He will finally destroy the evil scourge.[13]

Just when the repeated contrasts of heaven and hell, ascent and descent, success and defeat, seem to have firmly "placed" Richard, resolving any of the ambivalence that the audience may have felt toward him up to this point, Shakespeare overturns his audience's expectations in what Rabkin has called "a crucial moment both in the play and in Shakespeare's career."[14] Richard's final soliloquy is a complete departure from his earlier Vice-like soliloquies; like Faustus' very similar last speech, it offers the audience a genuinely tragic spectacle of internal conflict, spiritual struggle, and a fleeting moment of

[13] Richmond has sometimes been viewed as a noble and heroic figure in his own right: Robert Ornstein, for instance calls him a "spiritual leader who brings a new dispensation of mercy to England" in *A Kingdom for a Stage: The Achievement of Shakespeare's History Plays* (Cambridge, Massachusetts, 1972), p. 81. I would argue however, that Richmond is primarily significant as Richard's adversary. His role is to define Richard by being the opposite of him in every respect (cf. Champion, *Perspective in Shakespeare's English Histories*, p. 60).

[14] Rabkin, *Shakespeare and the Common Understanding* (New York, 1967), p. 25.

insight or recognition that comes too late and is insufficient to redeem the soul mired in guilt. Richard engages himself in dialogue, dramatizing the shifting relationship between the "I" and the "self" as he explores two different attitudes. The first, "I love myself," recalls his self-congratulatory manner in the first half of the play. The opposite attitude, "O no! Alas, I rather hate myself/ For hateful deeds committed by myself," introduces a new note of self-condemnation which, if pursued, could lead to repentance. Richard vacillates crazily between these two positions: "I am a villain; yet I lie, I am not./ Fool, of thyself speak well; fool, do not flatter." His conscience, with its "thousand several tongues," condemns him, and he arrives at the terrible realization of his utter isolation: "And if I die no soul will pity me." That he is divided from others is a logical consequence of his internal division: "And wherefore should they, since that I myself/ Find in myself no pity to myself?" (V, iii, 177-206.)

Richard's soliloquy has been described as a parody of the mature Shakespearean soliloquy, a case where the dramatist "has bitten off more than he can chew."[15] I find the speech interesting for precisely this reason. Its sing-song repetitions and conventional, homiletic imagery show a clear line of descent from the internal dialogues about the soul's state of election to the more philosophical and less obsessively self-absorbed soliloquies of a decade later. We can speculate that audiences accustomed to hearing, reading, and perhaps undergoing such dialogues would bring their knowledge of that process to the experience of the play. Certainly they would know that Richard, who began this speech by crying out "Have mercy, Jesu!" has not attained the certainty which the dialogue form could help the elect to attain. Richard backs off from moral awareness and, in the clear morning light, dismisses his "babbling dreams" with the epigrammatic pronouncement:

[15] Sanders, *The Dramatist and the Received Idea*, p. 107.

> Conscience is but a word that cowards use,
> Devis'd at first to keep the strong in awe:
> Our strong arms be our conscience, swords our law!
> March on, join bravely, let us to it pell-mell;
> If not to heaven, then hand in hand to hell.
>
> (309-13)

This Richard is closer to the one Richmond has just called "God's enemy," and "a bloody tyrant and a homicide" in his oration to his troops, than to the vulnerable, wretched soul who moments before had forced himself to confront the truth of his guilt and the knowledge that "there is no creature loves me" (200 ff.). With the return of the parallel structure, Richard once more becomes the antithesis of Richmond. His oration, in contrast to Richmond's, never invokes the support of God. It does, however, end with a stirring call for bravery which reminds the audience that Richard, damned soul though he may be, is still a heroic leader. This image is reinforced by Catesby's description of Richard enacting "more wonders than a man" and by Richard's wonderful last speech:

> Slave, I have set my life upon a cast,
> And I will stand the hazard of the die.
> I think there be six Richmonds in the field;
> Five have I slain to-day in stead of him.
> A horse, a horse! my kingdom for a horse!
>
> (V, iv, 9-13)

As Richmond and his followers celebrate the final restoration of peace and the union of the houses of Lancaster and York, the audience is left with two images of Richard that cannot be brought into focus. He is at once the heroic warrior resisting oppression to the very end, and the "bloody dog," the despised outsider, who is isolated from mankind by his dedication to evil. Unlike his fellow Vice and Machiavel Barabas, who degenerates into a comic, farcical figure in the later scenes of his play and so resolves the audience's dilemma for

263

them, Richard comes very close to being a tragic figure in his final moments onstage.[16] While the Elizabethan audience could not help but assent to the conventional expressions of divine purpose which give meaning to the events they have witnessed, their temporary engagement with the protagonist would not be easily forgotten. Richard, along with Faustus and Tamburlaine, remained fixed in their imaginations as embodiments, however perverse, of their own aspirations, and of the boldness and assurance that were both celebrated and condemned by the culture in which they lived.[17]

II. TRAGEDY OF A WEAK KING: *Edward II*

Edward II was twenty-three years old when he became King of England in 1307, but, as the chroniclers portray him, he seems much younger. In temperament and behavior, he resembles the self-indulgent, pleasure-loving morality play Youth figures, who are pulled in opposite directions by characters representing the principles of virtue and vice. Marlowe must have recognized the potential morality play structures which lay just beneath the surface of Holinshed's account of Edward's reign, for the design of his play deliberately emphasizes the conflicting claims of illicit private pleasure, represented by Gaveston, and public responsibility, represented at first by the barons and later by Kent and the Prince. The second half of the play more closely resembles the Heavenly Man - Worldly Man scheme, with Mortimer in the role of the unscrupulous and ambitious Worldly Man and Edward as the suffering, oth-

---

[16] Brooke observes that Richard, who derived his role from the Vice, in a sense becomes Mankind as well, "the human representative, bolder than ourselves, resisting oppression, and being destroyed." He is "the condemned outsider, rising to power by sheer force of will" (*Shakespeare's Early Tragedies*, pp. 79, 77).

[17] As Robert Y. Turner observes in *Shakespeare's Apprenticeship* (Chicago, 1974), "the plotting permits us to indulge some of our anarchic impulses within a narrative of poetic justice that exorcises them at the end . . ." (p. 127).

erworldly martyr. In Edward and Mortimer the audience is presented with the weak king and the tyrant, neither of whom shows any real concern for the country and its people. The ideal synthesis of these two extremes will be embodied in Prince Edward, who by the end of the play proves to possess the wisdom, maturity, and ability to exert control which his father lacks.

As a weak king, Edward stands apart from all of Marlowe's other protagonists, all of whom are strong, aspiring over-reachers.[18] Moreover, as Harry Levin has noticed, all are commoners, "self-made men."[19] Curiously, although Edward is more removed from the ordinary spectator in social status, he is ultimately more nearly like themselves. Setting aside the "otherness" that attaches to homosexuality, about which many Elizabethans may have felt ambivalent (particularly since Marlowe employs the classical idealization of friendship to elevate Edward's relationship with his favorites), Edward is a character whose vulnerability gradually commands more and more of the audience's sympathy.[20] We can speculate that the Elizabethans would have felt a closer bond of fellow-feeling with the thoughtful and devout Edward of the final scenes than they did with the fascinating but almost certainly reprobate Tamburlaine, Faustus, and Barabas. This aspect of the play's design is a significant departure from Marlowe's other plays; in effect, Marlowe has reversed the pattern of so many of the plays of the 1580s and 1590s, in which the audience's initial

[18] C. F. Tucker Brooke has suggested that so marked a change in Marlowe's approach to play and character construction might be due to a shift in acting companies; Tamburlaine, Barabas, and Faustus had all been played by Edward Alleyn, whose powerful presence was in large part responsible for the great success of Henslowe's company, The Lord Admiral's Men. *Edward II*, however, was performed by the Earl of Pembroke's company, and Tucker Brooke speculates that Marlowe created a different king of protagonist to suit the resources of a company without a star. "The Life of Marlowe," *The Works and Life of Christopher Marlowe*, ed. R. H. Case (London, 1930).

[19] Harry Levin, *The Overreacher* (Cambridge, 1952), p. 31.

[20] Cf. Paul H. Kocher, *Christopher Marlowe: A Study of His Thought, Learning and Character* (Chapel Hill, 1946), pp. 203-205.

inclination to identify with the protagonist gives way to a sense of detachment and sometimes even moral superiority in the final scene.[21] For this reason alone, *Edward II* signals an important development in the emergence of tragedy, despite its frequently discussed flaws.

These flaws are largely a result of the difficulties Marlowe faced in reducing twenty years' worth of intransigent chronicle material to a single play. Both Mortimer and Gaveston receive much more attention than they do in the chronicles, perhaps because both are examples of the aspiring minds Marlowe's audience had come to expect. Furthermore, Marlowe relies heavily on the audience's shifting judgments about these and other secondary characters to direct the audience's feelings about Edward himself. Instead of gradual transitions, characters undergo abrupt changes, and the play as a whole exhibits a pattern of antithesis.[22] Gaveston, whose opening speeches link him with the Vice tradition, becomes a sympathetic and even dignified figure as he approaches his death, as do his apparently ambitious and unprincipled counterparts, Baldock and Spencer. The Queen undergoes a contrary shift, from a devoted, suffering victim figure to the unscrupulous companion of Mortimer, the strong-willed baron turned ambitious villain. These dualities, unconvincing as they may seem at times, suggest an effort to rise above the morality technique of allegorical characterization and to investigate the contrary elements of which human beings are composed. Marlowe combines the most extreme types of saved and damned, self and "other," thus sacrificing the realism of his secondary char-

[21] For a discussion of the reversal of the pattern of response in *Edward II* see Judith Weil, *Christopher Marlowe: Merlin's Prophet* (Cambridge, 1977), p. 143. Weil is thinking specifically of the pattern in the Tamburlaine plays.

[22] Constance Brown Kuriyama notes in *Hammer and Anvil* (New Brunswick, New Jersey, 1980), that *Edward II* is dominated by the number two, in its pairing of characters, and in the elaborate antithetical or symmetrical motifs. She follows Steane in suggesting the play as a whole falls into two halves, each of which elicits a different response—disapproval toward Edward in the first, and pity toward him in the second (pp. 193-201).

acters, in order to achieve a complex audience response toward his protagonist.

As he had done elsewhere, Marlowe probes the psychology of aspiration in both its positive and negative aspects. Thus the Gaveston of Act I, scene i, joyfully anticipates his reunion with Edward not only because he holds the King so dear, but because it will enable him to bid "Farewell [to] base stooping to the lordly peers" (I, i, 18). Posed squarely against Gaveston in the struggle for Edward's "love" are the barons ("If you love us, my lord, hate Gaveston," Mortimer senior declares to Edward). Edward views "Aspiring Lancaster," Warwick, and the Mortimers as "haughty menaces" who threaten his identity as king: "Am I a king, and must be overruled?" (135.) To thwart them, he impulsively confers the symbols of power upon his friend, despite Kent's prudent warning that one title would suffice. Edward's behavior in these early scenes reveals that the presumptuousness of the aspiring mind can characterize a king as well as those who pursue kingly power. Yet Edward is a more complicated aspirer than Tamburlaine or Faustus, for, although he employs the characteristic rhetoric of aspiration, the political ambitions which this rhetoric articulates are projected by him onto Gaveston, whose rapid ascent in rank enrages the barons. Edward himself aspires downward, much as Henry VI had done; he is willing to divide up and give away the monarchy "So I may have some nook or corner left/ To frolic with my dearest Gaveston" (I, iv, 72-73). In a sense, Tamburlaine's role seems divided between two characters: Gaveston is the one whom the barons accuse of being a peasant "swoll'n with venom of ambitious pride," a Phaeton who "Aspir'st unto the guidance of the sun," yet it is Edward who responds with "I'll make the proudest of you stoop to him (I, ii, 31; I, iv, 15-16, 30). As a king Edward can rise no higher, so his aspirations are invested in his beloved. For himself he desires only pleasure and the freedom to love, and there is a certain poignancy in his response to Mortimer's question "Why should you love him whom the world hates so?" Edward's answer, "Because he loves me more than all the world," is a statement of the importance of loyalty as an antidote to the shifting political allegiances of the play (I, iv, 76-77). Whatever else it is, Edward's devotion to Gaveston is an example of genuine love in a world where that quality is in short supply.[23] As in his other plays, Marlowe uses the story he found in his source to speculate about what consitutes a damnable sin. Just as aspiration, in itself, is not altogether to be condemned, neither is homosexual love, even when it threatens the orderly relationships between man and wife or king and subjects.

Marlowe manipulates his audience's feelings about Edward through a number of techniques. Edward's inconsistent behavior, the treatment he receives from other characters, and Marlowe's deliberate allusions to topical issues all cause the audience to vacillate between engagement and detachment.[24] For example, in the long, event-filled Act I, scene iv, the audience is probably inclined to feel detachment from both sides during the noisy exchange of insults that begins the scene. But once the barons and the Archbishop of Canterbury have succeeded in forcing their King to banish his "minion," Edward becomes a more sympathetic figure, particularly when he appeals to the audience's anti-Catholic sentiments with a rousing speech that begins "Why should a king be subject to a priest?/ Proud Rome . . ." (96 ff.). Alone onstage, Edward and Gaveston arouse genuine pathos as they tearfully exchange pictures and farewells. When they are about to part, Edward's queen, Isabella, enters. Edward turns on her with cruel, ugly words, at which point the audience might begin to see the

[23] Clifford Leech, "Marlowe's *Edward II*: Power and Suffering," *Critical Quarterly*, I, 3, reprinted in *Edward II*, ed. Jacques Chwat (New York, 1974), p. 159. Leech's essay, written in 1958, contains one of the earliest discussions of the audience's ambivalence toward Edward.

[24] Cf. Joel Altman's excellent discussion of the audience's conflicting feelings about Edward. He notes, as I do, that Edward is at once the Protestant martyr and the reckless, despotic king because of the way Marlowe uses the Archbishop (*The Tudor Play of Mind* [Berkeley, 1978]). The pattern of audience response is also explored by Michael Manheim in *The Weak King Dilemma in the Shakespearean History Play* (Syracuse, 1973).

two friends from her perspective, which reduces Gaveston to a "bawd" who has "corrupted" the affections that properly belong to her. But if the Queen's formal lament makes her seem a pitiable victim, her privy conversation with Mortimer a few lines later recalls Edward's angry accusation that she is "too familiar with that Mortimer." This conversation, about the content of which the audience can only speculate, gives rise to the first of Mortimer's devious plots. Just as the barons have agreed to recall Gaveston and then suborn "some base slave" to murder him, Edward returns, mourning his friend's banishment. As he reacts to the news that Gaveston is repealed, the audience's relationship with him takes on a new complexity. From one viewpoint, they regard him somewhat ironically as a self-dramatizing, easily gulled victim, unable to see through Mortimer's plot. But, at the same time, his boyish gratitude and eagerness to reward the barons reveals a very human generosity which invites sympathy. Mortimer senior's thoughtful words to his nephew in the final moments of the scene, after everyone else has left the stage, sum up the audience's ambivalence: he observes that the King is "mild and calm," a "flexible" youth whose love for his friend places him among the honorable company of some of history's greatest kings and wise men. (387, 397.) If Mortimer junior were capable of accepting his uncle's advice to let Edward have his will, tragedy could be averted, but the spectacle of Gaveston's unchecked aspiration is too much for the younger baron to bear. Mortimer hates Gaveston because he is an overreacher, but, ironically, the play's greatest overreacher is Mortimer himself.

Marlowe further complicates the audience's mixed feelings about Edward by introducing the political consequences of his behavior. Mortimer and Lancaster raise the specter of foreign invasion so terrible to the Elizabethans with their vivid descriptions of "the haughty Dane [who] commands the narrow seas" and of "the Northern borderers, seeing their houses burnt,/ Their wives and children slain" by "unresisted" Scots (II, ii, 159 ff.). Their catalogue of evils rouses Edward's ire;

but, as he likens himself to the cruel and tyrannous lion, the audience will be more inclined to identify with the disapproving Kent, who finally decides that he can support his brother no longer.

Kent's shift of allegiance in Act II, scene iii, has frequently been viewed as a signal to the audience; his judgment, Kocher suggests, serves as the play's ethical norm.[25] By adopting his perspective, the audience can view the capricious King as an "other" who no longer deserves the loyalty of his subjects. In the aftermath of Edward's victory in Act III, Kent describes his brother as a "proud" and "unnatural butcher." Unlike the rebellious and vindictive Mortimer, with whom he has joined forces, Kent expresses sentiments of which the audience would wholeheartedly approve: "Would all were well and Edward well reclaimed,/ For England's honor, peace and quietness" (IV, ii, 57-58). Perhaps because it defies orthodox doctrine, Kent's disloyalty to the king is short-lived. During the battle in which Mortimer, Isabella, and the French oppose Edward, Kent once again changes sides. He now realizes that Mortimer is a "proud traitor" with no right to oppose "thy lawful king, thy sovereign" and prays:

> Rain showers of vengeance on my cursed head,
> Thou God, to whom in justice it belongs
> To punish this unnatural revolt.
> (IV, v, 12-18)

There is a direct connection between the audience's willingness to adopt Kent's view of Mortimer and the Queen as two dissembling villains who "do kiss while they conspire" (22) and their increasing engagement with Edward.

Kent's moment of recognition begins the final movement of the play. When the audience next sees Edward, he has be-

---

[25] Kocher, *Christopher Marlowe*, p. 205. See also Levin, who calls Kent "a sort of weathervane whose turnings veer with the rectitude of the situation" (*The Overreacher*, p. 98). For a contrary view, see Weil, who sees Kent as an unreliable figure, who "rarely knows what he is doing" (*Merlin's Prophet*, p. 145).

gun to assume some of the martyred saint's attributes. Disguised and hiding in a monastery, he can no longer take for granted his authority as King. At last, he seems able to view his past life with a detachment that suggests a new maturity, even as it reflects a traditional *de casibus* perception of fortune's overthrows.

> Whilom I was powerful and full of pomp;
> But what is he whom rule and empery
> Have not in life or death made miserable?
> (IV, vi, 13-15)

"This life contemplative is heaven," (20) he muses, as he longs for a quiet life and then, resting his head in the Abbot's lap, for a quiet death. At once he is betrayed into the hands of Leicester and Rice ap Howell by a mower, a harbinger of death. Thus Edward begins his painful journey to a far from quiet end.

The scene in which Edward unwillingly divests himself of his crown has no counterpart in the chronicles; rather, it comes from the tradition of interior debate which was contributing in significant ways to the depiction of the tragic protagonist. Both here and in the corresponding scene in *Richard II* the tense coexistence of the "I" and the "self" in the human psyche is presented as a dramatic encounter between the protagonist's two selves, the King and the man. Marlowe and Shakespeare may have been drawing upon their audience's familiarity with the Elizabethan legal doctrine of "the King's two bodies," which posited a "body natural," the mortal and fallible side of the King, annexed to and indivisible from the "body politic," which was wholly without defect or capacity for error.[26] Like the dichotomies of the saved and the damned or the "I" and the "self," the distinction between the "body natural" and the "body politic" provided a conceptual framework for expressing the

[26] This idea is discussed at length by Maynard Mack, Jr., in *Killing the King; Three Studies in Shakespeare's Tragic Structure* (New Haven, 1973), pp. 4-5. See also Ernst Kantorowicz, *The King's Two Bodies: A Study in Medieval Political Theology* (Princeton, 1957).

uncertainty about the nature of identity which haunted the tragic King as he embarked on the painful process of self-examination. Edward begins his deposition scene by trying on the role of the victim-turned-revenger. Like Hieronimo or Titus, he speaks of "soaring up to heaven/ To plain me to the gods," exhorting himself: "But when I call to mind I am a king,/ Methinks I should revenge me of the wrongs/ That Mortimer and Isabel have done." His thoughts do not pursue the idea of revenge, however; instead, they turn to the elusiveness of his identity as king: "what are kings when regiment is gone,/ But perfect shadows in a sunshine day?" (V, i, 21-27.) Although he is beginning to realize that kingship is a function of power, and not an intrinsic attribute, he nevertheless associates being King with being alive.[27] Like Faustus, he clings to life, succumbing momentarily to the illusion that if time stands still he will not have to undergo the dreaded change of identity symbolized by the physical act of removing the crown. Edward is also haunted by the realization that giving up the crown constitutes a foul crime against God's divinely appointed succession—that by deposing himself he runs the risk of committing a damnable act. Once the deed is done, however, he redefines his terms. With God's help, he will "despise this transitory pomp/ And sit for aye enthronized in heaven." Whether in death or in life, he seeks to escape the consciousness of self: "Come, death, and with thy fingers close my eyes,/ Or if I live, let me forget myself" (108-11). But he cannot forget his self, and with a self-indulgent theatricality that Richard II was later to share he sends the Queen a handkerchief wet with his tears, and rends Mortimer's name on a piece of paper. None of this is in Holinshed, which speaks of Edward's "marvelous agonie" without further elaboration.

---

[27] These lines should be compared with Richard II's reflective speech in III, ii, which begins "Let's talk of graves, of worms, of epitaphs." The recognition that within the hollow crown ... Keeps Death his court ..." is much like Edward's metaphor of the shadow. Note that "regiment" means government or control over oneself as well as rule or government of others (OED).

Holinshed's Edward does acknowledge and ask forgiveness for his errors, however. The chronicle relates that "he vtterlie renounced his right to the kingdome, and to the whole administration thereof. And lastlie he besought the lords now in his miserie to forgive him such offenses as he had committed against them."[28] Marlowe's Edward, in contrast, asks "Yet how have I transgressed,/ Unless it be with too much clemency?" (122-23.) He thus leaves the sphere of the morality play protagonist, who experiences regeneration after his life of sin, and enters a tragically ironic world where self-knowledge may remain forever out of reach. The audience's recognition of Edward's blindness prevents them from identifying too closely at this point,[29] but they clearly feel something quite different from the horrified detachment inspired by the bloodstained revenger at the end of *The Spanish Tragedy* or *Titus Andronicus*. Those feelings are reserved for Mortimer and the Queen, who at this very moment plot his death.

Although secondary characters continue to direct audience sympathy and identification toward Edward in the final scenes, the doomed King is also capable of inspiring pathos and even admiration on his own. After the pitiful moment when he asks for a drink and is shaved with filthy puddle water, he thinks of Gaveston, whose shade he addresses:

> For me both thou and both the Spencers died,
> And for your sakes a thousand wrongs I'll take.
> The Spencers' ghosts, wherever they remain,
> Wish well to mine; then tush, for them I'll die.
>
> (V, iii, 42-45)

[28] Raphael Holinshed, *Chronicles of England, Scotland, and Ireland* (London, 1807; rpt., New York, 1965), II, 585.

[29] Weil sees this question as tragic in spirit: "It characterizes a hero who is belatedly starting to know the world he is bound to by examining himself" (*Merlin's Prophet*, p. 147). Douglas Cole, in contrast, sees "this blind conviction of innocence" as "the ultimate irony" in Edward's tragedy, an irony which "helps to keep the response to his maltreatment from being one of total indignation" (*Suffering and Evil in the Plays of Christopher Marlowe*, pp. 177-78).

273

There is a generosity of spirit here which develops even in the course of the speech. Edward begins by asking the gods to punish his tormentors but ends by acknowledging his responsibility for his friends' death and accepting the consequences. Edward's final dialogue with Lightborn, the "Lucifer" who comes bearing death, displays several sides of his character. He is self-pitying and still insistent on his identity as King, yet he has risen above his earlier self-centeredness, for he wants his mind to be "steadfast on my God" in the moment of his death (V, v, 77). His almost childlike helplessness and fearfulness, as he places himself in the hands of one whom he instinctively suspects yet longs to believe in, must have had a powerful effect on the Elizabethan audience, whose preconceptions about the behavior of monarchs were being challenged by this lifelike display of human vulnerability. His is the natural weakness in the face of death characteristic of the ordinary Christian, and his final plea, "Assist me, sweet God, and receive my soul" (108), might have encouraged the audience to believe that his "hell of grief" on earth had purged him of his sins and earned him a place in heaven. Physically, Edward's death is bizarre and alienating, as critics repeatedly point out. But Edward's confrontation with death is intensely human and invites an engagement which, depending on the production, could conceivably outweigh the horror of the spit, featherbed, and table.

The final scenes of *Edward II* contain many villains, but Edward is not among them. Surrounded by Lightborn, Matrevis, Gurney, Mortimer, and the Queen, Edward has become a sympathetic figure against whom the cruelty of his persecutors stands out in sharp relief, and his death at their hands is perceived as a tragic ordeal. But it is also a self-wrought ordeal, as Edward seems at least partly to realize. This is an early, albeit incomplete, tragedy of self-realization, one in which the protagonist recognizes that he has brought on his tragedy and that his death is simultaneously just and unjust. Edward's tragedy is deliberately contrasted with Mortimer's fall from the top of Fortune's wheel. Mortimer's death is just in a very simple and direct way: the aspirer who said *"Major sum quam cui possit fortuna nocere"* ("I am too great for fortune to harm me") now realizes that in Fortune's wheel "There is a point, to which when men aspire,/ They tumble headlong down" (V, iv, 69; vi, 60-61). Edward's death is a more ambiguous example of justice, for it is both the punishment due to the sinner and the release due to the victim, a release from the long-shunned responsibilities of kingship leading to a better and more congenial existence in heaven. As such, it elicits both the sense of moral superiority the audience felt in the presence of the reprobate "other" and the sympathy and identification they had once felt for the Mankind or Youth figure. But, unlike the morality play ending, Edward's "reformation" is incomplete and insufficient to save him from suffering and eventual death.[30] Moreover, there are no merciful agents of God who miraculously avert tragedy, although there is a clearly elect Youth figure, King Edward III, who acts as God's agent in distributing justice and restoring order.[31]

III. *Richard II*

Edward II and *Richard II* have frequently been compared, and it is universally agreed that *Richard II* is both the better play and the more profound depiction of tragic character. Although Marlowe experiments with the idea of a protagonist whose own choices bring him to the point where tragedy becomes inevitable, as a playwright he falls back on the stark opposition of the conventional villain and victim archetypes

[30] Although it is possible to read the play as Cole does ("the suffering of Edward . . . is the suffering of a lost soul, a soul condemned to . . . material damnation"), I would argue that here, for the first time, Marlowe's audience was genuinely undecided about the protagonist's state of election (*Suffering and Evil*, pp. 173-74).

[31] For an extremely interesting discussion of Prince Edward's role, see Kuriyama, *Hammer and Anvil*, pp. 207-208. She sees an antithetical contrast between the King and his son: ". . . old Edward is ostensibly a man and a king, but actually a child; the Prince is physically a child, but has the character of a man and a king."

275

which the revenge tragedies had begun to dismantle. By the end of *Edward II* the protagonist has become a victim defined largely by his horrible suffering, while his antagonist has become a crudely over-simplified villain who persecutes the victim and is duly punished. Shakespeare took pains to avoid such easy moral distinctions in his study of the deposition of Richard II, despite the fact that earlier accounts of King Richard's reign seemed at times to reduce him to either the villain or the victim.[32] Using the situation presented by his sources, Shakespeare transformed the dual-protagonist play, with its Heavenly Man - Worldly Man scheme, into something quite different. Although Richard's and Bullingbrook's opposite qualities are dramatized through direct confrontation and contrast, the play provides no final assessment of their respective states of election. Indeed, *Richard II* is a thoroughly dialectical play, for it poses against one another two equally compelling but antithetical ways of perceiving the two major characters.[33]

To achieve this dialectical effect, Shakespeare made good use of his contemporaries' conflicting attitudes toward the events he dramatized. Bullingbrook was variously perceived as an unprincipled rebel against the Lord's anointed, a divinely appointed scourge who would himself be scourged, and as a leader who was chosen by the people to rescue England from chaos and who became King through the workings of Providence.[34] The duality of saved and damned is implicit in all of

---

[32] Ornstein notes that Shakespeare could have followed the earlier play *Thomas of Woodstock* in presenting Richard as a criminal, the puppet of sycophants, or the French chronicles in making him a saintly martyr. But he saw that there were neither heroes nor villains in Richard's fall (*A Kingdom for a Stage*, p. 107).

[33] Brooke suggests a tripartite scheme for *Richard II*: on the level of the divine, Shakespeare poses the king against the rebellious angel, on that of the political, the bad king against the competent rebel, and on the personal, the weak man against the strong man (*Shakespeare's Early Tragedies*, p. 128).

[34] Cf. Sanders' discussion of the attitudes contained in contemporary accounts (*The Dramatist and the Received Idea*, pp. 151 and notes). Irving Ribner, who regards Bullingbrook as "almost a passive instrument of destiny,"

these theories, but each offers a different judgment about which King is saved and which is damned. Just as the same attributes, under different circumstances, could characterize the reprobate and the elect, so the historical events surrounding Richard's deposition could be interpreted in entirely different ways. By refusing to commit himself to one interpretation, Shakespeare succeeded in transforming history into tragedy.

According to Holinshed, Richard was a youth much like the morality Youth figures, who, although of "good disposition and towardnesse," was of an age "readie to incline which way soeuer a man should bend it." Richard thus became corrupted by favorites who "brought him to tract the steps of lewd demeanour, and so were causers both of his and their owne destruction." Shakespeare includes the favorites in his play, but, compared with Marlowe, he makes very little use of them. Instead, he concentrates upon the disorder within Richard which caused him to alienate his subjects. Holinshed observes that Richard "did not behaue himselfe" in "discreet order ... but rather (as in time of prosperitie it often happeneth) he forgot himselfe, and began to rule by will more than by reason, threatning death to each one that obeied not his inordinate desires." Richard "abused his authoritie" by presuming upon his identity as King.[35] This identity, as Richard defines it in Shakespeare's play, is "the deputy elected by the Lord" (III, ii, 57), a special sense of self that the King shares with no other mortal. Richard's situation had a particular significance for his Elizabethan audience, who could see in the unique relationship between God and King an analogy to the relationship between God and his elect. For Richard, as for the ordinary believer, the problem was to discover what free-

---

(*The English History Play*, p. 162) suggests that the political issues contained in his sources led Shakespeare to the "discovery" of tragedy. Faced with the question: How could Shakespeare portray the ineffectiveness of Richard as a king and illustrate that England was better ruled by Bullingbrook without seeming to advocate rebellion? he arrives at this answer: by making Richard the author of his own downfall (p. 162).

[35] Holinshed, *Chronicles*, II, 715-16, 844.

doms and privileges this relationship entitled one to, and to accept the responsibilities and constraints that went with them. Shakespeare's Richard has forgotten himself in the sense that he does not accept the burden of responsibility that his election has conferred, although he is only too ready to presume upon the authority.

Richard's assurance in the opening scene reflects his secure belief in the divinity of the King, a form of election that carries with it unlimited worldly power. His formal, ceremonial tone as he speaks of "our sacred blood" and "the unstooping firmness of my upright soul" encourages the audience to accept his assurance as part of the dignity that attaches to the crown. Although the following scene confirms Richard's role in the murder of Gloucester (knowledge of which the audience presumably brought to the play), Gaunt's famous pronouncement against revenge reinforces the audience's sense of Richard's special status as "God's substitute" and "minister."

> God's is the quarrel, for God's substitute,
> His deputy anointed in His sight,
> Hath caus'd his death, the which if wrongfully,
> Let heaven revenge, for I may never lift
> An angry arm against His minister.
>   (I, ii, 37-41)

Gaunt counsels Gloucester's widow to leave revenge to heaven, the same heaven which Mowbray and Bullingbrook repeatedly invoke as they lodge their challenges against one another in the next scene. The ritualistic coupling of "God's name and the King's" in this scene elevates Richard still further, effectively anticipating the highly dramatic moment when, in a calculated yet almost casual display of authority, Richard throws down his warder and stops the combat. With god-like arbitrariness, Richard changes the course of his subjects' lives by banishing Mowbray forever, and Bullingbrook for ten years, soon changed to six, prompting Bullingbrook's comment: "Four lagging winters and four wanton springs/ End in a word: such is the breath of kings" (I, iii, 214-15).

278

Although Richard projects a certain exalted grandeur in these opening scenes, he can also be viewed as a version of the morality Youth figure, a flippant, careless young man who casually announces his intentions "to farm our royal realm" to raise funds for the Irish wars and responds to the news of Gaunt's illness with "Now put it, God, in the physician's mind/ To help him to his grave immediately!" (I, iv, 59-60.) Compared to Richard, Gaunt emerges as a personification of the virtue of patriotism, passionate and eloquent in his loyalty to "this blessed plot, this earth, this realm, this England" (II, i, 50). To the intensely patriotic Elizabethans, Gaunt becomes the norm against whom Richard's "otherness" is measured. Viewed from Gaunt's perspective, Richard's stature changes abruptly: he is "Landlord of England . . . now, not king" (113). A similarly damning contrast is later offered by York, another elderly, virtuous uncle, who compares Richard with his father, that "young and princely gentleman" who,

> . . . when he frowned it was against the French,
> And not against his friends. His noble hand
> Did win what he did spend, and spent not that
> Which his triumphant father's hand had won.
> His hands were guilty of no kindred blood,
> But bloody with the enemies of his kin.
>   (II, i, 178-83)

It is Gaunt who first suggests that Richard's actions are a crime against his "self," and that he will depose himself if he continues on his present course. Unwilling to accept correction, Richard takes hasty refuge in regal rhetoric. He condemns his uncle as a presumptuous fool who "Darest with thy frozen admonition/ Make pale our cheek, chasing the royal blood/ With fury from his native residence" (117-19). But such phrases no longer have the effect they had in scenes i and iii. When Richard responds to the news of Gaunt's death by seizing the possessions that rightfully belong to Bullingbrook, the audience concurs with York's judgment:

> Take Herford's rights away, and take from Time
> His charters and his customary rights;
> Let not to-morrow then ensue to-day;
> Be not thyself; for how art thou a king
> But by fair sequence and succession?
>
> (195-99)

Richard's actions are not appropriate to his "self"; they are the sins of an "other." When York warns "You pluck a thousand dangers on your head," he is making a similar distinction between the youthful will that acts and the head, or in other words, the crown, the self-as-king, which will suffer the consequences. Although Richard stubbornly refuses to heed York's warning, his judgment does not seem altogether blinded by folly. As he proceeds with his plans to appropriate Gaunt's estate, before lightheartedly embarking on an evening of merriment, he appoints York Lord Governor of England in his absence, observing, "For he is just and always loved us well" (221). This remark suggests to the audience that Richard is wiser than he seems. Perhaps they should therefore continue to withhold judgment, despite the severe criticism of his reign they are about to hear from Ross, Willoughby, and Northumberland, who also worries that "The King is not himself" (241).

While Richard is offstage engaged in his Irish wars, Bullingbrook returns. Like a conqueror figure, he is reported to be arriving "With eight tall ships [and] three thousand men of war." Northumberland, the bearer of this news, rejoices that "we shall shake off our slavish yoke . . . , Wipe off the dust that hides our sceptre's gilt,/ And make high majesty look like itself" (II, i, 286-95). For Northumberland, "high majesty" has become an "it," disassociated from the person of the King, and the King has become an object, a "slavish yoke." Northumberland's perspective is balanced in the following scene by the despairing Queen's sorrow, which is presumably included to elicit audience sympathy. The audience's sense of being pulled in contrary directions is articulated by York, whose slightly comic confusion stems from his realization that

> Both are my kinsmen:
> T' one is my sovereign, whom both my oath
> And duty bids defend; t' other again
> Is my kinsman, whom the King hath wrong'd,
> Whom conscience and my kindred bids to right.
>
> (II, ii, 111-15)

When Bullingbrook finally appears, the audience is immediately struck by the difference between his and Richard's temperaments. Critics have characterized the two men as the poet versus the pragmatic politician, or the embodiment of the medieval view of kingship versus the embodiment of the modern one.[36] It is also possible to see in the cousins two versions of the Elizabethan secure in his conviction of his election. Whereas Richard is arrogant, intensely self-conscious, and insistent on his elect status as King, Bullingbrook displays a much more understated conviction of election. His is the self-effacing humility of the proud man: "Of much less value is my company/ Than your good words"; "I count myself in nothing else so happy/ As in a soul rememb'ring my good friends" (II, iii, 19-20, 46-47). In his ominous silences, particularly in the desposition scene, there lurks a more dangerous kind of presumption than in Richard's garrulous posturing. Richard's belief that, as King, he can do no wrong, reveals the dangers inherent in the doctrine of election, but so does Bullingbrook's professed belief that God directs his steps. Though he claims to have returned to England to retrieve his

[36] For the view of Richard as poet-king, see A. R. Humphreys on the criticism of Pater and Yeats in *Shakespeare: Select Bibliographical Guides*, ed. Stanley Wells (Oxford, 1973), p. 260. See also Richard Altick's "Symphonic Imagery in *Richard II*," reprinted in *Twentieth Century Interpretations of Richard II*, ed. Paul M. Cubeta (Englewood Cliffs, New Jersey, 1971). For the contrast between the medieval and modern notions of kingship, see Tillyard, *Shakespeare's History Plays*, pp. 244 ff., and Ribner, *The English History Play*, p. 162.

lost patrimony, Bullingbrook immediately assumes the role of God's minister, plucking away the caterpillars of the commonwealth, Bushy, Bagot, and Green (the image is of a large hand reaching down from above). The execution of Bushy and Green as traitors is, as M. M. Reese has observed, tantamount to the assumption of sovereign power.[37] Bullingbrook's long speech to the prisoners casts him in the role of the strong, prudent King who has come to restore order to a kingdom languishing under the wrongs imposed by a capricious, easily led prince whom evil counselors have "unhappied and disfigured clean." But as Bushy and Green go off to their deaths, confident "that heaven will take our souls/ And plague injustice with the pains of hell," the audience is left wondering whether the picture that Bullingbrook has just painted for them is the distorted fiction of a deceitful Machiavel (III, i, 1-34).

Richard's return from Ireland offers an interesting contrast to Bullingbrook's return from France. In Act II, scene iii, Bullingbrook expressed his impatience with "the tediousness and process" of his travel through "high wild hills and rough, uneven ways." Richard, however, greets his kingdom's earth with a depth of feeling that hearkens back to Gaunt's long apostrophe to England, though the perspective is rather different. Gaunt viewed England with devotion and admiration, but from a remove, as "a seat of Mars," an Eden, a fortress, a little world, a "precious stone set in the silver sea" (II, i, 41-46). Richard, on the other hand, assumes the intimate and more limited viewpoint of "a long-parted mother with her child," addressing himself to the spiders, toads, nettles, and stones beneath his feet, and fancifully enjoining them to sting and annoy the feet of their sovereign's enemies (III, ii, 8-26). The Bishop of Carlisle gently takes him to task for presuming upon "that Power that made you king" instead of taking action to insure his own success. Richard is a little like the believer who

---

[37] Reese likens Bullingbrook to Cromwell, who also realized that he rises highest who knows not whither he is going (*The Cease of Majesty*, p. 251). See also Sanders, *The Dramatist and the Received Idea*, p. 164.

must make his election sure, rather than rest assured in his conviction of election. The Bishop preaches "The means that heavens yield must be embrac'd,/ And not neglected; else heaven would,/ And we will not" (29-31). But Richard remains convinced that he need do nothing but be King: in his imagination he becomes the eye of heaven rising in the east, exposing and punishing sin (50-62). At this moment, Richard genuinely believes that

> Not all the water in the rough rude sea
> Can wash the balm off from an anointed king;
> The breath of worldly men cannot depose
> The deput elected by the Lord;
> (54-57)

Richard's assurance begins to crack after he hears of the execution of his favorites. Meditating on the deaths of kings, he paints an utterly different picture of himself as King than the one he had constructed only moments earlier. Recognition of one's mortality is a traditional stage in the spiritual regeneration of the proud, but for Richard this recognition is accompanied by so complete a rejection of everything he had once believed in that it fails in its purpose:

> Cover your heads, and mock not flesh and blood
> With solemn reverence, throw away respect,
> Tradition, form, and ceremonious duty,
> For you have but mistook me all this while.
> I live with bread like you, feel want,
> Taste grief, need friends: subjected thus,
> How can you say to me I am a king?
> (III, ii, 171-77)

Properly speaking, Richard's deposition begins here, for once he loses his certainty about his identity as King, he in effect loses the ability to act as King. Moreover, he momentarily succumbs to the pragmatic premise that a man's claim to kingship rests on human political power alone, and that, lacking power, he has no choice but to depose himself. And so, when

283

he finally meets Bullingbrook in Act III, scene iii, he responds to his cousin's request for his inheritance by offering up his crown.

Thus Richard deposes himself, not as Edward did, in favor of his son, but in submission to one of his subjects before it is absolutely certain that he has no alternative. He is at once deposed and deposer, victim and villain, the protagonist with whom the audience identifies and the "other" from whom they feel detached. Their dual response to Richard reflects his own curiously divided sense of self. As he faces the prospect of his deposition, Richard's language reveals a growing distance between the "I" and the King which were once joined together as the royal "we." In the confrontation at Flint Castle Richard tells Northumberland, the go-between:

> What must the King do now? Must he submit?
> The King shall do it. Must he be depos'd?
> The King shall be contented. Must he lose
> The name of king? a' God's name let it go.
>   (III, iii, 143-146)

The "King" of these lines is and is not the Richard who speaks them.[38] Behind the jewels, the palace, the apparel, the goblets, and the scepter he offers to give up is an "I" waiting to be clothed in the costume of a hermit, but the only future he can envision for this "I" is death.

---

[38] In his introduction to the Arden edition of *Richard II*, Peter Ure points out that these lines seem to refer to a part that has been set down for Richard, which he cannot choose but play. A number of other critics have taken this approach, including Leonard Dean in "*Richard II*: The State and The Image of the Theatre" (both articles are reprinted in *Twentieth Century Interpretations of Richard II*). By viewing Richard as a passive actor in a play, these approaches run the risk, as Ure points out, of relieving Richard of his own responsibility for what happens (pp. 86-87). As Peter Phialas has observed in "Richard II and Shakespeare's Tragic Mode," *Texas Studies in Literature and Language*, 5 (1963), "the tragic hero must be in great part responsible for his suffering and death; and . . . he must discover and accept that responsibility before the play's end." Phialas regards *Richard II* as Shakespeare's first play to dramatize this recognition (p. 350).

Richard's belief that his existence and his identity as King are inextricably one is more urgently expressed in the deposition scene itself. Much as Richard tries to assume a new role, "To insinuate, flatter, bow, and bend my knee" (IV, i, 165), he nevertheless equates resigning the crown with being "nothing."[39] The all-nothing dichotomy pervades the scene, as do other dichotomies which direct the audience's feelings toward the two principal characters in subtle ways. The emblem of the crown as a "deep well," for example, poses Richard and Bullingbrook directly against one another—the full bucket and the empty one. Divested of everything else, even his cares, Richard is paradoxically full, but his fulness serves only to pull him down, and hence to elevate Bullingbrook. Richard's fulness is contrasted with his cousin's emptiness, an attribute that takes on moral implications. The cold, business-like Bullingbrook has just been called a "foul traitor" by the Bishop of Carlisle, who prophesies that "the blood of English shall manure the ground/ And future ages groan for this foul act" (IV, i, 135-38). The audience must decide whether they share Carlisle's view of the deposition, or whether Richard must bear much of the blame for deposing himself.

Shakespeare controls the audience's ambivalence toward Richard in several ways in the deposition scene. The Bishop's reminder that, as King, Richard is "the figure of God's majesty,/ His captain, steward, deputy, elect,/ Anointed, crowned, planted many years . . ." invites a very strong response. Richard himself takes up this theme, likening himself to Christ, who, he observes, "Found truth in all but one; I, in twelve thousand, none" (IV, i, 125-27, 170-71). Northumberland and the others are Pilates who "Have here deliver'd me to my sour cross . . ." (241). Yet as Richard pursues these analogies,

---

[39] In *The Drama of Speech Acts: Shakespeare's Lancastrian Tetralogy* (Berkeley, California, 1979), Joseph A. Porter notes that in Richard's mind "various types of nomenclature tend to coalesce so that to give up the name 'King' is also to give up the name 'Richard' bestowed at the font." Richard regards his name as an extension of himself; he concentrates on its importance to the exclusion of all else (pp. 20-21).

he finally turns his eyes upon himself and experiences a recognition of his own guilt:

> I find myself a traitor with the rest;
> For I have given here my soul's consent
> T' undeck the pompous body of a king;
> Make glory base, and sovereignty a slave;
> Proud majesty a subject, state a peasant.
>
> (248-52)

Richard is painfully conscious of having transformed himself into his opposite, from King to slave. In doing so, he has debased not only himself, but also the universal concepts of glory, majesty, sovereignty, and state. Richard's crime is like that of Faustus; it is a crime against himself. His acknowledgment of this leads to the desire for self-scrutiny which Shakespeare dramatizes in the mirror scene. The mirror will enable him to examine "the very book indeed/ Where all my sins are writ, and that's myself." The rather histrionic speeches that follow do fall short of the earnest self-scrutiny that leads to regeneration, but as Richard himself reminds us, they are only the "external [manners] of laments," mere "shadows to the unseen grief/ That swells with silence in the tortured soul" (296-98). Though Shakespeare has not yet found ways fully to express such unseen grief, he has convinced the audience that it exists, and so has created a character who more entirely engages the audience's sympathy than any of his previous creations.

When the audience next sees Richard, in his meeting with the Queen as he walks toward the Tower, he is calmly remote from his other self, and able "To think our former state a happy dream" (V, i, 18). He now understands "the truth of what we are," and his perception of this truth gives him, like Edward and Henry before him, the prophet's insight into the future. The forced parting of husband and wife reenacts the deposition; he is "doubly divorc'd," for the broken marriage oath corresponds in little to the oath of allegiance between subjects and King. Thus isolated and stripped bare, Richard is ready for his final scene in Pomfret Castle, which turns upon the most complex protagonist's soliloquy Shakespeare had yet written.

Richard begins by peopling his prison world with thoughts. Like Faustus in his opening soliloquy, surveying and rejecting the four professions, Richard probes and explores the shortcomings and failures of three attitudes, the religious, the ambitious, and the resigned. Out of his acknowledgment of his discontent with these roles and the roles of King and beggar comes the following insight:

> But what e'er I be,
> Nor I, nor any man that but man is,
> With nothing shall be pleas'd, till he be eas'd
> With being nothing.
> (V, v, 38-41)

For the Elizabethan audience, this nothingness may have sounded like the spiritual receptivity of the empty vessel waiting to be filled by the Lord, the obliteration of the worldly self in anticipation of the ascent of the spiritual self. Although it does not seem that Richard has attained this state of holy resignation, he has nevertheless arrived at an important realization. The King who had isolated himself from his fellow man, priding himself upon his sacred blood and upright soul, now understands that he is "but man." This is, in Derek Traversi's words, "something like a tragic statement about life,"[40] but it also hints at an acceptance of his condition which signifies a triumph over despair. A few lines earlier, Richard had been unable to envision any alternatives to the antithetical states

---

[40] Derek Traversi, *An Approach to Shakespeare* (1956; rpt., New York, 1969), p. 176. These lines have elicited a range of interpretations: Sanders, for example, sees nothing but nihilism and a desire for obliteration of consciousness in Richard's conclusion (*The Dramatist and the Received Idea*, p. 181), while Mack sees a recognition that "reality lies at last in the individual consciousness and only there" (*Killing the King*, p. 66). Part of the cause of this ambiguity, I would argue, is the Elizabethans' awareness that assurance and despair can be either opposite or kindred states.

of beggar or King (in a sense, these roles are worldly analogues to salvation and damnation). But now that he sees the possibility of being pleased and eased with being nothing, the word "nothing" means something different than it once did. Nothingness is a state of being, not non-being, from which a new "self" might conceivably emerge. Indeed, the process has already begun; Richard now possesses a "daintiness of ear," that is, an ability to distinguish order from disorder, true time from broken time. His meditation on proportion in music leads to a second insight: "I wasted time, and now doth time waste me" (49). This, too, is a partial recognition, one that lapses backward into self-pity, rather than leading him forward to self-knowledge. But, at least for a moment, before reverting to the preoccupation with complicated visual emblems that has characterized him all along, Richard acknowledges the relationship between action and reaction, guilt and retribution. Richard's final insight comes at the end of the soliloquy, when he discovers that the music which inadvertently chides him is in fact a sign of love. He is not, as he thought, universally hated and abandoned, as proved by the entrance of the loyal groom, whose heart communicates a love his tongue cannot.

No sooner does the groom leave but the keeper and murderers enter, and Richard is shaken out of his contemplative mood to become an actively heroic figure for the first time in the play. According to the stage directions, he beats the keeper and kills two of the murderers before he is struck down by Exton. His parting words affirm his identity as King for the last time.

> Exton, thy fierce hand
> Hath with the King's blood stain'd the King's own land.
> Mount, mount my soul! thy seat is up on high,
> Whilst my gross flesh sinks downward, here to die.
> (V, v, 109-12)

But they do more. They tell the audience that Richard's self-scrutiny has led to a traditional distinction between soul and body, and that he views his fall as merely the death of the body. As Richard urges his soul upward, the audience is confronted once again with the confidence of the elect, a confidence which enables Richard to take action against his murderers and affirm his right to a seat in heaven.

In the final moments of *Richard II* the audience's attention is focused on Bullingbrook. The worldly aspiration which successfully gained him the throne is nicely balanced against Richard's spiritual aspiration to a seat in heaven. As in *Edward II*, though with much more subtlety, the protagonist's "otherness" has been gradually transferred to his antagonist, so that Bullingbrook, a sympathetic figure at the outset, loses much of the audience's sympathy to Richard in the course of the play. Yet in Bullingbrook's success there is an element of tragedy, for he is acutely aware of his guilt once Richard is dead. In a sense, the buckets in the well are now reversed: as Richard's soul mounts, Bullingbrook's is weighted down, "full of woe." Bullingbrook's recognition of the implications of his actions complements Richard's acknowledgment that "I wasted time, and now doth time waste me."

> Though I did wish him dead,
> I hate the murtherer, love him murthered. . . .
> Lords, I protest my soul is full of woe
> That blood should sprinkle me to make me grow.
> Come mourn with me for what I do lament,
> And put on sullen black incontinent.
> I'll make a voyage to the Holy Land,
> To wash this blood off from my guilty hand.
>   (V, vi, 39-50)

These lines leave the audience feeling that the achievement of *Richard II* as tragedy is due to Shakespeare's depiction of Bullingbrook as well as Richard. Both, in their own ways, are tragic figures. With *Richard II*, Shakespeare brings the development of the dual-protagonist play to its logical conclusion; rather than a stark opposition of good and evil, self and "other," he offers his audience a pair of characters who are opposites

289

but who both inspire feelings of engagement and detachment. Whether or not they accept Tyndale's theories of kingship, the play's original audience probably concluded that Bullingbrook's actions were logical and inevitable, even if they were not "good" in any absolute moral sense. This attitude helped to preserve that element of emotional distance which enabled them to regard Richard's death as something that could not happen to people like themselves.

In the years following the first performance of *Richard II*, Shakespeare would continue to narrow the emotional distance between audience and protagonist, although that distance never completely disappeared. Shakespeare must have intuitively known that the sympathy one feels for the tragic protagonist must not become a self-serving identification which hopes for the averting of tragedy because the preservation of the self is imaginatively at stake. Hence an element of the "other" always remains in the magnificent protagonists of Shakespeare's major tragedies. In their most tragic moments, these characters acquire a self-knowledge which allows them to recognize the presence of the "other" within. The most moving example of this recognition occurs in the last scene of *Othello*. In his final, self-defining monologue, Othello poses the civilized "I" against the "malignant and turban'd Turk" that is the other side of himself. Not content to chastise and suppress the interior "other," as Rogers had done in his diary, Othello becomes the soldier once again. Tragically, in destroying the "other," he destroys himself as well.

CHAPTER IX

The Tragic Choice

The act of choosing has always been an important element in tragedy. The choices that tragic characters make are more often than not essentially moral ones, and their consequences both define and result from those characters' moral stature as perceived by the audience. In the fifteenth- and sixteenth-century morality plays, as we have seen, the playwright focused the audience's attention upon the conflicting claims of virtue and vice on characters who represented man's susceptibility to temptation but also his ability to reject evil and to choose good. From the 1560s onward, as the playwrights discussed in the preceding chapters moved beyond the relatively simple design of the morality plays to create more complex dramas derived from historical or fictional sources, their characters would continue to make life-shaping choices at crucial moments in the plays. But the alternatives from which these characters choose are not so easily equated with good and evil, nor is it invariably possible for them to reverse themselves in the latter part of the play, and so avoid the consequences of the potentially tragic choice. Nor, furthermore, does every dramatic structure turn upon a single crucial decision; the conqueror plays, for example, present a cumulative series of episodes in which deliberation and choice play little part. In contrast, a revenge play such as *The Spanish Tragedy* focuses upon the choice that confronts the protagonist, a choice imposed upon him by others. Hieronimo's decision to take revenge is the central event in the play, and the dramatic interest that he inspires stems largely from the ordeal involved in making that decision. Hieronimo's moral dilemma is transformed into a metaphysical one in *Hamlet*, where choice becomes not only an assertive act of self-definition but also an interpretation of reality.

291

The Elizabethan tragedy that most clearly dramatizes the tragic choice and its moral consequences is *Doctor Faustus*. Poised at a turning point in his life, Faustus knowingly elects a course of action that leads to damnation. Faustus' decision is easily made; indeed it is Mephostophilis, not Faustus, who hesitates before the enormity of the act of self-damnation. In this respect Faustus is a less interesting tragic protagonist than Hieronimo and others whose choices occur only after much soul-searching. Following the structure of the morality play, Marlowe offers Faustus several opportunities to reverse his decision and return to the path of virtue, but Faustus remains resolute. He is, in a very real sense, the last of the morality play protagonists. Seldom would subsequent tragic protagonists have the opportunity to undo the action that leads to tragedy; henceforth, the tragic sequence of events would have an irrevocable quality about it, and the possibility of a comic, redemptive ending would seem increasingly removed from the world of the play.

The tragic choice and its consequences are at the heart of *Macbeth*, a play that frequently invites comparison with *Doctor Faustus*. Although it was written a decade after most of the plays discussed in this book, I have included *Macbeth* for this reason: more than any other play of its age *Macbeth* is about the paradox of predestination. Ostensibly the doctrine of election would seem to deny the possibility of the tragic choice. But, as Milton would make clear in *Paradise Lost*, God's foreknowledge of an event does not make the agents thereof any less responsible for their actions. Adam and Eve deliberately choose a course of action to which they are predestined by a God whose motives are veiled in mystery. Much like tragic protagonists, they are at once victims of fate and responsible characters who knowingly commit a deed which will recoil upon them.

In writing *Macbeth*, Shakespeare probed the ambiguities inherent in the concept of predestination through the dramatic device of the witches, whom he found in his source, Holinshed's *Historie of Scotland*. The witches prophesy that Mac-

beth *will* become King but not *how* he will become King—
therein lies the tragic autonomy he shares with the morality
play Mankind figures and earlier tragic protagonists. As soon
as he hears the prophecy, Macbeth realizes that he has two
alternatives: he can wait for providence to act on his behalf or
he can take action. In a society where the godly were told to
make their election sure, and aspiring minds were esteemed,
to wait was not necessarily the right choice. Yet the action
Macbeth contemplates is an unnatural and terrifying one, as
he himself realizes:

> . . . why do I yield to that suggestion
> Whose horrid image doth unfix my hair
> And make my seated heart knock at my ribs,
> Against the use of nature?
> (I, iii, 134-37)

This recognition of his own susceptibility to evil is a quality
that Macbeth shares with other tragic protagonists. After his
first, horrified reaction, Macbeth considers leaving events to
chance: "If chance will have me king, why, chance may crown
me/ Without my stir" (142-43). It is significant that Macbeth
thinks in terms of chance, not providence or God. Without
confidence in a divinely ordained ordering of events that would
lead him naturally to the throne, he succumbs to the temptation to make the event occur by taking immediate action.
Shakespeare very carefully does not identify the witches as the
source of temptation; malevolent creatures though they are,
they do not function as tempters in the tradition of the morality play Vices, for they make no overt effort to lead Macbeth toward evil. The Vice's role is reserved for Lady Macbeth, who, as Holinshed describes her, "lay sore vpon him to
attempt the thing, as she that was verie ambitious, burning in
vnquenchable desire to beare the name of a queene."[1] Yet
Lady Macbeth's motives are different from the Vices', for she

---

[1] Holinshed, Rafael, *Chronicles of England, Scotland and Ireland* (London,
1807; rpt., New York, 1965), p. 269.

acts out of a desire to exalt her husband, not destroy him. Unlike Zenocrate, a more conventional female figure who provides the audience with a moral norm against which to view Tamburlaine's atrocities, Lady Macbeth violently casts off the role of the nurturing mother and scoffs at her husband's scruples. Her "we'll not fail" is the assurance of the godless sinner, and it sweeps Macbeth along on a course of action against which his better instincts recoil. Shakespeare associates her with the poisoners of *Hamlet* and *Othello* by having her speak of pouring her spirit into Macbeth's ear. Yet he also makes it clear that she would not have succeeded in compelling Maceth to kill the King had not his own inclination weakened his resistance.

For Macbeth, as for Hamlet, to kill a king was to risk damnation, although Hamlet's choice is more difficult: he must weigh the act of regicide against that of disobedience toward a ghost who claims the father's authority over his son. Shakespeare did not intend Macbeth's dilemma to arouse the ambivalence Hamlet's does, however, for he quite deliberately omitted all the references to Duncan's weakness as a king that he found in his source. Holinshed dwells at length on Duncan's negligence in punishing offenders, which led to many "seditious commotions." He relates how Macbeth and Banquo called the nobles together and after "speaking much against the kings softnes," succeeded in putting down the rebels and restoring law and justice to the land (p. 265). Shakespeare represents Duncan instead as a good and generous king whom Macbeth, contemplating the murder in the soliloquy of I, vii, describes thus:

> Besides, this Duncan
> Hath borne his faculties so meek, hath been
> So clear in his great office, that his virtues
> Will plead like angels, trumpet-tongu'd against
> The deep damnation of his taking-off.
> (I, vii, 16-20)

The use of the word "damnation" is revealing; as Richard Waswo observes, Macbeth's tragedy is terrifying and inexplicable because he begins with a precise and lucid moral awareness of the implications of the act he contemplates.[2] In this respect he resembles the elect, as described by Perkins:

> A wicked man, when he sinneth in his heart he giveth full consent to the sinne; but the godly though they fall into the same sinnes with the wicked, yet they never give full consent: for they are in their minds, coils, and affections partly regenerate and partly unregenerate, and therefore their wils doe partly will, and partly abhorre that which is evill. . . .[3]

Macbeth's soliloquy (I, vii, 1-28) constitutes a moment of self-scrutiny, culminating in a vision of pity come to life as "a naked new-born babe,/ Striding the blast, or heaven's cherubin . . ." broadcasting the horror of the deed. Had Lady Macbeth not interrupted him just as he seemed about to recognize the self-destructiveness and ultimate futility of "Vaulting ambition, which o'erleaps itself," Macbeth might have resumed his proper role as kinsman, subject, and host. But his resolution wavers when assaulted by her taunts; like the weak Christians of the Puritan tracts, he is not strong enough to withstand the persuasions of one more determined than he is. In acquiescing to evil, he must "bend up/ Each corporal agent to

---

[2] Waswo observes that in *Macbeth*, as in *Doctor Faustus*, tragedy occurs not because a good man does what he thinks is right, but because a man with moral knowledge inexplicably courts damnation. Waswo suggests that one way of understanding Macbeth's decision is to view it in light of the Calvinist concept of natural corruption, as articulated by Fulke Greville in "A Treatise of Religion": "So as what's good in us, and others too/ We praise; but what is evill, that we doe." "Damnation, Protestant Style: Macbeth, Faustus, and Christian tragedy," *Journal of Medieval and Renaissance Studies*, 4 (1974), pp. 66-77.

[3] Quoted by Charles H. and Katherine George, *The Protestant Mind of the English Reformation* (Princeton, 1961), p. 49.

this terrible feat," an act of physical distortion corresponding to the moral distortion within.

This distortion begins the process of transformation, in the course of which Macbeth becomes the bloody and tyrannical "other," as characterized by Macduff, Malcolm, and the other lords in the latter part of the play. Yet, unlike earlier tragic protagonists, who remain largely unconscious of their transformation into the "other," Macbeth fully realizes the tragic ironies that proceed from his choice:

> For Banquo's issue have I fil'd my mind;
> For them the gracious Duncan have I murther'd,
> Put rancors in the vessel of my peace
> Only for them, and mine eternal jewel
> Given to the common enemy of man,
> To make them kings—the seeds of Banquo kings!
>
> (III, i, 64-69)

The difference between Macbeth and Faustus is that Faustus never really acknowledges the paltriness of the privileges for which he sold his soul. Macbeth, by contract, is keenly aware that "to be thus is nothing" (III, i, 47). Or, as he says in the next scene, "Better be with the dead . . ./ Than on the torture of the mind to lie/ In restless ecstasy" (III, ii, 19-22). An even more dramatic representation of the increasing distance that separates Macbeth from normal humanity occurs in the banquet scene. There, Macbeth is isolated by the fact that he, and he alone, sees the terrifying spectacle of Banquo's ghost. Shaken by the vision, he resolves to return to the weird sisters, using a spatial image to describe the process of becoming the "other":

> I am in blood
> Stepp'd in so far that, should I wade no more,
> Returning were as tedious as go o'er.
>
> (III, iv, 135-39)

Watching Macbeth's painful and solitary journey toward an end from which there is no last-minute salvation, the audience is given very little sense of a healthy, benign society that resists

296

and opposes evil. As in the revenge tragedies, virtue seems weak and helpless in the tragic world, here symbolized by the slaughtered children who provide a recurring motif. Banquo, Macbeth's companion in the first encounter with the witches, occupies the Heavenly Man role very briefly. He immediately suspects that the witches may be instruments of darkness, and, with a consciousness of human frailty that Macbeth seems to lack, he prays to the "Merciful powers/ [to] Restrain in me the cursed thoughts that nature/ Gives way to in repose" (II, i, 7-9). In contrast to Macbeth, Banquo chooses not to act. When he dies a martyr's death relatively early in the play, the audience may well feel that virtue has been annihilated. Not until the scene between Malcolm and Macduff at the end of Act IV is there any sense that a restoration of order is possible.

When the restoration of order does begin, the audience's attention is directed much more powerfully to the psychological state of the tragic protagonist than to the victory of goodness over tyranny. Macbeth remains a complex character to the end, despite his countrymen's efforts to represent him as, in Macduff's words, a devil "damned/ In evils" whom not all "the legions of horrid hell" can equal (IV, iii, 55-57). Mired in blood though he is, Macbeth never altogether loses his awareness of the moral implications of his deeds; in this respect he is quite different from Richard III and the villains of the conqueror plays. Confronting Macduff in battle, he can still speak of his soul as "too much charg'd/ With blood of thine . . ." (V, viii, 5-6).

To a certain extent, Macbeth's complexity as a character is due to the complementary relationship between him and Lady Macbeth. Each side of his nature is balanced by hers: when he is weak and conscience-stricken, she is the bold assertive "other"; when he is reckless and determined, she becomes his guilt-ridden, self-destroying opposite. Shakespeare could have made Lady Macbeth's terrible madness and death an important part of Macbeth's tragedy, but he chose not to. Instead,

Macbeth's inability to react emotionally to the event causes him to recognize how much he has changed:

> I have almost forgot the taste of fears.
> The time has been, my senses would have cool'd
> To hear a night-shriek, and my fell of hair
> Would at a dismal treatise rouse and stir
> As life were in't. I have supp'd full with horrors;
> Direness, familiar to my slaughterous thoughts,
> Cannot once start me.
>   (V, v, 9-15)

This is a remarkable statement for a character to make about himself. The audience has watched Macbeth's transformation from the conscience-stricken sinner of Act II to a being "without sense and astonished like unto a stone," to use Perkins' description of the reprobate.[4] Yet, transformed though he is, Macbeth retains the tragic protagonist's acute self-awareness. To the very end, he can thoughtfully examine his own responses and pass judgment upon them eloquently. In his last moments he experiences neither Faustus' fear of hell nor Richard II's anticipation of heaven, but an extraordinary range of emotions that invites a corresponding range of responses. First, there is his haunting realization of what he has lost: "that what should accompany old age,/ I must not look to have . . ." (V, iii, 24-26). This fleeting image of normalcy makes the spectators intensely conscious of the distance between Macbeth and themselves. Next, there is his nihilistic vision of life as "a tale/ Told by an idiot, full of sound and fury/ Signifying nothing" (V, i, 26-28). This is the ultimate denial of meaning or order and the essence of despair, although Shakespeare nowhere uses that word.[5] Finally, there is the weakening of his

---

[4] I am indebted to Waswo for this passage from Perkins. Waswo suggests that Macbeth's punishment for abdicating his intelligence is the loss of his human capacity to discover meaning ("Damnation, Protestant Style," p. 97).

[5] Cf. Roland M. Frye, "Theological and Non-Theological Structures in Tragedy," *Shakespeare Studies IV* (1968). Frye argues that while Shakespeare

resolve: "I pull in resolution, and begin/ To doubt th' equiv-
ocation of the fiend/ That lies like truth" (41-43).

Macbeth's resolution, like Faustus', has been the reverse of
godly resolution, for it has resulted in a self-destructive commitment to a course of evil from which he cannot extricate
himself. Just as the elects' resolution is derived from the inner
knowledge of God's promises, so Macbeth's resolution has
been bolstered by the witches, whose prophecies seemed to
promise an election that would set him apart from mortal men.
His moment of *anagnoresis* comes when he finally realizes that
his assurance rests on false premises, and that his "charmed
life" must yield to Macduff's sword. But, rather than yield to
cringing despair, as a homiletic portrayal of a self-deluding
reprobate might have depicted him as doing, Macbeth remains as brave a soldier as one could hope for. He finally
understands that he has been deceived by fiends, but he goes
forward to battle, knowing that he is trapped and doomed to
die. His death is not merely the defeat of the tyrant; it is also
the tragic end of a life that could not have continued.

Of Shakespeare's great tragic protagonists, Macbeth is the
least likely to inspire audience identification. By committing
regicide for no reason except personal gain, he defies one of
the most sacred laws of God and man. And yet Macbeth is a
tragic figure in a way that Tamburlaine, Faustus, and Richard
III are not, despite the fact that he willfully damns himself.
Without holding out any hope that his protagonist is finally
repentant and hence among the saved, Shakespeare makes his
audience feel profoundly moved by the dilemma of a too easily swayed, impulsive, proud, desperate man—a man whose
tragedy is aptly summed up by one of the Scottish lords on
the march toward Birnam Wood. Responding to Angus's
striking description of Macbeth as the tyrant who "feel[s] his
title/ Hang loose about him, like a giant's robe/ Upon a dwarf-

---

uses theological material in *Macbeth*, the play contains a minimum of theological reference in the specific sense, particularly when compared with *Doctor
Faustus* (pp. 134 ff.).

ish thief," Menteith asks "Who then shall blame/ His pester'd senses to recoil and start,/ When all that is within him does condemn/ Itself for being there?" (V, ii, 20-25.) That state of self-condemnation is one the Elizabethans knew well. If their own guilt-stricken moments of recognition had never equaled Macbeth's, they nevertheless knew what it was like to live with the implications of their choices. As the Elizabethan audience watched Macbeth endure the final painful moments of his tragic life, we can speculate that they would have been conscious neither of his "otherness" nor of the emotional boundaries that circumscribed their own carefully protected selves. Instead, they found themselves drawn into an experience of intense and heightened engagement with a human being who was, and was not, an image of themselves.

BIBLIOGRAPHY

PRIMARY SOURCES

Adams, Joseph Quincy. *Chief Pre-Shakespearean Dramas.* Cambridge, 1924.

Anon. *The Anatomie of Sinne, Briefly discovering the braunches thereof, with a short method how to detect and avoid it.* London, 1603. STC #565.

——. *The copie of a leter wryten by a Master of Art of Cambridge to his friend in London.* . . . London, 1584. STC #1031.

——. *The Enterlude of Youth.* c. 1560-1562. Ed. John S. Farmer. London: Tudor Facsimile Texts, 1908.

——. *The First Part of the Reign of King Richard the Second or Thomas of Woodstock.* n.d. Ed. Wilhelmina P. Frijlinck. London: Malone Society, 1929.

——. *The First part of the Tragicall raigne of Selimus.* 1594. Ed. W. Bang. London: Malone Society, 1908.

——. *Hycke Scorner.* c. 1512. Ed. John S. Farmer. London: Tudor Facsimile Texts, 1908.

——. *Iacob and Esau.* 1568. Ed. John S. Farmer. London: Tudor Facsimile Texts, 1908.

——. *Impacyient Pouerte.* 1560. Ed. John S. Farmer. London: Tudor Facsimile Texts, 1907.

——. *New Custome.* 1573. Ed. John S. Farmer. London: Tudor Facsimile Texts, 1908.

——. *Nice Wanton.* 1560. Ed. John S. Farmer. London: Tudor Facsimile Texts, 1909.

——. *Respublica.* n.d. Ed. Leonard A. Magnus. London: Early English Text Society, 1905.

——. *The Triall of Treasure.* 1567. Ed. John S. Farmer. London: Tudor Facsimile Texts, 1908.

——. *The True Tragedy of Richard the Third.* 1594. Ed. W. W. Greg. London: Malone Society, 1929.

Anon. *The Wars of Cyrus*. 1594. Ed. John S. Farmer. London: Tudor Facsimile Texts, 1911.

————. *The worlde and the childe, other wyse called Mundus et Infans*. 1522. Ed. John S. Farmer. London: Tudor Facsimile Texts, 1909.

Aristotle. *On Poetry and Music*. Ed. Milton C. Nahm. Trans. S. H. Butcher. New York: The Library of Liberal Arts, 1948.

[St. Augustine]. *The glasse of vaine-glorie*. Trans. W. P. Doctor of the Lawes. London, 1585. STC #929.

Bale, John. *King Johan*. Ed. Barry B. Adams. San Marino, California, 1969.

Brawner, James Paul. *The Wars of Cyrus: a critical edition with introduction and notes*. Illinois Studies in Language and Literature, 28, Nos. 3-4. Urbana, 1942.

Brooke, C. F. Tucker, ed. *The Shakespeare Apocrypha: being a collection of fourteen plays which have been ascribed to Shakespeare*. Oxford, 1918.

Bullough, Geoffrey. *Narrative and Dramatic Sources of Shakespeare*. London, 8 vols., 1957-75.

Burton, William. *Davids Evidence or the Assurance of Gods Love*. London, 1592. STC #4170.

Calvin, John. *Institutes of the Christian Religion*. Trans. Ford Lewis Battles. Ed. John T. NcNeill. The Library of Christian Classics, Vols. XX and XXI. Philadelphia, 1960.

Campbell, Lily B., ed. *A Mirror for Magistrates*. London, 1938.

Chaderton, Lawrence. *An Excellent and godly sermon, most needfull for this time*. London, 1578. STC #4924.

————. *A Fruitfull Sermon upon the 3.4.5.6.7.8 verses of the 12 Chapiter of the Epistle of S. Paul to the Romanes*. London, 1584. STC #4926.

Chandos, John, ed. *In God's Name: Examples of Preaching in England from the Act of Supremacy to the Act of Uniformity: 1534-1662*. New York, 1971.

Crowley, Robert. *A Sermon made in the Chappel at the Gylde Halle*. London, 1575. STC #6092.

Cunliffe, John, ed. *Early English Classical Tragedies.* Oxford, 1912.

Dent, Arthur. *A pastime for Parents: or A recreation, to passe away the time: contayning the most principall grounds of Christian Religion.* London, 1606. STC #6622.

——. *The Plaine Mans Path-way to Heaven: Wherein every man may cleerely see, whether he shall be saved or damned.* London, 1607. STC #6629.

——. *A Sermon of Repentaunce.* London, 1583. STC #6650.

Dering, Edward. *M. Derings workes.* London, 1597.

Dod, John, and Cleaver, R. *Ten Sermons tending chiefly to the fitting of men for the worthy receiving of the Lords Supper.* London, 1634. STC #6949.

Eccles, Mark, ed. *The Macro Plays: The Castle of Perseverance, Wisdom, Mankind.* London: Early English Text Society, 1969.

Egerton, Stephen. *A Lecture preached by Maister Egerton, at the Blackefriers, 1589. taken by characterie, by a yong Practitioner in that Facultie and now againe perused, corrected and amended by the Author.* London, 1603. STC #7539.

Farmer, John, ed. *Early English Dramatists: Five Anonymous Plays.* 1908; rpt., New York, 1966.

Foxe, John. *Acts and Monuments of the Christian Martyrs, and matters Ecclesiastical, passed in the Church of Christ, from the Primitiue beginning to these our dayes.* 2 vols. London, 1610.

——. *A Sermon of Christ crucified, preached at Paules Crosse the Friday before Easter, commonly called Goodfryday.* London, 1570. STC #14921.

Fulke, William. *A Sermon preached on Sundaye, being the 17 of March Anno 1577, at St. Alpheges Church within Creplegate in London.* London, 1577. STC #11454.

——. *A Sermon Preached upon Sunday, being the twelfth of March, Anno 1581 within the Tower of London: In the hearing of such obstinate Papistes as then were prisoners there.* London, 1581. STC #1155.

Fulwell, Ulpian. *Like will to Like quoth the Deuill to the Collier.*

1587. Ed. John S. Farmer. London: Tudor Facsimile Texts, 1909.

Furnivall, F. J., ed. *The Digby Plays with an incomplete "Morality" of Wisdom, who is Christ*. London, 1896.

Garter, Thomas. *The most virtuous and Godly susanna*. 1578. Ed. B. Ifor Evans. London: Malone Society, 1936.

Gifford, George. *A Discourse of the subtill Practises of Deuilles by witches and Sorcerers. By which men are and haue bin greatly deluded*. London, 1587. STC #11852.

———. *Four Sermons upon the seven chiefe vertues or principall effectes of faith, and the doctrine of election: wherein everie man may learne, whether he be Gods childe or no*. London, 1582. STC #11858.

Gosson, Stephen. *The s[c]hoole of abuse, conteining a pleasaunt invective against poets*. London, 1579. STC #12097.

Green[e], R[obert]. *The Comicall Historie of Alphonsus, King of Aragon*. 1599. Ed. W. W. Greg. London: Malone Society, 1926.

———. *The Life and Works of Robert Greene*. Ed. Alexander B. Grosart. London, 1881-86; rpt., New York, 1964.

Greenham, Richard. *The Workes of the Reverend and Faithfull servant of Iesus Christ M. Richard Greenham*. 2nd ed. Rev. and ed. H[enry] H[olland]. London, 1599.

Gribalde, Matthewe. *A notable and marvellous Epistle of the famous Doctour, Matthewe Gribalde, Professor of the Lawe, in the Universitie of Padua: concernyng the terrible iudgement of God, upon hym that for feare of men, denieth Christ and the knowne verritie: with a Preface of Doctor Calvine*. Trans. Edward Aglionby. London, c. 1570. STC #12366.

Henslowe, Philip. *Henslowe's Diary*. Ed. R. A. Foakes and R. T. Rickert. Cambridge, 1961.

Holinshed, Raphael. *Chronicles of England, Scotland and Ireland*. London, 1807; rpt., New York, 1965.

Hooker, Richard. *A Learned and Comfortable Sermon of the certaintie and perpetuitie of faith in the Elect, especially of the Prophet Habukkuks faith*. Oxford, 1612. STC #13707.

Humphrey, Lawrence. *A view of the Romish hydra confuted in seven sermons*. Oxford, 1588. STC #13966.

Keltridge, John. *Two Godlie and learned Sermons, appointed, and Preached before the Jesuites, Seminaries, and other Adversaries to the Gospell of Christ in the Tower of London*. London, 1581. STC #14921.

Knappen, Marshall Mason, ed. *Two Elizabethan Puritan Diaries*. Chicago, 1933.

Kyd, Thomas. *The Spanish Tragedy*. Ed. Philip Edwards. Cambridge, 1959.

Linaker, R. *A Comfortable Treatise, for the reliefe of such as are afflicted in Conscience*. 2nd ed. London, 1607. STC #15640.

Lupton, Thomas. *All for Money*. 1578. Ed. John S. Farmer. London: Tudor Facsimile Texts, 1910.

Manningham, John. *The Diary of John Manningham of the Middle Temple: 1602-1603*. Ed. Robert Parker Sorlien. Hanover, New Hampshire, 1976.

Marlowe, Christopher. *The Complete Plays of Christopher Marlowe*. Ed. Irving Ribner. New York, 1963.

——. *Marlowe's Doctor Faustus: 1604-1616*. Ed. W. W. Greg. Oxford, 1950.

——. *The Jew of Malta*. Ed. N. W. Bawcutt. Manchester, 1978.

——. *Tamburlaine the Great*. Ed. J. S. Cunningham. Manchester, 1981.

Medwell, Henry. *Nature*. c. 1486-1500. Ed. John S. Farmer. London: Tudor Facsimile Texts, 1908.

Montaigne, Michel de. *Essays*. Trans. and ed. J. M. Cohen. Harmondsworth, England, 1958.

Palmer, Philip Mason, and More, Robert Pattison. *The Sources of the Faust Tradition from Simon Magus to Lessing*. New York, 1936.

Peele, George. *The Battell of Alcazar*. 1594. Ed. W. W. Greg. London: Malone Society, 1907.

——. *The Dramatic Works of George Peele*. Gen. Ed. Charles Tyler Prouty. New Haven, 1961.

Perkins, William. *A Case of Conscience, the greatest that ever was; How a man may know whether he be the childe of God, or no.* London, 1595. STC #19667.

———. *A Golden Chaine: or The Description of Theology.* London, 1635.

Phillip, John. *The Commodye of pacient and meeke Grissill.* n.d. Ed. Ronald B. McKerrow and W. W. Greg. London: Malone Society, 1909.

Pierce, William, ed. *The Marprelate Tracts, 1588, 1589.* London, 1911.

Pikering, John. *A New Enterlude of Vice Conteyninge the Historye of Horestes.* 1567. Ed. Daniel Seltzer. London: Malone Society, 1962.

Schell, Edgar T. and Schuchter, J. D., eds. *English Morality Plays and Moral Interludes.* New York, 1969.

Seneca, *Seneca His Tenne Tragedies.* Ed. T. S. Eliot. London, 1927.

Shakespeare, William. *The Riverside Shakespeare.* Ed. G. Blakemore Evans. Boston, 1974.

Skelton, John. *Magnyfycence: A Moral Play.* Ed. Robert Lee Ramsay. London: Early English Text Society, 1906.

Smith, G. Gregory, ed. *Elizabethan Critical Essays.* 2 vols. Oxford, 1904.

Smith, Henry. *Sermons.* London, 1593. STC #22719.

Travers, Robert. *A Learned and a very profitable Exposition made upon the CXI Psalme.* London, 1579. STC #24180.

Trinterud, Leonard J., ed. *Elizabethan Puritanism.* Oxford, 1971.

Udall, John. *The Combate between Christ and the Devill: Foure Sermons upon the temptations of Christ in the wildernes by Sathan: wherein are to be seene the subtile sleights that the tempter useth against the Children of God.* London, 1589. STC #24493.

———. *Two Sermons upon the Historie of Peters denying Christ.* London, 1584. STC #24503.

Wager, W. *Inough is as good as a feast.* c. 1565. Ed. Seymour de Ricci. New York, 1920.

———. *The longer thou liuest, the more foole thou art.* c. 1568. Ed. John S. Farmer. London: Tudor Facsimile Texts, 1910.

———. *The Longer Thou Livest and Enough Is As Good As A Feast.* Ed. Mark Benbow. Lincoln, Nebraska, 1967.

Wapull, George. *The Tyde taryeth no Man.* 1576. Ed. John S. Farmer. London: Tudor Facsimile Texts, 1910.

Waterhouse, Osborn, ed. *The Non-Cycle Mystery Plays, together with the Croxton Play of the Sacrament and The Pride of Life.* London: Early English Text Society. 1909.

Wever, R. *Lusty Iuuentus.* c. 1540. Ed. John S. Farmer. London: Tudor Facsimile Texts, 1907.

Whetstone, George. *The Right Excelent and famous Historye, of Promos and Cassandra.* 1578. Ed. John S. Farmer. London: Tudor Facsimile Texts, 1910.

Willis, Robert. *Mount Tabor, or Private Exercises of a Penitent Sinner.* London, 1639. STC #25752.

Woodes, Nathaniell. *The Conflict of Conscience.* 1581, 2nd issue. Ed. John S. Farmer. London: Tudor Facsimile Texts, 1911.

SECONDARY SOURCES

Adams, Barry B. "The Audiences of The Spanish Tragedy." *JEGP*, 6 (1969), 221-36.

Adams, H. H. *English Domestic or Homiletic Tragedy: 1575-1640.* New York, 1943.

Altman, Joel. *The Tudor Play of Mind: Rhetorical Inquiry and the Development of Elizabethan Drama.* Berkeley, 1978.

Ayres, Philip J. "Degrees of Heresy: Justified Revenge and Elizabethan Narratives," *Studies in Philology*, LXIX (1972), 461-74.

Babb, Howard S. "Policy in Marlowe's *The Jew of Malta*," *ELH*, XXIV (1957), 85-94.

Baines, Barbara J. "*Antonio's Revenge*: Marston's Play on Revenge Tragedy," *Studies in English Literature*, XXIII, 2 (Spring 1983), 277-94.

Baker, Howard. *Induction to Tragedy*. Baton Rouge, 1939.

Bamber, Linda. *Comic Women, Tragic Men: A Study of Gender and Genre in Shakespeare*. Stanford, 1982.

Barber, C. L. *Shakespeare's Festive Comedy: A Study of Dramatic Form and its Relation to Social Custom*. Princeton, 1959.

————. " 'the form of Faustus' fortunes good or bad.' " *Tulane Drama Review*, VIII, 4 (Summer, 1964), 92-119.

Barish, Jonas. "The Antitheatrical Prejudice." *Critical Quarterly*, LXVI, 329-48.

————. "Exhibitionism and the Anti-theatrical Prejudice." *ELH*, XXXVI, 1 (March, 1969), 1-29.

Barroll, J. Leeds. *Artificial Persons: The Formation of Character in the Tragedies of Shakespeare*. Columbia, South Carolina, 1974.

Battenhouse, Roy W. *Marlowe's Tamburlaine: A Study in Renaissance Moral Philosophy*. Nashville, 1941.

————. *Shakespearean Tragedy: Its Art and Its Christian Premises*. Bloomington, 1969.

Beckerman, Bernard. *Dynamics of Drama: Theory and Method of Analysis*. New York, 1970.

————. *Shakespeare at the Globe: 1599-1609*. New York, 1962.

Belsey, Catherine. "Senecan Vacillation and Elizabethan Deliberations: Influence or Confluence?" *Renaissance Drama*, N.S. VI (1973), 65-88.

Bennett, Josephine W., Oscar Cargill and Vernon Hall, Jr. *Studies in the English Renaissance Drama in Memory of Karl Julius Holzknecht*. New York, 1959.

Bercovitch, Sacvan. *The Puritan Origins of the American Self*. New Haven, 1975.

Berlin, Normand. *Thomas Sackville*. Twayne English Authors Series. New York, 1974.

Berry, Edward I. *Patterns of Decay: Shakespeare's Early Histories*. Charlottesville, 1975.

Bethell, S. L. *Shakespeare and the Popular Dramatic Traditon*. Durham, 1944.

Bevington, David. *From Mankind to Marlowe: Growth of Struc-*

ture in the Popular Drama of Tudor England. Cambridge, 1962.

———. *Tudor Drama and Politics: A Critical Approach to Topical Meaning*. Cambridge, 1968.

Blench, J. W. *Preaching in England in the Late Fifteenth and Sixteenth Centuries*. Oxford, 1964.

Boas, Frederick S. *An Introduction to Tudor Drama*. Oxford, 1933.

Bowers, Fredson. "Death in Victory: Shakespeare's Tragic Reconciliations," *Studies in Honor of DeWitt T. Starnes*. Ed. Thomas P. Harrison et al. (Austin, 1967), 53-76.

———. *Elizabethan Revenge Tragedy: 1587-1642*. Princeton, 1940.

Bradbrook, Muriel C. *English Dramatic Form: A History of its Development*. London, 1965.

———. *The Rise of the Common Player: A Study of Actor and Society in Shakespeare's England*. London, 1962.

———. *Themes and Conventions of Elizabethan Tragedy*. 1935; rpt., Cambridge, 1964.

Brockbank, J. P. "The Frame of Disorder—Henry VI." Reprinted in *Twentieth Century Views: Shakespeare: The Histories*. Ed. Eugene Waith. Englewood Cliffs, New Jersey, 1965.

Brockett, Oscar G., ed. *Studies in Theatre and Drama: Essays in Honor of Hubert C. Heffner*. The Hague, 1972.

Brooke, C. F. Tucker. "The Life of Marlowe." *The Works and Life of Christopher Marlowe*. Ed. R. H. Case. London, 1930.

Brooke, Nicholas. *Shakespeare's Early Tragedies*. London, 1968.

Broude, Ronald. "Roman and Goth in *Titus Andronicus*." *Shakespeare Studies*, VI (1970), 27-34.

———. "*Vindicta Filia Temporis*: Three English Forerunners of the Elizabethan Revenge Play." *JEGP*, LXXII (1973), 489-502.

Brown, John Russell. *Shakespeare's Plays in Performance*. New York, 1967.

Brown, John Russell and Bernard Harris, ed. *Elizabethan Theatre*. Stratford-Upon-Avon Studies IX. London, 1966.

Brucher, Richard T. "Comic Violence in *Titus Andronicus*." *Renaissance Drama*, N.S. X (1979), 71-91.

Burke, Kenneth. *Counter-Statement*. Chicago, 1931.

Bush, Douglas. *English Literature in the Earlier Seventeenth Century: 1600-1660*. Oxford, 1962.

Campbell, Lily B. "Doctor Faustus: A Case of Conscience." *PMLA*, LXVII (1952), 219-39.

————. "Theories of Revenge in Renaissance England." *Modern Philology*, XXVIII (1931), 281-96.

Chamber, E. K. *The Elizabethan Stage*. 4 vols. Oxford, 1923.

Champion, Larry S. *Perspective in Shakespeare's English Histories*. Athens, Georgia, 1980.

————. *Shakespeare's Tragic Perspective*. Athens, Georgia, 1973.

Clemen, Wolfgang. *A Commentary on Shakespeare's Richard III*. Trans. Jean Bonheim. London, 1968.

————. *English Tragedy before Shakespeare*. Trans. T. R. Dorsch. London, 1961.

Cole, Douglas. *Suffering and Evil in the Plays of Christopher Marlowe*. Princeton, 1962.

Collinson, Patrick. *The Elizabethan Puritan Movement*. Berkeley, 1967.

Cook, Ann Jennalie. *The Privileged Playgoers of Shakespeare's London 1576-1642*. Princeton, 1981.

Craig, Hardin. "Morality Plays and Elizabethan Drama." *Shakespeare Quarterly* I (1950), 64-72.

Craik, T. W. *The Tudor Interlude: Stage, Costume, and Acting*. Leicester, 1958.

Creeth, Edmund. *Mankynde in Shakespeare*. Athens, Georgia, 1976.

Cunningham, J. V. *Woe or Wonder: The Emotional Effect of Shakespearean Tragedy*. Denver, 1951.

Danby, John F. *Shakespeare's Doctrine of Nature: A Study of King Lear*. London, 1948.

Davies, Horton. *Worship and Theology in England*. Vol. I: *From Cranmer to Hooker: 1534-1603*. Princeton, 1970.

Dessen, Alan. *Elizabethan Drama and the Viewer's Eye*. Durham, 1977.

Doran, Madeleine. *Endeavors of Art: A Study of Form in Elizabethan Drama.* Madison, 1954.

Duvignaud, Jean. *Sociologie du Théâtre: Essai sur les ombres collectives.* Paris, 1965.

Edwards, Philip. *Thomas Kyd and Early Elizabethan Tragedy.* London, 1966.

――――. *Threshold of a Nation: A Study of English and Irish Drama.* Cambridge, 1979.

Ellis-Fermor, Una. *Christopher Marlowe.* 1927; rpt., Hamden, Connecticut, 1967.

Erikson, Kai. *Wayward Puritans: A Study in the Sociology of Deviance.* New York, 1966.

Esler, Anthony. *The Aspiring Mind of the Elizabethan Younger Generation.* Durham, 1966.

Farnham, Willard. *The Medieval Heritage of Elizabethan Tragedy.* Berkeley, 1936.

Fiedler, Leslie. *The Stranger in Shakespeare.* New York, 1972.

Fish, Stanley. *Self-Consuming Artifacts: The Experience of Seventeenth Century Literature.* Berkeley, 1972.

Freeman, Arthur. *Thomas Kyd: Facts and Problems.* Oxford, 1967.

Frye, Roland M. "Theological and Non-Theological Structures in Tragedy." *Shakespeare's Studies*, IV (1968), 132-48.

Garber, Margorie. " 'Vassal Actors': The Role of the Audience in Shakespearean Tragedy." *Renaissance Drama*, N.S. IX (1978), 71-90.

Gardner, Helen. "Milton's Satan and The Theme of Damnation in Elizabethan Tragedy." *Essays and Studies, I* (1948). Reprinted in Kaufmann, Ralph J., ed., *Elizabethan Drama: Modern Essays in Criticism.* New York, 1961.

George, Charles H. and Katherine. *The Protestant Mind of the English Reformation.* Princeton, 1961.

Godshalk, W. L. *The Marlovian World Picture.* The Hague, 1974.

Goldman, Michael. *The Actor's Freedom: Toward a Theory of Drama.* New York, 1975.

Gollancz, Israel. *The Sources of Hamlet*. 1926; rpt., New York, 1967.

Goodlad, J.S.R. *A Sociology of Popular Drama*. London, 1971.

Greenblatt, Stephen. *Renaissance Self-Fashioning from More to Shakespeare*. Chicago, 1980.

Greg, W. W. "The Damnation of Faustus." *Modern Language Review*, XLI (1946), 97-107.

Gunn, Giles. *The Interpretation of Otherness: Literature, Religion and The American Imagination*. New York, 1979.

Gurr, Andrew. *The Shakespearean Stage: 1574-1642*. Cambridge, 1970.

Hadyn, Hiram. *The Counter-Renaissance*. New York, 1950.

Hall, Basil. "Puritanism: The Problem of Definition." *Studies in Church History*, II (1965), 283-97.

Haller, William. *Foxe's Book of Martyrs and the Elect Nation*. London, 1963.

————. *The Rise of Puritanism, or The Way to the New Jerusalem as Set Forth in Pulpit and Press from Thomas Cartwright to John Lilburne and John Milton, 1570-1643*. 1938; rpt., New York, 1957.

Hallett, Charles A. and Elaine S. *The Revenger's Madness: A Study of Revenge Tragedy Motifs*. Lincoln, Nebraska, 1980.

Hamilton, A. C. *The Early Shakespeare*. San Marino, California, 1967.

Happe, Peter. "Tragic Themes in Three Tudor Moralities." *Studies in English Literature*, V (1965), 207-27.

————. "The Vice: A Checklist and An Annotated Bibliography." *Research Opportunities in Renaissance Drama*, XXII (1979), 17-36.

Harbage, Alfred. *Annals of English Drama: 975-1700*. Rev. Samuel Schoenbaum. London, 1964.

————. *As They Liked It*. 1947; rpt., Philadelphia, 1972.

————. "Innocent Barabas." *Tulane Drama Review*, VIII, 4 (Summer, 1964), 47-58.

————. *Shakespeare and the Rival Traditions*. 1952; rpt., Bloomington, 1970.

————. *Shakespeare's Audience*. 1941; rpt., New York, 1961.

Harding, M. Esther. *The I and the Not-I: A Study in the Development of Consciousness*. Bollingen Series LXXIX, Princeton, 1965.

Harper, J. W. *Tamburlaine the Great*. New Mermaid Edition. New York, 1971.

Harrison, G. B. *An Elizabethan Journal*. New York, 1929.

Hawkes, Terence. *Shakespeare's Talking Animals: Language and Drama in Society*. London, 1973.

Hazlitt, W. C., ed. *The English Drama and Stage under the Tudor and Stuart Princes 1543-1664*. London, 1869.

Heinemann, Margot. *Puritanism and Theatre: Thomas Middleton and Opposition Drama under the Early Stuarts*. Cambridge, 1980.

Herndl. George C. *The High Design: English Renaissance Tragedy and the Natural Law*. Lexington, Kentucky, 1970.

Herr, Alan Fager. *The Elizabethan Sermon: A Survey and a Bibliography*. Philadelphia, 1940.

Hill, Christopher. *Change and Continuity in Seventeenth-Century England*. Cambridge, 1975.

————. *Society and Puritanism in Pre-Revolutionary England*. 2nd ed. New York, 1967.

Hill, R. F. "The Composition of *Titus Andronicus*." *Shakespeare Survey*, 10 (1975), 60-70.

Hillman, Richard S. "Meaning and Mortality in Some Renaissance Revenge Plays." *University of Toronto Quarterly*, XLIX, 1 (Fall, 1979), 1-17.

Holloway, John. *The Story of Night: Studies in Shakespeare's Major Tragedies*. Lincoln, Nebraska, 1961.

Honderich, Pauline. "John Calvin and Doctor Faustus." *Modern Language Review*, 68, 1 (1973), 1-13.

Honigmann, E.A.J. *Shakespeare: Seven Tragedies: The Dramatist's Manipulation of Response*. London, 1976.

Hosley, Richard, ed. *Essays on Shakespeare and Elizabethan Drama in Honor of Hardin Craig*. Columbia, Missouri, 1962.

Hunter, G. K. *Dramatic Identities and Cultural Tradition: Studies in Shakespeare and his Contemporaries*. New York, 1978.

Hunter, Robert G. *Shakespeare and the Mystery of God's Judgments*. Athens, Georgia, 1976.

Jones, Emrys. *The Origins of Shakespeare*. Oxford, 1977.

Jones, Robert C. "Dangerous Sport: The Audience's Engagement with the Vice in the Moral Interludes." *Renaissance Drama*, N.S. VI (1973), 45-64.

Kahrl, Stanley J. *Traditions of Medieval English Drama*. Pittsburgh, 1974.

Kantorowicz, Ernst. *The King's Two Bodies: A Study in Medieval Political Theology*. Princeton, 1957.

Kauffman, Walter. *Tragedy and Philosophy*. New York, 1969.

Kernan, Alvin B. *The Playwright As Magician: Shakespeare's Image of the Poet in the English Public Theater*. New Haven, 1979.

————, ed. *Two Renaissance Mythmakers: Selected Papers from the English Institute, 1975-76*, N.S. 1. Baltimore, 1977.

Kiefer, Frederick. "Seneca's Influence on Elizabethan Tragedy: An Annotated Bibliography." *Research Opportunities in Renaissance Drama*, XXI (1978), 17-34.

Kimbrough, Robert. "*I Tamburlaine*: A Speaking Picture in a Tragic Glass." *Renaissance Drama*, VII (1964), 20-34.

Knapp, Robert S. "*Horestes*: The Uses of Revenge." *ELH*, XL, 2 (1973), 205-220.

Kocher, Paul H. *Christopher Marlowe: A Study of his Thought, Learning, and Character*. New York, 1962.

————. "The Early Date for Marlowe's *Faustus*." *Modern Language Notes*, 58 (1943), 539-42.

————. "The English Faust Book and the Date of Marlowe's *Faustus*." *Modern Language Notes*, 55 (1940), 95-101.

Kolve, V. A. *The Play Called Corpus Christi*. Stanford, 1966.

Kuriyama, Constance Brown. *Hammer or Anvil: Psychological Patterns in Christopher Marlowe's Plays*. New Brunswick, New Jersey, 1980.

Lawlor, John. *The Tragic Sense in Shakespeare*. New York. 1960.

Leech, Clifford, ed. *Marlowe: A Collection of Critical Essays*. Englewood Cliffs, New Jersey, 1964.

————. "Marlowe's Edward II: Power and Suffering." *Criti-*

cal Quarterly I, 3. Reprinted in *Edward II*. Ed. Jacques Chwat. New York, 1974.

———. "The Structure of *Tamburlaine*." *Tulane Drama Review*, VIII, 4 (Summer, 1964), 32-46.

Levin, Harry. *The Overreacher: A Study of Christopher Marlowe*. Cambridge, 1952.

Levin, Richard. *New Readings vs. Old Plays: Recent Trends in the Reinterpretation of English Renaissance Drama*. Chicago, 1979.

Lewalski, Barbara Kiefer. *Protestant Poetics and the Seventeenth-Century Religious Lyric*. Princeton, 1979.

Lewis, C. S. *English Literature in the Sixteenth Century excluding Drama*. Oxford, 1954.

Lewis, Charlton M. *The Genesis of Hamlet*. 1907; rpt., New York, 1967.

Logan, Terence P. and Denzell S. Smith, ed. *The Predecessors of Shakespeare: A Survey and Bibliography of Recent Studies in English Renaissance Drama*. Lincoln, Nebraska, 1973.

Mack, Maynard, Jr. *Killing the King: Three Studies in Shakespeare's Tragic Structure*. New Haven, 1973.

Maclure, Millar. *The Paul's Cross Sermons*. Toronto, 1958.

Mahood, M. M. *Poetry and Humanism*. London, 1950.

Manheim, Michael. *The Weak King Dilemma in the Shakespearean History Play*. Syracuse, 1973.

Margeson, J.M.R. *The Origins of English Tragedy*. Oxford, 1967.

Martin, Richard. "Tamburlaine and the Language of Romance." *PMLA*, 93 (1978), 248-64.

Masinton, Charles G. *Christopher Marlowe's Tragic Vision: A Study in Damnation*. Athens, Ohio, 1972.

Michel, Lawrence and Richard B. Sewall, ed. *Tragedy: Modern Essays in Criticism*. Englewood Cliffs, New Jersey, 1963.

Miller, Perry. *The New England Mind: The Seventeenth Century*. 1939; rpt., Boston, 1961.

Milward, Peter. *Shakespeare's Religious Background*. Bloomington, 1973.

Morgan, Irvonwy. *The Godly Preachers of the Elizabethan Church*. London, 1965.

Morris, Brian, ed. *Christopher Marlowe: Mermaid Critical Commentaries*. New York, 1968.

Motto, Anna Lydia and John R. Clark. "Senecan Tragedy: A Critique of Scholarly Trends." *Ren.•issance Drama*, N.S. VI (1973), 219-36.

Myrick, Kenneth O. "The Theme of Damnation in Shakespearean Tragedy." *Studies in Philology*, XXXVII (1941), 221-45.

New, John F. H. *Anglican and Puritan: The Basis of Their Opposition, 1558-1640*. Stanford, 1964.

Ornstein, Robert. *A Kingdom for a Stage: The Achievement of Shakespeare's History Plays*. Cambridge, 1972.

———. "Marlowe and God: The Tragic Theory of *Doctor Faustus*." *PMLA*, 83 (1968), 1378-85.

———. *The Moral Vision of Jacobean Tragedy*. Madison, Wisconsin, 1960.

Owst, Gerald Robert. *Literature and Pulpit in Medieval England*. Cambridge, 1933.

Pearson, A. F. Scott. *Thomas Cartwright and Elizabethan Puritanism: 1535-1603*. Cambridge, 1925.

Phialas, Peter G. "*Richard II and* Shakespeare's Tragic Mode." *Texas Studies in Literature and Language*, 5 (1963), 344-55.

Poirer, Michel. *Christopher Marlowe*. London, 1951.

Porter, Harry Culverwell. *Puritanism in Tudor England*. London, 1970.

———. *Reformation and Reaction in Tudor Cambridge*. Cambridge, 1958.

Potter, Robert. *The English Morality Play*. London, 1975.

Prosser, Eleanor. *Drama and Religion in the English Mystery Plays*. Stanford, 1961.

———. *Hamlet and Revenge*. Stanford, 1967.

Rabkin, Norman, ed. *Reinterpretations of Elizabethan Drama: Selected Papers from the English Institute*. New York, 1969.

———. *Shakespeare and the Common Understanding*. New York, 1967.

———. *Shakespeare and the Problem of Meaning*. Chicago, 1981.

Reese, M. M. *The Cease of Majesty*. London, 1961.

Ribner, Irving. *The English History Play in the Age of Shakespeare*. Rev. ed. New York, 1965.

——. "Greene's Attack on Marlowe: Some Light on *Alphonsus* and *Selimus*." *Studies in Philology*, 52 (1955), 162-71.

——. "Marlowe and the Critics." *Tulane Drama Review*, VIII, 4 (Spring, 1964), 211-24.

Riggs, David. *Shakespeare's Heroical Histories: Henry VI and Its Literary Tradition*. Cambridge, 1971.

Righter, Anne. *Shakespeare and the Idea of the Play*. London, 1962.

Rose, Elliot. *Cases of Conscience: Alternatives Open to Recusants and Puritans Under Elizabeth I and James I*. Cambridge, 1975.

Rossiter, A. P. *Angel with Horns*. London, 1961.

——. *English Drama from Early Times to the Elizabethans*. London, 1950.

Roston, Murray. *Biblical Drama in England*. London, 1968.

Sanders, Norman, Richard Southern, T. W. Craik, and Lois Potter. *The Revels History of Drama in English*, Vol. II, 1500-76. London, 1980.

Sanders, Wilbur. *The Dramatist and the Received Idea: Studies in the Plays of Marlowe and Shakespeare*. Cambridge, 1968.

Sasek, Lawrence A. *The Literary Temper of the English Puritans*. Baton Rouge, 1961.

Schwartz, Elias. "Detachment and Tragic Effect." *College English*, XVIII, 3 (December, 1956), 153-56.

Seaver, Paul S. *The Puritan Lectureships: The Politics of Religious Dissent 1560-1662*. Stanford, 1970.

Sibley, John. "The Duty of Revenge in Tudor and Stuart Drama." *A Review of English Literature*, VIII, 3 (July, 1967), 46-54.

Siegel, Paul N. *Shakespearean Tragedy and The Elizabethan Compromise*. New York, 1957.

Smith, Bruce R. "Toward the Rediscovery of Tragedy: Productions of Seneca's Plays on the English Renaissance Stage." *Renaissance Drama*, N.S. IX (1978), 3-38.

Snyder, Susan. "Marlowe's Doctor Faustus as an Inverted Saint's Life." *Studies in Philology*, LXIII (1966), 565-77.

Spence, Leslie. "The Influence of Marlowe's Source on *Tamburlaine I*." *Modern Philology*, XXIV (1926), 181-99.

Spivack, Bernard. *Shakespeare and the Allegory of Evil: The History of a Metaphor in Relation to his Major Villains*. New York, 1958.

Stampfer, Judah. *The Tragic Engagement: A Study of Shakespeare's Classical Tragedies*. New York, 1968.

Steane, J. B. *Marlowe: A Critical Study*. Cambridge, 1964.

Steiner, George. *The Death of Tragedy*. New York, 1961.

Stone, Lawrence. *The Causes of the English Revolution 1529-1642*. New York, 1972.

————. *The Crisis of the Aristocracy: 1558-1641*. Oxford, 1965.

Talbert, Ernest W. *Elizabethan Drama and Shakespeare's Early Plays*. Chapel Hill, 1963.

Tawney, R. H. *Religion and the Rise of Capitalism*. 1926; rpt., New York, 1947.

Thompson, E.N.S. *The Controversy between the Puritans and the Stage*. Yale Studies in English, XX. New York, 1903.

Tillyard, E.M.W. *Shakespeare's History Plays*. New York, 1946.

Toole, William B. "The Motif of Psychic Division in *Richard III*." *Shakespeare Survey*, XXVII (1974), 21-32.

Turner, Robert Y. *Shakespeare's Apprenticeship*. Chicago, 1974.

Ure, Peter. *Elizabethan and Jacobean Drama*, ed. J. C. Maxwell. New York, 1974.

van Beek, M. *An Enquiry into Puritan Vocabulary*. Groningen, 1969.

Vygotsky, L. S. *The Psychology of Art*. Cambridge, 1971.

Waith, Eugene. *The Herculean Hero in Marlowe, Chapman, Shakespeare and Dryden*. London and New York, 1962.

————. "Metamorphosis of Violence in *Titus Andronicus*." *Shakespeare Survey*, 10 (1957), 39-51.

Waldman, Milton. *Elizabeth and Leicester*. London, 1945.

————. *Sir Walter Raleigh*. London, 1928.

Walzer, Michael. *The Revolution of the Saints: A Study of the Origins of Radical Politics.* Cambridge, 1965.

Wasserman, Earl. "The Pleasure of Tragedy." *ELH,* XIV, 4 (1947), 283-307.

Waswo, Richard. "Damnation, Protestant Style: Macbeth, Faustus and Christian Tragedy." *Journal of Medieval and Renaissance Studies* 4 (1974), 63-99.

Watkins, Owen C. *The Puritan Experience: Studies in Spiritual Autobiography.* New York, 1972.

Weil, Judith. *Christopher Marlowe: Merlin's Prophet.* Cambridge, 1977.

Weimann, Robert. *Shakespeare and the Popular Tradition in the Theater: Studies in the Social Dimension of Dramatic Form.* Trans. and ed. Robert Schwartz. Baltimore, 1978.

Weiner, Andrew D. *Sir Philip Sidney and the Poetics of Protestantism: A Study of Contexts.* Minneapolis, 1978.

Weisinger, Herbert. *Tragedy and the Paradox of the Fortunate Fall.* London, 1953.

Weitz, Morris. *Hamlet and the Philosophy of Literary Criticism.* Chicago, 1964.

Weld, John. *Meaning in Comedy: Studies in Elizabethan Romantic Comedy.* Albany, 1975.

Wells, Stanley, ed. *Shakespeare: Select Bibliographical Guides.* Oxford, 1973.

Whale, John Seldon. *Victor and Victim.* Cambridge, 1960.

Whitaker, Virgil K. *The Mirror Up to Nature: The Technique of Shakespeare's Tragedies.* San Marino, California, 1965.

Wickham, Glynne. *Shakespeare's Dramatic Heritage: Collected Studies in Medieval, Tudor and Shakespearean Drama.* London, 1969.

Wilders, John. *The Lost Garden: Shakespeare's History Plays.* London, 1978.

Wilson, F. P. *Marlowe and The Early Shakespeare.* Oxford, 1953.

Wright, Louis B. *Middle-Class Culture in Elizabethan England.* Chapel Hill, 1935.

Ziff, Larzar. *Puritanism in America.* New York, 1973.

INDEX

Aaron (*Titus Andronicus*), 98, 183, 185, 195-96, 199, 207
Abrams, M. H., 111n
Acolastus, 82n
Adams, Barry B., 192n
Aglionby, Edward, 103
All for Money (Lupton), 98-100
allegorical characterization, in *Doctor Faustus*, 218, 234, 236; limitations of, 108; in the morality play, 75, 85-86, 91-92, 94, 98, 100-101, 203; of Richmond (*Richard III*), 260
Alleyn, Edward, 166, 265n
Alphonsus, King of Aragon, the Comicall Historie of, 163-66
Altman, Joel, 9, 37, 129n, 136n, 151n, 187n, 218n, 268n
Anatomie of Sinne, The, 57
Andrewes, Lancelot, 16
Antony and Cleopatra (Shakespeare), 37
Apologie for Poetry, An (Sidney), 25-26, 30, 37, 109
Appius and Virginia ("R.B."), 125-27, 108-109, 119, 181, 183
Aristotle, 32-34, 38, 75, 94n, 121, 178; *Poetics*, 32-34; *Rhetoric*, 33-34
aspiration, *see* pride *and* the aspiring mind
assurance, *see also* pride *and* the aspiring mind, 41-53, 67, 106, 168, 229; doctrine of, 42; as presumption or pride, 52, 56-64, 68, 139-40, 173, 259, 278; rhetoric of, 45-53, 140, 143-44, 163-65, 201, 205, 251; in *Richard II*, 278, 282-83, 287n, 289; as a sign of election, 43-45

aspiring mind, the, 52, 59-62, 64, 92, 114-18, 164-66, 164n, 167-68, 195, 248, 251; in *Doctor Faustus*, 210, 213, 217-18, 218n, 228; in *Edward II*, 265-68; Elizabethan ambivalence about, 60, 147, 168, 208, 210, 264; in *I Tamburlaine*, 137-39, 143-47, 165, 173
audience, anti-Catholic sentiments of, 103, 147, 204, 220, 232, 268; complaints about, 24; composition of, 16-17; expectations, assumptions, 4, 137n, 177-79, 211, 274, 277; overlapping, 15-16, 20, 23-24, 52; relationship with the protagonist, 3, 30-36, 60, 81, 135-36n, 208, 264, 290, 300; response (or dual response), 4, 7-10, 31-38, 63, 73, 84, 93-94, 94n, 122, 182-83, 198, 201, 207-208, 254-55, 268-69
Ayres, Philip J., 178

Baines, Barbara J., 178n
Baker, Howard, 109n
Baldwin, William, 156n
Bale, John, *see also King Johan*, 101
Bamber, Linda, 28n
Barabas (*The Jew of Malta*), 96, 170, 181, 183-85, 199-207, 263, 265
Barber, C. L., 3n, 223
Barish, Jonas, 22n
Barroll, J. Leeds, 71n
Battenhouse, Roy W., 30, 30n, 135n, 144n, 151n, 155n
The Battle of Alcazar (Peele), 134n, 166-70, 173
Beard, Thomas, 180n

than Calvinism, 4, 46n, 50-51, 112, 210n; in *Macbeth*, 292-93
prejudice, against blacks, Jews, and Moors, 196, 196n, 201-202, 202n
Preston, Thomas, *see* Cambises
pride, *see also* assurance *and* the aspiring mind, 22-23; and presumption, 52-61, 115, 163-65, 173, 210, 233-34, 258-59, 281; and the pursuit of knowledge, 57, 62-63, 222-23
Pride of Life, The, 77-78
Prosser, Eleanor, 177-78, 190n
protagonist, morality play, 75-107, 182, 203, 272, 292; absence of, 96-99; damnation of, 84, 87, 93-94; as "other," 88, 93, 105; potentially tragic, 86, 101-102
protagonist, tragic, *see also* tragedy: evolution or emergence of, 3, 15, 35-40, 76-77, 100, 110, 114, 117, 121, 125, 132-33, 226, 261, 264, 266, 275, 300; morality and hybrid play precursors of, 75, 81-82, 85, 92-94, 102, 105-108, 121, 127; as "other," 72-73, 116, 118, 121-22, 127, 129, 181-82, 187, 192-93, 203, 208-209, 284, 290; responsibility of, 73, 111-12, 121, 198, 240-41, 284n; self-knowledge of, 290, 298
psychomachia, 73, 95, 104, 108n, 149
Puritanism, 11, 12n, 17-18, 42-73, 85, 209-210, 214, 218, 240; influence on drama, 7n, 85; paradox of, 44-46, 45n; rise of, 18, 75; use of term, 5n, 18-19

Quez, 211n-12n, *see* entries for audience, Faustus, Greg, Haller, Sanders, Seneco, *I Tamberlaine*

Rabkin, Norman, 8, 37, 261

Raleigh, Sir Walter, 59-60, 147, 171
recognition, tragic (*anagnoresis*), 75, 121, 151, 162, 241, 259, 262, 270, 274, 283, 284n, 286-91, 296-99
repentance, 4, 45, 48-51, 66, 70, 72, 75, 79, 93, 240, 259, 262; and despair in *Doctor Faustus*, 70, 209-10, 220-21, 224-29, 234-35, 240-41, 246
reprobate, *see* "self" and "other"; election
Respublica, 117
revenge, *see also* revenger, revenge tragedy, 70, 117, 130-32, 168, 188, 272; as a character in *Horestes*, 123-24; as a character in *The Spanish Tragedy*, 186-89, 192; as divine justice, 125, 197-98; morality of, 109, 123-25, 123n, 174-80, 198, 200, 208; as a political act, 178-80
revenge tragedy, 5, 36, 70, 110, 122-23, 122n, 170, 175-208, 297
revenger, the, *see also* villain, 71, 128, 140, 174-208, 248-49, 272; audience attitude toward, 174, 178, 182, 188, 191, 193-95, 200, 207-208; damnation of, 180, 182, 198-99, 206; as hero, 185-86, 205; madness of, 182, 192, 194, 197; as scourge or agent of God, 176, 180, 198
Ribner, Irving, 165, 276n
Richard II (Shakespeare), 22, 39, 188, 251, 271-72, 272n, 275-90, 298
Richard II, King (*Richard II*), 250-51, 275-90; audience ambivalence toward, 276, 284-85
Richard III (Shakespeare), 121, 249-64, 299; idea of scourge of God in, 250, 253, 261; morality play devices in, 250-53, 259-61;

Library of Congress Cataloging in Publication Data

Rozett, Martha Tuck, 1946-
  The doctrine of election and the emergence of
Elizabethan tragedy.

  Bibliography: p.
  Includes index.
  1. English drama—Early modern and Elizabethan,
1500-1600—History and criticism. 2. English drama
(Tragedy)—History and criticism. 3. Election
(Theology)—History of doctrines—16th century.
4. Religion and literature. I. Title.
PR658.T7R68 1984   822'.3'09382   84-42565
ISBN 0-691-06615-9 (alk. paper)